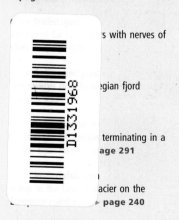

Hardangerfjord
Holiday in the midst of stunning scenery

BAEDEKER'S BEST TIPS

We have gathered together the most interesting of this book's Baedeker tips here. Discover and enjoy Norway at its most beautiful.

! Easter with the Sami
Each year at Easter, the Sami people gather together in Karasjok and Kautokeino. Wearing their traditional colourful costume, they celebrate marriages and put on competitions such as the reindeer sleigh races. The best Joik singers are discovered during the Sami Grand Prix.
▶ page 32

! Kongsvold Fjellstue
Delicious elk dishes, waffles and »smørbrød« are served at this cosy former staging inn. ▶ page 180

! Musk ox safari
To experience animals in the wild is one of the best travel experiences, especially when those animals are as unusual as the musk ox. ▶ page 182

! Sjoa rafting
A trip by inflatable boat on the wild Sjoa River is a sporting event as much as a wilderness experience. ▶ page 199

Sami culture
can be experienced especially close-up during Easter in Karasjok and Kautokeino.

Musk ox
can occasionally be quite aggressive, and are ideally approached only with an experienced guide.

🔢 Howling with wolves

Wolves, lynx, polar foxes and reindeer roam in the outdoor enclosures of the Langedrag Nature Park. ► page 208

🔢 Four in one

Four spectacular waterfalls are passed during a hike through the Kinso Valley. ► page 226

🔢 Fun in the water

There are many small bathing coves on the way to the Sørland cliffs near Mandal that are much less crowded than the Sjøsanden beach. ► page 281

🔢 The charming Edvardas hotel

Guest are made to feel at home and spoilt all round at the Edvardas Hus, close to Narvik. ► page 289

🔢 Ibsen's local

Eat like the bohemians in the historic Grand Café in Oslo. ► page 304

🔢 Grims Grenka Hotel

This design hotel in the heart of Norway's capital combines clear Nordic style with an oriental ambience. ► page 305

🔢 The Middle Ages brought to life

The medieval market during the Trondheim St Olav Days features demonstrations of traditional arts and crafts, and there are also ceramics, candles and carvings for sale. ► page 382

🔢 The Rallarvegen

The Rallarvegen hiking route leads down into the Flåm valley from Myrdal. The first section with its almost vertical rockfaces is the most spectacular. ► page 406

Arts and crafts
How the artful weavings for folk costumes are made is demonstrated each year during the St Olav Days in Trondheim.

A place in the sun
Norway's south coast is ideal for a beach holiday.

*Fish to take away: sardines
from Stavanger*
► page 357

BACKGROUND

PRACTICALITIES

Sculpture in Oslo's Vigeland Park.
► page 318

TOURS

SIGHTS FROM A to Z

Stunning island world: Lofoten
► page 269

*Modern art adorns
Norway's west coast.*
▶ **page 300**

Price categories

▶ **Hotels**
Luxury: over 120 €
Mid-range: 60 – 120 €
Budget: under 60 €
Two persons in a double room

▶ **Restaurants**
Expensive. over 30 €
Moderate: 12 – 30 €
Inexpensive: under 12 €
For a main course

*Sailing ships regularly chart a
course to Tromsø's islands.*
▶ **page 376**

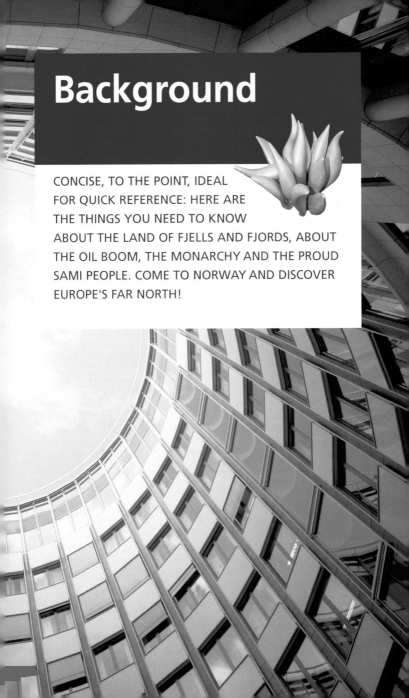

Background

CONCISE, TO THE POINT, IDEAL FOR QUICK REFERENCE: HERE ARE THE THINGS YOU NEED TO KNOW ABOUT THE LAND OF FJELLS AND FJORDS, ABOUT THE OIL BOOM, THE MONARCHY AND THE PROUD SAMI PEOPLE. COME TO NORWAY AND DISCOVER EUROPE'S FAR NORTH!

A LAND OF FJORDS

Nature is rarely as tangibly and closely experienced as it is in Norway. There are the great fjords: valleys plunging vertically down into the earth, filled with deep blue seawater. There are the fjells: uninhabited mountain regions across which run the migration routes of musk ox and elk. The midnight sun turns night to day and those in search of solitude will find their paradise in Norway, yet so will sun-seekers looking to stretch out on the beach.

Restless souls will quickly find peace in Norway. The hectic pace and stress of life are soon forgotten during a journey around this country, where progress is always slow on the narrow serpentine roads. Bit by bit, a new equanimity finds its way into the traveller's mind and the

Lofoten
Famous island chain in the high north

life's joys are rediscovered in a landscape whose beauty has few rivals in Europe. Three quarters of the country consists of mountains, and hiking and mountaineering number among the most popular outdoor activities. The landscape is also characterized by its coast and the skerries: a swarm of rock islands and islets, on some of which stand solitary huts painted in bright colours. Norwegians as well as visitors love to spend their holidays in such a »hytta«. Yet Norway does not only promise solitude: where people have settled, the scenery is characterized by farms, predominantly built of wood-frame turf-covered houses decorated with carvings; on the coast, meanwhile, stand colourful fishermen's cabins. The cities provide a contrast to the nature holiday: Oslo for example, with its promenades, nightlife districts and famous Vigeland Park; the historic Hanseatic town of Bergen, considered the secret capital of Norway; and, of course, the old royal city of Trondheim with its monumental Nidaros Cathedral. And from there, the gateways to the north open up.

Beyond the Arctic Circle

← Light in architecture: Oslo's government building

The Arctic Circle sits around the country's slim neck like an invisible necklace. During the summer months, darkness never falls, even at the level of Trondheim, while beyond the Arctic Circle the summer sun never sets at all. Some travellers report that this excess of light

Ascent
Norway's hiking regions are legendary.

Adventure
*With luck, you may meet the Sami people
and their reindeer.*

Short cuts
Ferries help cut mileage.

Plentiful harvest
Berries ripen en masse in autumn.

Peace and quiet
The clocks run more slowly in Norway.

Sheer romance
The glittering midnight sun over the dark sea.

makes them positively euphoric. With a little luck, the visitor at this time of year will experience the type of light that gives an atmosphere of unreality, seeing the landscape glow in warm colours and even discovering an unfamiliar sense of freedom. Suddenly it is no longer important when to set off on the hike or where to pitch the tent. On the other hand, those who come in the winter will see the aurora borealis: hovering curtains of colour that silently dance across a profoundly black sky.

Oil, Elk and Reindeer Roast

Fish, endless forests and natural resources of all kinds: Norway is indeed a blessed country. However, the wealth of the nation with one of the highest standards of living in the world comes mostly from the oil that rises from the seabed off its coasts. The Norwegians have invested their petrodollars – which, in the meantime, run into the billions – in a special fund, saving for the time when the oil wells run dry. The country rightly looks towards that day with trepidation, for oil and gas account for a third of its export income. Talking of money, the visitor to Norway will also experience the movement of currency: namely the Norwegian krone flowing out of his or her pocket! It is not only the astronomical prices charged for alcohol that empty the wallet either. Eating out, accommodation, petrol – everything is significantly more expensive here than in the rest of Europe. For that reason, many travel-

»The Seven Sisters«
Bizarre skyline of the Nordland coast

lers arrive in camper vans fully stocked with provisions from home. One of the most beautiful ways to travel the country is of course by a Hurtigruten ferry: the trip, »the most beautiful ocean journey of the world«, takes five days to pass along the endlessly jagged coast, from Bergen right up as far as distant Kirkenes. Along the way, the spiky mountain summits of the Lofoten Islands are passed, as well as the mighty plateau of Nordkapp and idyllic fishing villages. Talking of fish: in Norway you can catch them yourself in the numerous fjords and rivers. Salmon, halibut, fjord trout and cod are on the menu at many restaurants. So are elk sausage and reindeer roast, perhaps even traditionally prepared in a wood-fired oven in the style of the Sami. All this makes a holiday in Norway unique. Experience has proved that those who visit the country once are more than happy to come back.

Facts

Thousands of fjords cut into the backbone of Europe's longest country. Elk, reindeer and whales can be spotted moving from the southern tip up to Nordkapp and, depending on the time of year, the midnight sun or the unearthly spectacle of the aurora borealis can be marvelled at.

Nature

Europe's Longest Country

No other European country is as long as Norway. The port of Kris-   **Sharp relief**
tiansand in the far south is around **1700km/1062mi as the crow flies**
from Nordkapp. That is equal to the distance from Kristiansand to
Florence. Together with all the mountains and the fissured coast line,
this represents a considerable challenge to transport. From east to
west, the country measures no more than 430km/269mi at its widest
point (between the southern Norwegian Kappstad and the Swedish
border). At the level of Narvik, the east-west axis shrinks to **barely
7km/5mi**.

Norway is largely a mountainous country. More than half of its land
lies at elevations of over 500m/1640ft and a further quarter rises
above 1000m/3281ft. Considering the extreme northern latitude, this
feature is of defining significance as regards the possibilities of forestry and agriculture. Flatter land-
scapes can only be found in the
land surrounding the Trondheimsfjord and the Oslofjord, as
well as to the south of Stavanger.

The **Scandinavian Mountains** are
predominantly comprised of ancient sediment and volcanic stone,
as well as of gneiss. Morphologically, they are **fold mountains**,
which fused with the far older stone mass of the Baltic Plate to the
east in prehistoric times to form the bulk of Sweden and parts of
Finland. This approximately 400-million-year-old mountain range
has been greatly eroded over the course of millennia.

> **?** **DID YOU KNOW ...?**
>
> ■ ... that Europe's deepest lake and highest cliff
> are both in Norway? Hornidalsvatnet near the
> Nordfjord is 514m/1686ft deep, while not far
> from the mouth of the Nordfjord the mountain
> cliff Hornelen rises spectacularly from the
> water, towering 860m/2820ft into the air.

During the Ice Age all of Norway was covered by the giant, inland   **The power of ice**
ice blanket that extended across Scandinavia, many millions of
square miles wide. It is believed that during the coldest phase of the
Ice Age the **ice reached a depth of up to 3500m/11,483ft**. This
mighty ice sheet exerted enormous pressure on the underlying rock
stratum: the pressure generated at an ice thickness of 3000m/9843ft
would have been 2700t/sq m. As soon as the ice sheet began to melt,
the slow **rising** process of the continental shelf commenced, a process that continues to this day. At present, the section rising fastest is
along the Finnish Bay, at a rate of about 1cm/0.4in per year. The
coastal levels of the skerries have also risen, while expanses of water
in valleys and hollows have silted up.

← *Blue wonder: Briksdalsbreen in western Norway*

Coasts and skerries No other coast on earth is as **markedly fissured** Norway's. Its 2650km/1656mi coastline extends to 21,347km/13,342mi if the numerous fjord outlines are included. Countless skerries, tips of rocks and **small islands** that rarely reach a height of more than 50m/164ft above sea level, rise up out of the smooth water. Their number is estimated at between 50,000 and 150,000, though only around 2000 of them are inhabited. These rocky protuberances rising out of the sea are the offshore part of the coastal plate extending from the mountains. Today, the lowest points of the plate lie up to 50m/164m below the surface of the water. The region between the coast and the skerries is a popular area for amateur sailors with their motorboats and yachts, and numerous freight and passenger boats also travel within the protected channels created by the skerries.

The fjords: world class valleys Inland, the flat coastal strip is joined by the steeply rising bulk of the Scandinavian mountains, with summits reaching close to 2500m/8202ft. The mountains are edged by individual deeply cut valleys, the so-called **fjords**. Emblems of Norway, the two most beautiful have been under UNESCO protection since 2005: the **Geirangerfjord** and the **Nrøyfjord**, the most spectacular side-arm of the Sognefjord. Fjords, some of which cut up to 200km/125mi inland, are pre-Ice Age river valleys that were deeply eroded during the ice flows down to the sea during successive ice ages, and which then filled with sea water. They are often U-shaped in cross section, with **extremely steep** sides above and below the water. There is an almost complete absence of banks along the water's edge and human settlement could only take place where the confluence of side valleys caused a mound of sediment to accumulate. Depths of up to 1200m/3937ft (Sognefjord 1308m/4291ft) mean even ocean-going ships can travel all the way to the end of fjords. Some side valleys open into a fjord via a clear step and such openings are often recognisable as a »foss« (**waterfall**) crashing down from a great height. A seabed lip or fish bank usually seals the fjords morphologically from the coastal shelf.

Foss ▶

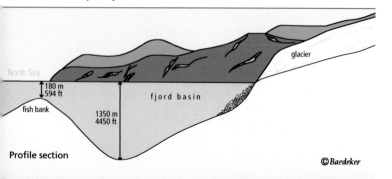

Fjord formation

North Sea

180 m
594 ft

glacier

fish bank

fjord basin

1350 m
4450 ft

Profile section

©*Baedeker*

Of course it is hard to develop overland routes near the fjords. Only where there are larger settlements at the end of fjords does a twisting **road** ascend the steep end of the valley in countless curves (for example the Trollstigveien near Åndalsnes or the Ørneveien near Geiranger) to reach the undulating highland plateau of the mountains – the so-called fjell that lies at 800m/2620ft–1000m/3280ft above sea level. In the Scandinavian region, the word »fjell« describes all land that lies above the tree line.

The Norwegians call the extensive and monotonous plateaus **»vidda«** (as in Finnmarksvidda and Hardangervidda). Due to the rising level of the Scandinavian landmass, rivers flowing from the edges of the vidda regions cut deep valleys into the highland plateaus. Thus the watershed towards the south and southeast of the fjells is characterized by broad, flattened out valleys, the so-called east Norwegian **farming valleys**, such as Østerdal, Gudbrandsdal, Valdres, Hallingdal, Numedal, Setesdal and Sirdal. These valleys too were broadened out by retreating ice sheets, but not nearly

> **?** DID YOU KNOW ...?
>
> ■ ... that although Norway has a lot of water, it has just one natural source of mineral water? The sulphuric salty spring called Kong Håkons kilde (King Håkon's well) bubbles up in the Oslofjord near Larvik and would attract spa guests from both home and abroad at the end of the 19th century. Today its waters are sold under the name of »Farris«.

as deeply as the fjords to the west. Typical vidda landscapes are in the districts of Trøndelag (Dovrefjell reaches elevations of up to 2286m/7500ft above sea level), Telemark, Hedmark and Akershus.

Alpine characteristics, such as ridges, cirques and sheer walls, dominate the high mountain ranges of the Lofoten and Jotunheimen. This is also where the highest elevations in Norway (and Scandinavia as a whole) can be found, such as the glaciated **Galdhøppigen (2469m/8101ft)** and **Glittertind (2452m/8045ft)**. Prior to the ice ages, the summits of the **Jotunheimen** (like those of the Lofoten) were rounded, but steep ridges and peaks were created by glacial erosion during the ice ages.

Alpine mountains

Despite the fact that Norway's glaciers have diminished in volume over the past two centuries – just as those of the European Alps – and that the area covered in ice has shrunk, the country still boasts **Europe's largest ice-covered area**. The largest glacier in the country is the Jostedal Glacier or **Jostedalsbreen**, lying at an altitude of around 1500m/5000ft–1700m/5600ft. It extends to the west from the Jotunheimen mountain range between the interiors of the Nordfjord to the north and the Sognefjord to the south. Its total area has shrunk in recent decades, going from more than 1000 sq km/400 sq mi to around 490 sq km/190 sq mi at present. With their many fingers trailing off, the glaciers are reminiscent of a mass of overflowing porridge.

Shrinking glaciers

Norway Five region-typical climate stations

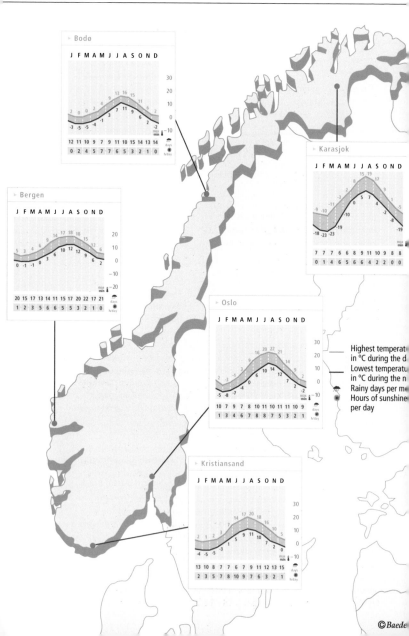

Bodø

J	F	M	A	M	J	J	A	S	O	N	D

Karasjok

Bergen

Oslo

Kristiansand

Highest temperat
in °C during the d
Lowest temperatu
in °C during the n
Rainy days per m
Hours of sunshine
per day

©Baede

In addition to these mountainous landforms, Norway also contains smaller lowland regions, which have been settled **and intensively farmed** since time immemorial. These are the regions around the Oslo basin and the Trondheimsfjord, as well the coastal landscape of Jæren to the south of Stavanger. The Oslo basin, stretching all the way to Lake Mjøsa, the country's largest lake, is part of the **huge tectonic rift valley** that cuts through Europe. The **Oslofjord** is therefore not truly a fjord. A flat bank has formed from marine sediment around the southern and eastern shore of the **Trondheimsfjord**, a cultural area that reaches altitudes of up to 200m/656ft due to the rising Scandinavian landmass. In **Jæren** the picture changes dramatically: the climatically mild Jæren plain south of Stavanger more resembles the Danish Jutland peninsular or southern Sweden.

Lowlands

Climate

Norway's geographical location, its huge length from north to south and the mountainous nature of its landscape ensure there is great variation in weather and climate. No country at a similar latitude has such a mild climate as Norway, a fact caused by the extensions of the Gulf Stream, which act as a »radiator« for the entire coast, keeping it ice-free right up to the extreme north even during the most severe of winters. They also ensure that most of Norway enjoys a maritime climate with moist, cool summers and mild winters. In contrast, to the east of the mountains that act as a weather divide, the climate is continental, and features great variation in temperature, depending on the times of year and day, and also less rainfall.

Warmed by the Gulf Stream

Norway's weather is better than its reputation. Though the west coast belongs to Europe's rainiest regions, precipitation declines rapidly east of the mountains, where there is also ever more sunshine. The reason for this typical west to east difference lies in the westerly winds that always bring clouds from the Atlantic, which deposit their rain on the mountain ranges. When this happens, there is dry high pressure weather on the rain shadow side of the mountains to the east. The highest precipitation and snowfall occurs in the southern fjord region, which has up to 3000mm/118in rainfall per year. The highest recorded levels of up to 5000mm/197in are only recorded in the most westerly glacier region. Generous amounts of rain also fall in the Saltfjell mountains and in the Lofoten. Those who hate rain should avoid the old Hanseatic town of Bergen, in which it frequently buckets down with rain (2250mm/89in per year on 202 days). The regions around Oslo, Finnmarksvidda and the Gudbrandsdal valley enjoy much more pleasant weather, and even have to rely in part on artificial irrigation for their agriculture.

Where does it rain the most?

Spring starts late after a long dark winter. Polar winds ensure that temperatures only increase gradually before the beginning of May,

Occasional Mediterranean temperatures

and even during the few summer weeks, the weather normally remains quite cool. In July and August, however, the thermometer is capable of recording temperatures of up to 30°C/86°F. When this happens, a positively Mediterranean atmosphere blossoms in the southern valleys of Norway and the normally ice-cold lakes transform into waters ideal for bathing with temperatures reaching up to 25°C/77°F. Traditionally, July is the warmest month and February the coldest. With an annual median of around 7.7°C/45.8°F, the coast between Stavanger and the Sognefjord is considered the **warmest region in Norway** and fruit and vegetables flourish here. The coldest temperatures are reached in Finnmarksvidda, where the annual average is −3.1°C/26.4°F.

Summer   In the valleys of southern Norway the temperatures between mid-June and mid-August normally hover between 18°C/64°F and 22°C/71°F, during prolonged heatwaves even reaching 30°C/86°F. Along the coasts the temperature is normally two to four degrees cooler. During the night temperatures drop to between 8°C/46°F and 12°C/54°F. For central and northern Norway, average maximum daily temperatures of 15°C/59°F–17°C/63°F are normal, though they can also be slightly higher in southern Finnmark. Along the coast and in the Lofoten mountains warm clothing is essential, as it rarely gets warmer than 12°C/54°F–15°C/59°F.

Winter   Winter commences after a short autumn, as early as mid-September in northern Norway. Away from the coasts, severe and snowy weather predominates from November to April, with temperatures between -6°C/21°F and -25°C/-13°F. It gets the coldest in Finnmark where, on 6 February 1998, a temperature of -55°C/-67°F was recorded in Kautokeino. Severe winters also characterize the valleys and highlands of southern Norway, with a continuous freeze-up of between -5°C/23°F and -10°C/14°F during the day and -10°C/14°F and -15°C/5°F during the night. With the exception of the coasts, Norway disappears under a thick blanket of snow during the winter, which reaches its greatest depth between March and April, when it can be between 50cm/20in and 2m/7ft thick. In northern Norway and in the mountains, this white wonderland lasts from mid-October to the beginning of June (over 200 days), while in the valleys of southern Norway it remains from mid-November to the beginning of May. In Lapland it can even snow in the summer.

Sunshine   The sun shines most frequently along the »Norwegian Riviera« between Kristiansand and Oslo, and in the Gudbrandsdal valley (1600hrs–1900hrs per annum). These figures equal Central Europe's top levels and, in Kristiansand during June, they can even exceed them with an average of 280 hours of sunshine (10hrs per day). But if the sun is shining in the east, the west coast is usually rainy. The best chances to experience the fjords in good weather exist between

You'll need a little luck to see the aurora borealis in such magnificence.

April and May or when there are easterly winds that disperse the clouds, creating high pressure.

Towards the north, Atlantic lows increasingly challenge the sunshine, although even coastal cities like Trondheim, Bodø or Tromsø can offer reasonable averages of 200hrs of sunshine per month between May and June. There is a great deal of bad weather and frequent coastal fog in **Nordkapp** precisely when the largest number of visitors come to the area in July, which obstructs views of the breathtaking landscape and the midnight sun.

Magical Polar Lights

The delicate dance of the polar lights is one of nature's most memorable spectacles. Named after the Roman goddess of the dawn, they are known as the »aurora borealis« in the northern hemisphere and the »aurora australis« in the southern hemisphere. Many people visit Norway, and especially Tromsø, during winter, with the sole purpose of witnessing the northern lights just once in their lifetimes. The shimmering veils of light display all kinds of patterns: shaped sometimes as wisps or bands, sometimes as broad curtains of light that illuminate the firmament. These light phenomena occur at between 100km/62mi and 300km/187mi altitude and can be viewed from many places at the same time, even thousands of miles apart.

Veils
of light

At one time the northern lights were understood as **harbingers of war**, catastrophes or times of economic hardship. Now that more scientific explanations are favoured it is believed that the northern lights are the result of astrophysical and geophysical processes. The effect is produced when the **rays of the sun** hit the outer layers of the earth's atmosphere, known as the **ionosphere**, where charged

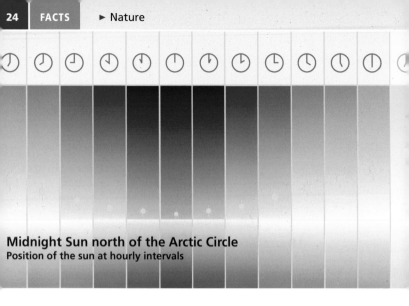

Midnight Sun north of the Arctic Circle
Position of the sun at hourly intervals

particles are then drawn in the direction of the magnetic poles. There they collide with electrons – among others with atoms of nitrogen and oxygen – setting off vibrations, and the result of this collision is the **illumination of the atoms**. Nitrogen atoms give off a somewhat red light, while the oxygen atoms glow blue and green. With luck, if the charged particles from the sun are particularly dense (normally once in an eleven-year cycle), the northern lights can even be seen in as far south as Ohio in the USA and southern Germany in Europe.

In the Land of the Midnight Sun

Where the sun never sets At the equator it is always day for twelve hours and night for twelve hours. The rest of the world experiences changeable lengths of day and night because the earth's axis is slightly tilted with respect to its plane of orbit. The Arctic and Antarctic Circles are found at 66.5° at the northern and southern latitude respectively. At the Arctic Circle to the north ((»polsirkelen« in Norwegian) the sun never sinks below the horizon during the summer; instead the so-called **midnight sun** shines.

Known as the **polar day**, this phenomenon can be observed at the precise latitude of the Arctic Circle alone during the summer solstice, on 22 June. On that date the presumed orbit of the sun reaches its greatest northern declination on the Arctic Circle, though there are also places south of the circle where it does not get dark, dusk excepted. As the dates for the midnight sun are drawn from astronomical data depending on sea level, there is a good chance of seeing the phenomenon from the tops of hills even in places a little to the south of the Arctic Circle. The further north you go, the longer the polar day lasts during sum-

mer. At the North Pole itself the polar day ought to last precisely half a year, but in fact lasts a little longer due to the curving of light rays in the earth's atmosphere. At that point the sun rises at the beginning of spring on 21 March and sets at the beginning of autumn on 23 September, a total of **187 days**. The polar night of winter is therefore correspondingly reduced. The Scandinavian regions north of the Artic Circle, the actual »Land of the Midnight Sun«, is referred to as the »North Calotte«.

Flora and Fauna

The plant world of northern Europe is rather species poor, since summers are short and cool. Only mountain flora less sensitive to cold survived during the ice ages, and then only in the region of the west coast warmed by the Gulf Stream, as far as the Lofoten Islands.

Few species

Flowers Impervious to Frost: Norwegian Flora

Around a quarter of Norway is covered in forest. In many areas of the country, however, the high mountains mean that forest is more or less limited to the sheltered valleys. There is little in the way of forest on the Atlantic coast. The skerries are normally pure rock and suffer significant erosion due to rainfall. **Many kinds of berries** (blueberry, cranberry and cloudberry) grow in the forests, as well as numerous mushroom species (for example, porcini and chanterelle). In the nature reservations of the Jotunheimen and Rondane mountains, the **tree line** is at 1000m/3281ft above sea level; by the Arctic Circle, the tree line has come down to 500m/1640ft, and the further north you go, the lower it sinks, until it reaches sea level itself.

Trees and berries

Mixed deciduous forests cover the southern regions of the country in particular. Red beech, oak, winter linden, ash, alder, elm, birch and a diverse variety fruit trees, such as cherry, are all common.

Deciduous forest in the south

Beech trees can be found right up to the mountains. **Oaks** can be found far into the north, as far as Trondheim. The further north you get, however, the more deciduous forest is replaced by coniferous forest.

Coniferous forest in the north

Extensive **moors** and dense spruce and pine forests are characteristic for central and northern Norway. Along the coast they reach right up beyond the Arctic Circle. In southern and eastern Norway **Norwegian spruce** predominates, while in western and northern Norway the **pine** is the most common species. The tree line of these forests reaches from 800m/2625ft in the Telemark and Hardangerfjord regions, to just 450m/1476ft in Finnmark. Here, in the north, only slim spruce and solitary pines are found.

Unique birch habitat

Low birch forests characterize the transitional zone of the pine trees in the arctic habitat. So called fjell birch raise the tree line by 100m/328ft–200m/656ft in mountainous areas. This **birch zone**, typical for all of Scandinavia, is unique on earth. The mountain valleys are greened by birch forests and willows, which are occasionally so thick as to be impenetrable. Ground cover in these northern forests is characterized by **berry bushes** and, in drier places, by **Icelandic moss** (despite its name a lichen).

Short summers in the tundra

Those who want to experience the tundra do need to travel very far north, for example to Spitsbergen or the Bear Islands. The extremely short **growth period of no more than three months** does not enable tree growth. The species-poor tundra can only sustain hardy dwarf birch and bushes, heather, moss and lichen.

Real alpine meadows can only be found in Norway's southern mountain region. The variety of flowering plants ranges from orchids to dry bushes, juniper and heather. Further north, the fjell highlands are similar to tundra: the landscape is characterized by **bushes and heather**, as well as mosses. At higher elevations, mosses, lichen and a few willow species predominate. Attentive mountain hikers will notice the numerous types of saxifrage (stone breaker). Annual plants are rarely found as their development is curtailed by the very short growing period. Because it is so cold on the Norwegian fjells, there are also very few **pollinating insects**, and most plants therefore have rather insignificant blossoms. The **snow bed willow** has proved itself to be especially adaptable. It grows very

> **? DID YOU KNOW ...?**
>
> ■ ...that alpine species *Ranuculus alpestris*, a type of buttercup, holds the altitude record for flowering plants? It manages to survive at up to 2370m/7776ft above sea level and can live for years under a blanket of snow without flowering at all.

← *Too cold: no trees grow on the highlands of the Jotunheimen mountains.*

slowly and only achieves a height of a few centimetres during the course of five decades.

Sugary anti-freeze ▶ Individual plants have adapted to their inhospitable environments in very interesting ways. Some develop sugary botanical juices not dissimilar to anti-freeze in their leaves and buds. The intense UV light on the fjell highlands inhibits the vertical growth of plants. Instead many plants here form rosettes, pads or even entire carpets, by that means taking advantage of the limited warmth emanating from the ground and also offering less surface area to wind. Very common flowering plants include primroses and, during summer in particular, the purple foxglove.

Reindeer, Wolf and Elk: Norway's Fauna

Fox and hare in the south Two climate and vegetation zones are of defining importance for Norway's animal kingdom. The forests of the southern regions belong to the temperate zone and are principally inhabited by the same species as in the forests of Central Europe: these include roe deer, red deer, foxes, rabbits and badgers. However, thanks to the low human population density and the limited cultural and industrial changes to the natural environment, Norway's variety of animal species is actually greater than that of Central Europe, and animals can often be found here that have long been marginalized or become extinct elsewhere.

Wolf and reindeer in the north The northern regions of Norway, especially Troms and Finnmark, belong to the arctic alpine zone. There is naturally a smaller number of animal species here than in other zones and the fauna is characterized by superb adaptation to the toughest living conditions. The most common animal is the reindeer. The snow grouse and arctic rabbit are also typical of this region along with the highly endangered species of otter, wolverine, wolf, and arctic fox.

! Baedeker TIP

On safari!

Those who don't want to leave elk sightings to chance should take part in an elk safari in the company of a ranger. These popular tours, which take place at dusk, are offered all over southern Norway. The region with the world's largest elk population is the coastal area of Sørlandet near Kristiansand.

The uncontested king of the northern forests is the **elk**, which can weigh up to 800kg/1760lb and grow to a length of almost 3m/10ft and a height of 2m/7ft. Elks are rarely seen as they are extremely shy animals. On the other hand, an elk may stumble in front of your car at dusk, even around Oslo. The consequences are often fatal. A consistent conservation policy over the past decades has increased the elk population, so that hunting is now permitted to the tune of more than 30,000 animals annually.

Norway's most widespread animal species is the reindeer, which grazes the barren north in huge herds. The indigenous Sami people keep reindeer for their milk, meat and furs. The nuclear catastrophe of **Chernobyl** (1986) was a particular disaster for the reindeer, as the largest part of their grazing habitat was contaminated by radioactive rain. Many animals had to be put down. After the Second World War, Greenland musk ox were repeatedly released into the wild in Norway and a significantly sized herd can now be observed on the Dovrefjell.

Reindeer and musk ox

Sheep and goats are very important suppliers of wool, milk and meat. In climatically suitable regions, cattle are also farmed. The rather small but tough and very nimble fjord horse was once a self-sufficient working animal and is now becoming ever more popular for horse-riding.

Goats, sheep, cattle & horses

Lemmings, rodents around 8cm/3in–15cm/6in in length, with a stunted tail, are members of the vole family that live in the arctic regions of Norway. Herbivorous, they are mostly active at dusk and during the night, when they create extensive underground dens. During winter, they live under the snow blanket and do not hibernate. There are several lemming species. The most common in Norway is the mountain lemming (*Lemmus lemmus*), which has a **strong tendency to mass reproduction**: a fertile female mountain lemming can produce three dozen young per year.

Lemmings

This massive increase in population triggers two major annual migrations. In the spring the males, especially, seek out new summer quarters en masse. During autumn all lemmings set off in search of new habitats. At the beginning of a good lemming year there is a variety of plentiful food available for these animals, but massive overgrazing leads to food shortages and the lemmings are forced to seek new homes. During the course of this effort they traverse streams, rivers and lakes; many perish during these mass migrations. It is a popular **myth** that they **willingly seek out death** by throwing themselves over cliffs into the sea. Such »good« lemming years are, of

The lemming: a member of the vole family

course, also advantageous for the population of their natural predators, in particular owls, buzzards and the south polar skua.

Sea life The coastal waters of Norway are home to diverse species of seal and sea lion, as well as whales (including the minke whale and the sperm whale; see ▶Baedeker Special p.400). So far, the only sea mammal that enjoys official protection is the dolphin.

Sea mammals ▶

Saltwater fish ▶ The coastal waters and the fjords are particularly rich in salmon, ocean trout and char. Out on the open seas, huge shoals of herring are sometimes encountered and large numbers of mackerel frequent the waters around the south and southwest coasts during summer. About one fifth of the fish that occur in the waters of Norway are cod. Their livers are highly prized as delicacies. However, the formerly huge stocks of cod, halibut, ocean salmon and herring have been badly decimated by over-fishing during recent decades.

Crustaceans ▶ Numerous crustaceans can be found along the coast, in particular diverse prawn and crab species, as well as **lobster**.

Freshwater fish Norway's most famous fish is without a doubt the salmon that can only be caught under certain conditions (▶Practicalities). The largest specimen so far caught by fly-fishing weighed in at 34kg/75lb. Each of the roughly 400 salmon rivers in Norway contains its own family of salmon, each distinct in terms of size and markings from all others. What counts for the passionate salmon fisherman is the battle with the fish, as it returns from many years in the Atlantic and climbs up the driving waters of its native river, never shrinking from any obstacle in order to reach its goal: the spawning grounds at the river's source.

Additional Norwegian freshwater fish include the rainbow and river trout, as well as char, perch, whitefish, pike and eel.

The deeply fissured cliffs of the Norwegian coast still offer protected breeding grounds to innumerable seabirds. Species include the guillemot and the endangered common murre, as well as other species that have become rare or extinct in Central Europe, such as the gyrfalcon, the **white-tailed eagle, the fish eagle, and the golden eagle**.

There are also those on the red list of endangered species, such as the cotton teal, the peregrine falcon, and the lesser black-backed gull. The **Atlantic puffin** has also come under threat in recent decades. The primary cause is the over-fishing of herring stocks which has deprived these fish-eating birds of their most important source of nourishment.

? DID YOU KNOW ...?

■ ... that the coastal tern flies a distance of 40,000km/25,000mi annually? It breeds in the northern Arctic, migrates to the southern hemisphere during winter and spends two months there, after which it sets off for the long journey north once more. No other bird covers such distances and no other life form enjoys so much light, because these animals benefit from the midnight sun twice a year.

Facts and Figures Norway

Norway

©Baedeker

Location
► Western Europe, at the western edge of the Scandinavian Peninsula

Geographical data
► Area: 386 958 sq km/149405 sq mi
► Distance north to south: 1756km/1097mi
► Physical distance of mainland coast: 25,148km/15,717mi
► Most northern point: Knivskjelodden (71° 11′ 9″ north)
► Most southern point: Mandal (57° 57′ 31″ north)
► Largest glacier: Jostedalsbreen (490 sq km/189 sq mi)
► Largest lake: Mjøsa: 362 km/226mi
► Highest mountain: Galdhøpiggen 2469m/8101ft
► Norway's widest point: 430km/269mi
► Norway's narrowest point: 6km/4mi

Population
► 4.604 million inhabitants
► Population density: 14 per sq km/0.38 sq mi
► Minorities: Sami (Laps) and Kvener (Kven)
► Foreign immigrants: 9.7% (especially from Poland, Germany, Sweden & Lithuania; also Pakistan, Iraq, Somalia, Vietnam & Denmark).
► Population growth: 0.5% per year
► Capital: Oslo
► Largest cities: Oslo (pop. 512,000), Bergen (236,000), Trondheim (153,000), Stavanger (111,000).
► Official languages: Bokmål (written language) and Nynorsk (new Norwegian)

Religion
► Protestant Lutherans (state church): 86%
► Other Christian faiths: 3%
► Without religion: 10%

State structure
► Parliamentary monarchy
► Head of state: King Harald V
► Prime Minister since 2001: Christian Democrat Kjell Magne Bondevik

Economy
► Land in agricultural use: just under 3%
► Employment: In industry: 22%, service sector: 74%, farming, forestry, fishing: 4%
► Gross Domestic Product (GDP): 1,520,728 million NOK Per capita: 335,108 NOK
► Unemployment: 4.5%
► Price increase: cost of living price index 2.6%

Oil and Gas
► Oil production: 3.23 million barrels per day (52% of Europe's oil production)
► Gas production: 73.1 million cubic metres
► Oil and gas exports: 61.2 % (3rd largest exporter of crude oil after Saudi Arabia and Russia).

Population · Politics · Economy

Paradise for hermits The country's impassability and rough climate has allowed for the creation of significant population densities only in a few places. Almost half of Norway's population lives in the favourable settlement areas around the Oslofjord. The least populated region is Finnmark, where there are barely two inhabitants per square kilometre.

Rural flight The transition of a society of fishermen and farmers into a modern industrial nation, which occurred at the end of the 19th century, initially took place peacefully and without the development of class divisions. For some time now, however, social change has not been being achieved without conflict. The country's development strategy is challenged by a marked imbalance between the centre and the periphery. Expensive infrastructure and subsidy programmes have had to be provided – especially for agriculture and fishing – to persuade the inhabitants of the sparsely populated and poorly served regions of western Norway's interior and all of northern Norway to remain where they are.

The oil boom and its consequences The structural changes that have appeared as a result of the exploitation of oil and gas deposits along the Norwegian coast since the 1970s have created new challenges for the state planners. Coastal settlements and cities such as Stavanger, Bergen and Trondheim have grown very rapidly, which has not only resulted in significant adaptation problems for their inhabitants, but has also led to environmental problems.

Increasing immigration Norway is traditionally a country that people leave. In the second half of the 19th century almost one million Norwegians emigrated, particularly to North America. However, in the last ten years the number of immigrants has almost doubled. While 1995 saw a total of 215,000 immigrants, in 2007 about 415,300 people migrated to Norway. Today, almost 9% of the population come from other countries, the majority from Sweden, Pakistan and Denmark.

The approximately 20,000-strong **Sami population** – which forms the most significant minority among Norwegian inhabitants and predominantly resides in the northern territories – meanwhile

---

! **Baedeker TIP**

Easter with the Sami

The liveliest experience of Sami culture and tradition can be enjoyed during Easter Week in Kautokeino and in Karasjok. That is when many Sami marry, and on Easter Saturday Sami from Norway, Sweden and Finland come together in colourful festive costumes for competitions including races on reindeer sleighs and snowmobiles, as well as putting their lassoing skills to the test. The cultural highlight during the Easter festivities is the Sami Grand Prix in the large hall on the edge of Kautokeino, when the best joik singers are celebrated.

A forest of antlers – reindeer remain the basis of life for many Sami.

has its own parliament, entrusted with representing the interests of this ethnic group. Every Norwegian must be able to speak the two official languages: »Bokmål« which is similar to Danish; and »Nynorsk«, which is an amalgam of 19th-century Norwegian dialects. Additionally, the Sami are now also offered **their own language, also called »Sami«, as a school subject** (for more on the Sami see ►Baedeker Special p.36).

A second significant minority in terms of numbers are the approximately 12,000 descendants of the **Kven**, immigrants from the Baltic and Finland. On the island of Spitsbergen, a significant number of **Russians** has settled alongside roughly 1500 Norwegians.

State and Society

Norway has been a constitutional **hereditary monarchy** since 1814. The king – Harald V since 1991 – nominates the executive with the help of the council of state (government), which is dependent on the support of parliament. The king can **veto** parliamentary decrees which can be resolved by electing a new parliament, which issues a new decree. Laws are made by the Storting (**parliament**), whose 165 members are elected for four-year terms. Proposed legislation is initially debated in the Odelsting (lower house) before being passed to the Lagting (upper house), to which a quarter of all parliamentarians belong.

A king at the helm

A Norwegian administrative anomaly is formed by Svalbard in the Arctic Ocean. This administrative entity includes Spitsbergen and

Svalbard, a special case

Norway *Administrative provinces and regions*

North Norway
Central Norway
West Norway
East Norway
South Norway

Hammerfest

Finnmark

Tromsø

Troms

Narvik

Bodø

Nordland

Arctic Circle
Polsirkelen

Mo i Rana

Nord-Trøndelag

Trondheim

Møre og Romsdal   **Sør-Trøndelag**

Hedmark

Song og Fjordane   **Oppland**

Lillehammer

Bergen

Hordaland   **Buskerud**

OSLO   **Oslo**

Akershus

Rogaland   **Telemark**

Vestfold   **Østfold**

Stavanger

Aust-Agder

Vest-Agder   Kristiansand

Bouvet Island. Norway has had sovereignty over this island group since the 1920 Svalbard Treaty. However, there are also many Russian citizens living here.

Government   The parliamentary elections in 2005 were won by the opposition centre-left red-green coalition headed by Jens Stoltenberg. The largest party in the coalition is the social-democratic Norwegian Labour Party (Det norske Arbeiderparti), which claimed nine ministerial positions in the Norwegian government. These include the prime minister Jens Stoltenberg, the foreign minister Jonas Gahr Støre and the justice minister Knut Storberget. The finance minister is Kristin Halvorsen of the Socialist Left Party (Sosialistisk Venstreparti), which holds five positions in government. The Centre Party, dedicated to the farming community, has four. The right-wing, populist Progress Party took 22.1% of the votes at the elections, the Conservative Party (Høyre) 7.1%, and Kjell Magne Bondevik's Christian Democratic Party 6.8%.

Extensive state power

The state owns, in whole or in part, numerous major industries. The tremendously important energy industry is controlled by the state, with a dedicated oil and energy ministry underlining the significance of this industrial sector. The monopoly of control over public services vital to society, along with the massive subsidy programmes for the fishing and agriculture sectors, has further contributed to the **concentration of power** in the state's hands – one of the reasons for the high level of taxes in Norway.

No to Europe

Norway's foreign policy focuses on the **United Nations**. As a result of its experiences during the Second World War, Norway renounced its traditional neutrality and became a founding member of **NATO** in 1949. The Norwegian parliament voted to accept the constitution of the European Economic Area (EEA) in 1993, and in that respect the states of the European Free Trade Association (EFTA) and the **European Union (EU)** were able to come to an understanding regarding the formation of the European Economic Area (EEA). However, the Norwegian population voted against full membership of the European Union in 1972 and in 1994. As a member of the European Economic Area the country has to accept all decisions made by the European Union, but as a non-member of the EU exerts limited influence over these decisions. Norway's international policy is developed in line with the **Nordic Council**, whose members also include Sweden, Denmark and Finland.

The role of women

The position of women has traditionally been very strong in Norway, one of the first countries in the world to give **women the right to vote**, back in **1913**. In 1986 Gro Harlem Brundtland (▶Famous People) became Norway's first woman prime minister, and a further eight women joined her cabinet. A comprehensive consolidation of child care services has enabled three quarters of Norwegian women to be in full or part-time work. From 2005 on, the boards of Norway's companies have been required to meet a quota of 40% women.

Children

Children are highly valued in this society, a fact that is evident not only on 17 May (a national holiday), when thousands of singing children parade past the royal family. A »children's ombudsman« is entrusted with ensuring conditions for a good and safe childhood, for example by improving the position of families with children. The holder of this post is also charged with protecting the rights of children at school or in the playground.

THE MARSH PEOPLE OF THE HIGH NORTH

The Sami people migrated to northern Scandinavia from the Ural region as early as four thousand years ago. They consider themselves the indigenous population in Norway, Sweden and Finland, yet they are an ethnic minority there today. Only a few still keep reindeer like their forefathers did, but Sami language and culture is maintained: joik singing still survives and the beautiful Sami costume is worn during traditional festivals.

The inhabitants of northern Norway call themselves the »Marsh People« (Sámi, Sapme, Sámit, Samen). The number of people with more or less Sami blood is estimated to be around 40,000, of which around half are settled in Norway and a quarter respectively in Finland and Sweden. As early as AD 100, Tacitus mentioned this **reindeer herding**, hunting people who walked using snow shoes, and the Sami also feature in the Icelandic sagas.

Shamans and bus drivers

Originally the Sami were hunters and herders with an animist religion. A **shaman** mediated between people and the gods with his drum, the Noai'di. An increasingly strong **Scandinavian colonization** of Sami territories took place from the 16th century onwards. Christianization, territorial disputes and a gradual settlement of the high north marginalized the Sami, their

way of life and their shamanism-infused culture ever more. This process also led to the gradual decline of the Sami language, a development that was only halted in the 1960s. Since then, teaching Sami – a language that is not related to the Germanic group, but to the Finno-Ugric group – at schools has been permitted. The **indigenous language** is an important facet of growing up with a Sami identity. Norwegian and Sami were given equal status as official languages in various north Norwegian provinces in 1990. In this way the Sami were granted the right to maintain their culture once more. As a result of the many centuries of assimilation, most Sami now live from agriculture or fishing, like other Norwegians, and even follow careers as school teachers and bus drivers. Less than one tenth of Norwegian Sami people still travel through the land of Sámpi or Sámiid eanan (Land

The Sami wear their colourful costumes to traditional festivals.

of the Sami) as reindeer herders, as of yore. But it is this tenth, in particular, who maintain the Sami cultural heritage. Most Sami only live in their small wooden or earth huts or in tents with an opening for smoke at the top during the summer. Occasionally, during winter, the boat-shaped reindeer-drawn sleigh, known as a »pulk«, is still used for transport. Quite a few Sami cultural goods are also very popular with tourists. Reindeer furs and pewter works are popular purchases, as are colourful ribbon weavings, carpets, carved horn and bone, as well as birch bark items. **Sami traditional costume** is a knee-length skirt with red and yellow borders and tight cloth trousers. A cloth hat is also part of the ensemble which, for Norwegian Sami men, has several points. Shoes are made of soft leather and end with a turned-up point.

More than anything, the joik is an important element of Sami tradition. The monotonal, but very rhythmic, harmonic singing describes places, people and landscapes. Its roots probably reach back as far as Stone Age. The Christian church prohibited joik singing at the beginning of the 17th century, fearing devilish magic. This proscription was only lifted in the 1980s, since which time it has also been permitted during music lessons in the Sami lands.

Confident and proud

The world was made aware of the Sami around 1980, when the Norwegian government drew up plans for the building of a **dam** along the north Norwegian Altaelv river that would have flooded a large area. Together with environmentalists, the Sami resisted this prestige project for years, and it was eventually realized on a much smaller scale than originally proposed. This success fomented a new solidarity among the Sami, and a new-found pride in their own culture and tradition. As a result a **Sami parliament** was established in Karasjok. Those employed in this and other institutions now have better opportunities to ensure that their interests receive a fair hearing in the Norwegian government.

Economy

The world's second richest nation

With a per capita income of 43,000 US dollars per year, Norway is the second richest country in the world after Luxembourg. Oil and gas, shipping and fishing are the most important economic sectors. Norway's economic growth of on average 3% is thanks to North Sea oil. Almost half of Norway's exports originate from the oil industry and its supply industries. The shipping and fisheries sectors, in contrast, have been suffering from tough conditions in recent times.

Norwegian **employment costs** are the highest in the world and no other country in the world has less working hours per year. Everything is **very expensive** in Norway, and taxes are high (a fact relevant for tourists, too). Nevertheless, the Norwegian economy is thriving. In contrast to the general trend for European Union states, Norway's **unemployment rate** has stabilized at 3.5%.

Oil and gas

Even though exploration in the Norwegian North Sea in search of oil only began in 1963, oil and gas extraction now plays a dominant economic role. In the meantime, Norway has become the third largest exporter of oil after Saudi Arabia and Russia, and the world's fourth largest gas exporter after Russia, Canada and Algeria. The financial blessings provided by the oil industry are controlled by the state. Almost one quarter of tax income flows to the state coffers, while the rest goes to an oil fund intended to finance the pensions of future generations.

The port of Bergen: Norway has one of the world's largest merchant fleets.

It is now known that about 1% of the world's oil reserves are located off Norway's shores. The largest oilfield, known as the **Troll field**, covers a seventh of European demand for oil. The **Ekofisk field** 240km/150mi southwest of **Stavanger** is also of great economic significance, as are the **Frigg field** to the west of Bergen, the **Statford field** at the level of the Sognefjord estuary, and the **Snøhvit (Snow White)** and **Goliath** fields near Hammerfest.

In the meantime, exploration and extraction activities have extended north to the Artic Sea, which according to American scientists could conceal a quarter of worldwide oil and gas reserves. The largest natural gas field in the world is the **Stockmann** field on the Russian border.

Dependent on oil

Technological developments and altered market conditions have led to once significant industrial sectors, such as shipping, wood, glass production and food products losing out; Norway has so far not succeeded in establishing greater economic diversification and reducing its dependency on two sectors: North Sea oil and gas, and the fishing industry.

Shipbuilding

The most important centres of shipbuilding today are in Stavanger, Bergen and Trondheim, where this traditional economic sector has greatly benefited from the oil boom. The strong demand for **offshore equipment**, such as drilling platforms and tank equipment, has resulted in dynamic development. Norway has also proved itself to be a pioneer in this sector: Norwegians were the first to build **oil tankers** with double hulls. However, the demand for Norwegian ships is presently on a steady downward spiral.

Traditional seafaring nation

Norway is an extremely important seafaring nation. It maintains one of the world's **largest merchant navies**, with a total tonnage of almost 23 million gross register tons (GRT). The Norwegian fleet of oil tankers alone accounts for a capacity of around 10.5GRT. International passenger shipping, especially the lucrative **cruise market**, is dominated by Norwegian shipping companies. Norwegian luxury liners travel all the world's oceans and major Norwegian shipping companies also dominate the American market. There are plans to become the pre-eminent force in the European market for cruises.

Aluminium and paper

Norway's wealth of cheap hydro-power has led to a flourishing aluminium industry, which requires high levels of energy. Other branches of the Norwegian steel and the paper industry have greatly profited from this plentiful source of energy.

Hydroelectric power

Despite Norway's massive natural oil and gas resources, thermal power stations are only of limited significance. Thanks to high mountains and plentiful water, Norway is able to meet **99% of its electricity needs** from hydroelectric facilities.

Agriculture High mountains, fjell landscapes and barren soil mean that only 3% of the nation's territory can be exploited for agriculture. These areas are found, for example, in the fertile lime and clay fields around the Oslofjord, the Trondheimsfjord and Lake Mjøsa, as well as in the region south of Stavanger. To the west, agriculture is limited to the 40km/25mi–60km/37mi-wide coastal area, as well as to narrow strips along the lower fjord valleys. **Cereals, potatoes** and greenhouse vegetables are cultivated here. In the region around the Hardangerfjord, **fruit cultivation** also has a role to play. The extremely short growing season in the north is also a limiting factor – only 140 days per year in northern Norway for example. Arable agriculture therefore gives way to animal husbandry moving further north. North of the Arctic Circle, therefore, only **reindeer herding**, sheep farming and the breeding of animals for fur have any economic significance. 80% of foods and semi-luxury foods have to be imported. Norwegian agriculture today can only be kept alive by means of **high subsidies**.

Forestry In contrast to the neighbouring countries of Finland and Sweden, Norway's forestry sectors are in decline, because only 22% of the total national territory (7 million hectares or 17 million acres) are of commercial use. Norway is therefore keen to develop long-term aforestation programmes to increase its forest areas.

Fishing industry After natural oil and gas, fish and fish products are Norway's most important export items. 44% of export income in this sector comes from the export of **farmed salmon and trout** produced by **fish farms**. The salmon business, in particular, is booming: in Britain, Germany, Poland, Russia, Japan and even Sweden, Norwegian salmon is in great demand. Going by the annual catch of around 2.8 million tons, Norway is the most significant fishing nation in Europe, especially with regard to deep-sea fishing. The main species caught at present are capelin (a type of salmon), cod, mackerel, shellfish and coley (▶Baedeker Special p.276). The fish processing industry's main products are fishmeal, fish oil and tinned fish, though the number of fish processing factories has reduced from 860 to 500 during the past two decades. Coastal fishing is in decline, especially in the region of the Lofoten. Herring and cod have also lost a great deal of their significance for the deep-sea fishing industry. The percentage of the annual catch consisting of these species has been reduced to between 10 and 15%.

Due to international pressure, **whaling** (▶ Baedeker Special p.400) has all but collapsed in recent years. Despite loud protests by environmental protection agencies, however, Norway increased its annual quota for minke whale from 670 to 797 animals in 2005.

Fish farming Fish farming in massive aqua farms has expanded at a tremendous rate over recent decades, especially for salmon and trout. Modern fish farming is considered an innovation in Norway. There are now

Salmon from the aquaculture industry has flooded the market and caused prices to collapse.

around 1200 such businesses, producing more than the market consumes. The collapse in the prices for salmon and serious marketing problems brought economic ruin for many fish farmers. The monoculture of mass fish keeping, uncontrolled use of antibiotics and use of beta-carotene to increase the red colour of salmon meat all combined to bring aqua farming into disrepute. These days, antibiotics are hardly used. Furthermore, farming in narrow fjords is avoided, in order to avoid over-fertilized waters. Nevertheless, biotechnological research continues. A new type of farmed fish is the arctic char and, in the meantime, halibut, Dover sole and a variety of crustaceans and mussels are also farmed.

Back in the 18th century, it was salmon that attracted the first tourists to Norway – mostly those members of the British nobility that were not frightened by the challenging journey. Today the journey is much easier and Norway enjoys great popularity as a tourist destination. The British are the fourth most significant visitor group after the Swedes, the Germans and the Danes, and contribute 8% of Norway's tourist visitors annually. Additional employment is created by tourism, especially in the regions of central and northern Norway with weak infrastructure. At present, tourism accounts for over 10% of all Norwegian jobs. There is much optimism for a major increase in visitors who like to be active on holiday, with trekking, canoeing, kayaking, sailing and winter sports on offer.

Tourism

NORTH SEA OIL

The exploitation of gas and oil in the North Sea has particularly benefited Stavanger and Bergen, which have developed into genuine boom towns. Wages are high and the population is rising dramatically. Only around 16,000 people earn their living on the oil platforms, but the national importance of the shipping companies, dockyards and supply industries is enormous.

A deafening noise can be heard in the middle of the North Sea, barely 170km/106mi southwest of the Norwegian port of Stavanger. Heavy diesel-powered engines drone, metal railings vibrate, helicopter blades whip the rough air and heavy breakers lash against 16 metal posts. 26 Norwegians reach this, their workplace, after a flight of just under one hour. The »Ocean Viking« drilling platform is a monster of iron and steel that is one of several dozen similar constructions looking for oil in the North Sea: 112m/367ft long, 91m/299ft wide, and weighing 4860 tons.

Striking it lucky 15,000ft down

It happened on 2 August 1969: the diamond-tipped drill point of the »Ocean Viking« struck oil at a depth of 4500m/14,764ft. This newly discovered oilfield was to become famous around the world as the **Ekofisk field**, and a new epoch in Norwegian history had begun. Oil exploitation in the North Sea was fraught with danger and therefore very expensive, but it soon started to pay: substantial profits were already being made from oil and gas exports by 1975. Between 1980 and 2000, offshore oil exploitation more than quadrupled. Present extraction rates lie at over 3.2 million barrels per day (1 barrel = 159 litres). Despite massive reserves, gas exploitation has only been developed gradually. In 1979, the Norwegians produced 25 billion cubic metres of gas from fields in the North Sea. That has increased by 20% today, Germany being the major buyer of Norwegian gas. Floating platforms with hydraulic legs that sit on the seabed are used up

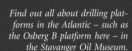

Find out all about drilling platforms in the Atlantic – such as the Osberg B platform here – in the Stavanger Oil Museum.

to a depth of 100m/328ft. The **working platform** is about 30m/98ft above the water. For depths of 100m–250m/328ft–820ft semi-submersibles with mighty ballast tanks are used. These are propelled by engines and positioned over the drilling spot by anchors. For depths of over 250m/820ft, drilling ships with **dynamic positioning systems** are used.

Towns at sea

The production platforms together with the accommodation platforms, work ships, loading stations and pipelines form veritable towns at sea. One of the largest offshore projects ever is the oil and gas field of **Troll Olje** (70km/44mi northwest of Bergen), where half of Norway's presently-known gas reserves are located. The **world's largest production platform** was inaugurated here in 1996, with a daily production capacity of 150,000 barrels of crude oil.

Life-threatening job

The Norwegian technology used to deal with the difficult offshore extraction conditions is in demand all around the world. Yet the dangers of the offshore drilling business are not to be underestimated. There is a permanent danger of oil spillage, with all the associated damage to the environment. The Bravo drilling platform tipped over in the Ekofisk oilfield in 1979, and only the dedicated deployment of the Texan Red Adair's oil brigade limited environmental damage as much as was possible. Three years later, the Alexander Kielland platform was ripped from its anchorage by the tempestuous North Sea, a disaster that cost over 100 people their lives.

History

Ice Age hunters roamed the tundra, Vikings ruled the waves, but then the country had to bow to its neighbours: for many centuries Norway remained under the control of Denmark and Sweden and it only became an independent country in 1905. Now however, shored up by petrodollars, Norway takes a very self-confident stand in Europe.

Hunters, Farmers and Germanic Tribes

10000–2500 BC	Hunter-gatherers in Norway
from 2500 BC	First farmers
1800–500 BC	Bronze Age: rock paintings
AD 200	Runic writing is invented

Stone Age

As the ice of the glaciers retreated, the first humans migrated to the area. Archaeological finds of fishing and hunting tools prove that man lived along the Norwegian coast as early as 10,000 years ago. While the interior of the Scandinavian Peninsula was still under ice, the settlement areas along the coast reached all the way up to Finnmark. It is unclear if these hunter-gatherers were ancestors of the Sami people (once known as the Lapps or Laplanders).

Nordic Bronze Age

There are also significant finds dating from the Nordic Bronze Age(Nordic Circle) originating in southern and western Norway. The **rock paintings**, found predominantly along the west side of the **Oslofjord** and along a strip of land heading into Sweden to the east of Trondheim, date from this time. Animals hunted for food, such as reindeer, deer and fish are portrayed, as well as occasional images of humans and boats. The **burial mounds** also date from this epoch, complete with elaborate tombs for the dead of chieftain families.

Germanic tribes

In Norway, the Germanic tribes spread all the way to the Arctic Circle during the **Ice Age**. Kinship groups, headed by chieftains, emerged in the fjord valleys. The era of the **great migrations** (AD 400 – AD 550) appears to have been an unsettled time for Norway, because many tribes created defensive systems, some of which were virtual fortresses. Even today, the remains of fortifications can be seen spread over 50km/30mi along the eastern shore of Lake Mjøsa. During the Iron Age, **iron extraction** from bog ore became ever more widespread. In particular the techniques of weapon production were improved. The art of writing also caught on and, from AD 200, **runic inscriptions** became common on jewellery and tools. Around the 4th century AD, people in Norway also began to carve runic script into stone, among other places into rock walls, standing stones and onto tomb covers. While the name »Scandinavia« was first used by Pliny the Elder (around AD 75), and Tacitus also mentioned Swedes (Suiones) and Finns (Fenni), ancient songs give no evidence of a common name for the Norwegian tribes. The later word »Norvegr« simply means »the way to the north«.

← *Three swords near Stavanger recall the battle of 872, when Harald Fairhair vanquished the minor kings at the Hafrsfjord.*

THE VIKINGS ARE COMING!

This call inspired fear and loathing all over Europe for over three hundred years. The Vikings' extensive war and looting campaigns have been the foundation of their reputation to this day. However, they were also traders, explorers and talented boat builders.

The Vikings made their first bloody entry into the history books in AD 793, when they attacked the English monastery of Lindisfarne. In 845 they conquered Paris, in 862 Cologne and in 882 they ransacked the city of Trier. The great era of the Vikings (from the old Norse »vik« = bay), as the northern Germanic tribes of the early Middle Ages are referred to today, spanned the 8th to 11th centuries. The »Nortmanni« (Northmen), as contemporary reports refer to the northern Germanic people, left their Nordic homeland and penetrated into the rest of Europe and far beyond.

The first in America

The so-called »Rus« (probably the Finnish word for the eastern Northmen, or the Swedes), headed south-east to trade with the Slavic tribes, and they also settled in this region. They founded a **new »Rus(s)ian« state** and expanded their sphere of influence as far as Constantinople and Bagdad. The western Northmen (Norwegians) moved to the south-west, settling in almost uninhabited regions of Scotland, as well as on the Shetland Islands, the Orkneys and the Hebrides. From there they attacked Ireland and England. For decades they exacted tribute payments from the inhabitants of the French northwest coast, until the French king gave them the land in fief and it became known as **Normandy** (»the land in which the Normans rule«). They attacked Spain and Italy and pushed on as far as Antioch; they settled Iceland, which had been uninhabited until then, and brought northern Germanic culture to its greatest flowering there. Their

»Leif Erikson discovers America«, a painting by Christian Krohg (1893) exhibited in the Seafaring Museum in Oslo.

sense of adventure pushed them ever further. Erik the Red discovered Greenland while based in Iceland, and many Norwegians soon settled there. **Leif Eriksson**, his son, left Greenland in 992 heading west, and landed in Newfoundland, now the easternmost province of Canada. The Vikings therefore discovered America **500 years before Columbus**.

Setting off into the world

What suddenly impelled the Northmen to head off into the world, having lived relatively peacefully for a long time? An important feature of agricultural Nordic society was inheritance. **The oldest son inherited** the estate while the other sons had to make their own way. Furthermore, the climate became warmer towards the end of the 8th century, which

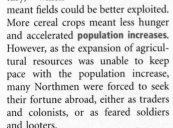

meant fields could be better exploited. More cereal crops meant less hunger and accelerated **population increases**. However, as the expansion of agricultural resources was unable to keep pace with the population increase, many Northmen were forced to seek their fortune abroad, either as traders and colonists, or as feared soldiers and looters.

Brilliant seafarers

The Vikings' ability to conquer the world so successfully lay first and foremost in their superiority at sea. They were at home on the world's oceans, they proved themselves to be outstanding seafarers and their long, yet manoeuvrable **dragon boats** were the most seaworthy craft of their day. The 20m–25m/66ft–82ft-long and 3m–5m/10ft–16ft-wide hull had an identical bow and stern which allowed for forward and backward steering with equal ease. These light yet tough wooden boats did not lie deep in the water and could quickly be pulled to shore or even across land. Superior boat-building technique alone, however, does not quite explain the Vikings' military success. Ideology may have been a deciding factor. All of Scandinavia had remained heathen until far into the Middle Ages. Odin, the god of poetry and war, ruled in the Northmen's celestial heavens. He decided who would die on the battlefield and took the bravest to join him in paradise, or Valhall (Walhalla). The Vikings therefore positively sought out battle and death by the sword, so that they might reach Valhall where they would join the gods in one **last battle** against the dark forces of the cosmos.

The Creation of Norway

around 872	Harald Fairhair unifies the country
8th–11th century	Vikings spread fear and horror.
10th–11th century	Violent Christianization of the population
around 1250	Norway reaches the height of its power under Håkon Håkonsson

One all-powerful ruler

Dozens of small kingdoms were created up to the 8th century AD. But around the year 872 Harald Hårfagre (»Fairhair«; 872–930), who came from an old Oslofjord ruling dynasty, conquered all the other minor kings and united western and southern Norway under his rule. After his death, however, the minor kingdoms partly revived. During this same period, the **Vikings** also undertook their spectacular warring campaigns and raids, penetrating into distant parts of western and central Europe, as well as into the Atlantic region.

Christianization

It took about two centuries before the entire heathen population had accepted the Christian faith. The minor kings (Jarle) of Trondheim, who wanted to keep their ancient traditions, proved to be particularly stubborn opponents of the missionary work that began at the end of the 10th century. Yet with a firmness that often bordered on the brutal, Olav Haraldsson (1015–30) established both unification and **Christianity**. He fought against the Danes and the Trondheimers and was exiled in 1028. Attempting to return, he fell at the **Battle of Stiklestad** in 1030. Soon afterwards, he was honoured as a martyr and raised to the status of a Norwegian national hero, as well as being made a saint. He went down in history as **Saint Olav**, Norway's eternal king. His body was brought to Nidaros (the present-day Trondheim) and buried there. **Nidaros Cathedral**, the largest medieval construction in Scandinavia, was erected over his tomb. Shortly before 1100, the first bishoprics emerged in the kingdom, including the bishopric

The Saga Column at Elveseter presents Norwegian history you can touch, beginning in 872.

of Nidaros that became an archbishopric in 1152 and took the lead in establishing a national church. The power of the church soon grew to such an extent that it was able to demand the right to grant land in fief.

Under Håkon Håkonsson (1217–63) the Norwegian kingdom achieved the height of its power, having secured itself as a hereditary monarchy. The crown controlled the nobility, administration was re-organized, the population increased, towns and cities were built or developed further, and Norway achieved its **greatest territorial gains** with the annexation of Iceland, Greenland, the Faroe Islands, the Hebrides, and parts of Sweden.

Unified kingdom

Under Danish Rule

1319	Norway initially falls to Sweden
1397	Kalmar Union unites Norway, Denmark and Sweden
1387–1814	Norway belongs to Denmark
1536	Reformation

Having already been under Danish rule for a short period in the 11th century, Norway entered into a personal union with Sweden after the extinction of its royal lineage in 1319. According to royal inheritance, the Swedish crown prince **Håkon VI** (1340–80) was the rightful heir to the Norwegian Crown. In 1349, the plague reduced Norway's population by two thirds. As a result, the country was in a severely weakened state when Håkon VI married **Margrethe of Denmark**, daughter of the Danish king Waldemar IV Atterdag. It was therefore child's play for Margrethe to take control of Denmark, Sweden and Norway after her husband's death in 1389. Queen Margrethe created the constitutional basis for this union of states, during which Norway finally lost its independence, by establishing the **Kalmar Union** in 1397, which was intended to unite the Nordic countries against the German Empire.

Loss of independence

While Sweden successfully fought for its independence from 1433 onwards, finally escaping the union of states in 1523, Norway remained tied to Denmark until 1814, officially declared a Danish province. The dissolution of the Norwegian state council took place in 1536, and a **Danish governor** ruled in Norway from 1572 onwards. The **Reformation** spread from 1536 onwards, and in the succeeding era Danish became the official state language, including in church and school. The old Norwegian language only survived in di-

A Danish province

alects. Economically, Norway experienced an upturn. However, trade in the 15th and 16th centuries was almost entirely dictated by the German **Hanseatic League**. Mining was of increasing importance from 1624 onwards, for which miners from the German-speaking lands were also brought in. Silver mining was begun near Kongsberg, and copper was mined in Røros from 1644 onwards. Revolt against Danish hegemony only emerged at the beginning of the 19th century. The continental blockade against England established by **Napoleon I** in 1806 resulted in a counter-blockade of the Norwegian coast by the British, which inhibited seafaring and soon caused economic hardship in the country. Understandably, Norway sought to disassociate itself from Denmark, which was aligned with Napoleon.

After Napoleon I's defeat, Denmark had to cede Norway to Sweden in the **Treaty of Kiel**. Copenhagen was only allowed to keep the Faroe Islands, Iceland and Greenland. The Norwegian islands of Orkney and Shetland had already been pawned to Scotland by the Danish King Christian I, in the 15th century.

Union with Sweden

1814	Norway writes itself a liberal constitution on 17 May (a national holiday)
1814–1905	Personal union with Sweden
1854	Railway link between Oslo and Eidsvoll

Independent constitution

The Norwegians did not accept the Treaty of Kiel, however, declaring independence and giving themselves a liberal constitution at Eidsvoll on 17 May 1814, now a national holiday. Norwegians were only persuaded to accept the personal union with Sweden after **Swedish troops invaded** their country, but they were allowed to keep their constitution.

Upswing in the economy

Norway experienced a general upturn in the economy from the beginning of the 1830s. The first textile factories and machine workshops were founded in the 1840s, which formed the foundation of Norway's modern industries. Norway also rose to become an important **seafaring nation** between 1850 and 1880, thanks to its ever-expanding merchant fleet.

Norway becomes independent

Swedish concessions meant that the Norwegians achieved home rule. The Norwegian national assembly (the »Storting«) was empowered to nominate the government and pass laws, though these could always be vetoed by the Swedish king. In 1880, though, the Storting successfully campaigned to have the Swedish right of veto annulled. From then on, Norway's domestic politics were under its own control and only the personal union's foreign policy continued to be dictated by Stockholm alone. But when the now mighty seafaring nation of Norway demanded to have its own economic consulates abroad and the Swedes rejected their wishes, the Storting threatened a split in **1905**, and Stockholm responded by demanding a **popular referendum** that was to decide the future of the union. 368,392 Norwegians voted for the dissolution of the Union, while only 184 voted for its continuation, and Sweden granted Norway its **independence** without further objection. In a further referendum the Norwegians voted to keep the monarchy and shortly afterwards Prince Karl of Denmark took the name of Håkon, after having been elected Norwegian King. Håkon ruled from 1905 to 1957.

The World Wars

1911	Roald Amundsen is the first to reach the South Pole.
1913	Female suffrage is established.
1914–18	Norway remains neutral during World War I.
1925	Norwegian rule over Spitsbergen
1940	Norway is occupied by German troops.
1945	King Håkon VII returns from exile.

Pre-war era

Norway was enjoying an economic upturn at the time of the union's dissolution. It had cheap energy through hydroelectric power, foreign investment was flowing into the country, and electro-chemical and electro-metallic factories were established for the first time. Politically, Norway also developed into one of the most advanced and liberal nations in Europe.

First World War

Norway remained **neutral** during the First World War, though it suffered greatly from the **submarine war** waged by the Germans in the North Atlantic. The merchant fleet, vital for the supply of goods to the nation, was halved with losses of over 800 ships to submarines and mines. But the Norwegians also made a great deal of money from the wartime economy: their fish and ores (especially copper) were highly prized by the warring nations.

Second World War

Norway also attempted to remain neutral during the Second World War. However, both the Germans and the Allies had a strong interest in controlling the Norwegian coast. There was a particular focus on the port of Narvik, from which iron ore was shipped to Germany via Swedish Kiruna. After British forces had **mined Norwegian waters**, an ambush-style occupation of Norway followed by German troops in April 1940, who were intent on pre-empting a British landing. The Norwegian army offered considerable resistance, despite withdrawing, and was supported by British, French and Polish expeditionary corps. Particularly costly battles took place around the **iron ore port of Narvik** and, in June 1940, the Norwegian forces capitulated. The royal family and the government fled into **exile in London**, where the exiled Norwegian government set up shop. From then on, **Vidkun Quisling**, the leader of an insignificant fascist association, was imposed as prime minister of a puppet regime by the Germans. Quisling – who was to be condemned by the Norwegian courts after the war and executed – was soon replaced by a state governor, again appointed by the Germans.

Resistance

Large sections of the Norwegian population offered fierce resistance from early on in the war, but the German occupying forces held the country in a firm grip. Nevertheless, when compared to other countries subjected to the Nazi terror, Norway emerged more or less unscathed from the Second World War. The German troops were forced to withdraw from Norway at the end of 1944 and their final capitulation took place on 8 May 1945. A total of 10,262 Norwegians were killed in battle during the war or lost their lives as prisoners. Many cities and municipalities were destroyed in bombing raids or by fire. The Norwegian King Håkon VII, returned from his London exile as early as one month after the end of the Second World War.

Into the 21st Century

from 1946	Swift reconstruction and upturn
1969	The legendary Ekofisk oil field is discovered
1972/1994	Norway says no to membership of the EC/EU
1981	Gro Harlem Brundtland is the first woman to become prime minister

Welfare state and oil nation

Reconstruction after the war was unexpectedly rapid. By 1946 industrial production and gross national product were already higher than in 1938, which enabled the development of a welfare state based on the Swedish model. The oil age began in 1969, when natural oil and gas was discovered at the Ekofisk field in the North Sea (▶Baedeker Special p.42).

Norway and Europe

In terms of foreign policy, Norway exhibited extreme restraint during the early years after the war. However with the onset of the Cold War and the increasing tension between East and West, a new stand was taken. A founding member of the United Nations, it joined the North Atlantic Treaty Organization (NATO) in 1949. Unlike in Sweden and Finland, the Norwegian people voted against full membership of the European Community in 1972 and then of the European

Crown Prince Håkon with his wife Mette-Marit and their first child Ingrid Alexandra. Their marriage was highly controversial at first.

Union in 1994. It seems that after the trauma of centuries of forced union with Denmark and Sweden, as well as of the German occupation, this small nation's fear of unions of any kind was just too strong. Many also feared that Europe would use the country's oil wealth as a ready source of contributions.

When Håkon, the Norwegian heir to the throne, announced his plans to marry Mette-Marit Tjessem Høiby in the summer of 2001, there were cries of outrage the like of which had not been seen for a very long time. But it was not the fact that his chosen bride was a commoner that made the Norwegian people hot under the collar – after all, King Harald himself had also once chosen a non-royal. It was more Mette-Marit's earlier life: wild parties, an illegitimate child by a playboy with criminal convictions, her humble family background, and summer jobs as a waitress and strawberry picker. »Someone like that«, according to many Norwegians, should definitely not become queen. Suddenly only 62% were still in favour of keeping the monarchy. But when the wedding took place in August 2001, all was forgiven and forgotten: the rejoicing by the Norwegian people knew no limits. Her Royal Highness Princess Ingrid Alexandra was born on 21 January 2004. Since absolute primogeniture was established in Norway in 1990, Princess Ingrid Alexandra could one day follow her father onto the Norwegian throne, a fate denied to Princess Märtha Louise, the present King Harald V's first-born child. The Norwegian Crown Prince's second child, Prince Håkon Sverre Magnus, was born 3 December 2005.

Monarchy in the firing line

Arts and Culture

Norway's Viking ships and stave churches are unique, and those who want something special to take home can stock up on plays by Henrik Ibsen and dramatic crime novels by Norwegian authors, not forgetting the renowned philosophical novel, *Sophie's World*.

Art History

Ancient Art

The era of the early Stone Age, during which the transition from hunting and gathering to settled agriculture took place, occurred in Scandinavia around 1800 BC. The **rock paintings** of the Arctic Circle were created at that time. Many of these rock paintings display images of game animals, with relatively few pictures of humans. Some researchers have interpreted the images as **magical paintings** that were somehow intended to bring good fortune when hunting, but the true motivation that inspired the archaic artists will probably never be known.

Early Stone Age

Germanic art in Scandinavia spans almost three millennia, from the Bronze Age, which lasted from 1800 BC to 600 BC in this region, all the way to the first century AD. The Bronze Age is characterized by technical innovation: the extraction, smelting and working of **bronze**. The weapons, tools and jewellery that were made of stone during the Stone Age were now made of metal; expressive art from the Bronze Age has also survived in the form of **rock paintings**, with schematic cultural illustrations of such events as festive processions, ritual war games and sleigh processions, as well as images of boats and pilgrims.

Germanic art

◀ *Bronze Age*

Germanic art flowered when the originally rather sober illustrations developed into lively zoomorphic (animal) ornamentation. There is a penchant for filigree art from early history right up to around AD 350, and fibulas or clasps are embellished with granular gold and silver wires. Later, the technique of **chip carving in bronze and silver** was popular until the 6th century. This style of art involved making intricate decorative indentations into the metal with a sharp point. Originally, this technique probably came from wood carving and has survived in folk art to this day. Abstract **zoomorphic ornamentation** and ribbon-like tracery predominate from the 6th century to around 800. The »**Animal Style**« of various regions is characterized by a development from highly abstract animal forms to intricate ornamental compositions. A tip for those trying to recognize the animal in any one of these decorative works: if you first find the easily identified eye, the rest can be deciphered much more easily.

◀ *Early history*

Viking art (approx. 800–1100) is also characterized by zoomorphic ornamentation. The Viking's greatest technical achievement was replacing the old rowing boats with ocean-going **keel boats**, which had reinforced hulls, masts and a keel. It was this superior ship construction that made possible the Viking's great success. An impres-

Viking art

← *Kings are crowned in the Nidaros Cathedral in Trondheim.*

sive example of this innovative type of vessel is the **Oseberg ship** (in the Viking Boat Museum in Oslo), used as a burial ship for a **Norwegian princess** (▶p.322) in AD 834. Another clinker-built ship is the **Gokstad ship** from the grave mound of Kongshaugen, located near Sandar in the district of Vestfold (today also in the Viking Ship Museum, Oslo). The 24m/79ft-long boat contained (among other things) the grave of a dressed man lying on a magnificent bed accompanied by a wealth of burial objects. When Christianity finally superseded the Germanic heathen religions, zoomorphic ornamentation also disappeared. The last examples date from around 1100 and can be seen, for example, in the **stave church at Urnes** (around 1090).

Romanesque (11th–12th century)

Stone churches
Christianization, which took place around AD 1000, marks the end of the Germanic and Viking artistic heyday. Building using bricks was established around 1160. Churches built of stone signified the **power of the new religion** and are now the best-preserved architectural monuments from the Romanesque era, chalk and granite being the favoured building materials. The stone buildings from the Romanesque era, including **Stavanger Cathedral** (around 1130) and the **Lyse monastery church** (around 1146) were modelled on English examples.

Stave churches
Wood is Norway's traditional building material and craftsmen exhibited great artistry very early on. The **influence of shipbuilding techniques** can be seen in the stave churches (▶ Baedeker Special p.175), whose walls are made up of vertically placed posts in the stave building style. One of the oldest wood churches, the **stave church of Urnes**, dates from around the year 1090. Most of the stave churches still surviving today can be found in the triangle between Oslo, Bergen and Trondheim.

Gothic (13th–15th century)

Architecture
The architectural style of Norway's Gothic churches often follows the Franco-Spanish examples. Several sacred buildings also recall German **red-brick Gothic** church building. The influence of the English style in that era also left a lasting impression, as can be seen, for example, in Trondheim Cathedral (new building phase from 1152).

Painting and sculpture
Norwegian painting and sculpture from the Middle Ages displays very little originality and is predominantly preserved in the form of church frescoes. **Historic Germanic ornamentation techniques** have survived in the carvings of the stave churches. During the late Middle Ages, paintings, winged altars and alabaster reliefs were imported from the Netherlands, Lübeck and England.

Norway's stave churches

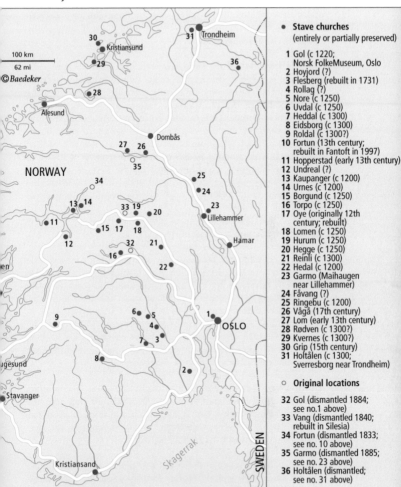

100 km
62 mi
© Baedeker

NORWAY

SWEDEN

Skagerrak

- **Stave churches**
  (entirely or partially preserved)

1 Gol (c 1220;
  Norsk FolkeMuseum, Oslo
2 Hoyjord (?)
3 Flesberg (rebuilt in 1731)
4 Rollag (?)
5 Nore (c 1250)
6 Uvdal (c 1250)
7 Heddal (c 1300)
8 Eidsborg (c 1300)
9 Roldal (c 1300?)
10 Fortun (13th century;
   rebuilt in Fantoft in 1997)
11 Hopperstad (early 13th century)
12 Undreal (?)
13 Kaupanger (c 1200)
14 Urnes (c 1200)
15 Borgund (c 1250)
16 Torpo (c 1250)
17 Oye (originally 12th
   century; rebuilt)
18 Lomen (c 1250)
19 Hurum (c 1250)
20 Hegge (c 1250)
21 Reinli (c 1300)
22 Hedal (c 1200)
23 Garmo (Maihaugen
   near Lillehammer)
24 Fåvang (?)
25 Ringebu (c 1200)
26 Vågå (17th century)
27 Lom (early 13th century)
28 Rødven (c 1300?)
29 Kvernes (c 1300?)
30 Grip (15th century)
31 Holtålen (c 1300;
   Sverresborg near Trondheim)

○ **Original locations**

32 Gol (dismantled 1884;
   see no.1 above)
33 Vang (dismantled 1840;
   rebuilt in Silesia)
34 Fortun (dismantled 1833;
   see no. 10 above)
35 Garmo (dismantled 1885;
   see no. 23 above)
36 Holtålen (dismantled;
   see no. 31 above)

Renaissance and Baroque (16th–18th century)

Only a few examples of Renaissance architecture can be found in Norway, but there are significant Baroque buildings. Cities are still dominated by their Baroque fortifications today, their military significance a dim and distant memory. Outstanding examples of Baroque fortress building include the **Akershus** in Oslo, built in 1660; the **Kristiansten** fortress of 1681 in Trondheim; the **Håkonshalle** in Bergen, built in 1700; the **Vardøhus** (northern Norway) built in 1738; and the **Fredriksten** fortress in Halden (southern Norway). A complete 17th-century garrison town can be seen in the historic centre (Gamlebyen) of **Frederikstad**.

Wooden architecture
With the **invention of the band saw** at the end of the 16th century, it became possible to divide tree trunks into individual boards. In this way wood cabins could be given a protective shield against the weather and their design could also follow styles for façades from other parts of Europe. Thus wooden houses were created in the 17th and 18th centuries that mirrored the formal designs of stone buildings in their detail. Much-discussed examples that can still be seen today are the old wooden houses of the mining town of Røros, as well as the Hanseatic merchant homes on the Bryggen at Bergen. Norway's largest wooden building, the **Trondheim Stiftsgården**, displays an extremely impressive copy of what would be a Baroque stone façade elsewhere.

Art in the 19th and 20th Centuries

Classical art
A large array of public buildings was created in the Classical style after the dissolution of the union with Denmark. H.F.D. Linstow built the royal palace at Kristiania (today Oslo) between 1824 and 1848, and also redesigned the Karl Johansgate, the main thoroughfare of the Norwegian capital. The university buildings were built in 1852 according to designs by Christian H. Grosch.
Romantic German castle building also made an impression here, its influence particularly noticeable in the market hall next to the Oslo cathedral, designed by Christian H. Grosch in 1849.

Swiss style
The so-called Swiss style spread throughout Norway like wildfire, although transformed by Nordic motifs it did develop into the Norwegian **Dragon style**. One of the most beautiful examples of this building style is the »**Frognerseteren**« restaurant, built on the Holmenkollen hill by Holm H. Munthe in 1890.

Sculpture
Renowned representatives of the younger generation of Norwegian artists include the sculptors **Stephan Sinding** (1846–1922), **Ingebrigt Vik** (1867–1927; ▶ Hardangerfjord, Øystese) and, in particular, **Gustav Vigeland**, whose sculptures attract many visitors to Vigeland Park in Oslo.

Decorative painting
It is Norway's folk art scene that produces art and craft works of the greatest character. This is especially true of the rural tradition of »**rose painting**«, in which furniture and parts of houses are decorated. Rose motifs are rarely used, however. Wall hangings, usually of cloth or paper, are normally produced for festivals, but walls and ceilings are also very popular surfaces for painted decoration.

They always inspire conversation: the sculptures in Oslo's Vigeland Park.

Impressive works can also be found in Norwegian painting. The Ro- **Painting**
mantics Johann Christian Dahl (1788–1857) and his pupil Thomas
Fearnley (1802–42) were at work in the 19th century. The artists J.
Eckersberg (1882–70) and Hans Gude (1825–1903) belong to the so-
called Düsseldorf School, while Gerhard Munthe (1849–1929), Erik
Werenskiold (1855–1938) and Christian Krohg modelled their work
on French art. **Edvard Munch** (▶ Famous People), who is considered
to be one of the founders of **Expressionism**, is of international
significance.

Folk Art

In Norway, as elsewhere, there are innumerable stylistic forms of folk
art. The three most famous are wood carving, rose painting and the
making of the colourful folk costumes.

The art of wood carving goes back to the Vikings. Their famous **Wood carving**
ships were decorated with carved animal heads, usually dragon
heads, and other figures from the bow to the waterline. Domestic
items and tools were also decorated with carvings. In the 12th century, by which time the country had been Christianized, church
building began in Norway, and the new stave churches (▶ Baedeker
Special p.175) provided wood carvers with a wealth of surfaces to
work on. Some of the most beautiful examples of this medieval
handicraft are seen on the carved doorways and window frames of
farmhouses, and this art form in particular has survived right up to

Not only girls love their national costume.

the present day. Wooden houses, including newly erected ones, are usually embellished with carvings on their exterior walls. A particularly beautiful example is the Frognerseteren restaurant built in the hills above Oslo in 1891 (▶p.324).

Another major folk art form is so-called »rosemaling« or rose painting, a form of rural painting that involves decorating parts of houses, furniture and everyday domestic items. Rose motifs and variations thereof do occur but, in addition, geometric patterns, portraits and landscapes are also featured. The oldest surviving paintings of this form date from the 17th century. There are countless theories on the origins of rose painting. Every settlement developed its own style due to the remoteness of the valleys, and these differences in style are so marked that experts today are able to give very precise information on the age and origin of rose painting works. Pieces of furniture adorned with rose painting are among the most desirable items in the Norwegian antiques market.

Folk costumes The third great artistic form in Norwegian folk art is costume-making and the wearing of traditional costumes is still popular today. Whatever the occasion, Norway's traditional garb is always guaranteed to be acceptable attire. Costumes are handed down through the generations, the silver belt traditionally being presented to daughter-in-laws, a gift from their husband's parents.

Literature

Old Norse poetry Early Old Norse poetry takes three well-known forms: the pagan Eddaic poems, the sagas, and skaldic verse. Most of these works were composed in Norway, centred around the Norwegian royal court. Iceland was settled during the Viking period, where a rich culture soon developed, and this lies at the root of the close relationship between Old Norse and old Icelandic literature.

During the personal union with Denmark between 1387 and 1841, Danish became the official language of state, church and school. Norwegian was obliterated and only survived in rural dialects. The century of the Reformation signified not only the loss of the national language, but also a cultural loss. Churches and monasteries were looted, and valuable manuscripts, including many sagas, fell victim to the flames. The Norwegian language was put to the test, and only humanism revived consciousness of Norway's native roots and culture. National poetry experienced a heyday with the works of Claussøn Friis (1545–1614) in the 16th and 17th centuries. He also translated *Heimskringla*, the medieval stories of the Icelandic writer Snorri Sturluson, which was Norway's most-read book next to the bible during the 18th century.

Danish period

◄ Humanism

A central figure in Norwegian as well as Danish literature is Ludvig Holberg (1684–1754). The comedies he wrote for the newly established Danish theatre in Copenhagen were soon performed outside Denmark and remain the foundation of the repertoire of Danish comic plays to this day.

Ludvig Holberg

After liberation from Danish hegemony in 1814, the foundations of Norwegian literature could be laid. This occurred at the time of the Romantic epoch. The most important proponent of Norway's national Romantic literature was Henrik Wergeland (1808–45), who remains Norway's most famous lyricist to this day. His poems, dramas and essays reflect his deep commitment to cultural independence.

Henrik Wergeland

Norway's great epoch of literary realism, its golden age of literature, began at the end of the 19th century. Norwegian realism's outstanding works were written by the »Big Four«: **Jonas Lie** (1833–1908); **Alexander Kielland** (1849–1906); **Bjørnstjerne Bjørnson** (1832–1910); and Henrik Ibsen (1828–1906; ►Famous People).

The Big Four

Knut Hamsun (►Famous People) was honoured with the 1920 Nobel Prize in Literature for his novel *Growth of the Soil* (1917). **Sigrid Undset** (1882–1949; ►Famous People) is another of the outstanding figures of Norwegian literature and received the Nobel Prize for her trilogy *Kristin Lavransdatter* in 1928.

Nobel Prize in Literature

As far as contemporary Norwegian literature is concerned, a book for teenagers has achieved the greatest success: Jostein Gaarder's (born 1952) ***Sophie's World***, a novel on the history of philosophy, became a bestseller that has so far been translated into forty languages. Norwegian crime writers also enjoy great popularity today (►Baedeker Special on the following pages).

Contemporary literature

Anne Holt numbers among the most successful Norwegian crime authors.

MURDER IN NORWEGIAN

When, in 1991, Jostein Gaarder published *Sophie's World*, his history of philosophy in the form of a novel, everyone was surprised by its success. In the meantime, however, Norwegian authors, especially crime writers, are firmly established as bestsellers in the book trade – a trend that is set to continue.

The success of *Sophie's World* opened doors, and it ensures that an increasing number of Norwegian authors are translated with every year. One reason for this success is no doubt that the next generation of Norwegian literary figures are not usually starving poets; instead they are able to develop their ideas with the help of generous state subsidies. Modern Norwegian crime novels are the foundation of this success. They bewitch with a great deal of local colour, as most of the murders occur in Oslo, Bergen or Trondheim. They are often socially critical and contain believable settings, with headstrong yet loveable protagonists. Everything therefore feels uniquely Norwegian.

American inspiration

Jon Michelet popularized the crime novel in Norway in around 1970. His hero, the Oslo detective Vilhelm Thygesen, also fought economic crime. The contemporary crime novels by **Kjartan Fløgstads** were also heavily influenced by American detective novels.

Strong women

Kim Småge was the first woman to challenge the success of male authors and for her first book, *Night Dive* from 1983, she consciously chose a female perspective. **Pernille Rygg** and **Kjersti Scheen** equalled her literary quality and success, both using female heroines, or rather detectives, to solve their cases. The Oslo crime writer **Anne Holt** is not only an extremely successful author, but also a lawyer and ex minister of justice. In *The Eighth Commandment* she tells of a man who is said to have stood by while his own wife was decapitated. *In Cold Blood* is no less riveting: a story in which parents receive their son's corpse in the post with the message »You have got what you deserved«. Chief inspector Ingvar Stubo is faced with a mystery and tries to secure the services of university lecturer Inger Johanne Vik for the profiling work. Another jewel in the crown of the Norwegian crime writing is **Karin Fossum**, whose unembellished, realistic style is nevertheless fascinating to

the last page. In *Eve's Eye*, a young woman is sucked into the maelstrom of a crime that she witnesses because of her inquisitiveness. In *Don't Look Back*, the author also succeeds in presenting several suspects in a highly interesting manner: the reader is rivetted throughout.

Unni Lindell's *Careful what you Dream* is nerve-wracking to the very end. The Oslo detective Cato Isaksen desperately tries to solve the mysterious murder of the 18-year-old Therese, but not even her twin sister can help him. When a second murder occurs, a race against time begins. Unni Lindell won the 1999 Riverton Prize for the best Norwegian crime novel with this book, a prize she had received once before.

The detective drinks aquavit

Gunnar Staalesen has his cases solved by the Bergen private detective Varg Veum, who is a little more sentimental than his American counterparts, drinks aquavit instead of whiskey while waiting for new clients, and endures Bergen's constant rain.

If **Jon Ewo** is to be believed, Oslo has long since stopped being a sleepy village on the edge of Europe, and is instead becoming a centre for all kinds of drugs and alcohol-inspired illegal activity. Born in Oslo, Ewo has had a varied life so far: he has been a librarian, producer, publisher, and a singer in a punk band that never performed a single concert. He wrote books for children and teenagers before sending his hero Alex Hoel to wander through the capital's criminal milieu.

The list of successful Norwegian authors is much longer than this though, and books by writers such as Jan Kjaerstad, Ingvar Ambjørnsen, Toril Brekke, Lars Saabye Christensen, Erik Fosnes Hansen, Jan Mehlum and Frederik Skagen are certainly worth reading.

Famous People

Who discovered America? Why did Nobel Prize winner Knut Hamsun fall from favour? Who was Norway's foremost pomologist? Which tragic race did Roald Amundsen win? Find out in these miniature monuments to those who have made their mark in the land of the fjords.

Roald Amundsen (1872–1928)

The great polar explorer Roald Amundsen conducted research on both the northern arctic zone and the South Pole region. From 1897 to 1899 he took part in a Belgian expedition to the region of the South Pole. After scientific studies in Germany, where he specifically focused on techniques associated with measuring the earth's magnetism, he explored the northern magnetic pole. From 1903 to 1906, Amundsen was the first to sail the North West Passage, the shortest link between the Atlantic and Pacific Oceans cutting through to the north of North America. He then participated in the race to reach the South Pole, a feat not yet achieved by man at that time. In January 1911 Amundsen landed on the Antarctic coast at the Ross Barrier and penetrated the ice pack by dog sled, and on 14 December 1911 he became the first man to reach the South Pole. When his British rival, Robert F. Scott, reached the South Pole using ponies on 17 January 1912, the Norwegian flag was already flying there. All the members of Scott's expedition were to perish, just 18km/11mi from their base camp. In contrast, Amundsen returned safely from the pole, discovering the Queen Maud Mountains on the way. Between 1918 and 1920 Amundsen successfully travelled the North East Passage which also links the Atlantic and Pacific Oceans, but which leads north of Siberia; he was the second to do so, after Adolf Erik from Nordenskiöld. His real goal had been the ice floes at the North Pole, which failed to reach. On 12 May 1926, after several failed attempts to reach the North Pole by air, he flew over the floes with two companions in the airbus »Norge«. Roald Amundsen disappeared during a flight to Spitsbergen in June 1928.

Polar explorer

Bjørnstjerne Bjørnson (1832–1910)

Born in Kvikne (Østerdalen), Bjørnstjerne Bjørnson had already begun writing reviews and articles during his studies in Christiania (Oslo today) and was the »literary speaker of his generation«. Bjørnson was one of the great realists of Norwegian literature and was a proponent of the artistic idea that nature and poetry should be seen as one entity, far from false aestheticism and radicalism. His bucolic stories, such as *Synnøve Solbakken* (1857; also known in English as *A Girl of Solbakken*), *Arne* (1859) and *En glad gut* (1860; *A Happy Boy*), were very successful and influenced literary trends elsewhere. His epics, such as *Arnljot Gelline* (1870), recalled the old sagas and were a popular read. As a journalist, he was just as committed to Norway's independence from Denmark's cultural influence as he was to Norway's move away from Sweden's political influence, and he was an energetic campaigner for an independent republic of Norway.

Writer

← *The actress Liv Ullmann became famous mostly through her roles in films directed by Ingmar Bergman.*

He made passionate speeches for world peace, as well as for the freedom and independence of the individual and of nations. The text of Norway's national anthem was written by Bjørnstjerne Bjørnson: »Ja, vi elsker dette landet« (»Yes, we love this country«). He was honoured with the Nobel Prize in Literature in 1903. Bjørnson died in Paris in 1910, having spent a lifetime travelling and having spent many years in Germany, Italy, France and America.

Gro Harlem Brundtland (born 20 April 1939)

Politician

The politician Gro Harlem Brundtland was born in Oslo and had already joined the social-democratic Norwegian Labour Party as a schoolgirl. She studied medicine and after completing her first medical degree she attended Harvard, the elite American university, for two years in 1963. She was elected Norwegian Minister for the Environment in 1974 and party chairwoman of the workers' party in the following year; in 1977, she was called to serve in the Storting, the Norwegian parliament. She achieved great recognition as president of an international commission for environment and development. When the Norwegian central-right coalition government was forced to step down, she became the prime minister of the minority government headed by the Labour Party. She caused a stir – even in the relatively emancipated Norway – by appointing no less than eight women (from a total of 18) to serve in her cabinet. After 15 years in government, Prime Minister Brundtland resigned unexpectedly from her post in 1996.

Erik the Red (approx. 950–1007)

Discoverer of Greenland

The Vikings, also known as Normans or Northmen, spread from Scandinavia throughout Europe's coasts as pirates, merchants and conquerors between the 8th and 11th centuries. A Norwegian Viking, Erik the Red reached the island of Greenland during his voyage to Iceland in 982, which he named »Grönland« (»green land«). He established the first settlement with his followers in the southwest of the island in 985, and Greenland submitted to the authority of the Norwegian king in 1261. Today the island is an autonomous region belonging to Denmark. Erik's son ► Leif Eriksson discovered the coast of the North American continent.

Edvard Hagerup Grieg (1843–1907)

Composer

Born in Bergen, the composer Edvard Grieg studied music at the Leipzig Conservatory before continuing his studies with N. Gade in Copenhagen, who was then the leading Danish composer. He received defining inspiration from Richard Nordraak, through whom he discovered Nordic folk music. In 1866 in Christiania, the present-day Oslo, Grieg gave his first concerts of his own compositions of piano and violin sonatas, as well as songs. He met Franz Liszt in Rome and, after his return, he joined a circle of young musicians and writers who wanted to create a national art movement. In his re-working of folk songs, Grieg established world renown for Norwegian music by combining native musical forms with his century's compositional forms. He composed piano music, chamber music and orchestral works (the Holberg Suite is a celebration for the 200th anniversary of the playwright Ludvig Holberg's birthday).

Along with his orchestral pieces for Bjørnstjerne Bjørnson's *Sigurd Jorsalfar* (1872), his music for Henrik Ibsen's *Peer Gynt*, composed on the playwright's request between 1874 and 1876, is of particular significance. The music reflects the atmosphere in the high mountains, the rage of the wedding guests when the bride is stolen and, finally, Peer Gynt's dramatic homecoming and the peace of life with Solvejg, who has waited for him (*Solvejg's Song*).

Knut Hamsun (1859–1952)

Knut Hamsun (actually Pedersen) was the son of poor tailors of rural origin. The family moved to the Hamsund farming estate in Hamarøy across from the Lofoten Islands in 1862, and it is from here that the writer took his name. His youth was spent in restless wandering during which he earned his living as a casual labourer and assistant teacher, among other things. He travelled to North America **Author**

twice, visits which resulted in his pessimistic judgement of America's highly technological culture. After further travels, from 1918 onwards he lived on the Nørholm estate near Grimstad in southern Norway. He was awarded the Nobel Prize in Literature in 1920. He first caused a stir with his novel *Hunger* (1890), in which he describes the privations experienced by a young writer seeking success, which lead to physical and emotional exhaustion. Hamsun's works exhibit a profound feeling for nature and the belief in an all-pervading life force. He frequently portrayed the irrational in the actions of his characters and his literary work is seen as an attempt to overcome naturalism. Hamsun remains a controversial figure to this day, because he welcomed the German occupation of Norway in 1940. Furthermore, he published articles in Nazi-collaborator Vidkun Quisling's party newspapers. After the Second World War the author was arrested and sentenced to pay a fine, leaving him financially ruined.

Thor Heyerdahl (1914–2002)

Explorer   The zoologist and ethnologist Thor Heyerdahl made it his goal to prove that early trans-oceanic contact between peoples had been possible. For this purpose he crossed several oceans in simple boats. He sailed alone and used only ocean currents and winds. For his first expedition in 1947, Heyerdahl bravely crossed the Pacific on a raft called *Kon-Tiki*. He set off from the coast of Peru and finally reached Polynesia (Tahiti) after 101 days, having covered 8000km/5000mi. In 1955–56 he researched the culture of Easter Island. Between 1969 and 1970, his expedition entitled »Ra« led him from Morocco to the Caribbean island of Barbados. In 1977–78, he travelled through the Persian Gulf from Basra to Djibouti on a reed boat called *Tigris*, modelled on Sumerian craft. In 1983, he discovered the remains of an ancient sophisticated culture in the Maldives. Thor Heyerdahl recounted his expeditions in several books.

Across the open sea on the Ra II?

Henrik Ibsen (1828–1906)

Playwright   Henrik Ibsen, Norway's greatest playwright, was born in Skien and died in Christiania (Oslo). After completing basic schooling he began a pharmacy apprenticeship in Grimstad, his father having become impoverished. In 1850 he began studying medicine, but from 1851 Ibsen worked as playwright at the theatre in Bergen. Afterwards he was employed as the artistic director of the theatre in Christiania. Ibsen left Norway in the spring of 1864 under a cloud and spent many years living abroad, mainly in Rome, Dresden and Munich. Ibsen, who had already written plays as a young man, began his career with the Roman play *Catilina* in 1850. The plays that were created in the following years were written under the pervading influence of Norwegian national Romanticism, whose conservative tendencies Ibsen criticized. Following on from his historical dramas and theatre of ideas, Ibsen created a new type of theatre with »realistic drama«, whose radical criticism of social conditions marked the beginning of modern drama. In his piece *Pillars of Society* (1877) and following works, Ibsen illustrated life's illusions and the often hidden fragility of human relationships in stories from the everyday lives of ordinary people. Ibsen achieved world fame with his marital drama entitled *The Dolls House* (1879), in which the woman claims equal status in the partnership. This play, as well as the later marriage drama *The Ghosts* (1881), caused violent discussions in the Nordic countries. Ibsen's work had a powerful influence on the drama of the outgoing 19th century and the beginning of the 20th century. Edvard Grieg composed his *Incidental Music* for the play *Peer Gynt* (1867), which was written in Italy but is set in Gudbrandsdal and the highlands of Norway.

Knud Knudsen (1831–1915)

Presumably half of Norway still bites into the Hardanger apples that Knud Knudsen cultivated. Knudsen travelled as far as Swabia in Germany in 1862, to pursue his passion as photographer, basket weaver and apple tree fanatic.

Pomologist and photographer

It is not known what inflamed Knudsen's passion for pomology (the study of apples), but he did grow up in a corner of Norway whose climate is uniquely suitable for growing fruit: the Hardangerfjord region. Born in Odda in 1831, he initially completed a sales apprenticeship in Bergen, and then trained as a basket weaver. Afterwards he repeatedly returned to his parent's farm where he planted an apple tree nursery – a novelty in those days – which he stocked with foreign fruit varieties. He quickly enjoyed success. In 1860, he won the prize for the greatest species variety in a fruit exhibition in Bergen. The state granted the talented young man who promised to develop innovative ideas a stipend to study abroad. So Knudsen went to Reutlingen in Germany, to one of the most famous fruit growing institutes. His luggage will have raised some eyebrows. For, along with his photographic apparatus (very bulky in those early days), it also included a giant tent for use as a dark room, and countless glass plates for creating images. Knudsen studied at the institute for six months and in his free time took the first ever photographs of Reutlingen.

Back at home, Knudsen chose not to tend to his fruit orchards but to open a photographic studio in Bergen instead. Nobody knows why he so resolutely turned his back on his beloved apple trees. Perhaps the two bad harvest years that followed his return permanently disillusioned him. However, he went down in Norwegian history as the founder of the first fruit plantations in the country, and Reutlingen, too, is grateful to him to this day, for providing invaluable historic photographic documentation of their town.

Leif Eriksson (approx. 975 – approx. 1020)

Discoverer of the Americas The Norwegian seafarer Leif Eriksson, whose father was ▶ Erik the Red, was blown off course during his journey to Greenland in around 100. He ended up reaching the coast of North America. Presumably he landed in the area of Nova Scotia, a peninsula that today belongs to Canada. Leif Eriksson, who discovered America before Columbus and therefore counts as the first European who set foot in the New World, called the land he found on the east coast of North America »Vinland« (»fertile, meadow country«).

Edvard Munch (1863–1944)

Painter Scandinavia's greatest painter Edvard Munch was born in Løten near Hamar, and died in Ekely near Oslo. He spent his childhood in Oslo (then called Christiania); his mother died of tuberculosis when he was five years old. With occasional breaks, Munch lived in Paris from 1885 onwards, where he was influenced by Van Gogh and Paul Gauguin. Later, he spent a good deal of time in Germany, especially Berlin. In 1909, he suffered a nervous breakdown and returned to Norway, where he created the frescoes for the University of Oslo in 1916. During his final years, which were marred by an eye problem, the painter frequently stayed in Åsgårdstrand.

Lost and found: »The Scream«.

The coast and the sea are the setting for many of his paintings. Munch created paintings, drawings, lithographs and woodcuts that occasionally reflect influence from the art nouveau and Symbolism movements. In his landscapes, whose shapes he created in simplified, darkly glowing areas of colour, an early Expressionist art form is recognizable. His portraits of people are usually grim and express universal human experiences, such as fear, death and erotic love. Numerous themes exist in several versions. Munch began his cycle entitled *The Frieze of Life*, which consists of twelve paintings, for Max Reinhardt's Berlin Chamber Theatre in 1893. His most famous pictures include *The Sick Child* (1885–86), *The Scream* (1893), *Dance of Life* (1899–1900) and *Girl on the Bridge* (1900). In later life, he turned away from the portrayal of the darker side of life to more positive picture themes. In his will, Munch left his entire estate of 1000 paintings, 15,400 prints, 5400 watercolours and drawings, and six sculptures to the city of Oslo. Today most of these artworks can be viewed in the Oslo Munch Museum, as well as in the National Gallery. The Nazis, by the way, had no time for Munch: around 80 of his paintings were labelled »perverted art« by the National Socialists in 1937 and removed from public collections.

On 22 August 2004 armed and disguised robbers stole *The Scream* and *Madonna* from the Oslo Munch Museum. Two years later six of the assumed seven culprits were arrested. They were all members of the Norwegian answer to the Mafia, the Tveita gang, named after a quarter of Oslo. During his appeal proceedings of one of the criminals, David Toska, he offered to return the paintings to the police in exchange for remission of his 19-year prison sentence. On 31 August 2006 both paintings were seized in a raid. But the robbery left its traces: *The Scream* in particular has been so badly damaged by damp that it is impossible to restore it fully.

Fridtjof Nansen (1861–1930)

Polar explorer Fridtjof Nansen was born on a farm near Christiania (Oslo). In 1888 he and fellow Norwegian Otto Sverdrup (1854–1930) became the first men to cross Greenland from its east coast to its west coast on skis and by sleigh. In 1893, Nansen set off on a scientific expedition on his ship the *Fram* (»Ahead!«) through the North Polar Sea, departing from the north Siberian islands of »Nowaja Semlja«. In 1895, he reached a northern latitude of 86° 14' during an attempt to reach the North Pole, setting off by sleigh from the *Fram*. A year later Nansen returned to

Polar explorer

Norway via Franz Josef Land. He became a professor of zoology in 1896, and of oceanography in 1897. He led several expeditions into the North Atlantic between 1900 and 1914 and he wrote about his experiences in numerous books, including *Farthest North*, *In Northern Mists* and *The First Crossing of Greenland*. His scientific exploration ship, the *Fram*, is today exhibited in the museum of the same name on the peninsula of Bygdøy near Oslo. Nansen also held political office in later life. In 1920, he oversaw the return of prisoners of war from Russia; in 1921–23, as High Commissioner for the League of Nations, he organized emergency aid to the starving in the former Soviet Union. On Nansen's instigation, a travel document was established for Russian refugees without papers, later known as the »Nansen passport«, which was also used for other refugees. In 1922 Fridtjof Nansen was honoured for his committed work with the Nobel Peace Prize.

Birger Ruud (1911–98)

Skier Birger Ruud, born in Kongsberg, is a legendary figure in international skiing. The younger brother of Sigmund Ruud, who won silver at the Olympic Winter Games of 1928 in St Moritz, Birger Ruud was a talented ski jumper and downhill racer. He won Olympic gold at Lake Placid in 1932, achieved the same feat in Garmisch-Partenkirchen in 1936, and took the silver medal in the Olympics at St Moritz in 1948. An outstanding sports personality, Ruud made Nordic and Alpine skiing, including ski jumping, famous throughout the world. Contemporaries remember him wearing highly fashionable, dark ski pants along with Norwegian knitted gloves and hat to take off from the Olympic ski jump on parallel skis with his arms outstretched before him. As if all that were not enough, he also won downhill ski races.

Liv Ullmann (born 1938)

Actress The stage and film actress Liv Ullmann first saw the light of day in Tokyo. After studying theatre in London and Stavanger, she began her career in the theatre and as of 1957 joined film productions too (▶photo p.64). Her first major role in film was as Elisabeth Vogler in *Persona*, directed by Ingmar Bergman, with whom she made a whole series of films. Bergman and Ullmann were together for years and have a daughter, the writer Linn Ullmann.

Liv Ullmann has frequently portrayed women who only give the appearance of being psychologically grounded, and who are exposed to great challenges. The actress has appeared in more than five dozen films and has twice been nominated for an Oscar. She has enjoyed great success in the USA, not just in Hollywood but also on Broadway. Meanwhile, she has also proved herself as a director. In 1995, for example, she filmed the Norwegian literary classic *Kristin Lavransdatter* by Sigrid Undset, which tells the dramatic story of a woman in medieval Norway. She has also made a name for herself as a writer, with respected works such as *Changing* and *Choices*. Liv Ullmann has also involved herself in political and social issues and became a UNICEF Goodwill Ambassador in 1980. In her memoirs, which at the time of writing have yet to be published in the UK, she describes an enigmatic but glittering life, complete with personal crises and professional challenges.

Sigrid Undset (1882–1949)

Writer The Nobel Prize winning author Sigrid Undset originally came from the Danish town of Kalundborg, and grew up in Oslo from the age of three. She was forced to abandon her studies after the premature death of her father, and worked as a secretary. She was married to the painter A.C. Svarstad from 1912 to 1925. Having warned against

National Socialism in the 1930s, she fled to America in 1940. One of her sons was active in the resistance against Hitler. Undset returned to Norway in 1945. In her fiction, she created deeply intuitive, realistic portrayals of apparently uncomplicated, average people. She was particularly fascinated by the question of whether women should seek their life's happiness in work, in erotic love, or as mothers. After her conversion to Catholicism in 1925, she herself found human fulfilment in a campaigning life based on faith. Sigrid Undset began her literary career with novels and short stories portraying contemporary life. Later she turned to the style of old Icelandic sagas and her novels took their themes from the Norwegian past. It is these works that gained her international fame. Her trilogy *Kristin Lavransdatter* was written between 1920 and 1922, and in 1925 and 1927 she wrote *Olav Audunssøn i Hestviken* and *Olav Audunssøn og hans børn* respectively. She received the Nobel Prize in Literature for her life's work in 1928.

Adolf Gustav Vigeland (1869–1943)

Adolf Gustav Vigeland first saw the light of day in the southern Norwegian settlement of Mandal. The artistically highly talented young man received his training in Oslo, Copenhagen, Paris, Rome and Florence. Vigeland created portraits and especially busts. During his early period, he was greatly influenced by Auguste Rodin. This is most apparent in one of his best known busts, the study of N.H. Abel made in 1905. During his later working life, Vigeland turned to a more classically influenced style of work. Among his most famous works from this later period are the monumental sculptures in Oslo's Frogner Park, for which he made around 100 symbolic figural groups and reliefs of granite and bronze. Vigeland died in Oslo in 1943, after which his studio was opened to the public as a museum.

Sculptor

WHAT SHOULD YOU REMEMBER TO TAKE? WHERE CAN YOU FIND THE BEST SOUVENIRS? HOW DO YOU HANDLE NORWAY'S ROADS? FIND OUT HERE – IDEALLY BEFORE YOU LEAVE!

Accommodation

Camping and Caravanning

Camping wild Note: camping in nature reservations and on military training grounds is prohibited. Those who wish to camp in the open countryside should always ask permission from the owners of the nearest private properties. Along the coast and at fjords it is recommended to position tents so that entrances are facing out of the wind. In the northern regions, a **mosquito net** is essential.

Open access In Norway, everyone has the right to use beaches, shorelines, forest and meadows, even if they are privately owned. This is based on an ancient and universally respected traditional right whose limits are flexible. To avoid causing offence, however, camping on other people's property should always be predeed by a polite request; the same goes for making fires. Mobile homes, camper vans and tents must never be positioned less than **150m/164yd from any building** or hut, and the site must be vacated after **48 hours**. No sewage or rubbish should be left at the site.

Sadly, thoughtless campers and mobile home owners have made themselves very unpopular in many places in recent years. The result is that while an entire network of sanitary posts has been developed and the number of campsites increased, there have also been an increased number of **fines** issued by the authorities to inconsiderate holidaymakers.

> ! **Baedeker TIP**
>
> **A night in a lighthouse**
>
> Care to spend a night in a lighthouse? No problem in the Nordfjord region in summer. Dramatically positioned atop cliffs, the Kråkenes Fyr weather station offers a bridal suite and four double rooms. For small groups the Ulvesund Fyr is ideal, with 30 beds in two houses. Those looking for total seclusion should head for Skongenes Fyr, which is fully furnished – though there is no food and drink on offer (www.nordfjord.no).

Outdoor fires Outdoor fires near forests are prohibited from 15 April to 15 September. Severe fines are imposed for ignoring this rule.

Campsites Norway has made excellent provisions for the needs of campers. The official campsites (»campingplass« in Norwegian) are open to anyone for a fee, though international and national camping passes are sometimes required. The tourist office, automobile clubs and camping organizations publish annually updated listings which provide information on location, size, facilities and quality for individual sites. The roughly 1400 campsites are divided into five categories (1–5 stars). At larger sites there are also shops and cafeterias. Furthermore, many campsites also have cabins (simple wooden huts with

It is human instinct to seek a roof over one's head. Along with simple Sami tents, Norway offers everything from lonely cabins to luxury hotels.

bunks). The national camping organization and tourist office sell the Camping Card Scandinavia (formerly the Norsk Camping Kort), akin to a credit card. Camping holidaymakers can use it for reductions and quicker checking in procedures at campsites. The card costs 90 NOK.

◄ Camping Card Scandinavia

Not all roads are open to caravan-towing vehicles. Mobile homes can only be a maximum of 2.3m/7.5ft wide. Towing vehicles with a caravan cannot be longer than 18.5m/60.70ft and the caravan must not be wider than the car, and in all cases it must not be wider than 2.5m/8.2ft. The Norwegian transport authorities publish a map specifically for holidaymakers with mobile homes that indicates all prohibited routes for trailers, caravans and mobile homes. Furthermore, this map shows all sanitary posts for mobile home and caravan owners (see address box for where to buy it).

Caravans and mobile homes

Hotels

The comfort and service provided by Norwegian hotels matches international standards for similar price ranges. Luxury hotels can be found in the large towns and cities, but many smaller places also

Comfort, even in the far north

ACCOMMODATION ADDRESSES

CAMPING

▸ **Reiselivsbedriftenes Landsforening (RBL)**
Essendropsgt. 6
N-0305 Oslo
Tel./fax 23 08 86 21
www.camping.no

FARMSTAYHOLIDAYS

▸ **Useful websites:**
www.eurotourism.com
www.visitnorway.com
www.accommodation-scandinavia.com

CABINS, HOLIDAY HOMES

▸ **NOVASOL AS**
Nedre Vollgate 3
N-0158 Oslo
Tel. 81 54 42 70
Fax 23 35 62 75
www.novasol.no or
www.novasol.co.uk
Tel. +45 73 75 66 11
(head office in Denmark)
novasol@novasol.co.uk

YOUTH HOSTELS HIKING HOSTELS

▸ **Norske Vandrerhjem**
Torggata 1
N-0181 Oslo
Tel. 23 13 93 00
Fax 23 13 93 50
www.vandrerhjem.no

▸ **Den Norske Turistforening (DNT)**
Storgaten 3
Postboks 7
N-0101 Oslo
Tel. 22 82 28 00
Fax 22 82 28 01
www.turistforeningen.no

▸ **International Youth Hostel Federation (IYHF)**
Trevelyan House
Dimple Road, Matlock
Derbyshire, DE4 3YH
Tel. 0 16 29 / 59 26 00
Fax 59 27 02
www.yha.org.uk

have excellent hotels. There are even good hotels in the far north, as well as cosy guesthouses. Numerous private homes offer so-called family rooms with 3–5 beds. Some mountain hotels are only open during the summer and winter holiday season. Many Norwegian hotels have disabled access and some of them offer specific installations for allergy sufferers. By the way, hotel beds are often slightly smaller than normal, as are the sanitary facilities such as showers and toilets.

Room reservations It is advisable to book ahead for hotel rooms during the easter and summer holidays. An up-to-date list of accommodation is published by the Norwegian Tourist Board (▸Information).

Accommodation classification There are luxury hotels in the large cities and at some other special locations. Comfortable accommodation in the mountains outside settlements is referred to as »turisthotell« or »høyfjellshotell«. Average levels of comfort are offered by so-called »pensjonater«, usually small hotels, while guesthouses and inns are called »gjestgiveri«.

Norwegian hotels are very expensive. In the section entitled Sights from A to Z, accommodation is divided into **three categories**: luxury (double room over £100); mid-range (double room for £50–£100); budget (double room up to £50). Many first-class hotels offer price reductions during the summer season or during weekends all year round, however. See also the section on special offers and prices, p.107.

Prices

Huts, Holiday Homes and B&Bs

In some towns and regions heavily frequented by tourists rooms with breakfast are offered at reasonable prices. Information is supplied by the regional tourist offices. A brochure entitled *Bed & Breakfast*, containing current addresses and prices for all of Norway, can be purchased in book shops or online at www.bbnorway.com or at www.bedandbreakfastinnorway.com.

Bed & breakfasts

Huts, lodges (hytter) and holiday homes offer good value for money. The accommodation ranges from spartan fishing huts (rorbu) and simple mountain cabins (fjellhytte), to comfortable cabins on camp-sites and luxury private holiday homes.

Huts and holiday homes

In Norway too, »farmstay holidays« are an **affordable** way for families to have a holiday. An annual brochure for on the subject of holidays on farms is published in Norway.

Farmstay holidays

Youth Hostels and Hiking Cabins

Forgoing certain comforts, it is possible to stay the night in affordable youth hostels (not only for teenagers) and hiking cabins and lodges. Reservations are recommended. The Norwegian youth hostel association (Norske Vandrerhjem) publishes a list of the country's approximately 80 youth hostels. Furthermore, the accommodation listing *Hostelling International, Volume 1, Europe* is published annually, which also lists hiking cabins, and is available in book shops. In many places, children and teenagers and members of hiking associations receive price reductions at private huts and cabins. Information is available from the regional tourist offices.

Not just for the young

The Norwegian mountaineering and tourist association DNT maintains around 300 hiking hostels and cabins. There are simple cabins for self-caterers, some also stocked with provisions, and there are also staffed cabins and hiking hostels with varying degrees of comfort offered. It is not possible to make prior reservations, but the staffed cabins will always supply at least a mattress in emergency cases.

DNT Hiking hostels

Arrival · Before the Journey

Arrival

By air Flights from the UK to Norway tend to operate to the capital Oslo, but there are also direct connections to cities along the country's North Sea coast. For the no-frills, low-cost flights, Ryanair (www.ryanair.com) and local budget airline Norwegian (www.norwegian.no) are the carriers to check out. Prospective travellers in the north of England may also be interested in the low-cost airline Jet2's (www.jet2.com) service to Bergen from Newcastle Airport.

Ryanair flies direct to Haugesund Karmoy and Oslo Sandefjord Torp airports from London Stansted. There are also daily Ryanair flights from Newcastle to Torp. The budget airline also flies to Oslo from Glasgow Prestwick, Liverpool and London Stansted airports, as well as operating flights between Stansted and the western Norwegian city of Haugesund. Norwegian offers direct flights from Stansted to Oslo, Rygge, Bergen, Trondheim, and Tromsø, from Gatwick to Oslo and Stavanger, and from Edinburgh to Oslo. The routes Stansted to Stavanger, and Edinburgh to Bergen, Bodø, Stavanger, Tromsø, and Trondheim, require a stop in Oslo. British Airways (www.ba.com) flies direct from Heathrow to Oslo, and SAS Scandinavian Airlines (www.flysas.com) also offers direct flights to Norway: from Gatwick to Bergen, from Heathrow to Stavanger, and from Newcastle to Stavanger. There are bmi (www.flybmi.com) flights between Heathrow and Stavanger too, as well as a direct connection between Oslo and Heathrow. Oslo's Torp Sandefjord airport is 130km/80mi from the city centre. A shuttle bus brings passengers free of charge to the railway station to board the regional train for the lengthy journey into the capital. Oslo Gardermoen airport is 47km/29mi from the city, but the high-speed »Flytoget« train carries passengers to the centre within 20 minutes. For internal flight connections please see ▶Transport.

By car Since the opening of the 16km/10mi-long Öresund bridge between Copenhagen and Malmö (Sweden), it is possible to reach Norway overland. The bridge toll is €36 for cars, €71 for mobile homes (2008); www.oresundsbron.com. Those driving from the UK can use the Eurostar service through the Channel Tunnel or make the crossing by car ferry, either across the Channel or to the western coast of Denmark (see below).

By ferry Due in part to rising fuel costs, DFDS Seaways announced the complete withdrawal of its historic Newcastle to Norway ferry routes as of September 2008. For the first time in a century, there is currently **no ferry service from the UK to Norway**. However a DFDS Seaways ferry, M/S Dana Sirena, does sail every other day from Harwich in Essex to Esbjerg in the Ribe region of western Denmark.

► FERRIES

► **Harwich – Esbjerg
(M/S Dana Sirena)**
DFDS Seaways, 19hrs

► **Frederikshavn – Oslo**
Color Line, 9–14hrs
(M/S Color Festival)
Stena Line, 9–14hrs
(M/S Stena Saga)

► **Hanstholm – Egersund/
Haugesund/Bergen**
Fjord Line, 8hrs to Egersund,
13hrs to Haugesund, 18hrs to
Bergen (M/S Atlantic Traveller)

► **Hanstholm – Kristiansand**
Master Ferries, 2hrs (Mastercat)

► **Hirtshals – Larvik**
Color Line, as of May 2008: 4hrs
(Super Speed 2)

► **Hirtshals – Kristiansand**
Color Line, 4.5hrs or 6hrs
(M/S Christian IV) and 3.5hrs
(Super Speed 1)

► **Hirtshals – Stavanger/Bergen**
Color Line, approx. 12hrs to
Stavanger, 18–20hrs to Bergen
(M/S Prinsesse Ragn-hild)

► **Copenhagen – Oslo**
DFDS Seaways, approx. 16hrs
(M/S Crown of Scandinavia)

► **Kiel – Oslo**
Color Line, approx. 20hrs
(M/S Color Magic, M/S Color
Fantasy)

► **Puttgarden – Rødby
(Denmark; Fugleflugtslinien)**
Scandlines, approx. 1hr

► **Rostock (international port) –
Gedser (Denmark)**
Scandlines, 2hrs

► **(Copenhagen –) Helsingør –
Helsingborg**
Scandlines, 1.5hrs

► **Frederikshavn – Göteborg**
Stena Line, 2–3.5hrs

► **Grenå – Varberg**
Stena Line, 4hrs

► **Color Line**
www.colorline.com
Tel. +47 (0) 22 94 42 00

► **DFDS Seaways**
www.dfdsseaways.co.uk
Tel. 0871 522 9955

► **Fjord Line**
www.fjordline.com
Tel. +47 (0) 815 33 500

► **Kystlink**
www.kystlink.no
Tel. +47 (0) 815 56 715

► **Master Ferries AS**
www.masterferries.com
Tel. +47 (0) 815 26 500

► **Scandlines**
www.scandlines.com
Tel. +49 (0) 381 5435-0

▶ **Stena Line**
www.stenaline.com
Tel. +46 (0) 31 85 80 00

▶ **For journeys on the Hurtigruten line**
Hurtigruten Ltd. 3 Shortlands,
London, W6 8NE

Tel. 020 88 46 26 66
www.hurtigruten.co.uk

The historic DFDS Seaways Newcastle to Norway route was scrapped in September 2008.

Those in continental Europe can travel easily to western Norway from Hirtshals at the northern tip of Denmark; Kristiansand is just a short ferry journey away. There is also a ferry connection to Bergen from Denmark's Hanstholm. These routes are heavily frequented during the high season – make sure you book well in advance.

By rail   It is of course possible to travel from London to Oslo by rail. Take the Eurostar through the Channel Tunnel to Brussels, board a connecting Thalys or Deutsche Bahn ICE train to Cologne, and then travel overnight on the City Night Line sleeper to Copenhagen. From here, there is a high speed Linx train to Gothenburg (3hrs 30mins), from which Oslo is another 4hrs 15mins away. A good source of information for those who wish to take the train is www.seat61.com.

By bus   National Express coaches leave London Victoria coach station for Oslo three to five times weekly. The journey takes around 32hrs, with half-hour waits in Brussels and Copenhagen (www.eurolines.co.uk).

Travel Regulations

Travel documents   Though not a member of the EU, Norway has signed the Schengen Agreement which is intended to do away with border controls within the European Union. The UK and Republic of Ireland apply the Schengen provisions regarding police and judicial cooperation, but have not ended border controls with EU states, so UK and Irish nationals, as well as those from outside the EU, will need a valid **passport**. Those wishing to remain in Norway for over three months or to seek employment there must apply for a residency permit.

Driving licence ▶   National driving licences and vehicle registration documents of European Union nationals are recognized in Norway. In the case of traffic incidents involving damage to vehicles, the **international green car insurance card** is required. All cars must display the blue European Union sticker or the oval European national stickers. Healthcare needs should be covered by private travel and health insurance. European Union citizens should also remember to bring their **European Health Insurance Card** (EHIC) which replaced the E111 form in 2004 (see www.ehicard.org).

Healthcare ▶

Dogs and cats can be brought to Norway as long as they have been
vaccinated against rabies and have been issued with a pet passport. A
period of six months should be planned for required vaccinations.
See www.pettravel.com or contact the Norwegian tourist office for
more information (►Information).

Pets

Customs Regulations

The following **alcoholic beverages** can be imported duty free: 1 litre/
0.26 US gal of wine, 1 litre spirits (minimum age 20) and 2 litres/0.5
US gal of beer; or 2 litres of wine and 2 litres of beer. 200 cigarettes
or 250g/9oz of tobacco (minimum age 18) can be imported, along
with gifts to a value of £600/6000 NOK. Duty can be paid to import
an additional 4 litres/1 US gal of wine or spirits, or 10 litres/2.6 US
gal of beer and 400 cigarettes. The minimum age for importing spirits is 20; it is 18 for wine. The importation of **hunting weapons** is
governed by special regulations.
The importation of drugs, poisons, weapons, ammunition and explosives (with the exception of hunting materials), fishing nets and
lobster and crab catching equipment is **prohibited**.

Arrival

Travellers returning to the UK from Norway, a non-EU country, can
bring the following quantities duty free for personal use: 200 cigarettes (or 100 cigarillos, 50 cigars or 250g/9oz tobacco); 2 litres/0.5
US gal of still table wine, 1 litre/0.26 US gal of spirits with more than
22% alcohol content or 2 litres/0.5 US gal of fortified wine, sparkling
wine or other liqueurs, 60cc/2 fl oz of perfume, 250cc/8.5 fl oz of
eau de toilette, plus goods to a value of £145/1400 NOK.

*Returning to
the UK*

Mosquito Plague

The plague of mosquitoes during the warm seasons particularly af-
fects Norway's damp and lower-lying regions. Myriads of inscets, including the ones that bite, buzz and whirr through the air in the river valleys, along lakes and especially in the high north, where the sun
never sets for almost half the year. It is therefore imperative to pack
insect repellent and even mosquito nets. Salt water is unattractive for
mosquitoes, so those travelling near the sea and the fjords should escape torment.

*Insect repellent
a must!*

Children in Norway

Norway is known to be an **extremely child-friendly country** and for
many parents this is an important factor in making the decision to
choose a holiday there. Pure and unspoilt nature awaits in Norway,

*Children are
welcome*

with mountains, lakes, seaside beaches, and climbing rocks, as well as trees, playgrounds, and adventure, leisure and entertainment parks; there are child-friendly campsites, holiday homes, hiking hostels and hotels, and numerous options for farmstay holidays. Campsites have playgrounds as do many rest stops, and the Norwegian State Railway even has various trains equipped with play compartments for children.

Numerous museums and galleries offer **children's programmes**. Most restaurants have children's menus, high chairs and nappy changing facilities.

Electricity

The Norwegian mains supply is generally 220 volts. Visitors who are not from mainland Europe are advised to take an **adapter**.

Emergency

▶ USEFUL PHONE NUMBERS

GENERAL EMERGENCIES

▶ **Emergency doctor**
Tel. 113

▶ **Fire services**
Tel. 110

▶ **Police**
Tel. 112

▶ **Automobile Association**
Tel. 00 44 8705 33 22 11

▶ **Cega Air Ambulance (worldwide service)**
Tel. +44(0)1243 621097
www.cega-aviation.co.uk

▶ **Call centre for members of Norwegian automobile clubs**
Tel. 81 00 05 05, www.theaa.com

▶ **US Air Ambulance**
Tel. 800/948-1214 (US; toll-free)
Tel. 001-941-926-2490 (international; collect)
www.usairambulance.net

Etiquette and Customs in Norway

Reserved people   Part of a successful holiday is making an effort to avoid misunderstandings that can otherwise spoil the atmosphere. Norwegians may appear somewhat reserved, even unfriendly, but as a rule this is not the impression your hosts wish to give. Instead it is typical of many a Norwegian's characteristically **reticent nature**. Conversely, Norwegians value tactful and discrete behaviour.

Shaking hands is not common in Norway and a short »hei« is normally sufficient when greeting a local. Another Norwegian phrase that is essential is **takk – thank you**. Without »takk«, nothing gets done in this country.

The modest Norwegians do not make much of their titles or honours: no one here would ever think of introducing themselves or booking a hotel room as »Dr. Knudsen«, for example.

Remove your shoes before setting foot in someone's house: it is considered the height of bad manners to enter a home with street shoes on. This also goes for many mountain huts, where walking boots should remain outside. There are really only two conversation topics that are risky: **patriotism and whaling**. As regards the former, Norwegians are proud of themselves and their small country and show national pride unreservedly. It is quite normal to hoist the patriotic Norwegian flag outside the summer home and to celebrate national holidays with the royals accompanied by much flag waving and the donning of traditional dress. If you dare to broach the subject of whaling in the far north, it will quickly become clear that Greenpeace sympathizers are few and far between in this region.

Potential blunders

Social contact is easily made during festivals, such as the Shellfish Festival in Mandal.

Limits on freedom

The increasing number of foreign mobile homes and camper vans has become a problem. **Rubbish** in the countryside and dirty toilets have led to a prohibition of overnight camping on the open road almost everywhere, including popular areas such as the Jotunheimen mountains.

The **right of public access** (generally free access to land – fenced or not – and permission to camp at least one night) typical of Scandinavia that existed before mass tourism was only really intended for hikers. In fact, there are already those demanding drastic restrictions on this historic right. To encourage a continuation of this almost limitless freedom of the open road in Norway for the future, it is a good idea to follow the local example and ensure no damage is done to the sensitive Norwegian environment, and to leave no traces of your visit (for more information see 'Right of Public Access' on the official Norway website: www.norway.org.uk).

Norway by night?

Norwegian nightlife cannot be compared with that in central European and the Mediterranean, not least because of the extremely restrictive laws on the consumption of alcohol and tobacco. **Bar opening times and drinks licences** are highly regulated. The most highly developed nightlife so far is found in Olso, where there are countless nightclubs and bars. Night owls will also find nocturnal entertainment in Bergen, Stavanger, Tromsø and Bodø.

No smoking!

In recent years, the Norwegian government has continuously refined the laws directed against tobacco consumption. There is a strict no-smoking policy for all public buildings and transport, in restaurants, cafés and bars. In urban areas smoking while driving is prohibited. The minimum age for buying tobacco is 18.

Tipping

Those providing standard services do not normally expect a tip in Norway, although it is worth remembering that although prices are high in Norway, salaries in the service sectors are certainly not. For many city and tour guides, for example, tips represent a significant portion of their income. In restaurants it is customary to round up the final bill, and taxi drivers also receive a small tip for their services.

Festivals, Holidays and Events

Norwegians like to party. Many offices and shops are only open in the mornings on the day before bank holidays. The regional and local tourist offices (▶ Information) maintain reasonably extensive events programmes. The daily newspapers also publish regional events calendars. A summary of all festivals and events can be found on the internet at www.norwayfestivals.com.

⏵ BANK HOLIDAYS IN NORWAY

OFFICIAL HOLIDAYS

▸ **1 January**
New Year

▸ **1 May**
Labour Day

▸ **17 May**
National holiday

▸ **25 and 26 December**
Christmas

▸ **31 December**
New Year's Eve

▸ **Moveable Holidays**
Maundy Thursday, Easter Friday, Sunday and Monday, Ascension Day, Whitsun and Whitmonday

JANUARY

▸ **Tromsø**
The music on offer during the Northern Lights Festival ranges from Baroque and classical music to jazz and works by contemporary composers. An international film festival takes place at the same time.

FEBRUARY

▸ **Kristiansund**
Opera week with operas, musicals, church music and ballet performances

MARCH

▸ **Lillehammer**
The »Birkebeiner« international Nordic ski race from Rena to Lillehammer (58km/36mi) has a long tradition.

▸ **Oslo**
Famous ski festival at the Hol-

menkollen with World Cup events in cross-country skiing, Nordic skiing and ski jumping.

▸ **Alta**
Europe's longest race for husky racing in the Nome style, the »Finmarksløpet«, starts in Alta and crosses Finnmark on old post routes for around 400km/250mi

EASTER

▸ **Kautokeino**
Traditional Sami singing, known as »Joik«, is performed at the Sami Grand Prix; highlight on Easter Saturday are the reindeer sleigh races.

▸ **Karasjok**
In Karasjok there are also reindeer and dog sled races on Easter Saturday at midday – the symbolic end of the winter – on the frozen Karasjohka river. Tourists can also participate.

MAY

▸ **17 May (everywhere)**
National holiday with processions and military music, during which children also don their Sunday best

▸ **Oslo**
Relay racing from the Holmenkollen: Oslo street race

▸ **Kristiansand**
Church festival with services, sacral music choirs, gospel singing and African rhythms

MAY / JUNE

▸ **Bergen**
The port renews itself each end of

A joy for the ears and eyes at many festivals:
the Hardanger violin

May, in time for its festival week.
A varied programme is offered
during which renowned inter-
preters of classical and modern
music, as well as theatrical arts,
can be seen and heard.

JUNE

▶ 23 June (everywhere)
Midsummer is celebrated on St
John's Day (St Hans) all over
Norway, often with large fire-
works.

▶ Bergen
Market days at the port of Bergen,
along with folklore and lots of
entertainment

▶ Harstad
North Norwegian music festival
with music, theatre, dance and art
exhibitions

▶ Honningsvåg
Nordkapp Festival with folklore,
concerts, dance, ships' parades and
weight lifting/throwing

▶ Oslo
Færder Seilas: sailing regatta on
the Oslofjord
Summer concert with classical,
ballet and folk music at the ski
jump at Holmenkollen

JULY

▶ Molde
Norway's largest international jazz
festival has already hosted many
famous musicians from all over
the world.

▶ Førde
International Folklore Festival:
Norway's most important folk
music festival with participants
from all over the world

▶ Stiklestad
History play on the Battle of
Stiklestad and St Olav

▶ Vinstra
Peer Gynt Festival: open-air theatre performance of Ibsen's *Peer
Gynt* with music by Edvard Grieg,
folk costume processions and
more

JULY / AUGUST

▶ Risør
International wooden boat festival
for traditional and modern
wooden craft, as well as regattas

▶ Bodø
(till the beginning of August)
Nordland Music Festival with
classical, jazz, rock, and folk
music

▶ Trondheim
St Olav Festival

AUGUST

▶ Oslo
Jazz festival: internationally acclaimed artists appear here.

▶ Skien
Festival in honour of Henrik
Ibsen with theatre, markets and
lectures

► **Mandal**
Shellfish festival: a long table laden with fresh shellfish and other seafood is set up in the old town.

► **Haugesund**
Norwegian film festival during which the Amanda Prizes are announced

► **Trondheim**
High calibre chamber music festival

► **Bergen**
Guitar festival with Norwegian and international artists

Why complain about the weather, when you can celebrate it at the Rain Festival: parade with people dressed in wet weather gear and carrying umbrellas

► **Oslo**
Ultima: Norway's largest festival for contemporary music

► **Oslo (10 December)**
Ceremony for the Nobel Peace Prize

► **31 December
(all over the country)**
Prime Minister's television address

Food and Drink

Going out for a meal in Norway is extremely expensive. Restaurant prices lie at approximately 50–100% above the European average.

Pricey restaurants

Food

In Norway, the cold buffet is an obligatory feature of any hotel dining hall. A large table laden with a range of delicious titbits is normally displayed during breakfast and for the evening meal.

Cold buffet (Kolbord)

Fish plays a predominant role in traditional Norwegian cuisine and is offered in all variations. More or less the basic foodstuff in Norway, the fish here is always fresh thanks to the short distance from the boat to the kitchen. Steamed or fried **wild salmon** with fresh herbs (parsely, chives, chervil, dill, thyme, basil and fennel), usually served with boiled potatoes, is a sheer joy. The **farmed salmon** that is cultivated in great aqua farms along the coast does not taste nearly as good as that caught wild. Farmed salmon is predominantly destined for the fish counters of supermarkets. Norwegian **smoked salmon** and »graved laks« are famous, though the introduction of industrial production methods has led to a marked variation in quality. Ideally, smoked salmon should be bought unpacked directly from the smoke houses. Products sealed in plastic do not taste as good; furthermore, they can be bought in any supermarket back home.

Fish

KONTROLLERTE
BLÅSKJELL
KR. 52,- PR. KG

SCAMPI
KR. 180,-
PR. ½ KG

FERSK
KVEITE
KR. 179,-
PR. KG

FERSK
STEINBIT
KR. 110,-
PR. KG

Norway is a paradise for fish lovers.

In recent years, **cod** has become quite rare due to overfishing, and is therefore often more expensive than salmon. Cod was once everyday food for Norwegians; the liver is especially popular. **Herring** is another Norwegian fish speciality that has become rarer in recent times, while boiled monkfish fillets and fried halibut slices are another Norwegian delicacy. Of the freshwater fishes, **trout** is highly prized in Norwegian cuisine, and fillets smoked over pine cones are exquisite. Between the end of July and the beginning of September, boiled **crabs**, served with a dill sauce, are on the menu.

Meat   Norwegian cuisine without lamb and mutton is unthinkable. Next to joints and cutlets of mutton, a speciality known as »spekamat« is served, which is air-dried leg of mutton. Lamb is also turned into delightful dishes with particular finesse and served with a range of herbs. **Reindeer meat** is offered as a special, but rather expensive, delicacy and in many places it is possible to try roast reindeer in cranberry sauce. Smoked reindeer meat also tastes excellent.

There are only a few **sausage varieties** that appeal to European tastes. In contrast, ham and cold meats are very tasty. The dark and normally very spicy **lamb sausage** is also a Norwegian speciality.

i **Be sure to try**

- Wild salmon with herbs
- Rømmegrøt
- Reindeer meat
- Lamb sausage

Goat's cheese (geitost) is very common in Norway, as is **»Mysost«**, a brown, sweet cheese that is eaten in very thin slices on bread. Preserved fruit covered in sweetened liquid cream is very often served as dessert. The Norwegian national favourite is **»rømmegrøt«**: a porridge type dish drenched in hot butter with cinnamon and sugar.

Other specialities

Drinks

Milk (melk) is very popular in Norway and is often served for breakfast without extra charge; also popular are cream (fløte) and sour cream (rømme). Coffee (kaffe) is made well and happily served at virtually any time of day. A lemonade especially popular among children is called »Gøy«.

Alcohol free

Norway has very restrictive alcohol laws. Private distilleries are prohibited and the sale and service of alcoholic drinks is strictly regulated. Beer can be bought at supermarkets. On the other hand, wine and spirits can only be bought at state-run outlets (»Vinmonopolet«, meaning »the wine monopoly«) which can only be found in larger towns and cities. Most restaurants have a permit to serve beer and wine. Hard liquor (»brennevin«) can be purchased in the bars of larger hotels, but there is a complete ban on serving spirits on Sundays and bank holidays.

Strict alcohol regulations

Understandably, Norway is no place for wine drinkers. Good wine can be purchased, but the pleasure of consuming a bottle that cost roughly £25 is slightly dampened by the fact that it is sold for a fiver at home. So-called house wine (»husets vin«) is a little more reasonable and is normally served in carafes. Lagers are sold in small bottles; draught beer is the rather the exception. The northernmost brewery in the world was founded by Ludwig Mack from Germany in Tromsø, in 1877, and beer and pilsner have been brewed up there according to German purity rules ever since, using German and Czech hops.

Wine and beer

Health

In Norway initial medical care and emergency care normally take place via the hospitals (sykehus, sjukehus) or emergency surgeries (legevakt) and only rarely at private doctors' practices. As virtually every Norwegian is familiar with this system, it is easy to get information on the nearest hospital.

Medical care

The **phone numbers** for doctors are on page 2 of Norwegian phone books (search under »Legevakten« for doctors, »Tannleger« for dentists). See also ▶Emergency.

Health insurance | The European Health Insurance Card is acceptable for medical consultations in Norway (▶p.82).

Pharmacies (Apotek) | There are numerous pharmacies located in all cities and major settlements in the country. They are open during normal shop opening hours, and there are also emergency pharmacies that open at other times in the towns. Medication can only be purchased by presenting a Norwegian doctor's prescription in a pharmacy.

Hiking

Hiking season | The Norwegian mountains offer ample opportunity for mountaineering and hill walking, as well as mountain and glacier touring. Appropriate equipment is needed, however, as well as careful planning before you go. As far as the weather in Norway goes, the best months for a »fjelltur« (mountain tour) are June, July and August. The country's landscapes are covered by an extensive network of footpaths, all signposted with the generally recognizable red »T«. Information and suggested tours can be supplied by local tourist offices and by the Den Norske Turistforening or DNT (Norwegian Trekking Association).

Hiking cabins | Numerous hiking cabins are dotted throughout the land. The distance between two huts is, on average, the equivalent of a day's walking (between four and nine hours). The comfort levels of these accommodations ranges from simple block houses with a grassed roof, where personal provisions and a sleeping bag must be brought, to catered rustic mountain cabins and luxurious mountain lodges.

● HIKING INFORMATION

▶ **Den Norske Turistforening (DNT)**
Storgaten 3, Postboks 7
N-0101 Oslo
Tel. 22 82 28 00, fax 22 82 28 01
www.turistforeningen.no

▶ **Norsk Tindeklubb**
Postboks 7 Sentrum
N-0101 Oslo
Tel. 22 64 95 91

The red »T« of the DNT trekking association marks out footpaths.

Climbing fans have ample opportunity to pursue their passion in Norway, and at all levels of difficulty. The current mecca for adventurous climbers is the almost 1000m/3281ft high, virtually vertical rock face of Trollveggen in Romsdal (►Sights from A to Z). Information is available from the DNT.

Mountaineering

Guided glacier tours are offered by a number of mountain huts during the main hiking season. For example, setting off from Spiterstulen and Juvasshytta, it is possible to climb onto the »eternal ice« of Galdhøpiggen (2468m/8097ft), Norway's highest mountain. Other impressive glaciers can be found in Sognefjell, the Jotunheimen region, Jostedalsbreen, Hardangerjøkulen and Svartisen. Information on guided glacier tours and glacier lectures are provided by the DNT.

Glacier touring

Those travelling or trekking through the tundra would do well to keep in mind that they are coming into contact with an extremely sensitive ecosystem, where it takes years for damaged vegetation to recover; it may take decades for a discarded tin to rust away. Take extreme **care with open fires** during the dry summer period.

Trekking in the tundra

Hiking in the tundra necessitates the relevant equipment and clothing. In addition to good footwear, all-weather clothing, sufficient provisions, a map and a compass are essential requirements. No one should ever set off alone. Unexpected weather changes are the rule rather than the exception, and biting insects thrive here (remember the insect repellent). Encounters with reindeer, elk, lynx and brown bears are also possible.

Information

 USEFUL ADRESSES

IN THE UK AND REPUBLIC OF IRELAND

► **Innovation Norway (Norwegian Tourist Board)**
5th Floor, Charles House
5 Lower Regent Street
London SW1Y 4LR
Tel. 020 7389 8800
www.visitnorway.com
infouk@invanor.no

IN THE USA

► **Norwegian Tourist Board**
655 Third Ave
10017 New York
Tel. +1 212 885 9700
Fax +1 212 885 9710
www.visitnorway.com/
foreign_offices/usa/
usa@ntr.no

IN CANADA

▸ **Tourist information provided by the Norwegian Embassy**
See embassy contact information
www.emb-norway.ca/travel/ or
www.emb-norway.ca/faq/tourism/

IN AUSTRALIA AND NEW ZEALAND

▸ **Scandinavian Tourist Board**
Contact: Carpe Diem
Level 1, 16 Foster Street
Surry Hills, NSW 2010
Tel. + 61 (0) 2 9212 1332
www.visitscandinavia.com.au
info@visitscandinavia.com.au

EAST NORWAY

▸ **A/L Gudbrandsdal Reiseliv**
Vinstra Skysstasjon
N-2640 Vinstra
Tel. 61 29 47 70
www.gudbrandsdalen.no

▸ **Hedmark Reiseliv BA**
Grønneg 11, N-2317 Hamar
Tel. 62 55 33 20
hedmreis@online.no
www.hedmark.com

SOUTH NORWAY

▸ **Telemarkreiser AL**
Nedre Hjelleg. 18
N-3724 Skien
Tel. 35 90 00 20, fax 35 90 00 21
www.telemarkreiser.no

▸ **Vest-Agder Fylkeskommune**
Tordenskjoldsgate 65
N-4614 Kristiansand
Tel. 38 07 45 00, fax 38 07 45 01
www.vaf.no

WEST NORWAY

▸ **Fjord Norge AS**
P.O. Box 4108, N-5835 Bergen
Tel. 55 30 26 40, fax 55 30 26 50
www.fjordnorway.no

▸ **Hordaland Reiseliv**
Strømgaten 4, Pb. 416 Marken
N-5828 Bergen
Tel. 55 31 66 00, fax 55 31 52 08
www.visithordaland.no

▸ **Møre og Romsdal Reiseliv**
Fylkeshuset, N-6404 Molde
Tel. 71 24 50 80, fax 71 24 50 81
www.visitmr.com

▸ **Sogn og Fjordane Reiseliv**
P.O. Box 299
N-6852 Sogndal
Tel. 57 67 23 00, fax 57 67 28 06
www.sfr.no

CENTRAL NORWAY

▸ **Trøndelag Reiseliv**
P.O. Box 65, N-7400 Trondheim
Tel. 73 84 24 40, fax 73 84 24 50
www.trondelag.com

NORTH NORWAY

▸ **Nordland Reiseliv**
P.O. Box 434, N-8001 Bodø
Tel. 75 54 52 00, fax 75 54 52 10
www.visitnordland.no

▸ **Finnmark**
Finnmark Reiseliv
Sorenskriverveien 13
N-9511 Alta
Tel. 78 44 00 20, fax 78 43 51 84
www.visitnorthcape.com

NORWEGIAN EMBASSIES

▸ **In the UK**
25 Belgrave Square
London SW1X 8QD
Tel. 020 7591 5500
emb.london@mfa.no

▸ **In the Republic of Ireland**
34 Molesworth Street
Dublin 2
Tel. +353 1 662 1800
emb.dublin@mfa.no

► **In the USA**
2720 34th Street, N.W.
Washington, D.C. 20008
Tel. 202 333 6000
washington@invanor.no

► **In Canada**
150 Metcalfe Street, Suite 1300
Ottawa, Ontario K2P 1P1
Tel. (613) 238 6571
emb.ottawa@mfa.no

► **In Australia**
17 Hunter Street
Yarralumla ACT 2600
Tel. +61 2 6273 3444
emb.canberra@mfa.no

A listing of Norwegian embassies
and consulates is available at
www.embassies.mfa.no.

EMBASSIES IN NORWAY

► **British Embassy**
Thomas Heftyes gate 8

N-0244 Oslo
Tel. 23 13 27 00
www.britishembassy.gov.uk

The British Embassy also handles
Australian consular affairs.

► **Irish Embassy**
4th Fl, Håkon VII's gate 1
N-0212 Oslo
Tel. 22 01 72 00

► **United States Embassy**
Drammsveien 18
N-0244 Oslo
Tel. 22 44 85 50
www.usa.no

► **Canadian Embassy**
Wergelandsveien 7
N-0244 Oslo
Tel. 22 99 53 00
www.dfait-maeci.gc.ca

Language

In many places in Norway it is perfectly possible to communicate in
English, but in remote areas, especially in central and north Norway,
it is useful to know the most important words and phrases. The following explanations and vocabulary offer just the basics. For a deeper understanding of the Norwegian language, the purchase of a
language guide is recommended.

Norwegian belongs to the North Germanic or Scandinavian language   Indo-Germanic
group. It has a curious proclivity to suffixes, as shown in the added   language
on articles and in the formation of the passive, for example: veien =
the path, huset = the house, hjelp søkes = help needed. In the Norwegian alphabet, æ, ø and å follow on from z.

The Norwegian language today is split into the Danish-rooted   Two languages
Bokmål and Nynorsk (new Norwegian), which was borne of various
dialects and which was also known as Landsmål until 1929. The increased national consciousness of the population inspired by inde-

pendence from Denmark in 1814 led to a rediscovery of the old Norwegian language. While Nynorsk is predominantly spoken in the southwest and west of the country, Bokmål is spoken in the country's east and in the cities; both languages have equal status.

Pronunciation

Norwegian pronunciation presents a challenge to native English speakers. Vowels have a long and a short version, so that a can be pronounced like the u in cut or like the a in father; å is either like the o in pot, or the aw in law; e or æ is short as in bet or long as in the British received pronunciation of day; i is either like the i in police or the double-e in seethe; o is pronounced short like pot or put, or long as in zoo or or; ø is like the e in her; u is like the u in put or the double-o in soon; and y is spoken as if saying ee with pursed lips. As for consonants, d is usually silent before s, after n and l, also as the final consonant after r; g is spoken as in go unless before ei, i, j, øy, or y when it is like the y in yard; j is always like the y in yard; egn is pronounced as the ine in fine; ng is like the ng in sing; r is normally trilled as in Spanish, while in southwest Norway it is like the r in the French word rien; and s is like the s in so, except when sk is followed by ei, i, j, øy, or y, when it becomes a sh sound, making the Norwegian pronunciation of ski more like she.

NORWEGIAN LANGUAGE GUIDE

At a glance

Yes/No	Ja./Nej.
Maybe	Kanskje.
Please	Vær så snill.
My pleasure (answer to thanks)	Ja takk!
Thanks	Takk.
My pleasure	Det var da så lite.
Sorry	Unnskyld!
What did you say?	Unnskyld!
I don't understand you	Jeg forstår deg ikke.
I only speak a little ...	Jeg snakker bare litt ...
I like that (not)	Det liker jeg (ikke).
Do you have ...?	Har dere/du ...?
How much is it?	Hva koster det?
What time is it?	Hvor mye er klokka?

Greetings

Good morning	God morgen!
Good day	God dag!
Good evening	God kveld!

Hallo!	Hallo!/Hei!
My name is …	Navnet mitt er …
What is your name?	Unnskyld, hva var navnet?
How are you?	Hvordan har du det?
Thanks. And you?	Takk, bra. Og du?
Goody bye	På gjensyn!
See you soon	Vi sees!

Travel information

left/right	til venstre/til høyre
straight ahead	rett fram
near/far	nær/langt
Excuse me, where is …?	Unnskyld, hvor ligger …?
Railway station	hovedstasjon
Metro	T-bane
Airport	flyplass?
I want to rent…	Jeg ville gjerne leie …
… a car	…en bil
… a bicycle	…en sykkel

Breakdown

I have broken down	Jeg har en skade på bilen.
Where is there a car mechanic workshop near here?	Fins det et verksted i nærheten?

Petrol station

Where is the next petrol station please?	Unnskyld, hvor er nærmeste bensinstasjon?
I would like …liters.	Jeg skal ha …liter …
… petrol.	…normalbensin.
…premium petrol.	…super.
…diesel.	…diesel
…unleaded/leaded.	…blyfri/ …blyholdig
Fill it up, please	Full tank, takk

Accident

Help!	Hjelp!
Watch out!	Se opp!/Forsiktig!
Please quickly call …	Vær så snill og ring etter …straks.

…an ambulance.	…en sjukebil.
…the police.	…politiet.
…the fire brigade.	…brannvesenet.
Please give me your name and address.	Kan jeg få navnet og adressen din.

Eating/Entertainment

Where is there …	Hvor er det …
…a good restaurant?	…en god restaurant?
…an affordable restaurant?	…en ikke altfor dyr restaurant?
Cheers/To your health!	Skål!
The bill please	Kan jeg/vi få betale!
The meal was very good.	Maten var utmerket.

Shopping

Where do I find …	Hvor finner jeg …?
pharmacy	apotek
bakery	bakeri
photographic shop	fotoforretning
department store	varehus
provisions shop	dagligvareforretning
market	marked

Accommodation

Can you please recommend…?	Kan du anbefale meg …?
…a hotel	…et godt hotell

Har dere noe ledig rom?

…a guesthouse	…et pensjonat
I have booked a room with you.	Jeg har reservert et rom hos dere.
Do you still have a room?	Har dere noe ledig rom?
a single	et enkeltrom
a double	et dobbeltrom
with shower/bath	med dusj/bad
for one night/week	for ei natt/uke
How much is the room with breakfast?	Hva koster rommet med frokost?
…half board?	…halvpensjon?

Doctor

It hurts here.	Jeg har vondt her.

Bank and post office

Where is there …	Unnskyld, hvor finner jeg …
…a bank?	…en bank?
…a foreign currency exchange booth?	…et vekslingslkontor?
I would like to change …into Krone.	Jeg ville gjerne veksle… i kroner.
How much is …	Hvar koster …
…a letter …	…et brev …
…a post card …	…et postkort …
to England?	til England?

Days of the week

Monday	mandag
Tuesday	tirsdag
Wednesday	onsdag
Thursday	torsdag
Friday	fredag
Saturday	lørdag
Sunday	søndag

Numbers

0	null
1	ehn/ett
2	to
3	tre
4	fire
5	fem
6	seks

7	sju (syv)
8	åtte
9	ni
10	ti
11	elleve
12	tolv
13	tretten
14	fjorten
15	femten
16	seksten
17	sytten
18	atten
19	nitten
20	tjue (tyve)
21	tjueen
22	tjueto
30	tretti (tredve)
40	førti
50	femti
60	seksti
70	sytti
80	åtti
90	nitti
100	hundre
200	tohundre
1000	tusen
2000	totusen
10 000	titusen
1/2	en halv
1/4	en fjerdedel

Spisekart/Meny (Menu) Frokost (Breakfast)

svart kaffe	black coffee
kaffe med melk	coffee with milk
koffeinfri kaffe	decaffeinated coffee
te med melk/sitron	tea with milk/lemon
urtete	herbal tea
sjokolade	chocolate
fruktsaft/juice	fruit juice
bløtkokt egg	soft egg
eggerøre	scrambled egg
egg og bacon	egg and bacon
brød/rundstykke/ristet brød	bread/roll/toast
horn	croissant
smør	butter
ost	cheese

pølse	sausage
skinke	ham
honning	honey
syltetøy	jam
mysli	muesli
yoghurt	yoghurt
frukt	fruit

forretter og supper (starters and soups)

tøndersodd	meat broth with vegetables and meat balls from Trøndelag
ertesuppe	pea soup
fersk suppe	soup with fresh meat and vegetables
fiskesuppe	fish soup
gravlaks	salt and sugar cured salmon
kryddersild	spiced herring
rekecocktail	prawn salad in mayonnaise
røkelaks	smoked salmon
rømmegrøt	cream porridge with high fat content (35%); also served as main dish
speket reinsdyrkjøtt	pickled reindeer meat
salater	salads
tomatsild	tomato herring

Kjøttretter (meat dishes)

elgsteik	roast elk
fårikål	mutton and cabbage casserole
ferskt kjøtt	boiled beef with vegetables and a light sauce
flesk	pork
hjortesteik	roast stag
kalkun	turkey
kjøttkaker	meat balls in brown sauce
knackpølse	knackwurst sausage
kylling	chicken
lammefrikassé	fricassee of lamb
lammekoteletter	lamb cutlet
lammesteik	roast lamb
oksesteik	roast beef
rådyrsteik	roast deer
reinsdyrsteik	reindeer roast
spekemat	cold pickled or dried smoked meat
svinekotelett	pork cutlet
svinesteik	pork roast

vilt	game
wienerpølse	wiener sausage

Fisk og skalldyr (fish and shellfish)

ål	eel
blåskjell	mussel
fiskeboller	fish dumplings
fiskepudding	fish pudding
gjedde	hake
hummer	lobster
kreps	river crab
kveite	halibut
laks	salmon
makrell	mackerel
ørret	trout
rødspette	plaice
sei	coley
sik	vendace
spekesild	pickled herring
steinbit	spined loach
torsk	cod

Grønnsaker (vegetables)

agurksalat	cucumber salad
bakte poteter	baked potatoes
blandet salat	mixed salad
blomkål	red cabbage
champignon	mushrooms
erter	peas
gulrøtter	carrots
hodekål	white cabbage
kål	green cabbage
kantarell	chanterelle mushrooms
løk	onions
potet(mos)	mashed potatoes
rødkål	red cabbage
salat	salad
sopp	mushroom
steinsopp	porcini mushroom

Smørbrød (open sandwiches)

egg og ansjos	bread with boiled egg and anchovies

fiskekabaret	bread with fish and vegetables in aspic
karbonade	bread with meat balls
leverpostei med syltede agurker	bread with paté and pickled gherkin
patentsmørbrød	bread with fried egg and bacon
rekesmørbrød	bread with prawns in mayonnaise
roastbiff	bread with roast beef
svinesteik	bread with roast pork

Bakverk (pastries and cakes)

boller	sweet rolls with raisins
bløtkake	torte
eplekake	apple cake
julekake	raisinbread
lefse	soft, thin patty made of potatoe and flour
rulade	biscuit rollade
småkaker	biscuits
vannbakkels	cream puff
wienerbrød	Danish pastry

Dessert (desserts)

fruktkompott	stewed fruit
fruktsalat	fruit salad
is	ice
sjokolade	chocolate
jordbær	strawberry
vanilje	vanilla
jordbær med fløte	strawberries and cream
karamellpudding	caramel pudding
moltekrem	cloud berries and cream
osteanretning	cheese plate
riskrem	rice pudding with cream and red sauce
rødgrøt med fløte	red jelly with cream

Vinkart (wine list) Alkoholholdig (alcoholic drinks)

akevitt	aquavit
fatøl	draught beer
hvitvin	white wine
likør	liquor
øl	beer
rødvin	red wine

Alkoholfritt (non-alcoholic drinks)

alkoholfri vin	alcohol-free wine
brus	lemonade
kaffe	coffee
kakao	cacao
melk	milk
saft	fruit juice
juice	fruit drink
sjokolade	hot chocolate
te	black tea
med sitron	with lemon
vann	water

Media

Newspapers & magazines The top selling newspaper in Norway is the daily *Aftenposten*. As a rule the major newspapers and magazines in English are available in the larger towns one day after publication.

Radio During the summer months, as a service for tourists, Norwegian Broadcasting (NRK) provides news programmes on the radio in English between 10am and 11am. The **BBC World Service** can be received on short wave or cable FM. Offering regular news bulletins as well as cultural and entertainment programmes, it broadcasts on 9410 kHz on the 31m waveband and on 6195 kHz on the 49m waveband. Full details can be found at www.bbc.co.uk/worldservice. Voice of America is also available on short wave (www.voanews.com).

Television Norwegian television usually transmits films and series in the original language with subtitles in the local language. The weather report at the end of the evening news is of no little interest; the symbols used are internationally recognizable, high and low pressure weather fronts being indicated by »H« and »L« as appropriate.

Money

The national currency is the Norwegian krone (1 NOK = 100 øre). There are 50, 100 and 1000 krone notes, and coins to the value of 50 øre, as well as 1, 5 and 10 krone. The import and export of both national and international currency is unrestricted, though the export of more than 25,000 NOK must be declared by filling in a customs form. There are no limits on travellers' cheques.

INFORMATION

EXCHANGE RATES

1 NOK = 0.10 £
1 £ = 10 NOK
1 NOK = 0.19 US$
1 US$ = 5.5 NOK
1 NOK = €0.13
1 € = 7.87 NOK

LOST OR STOLEN CARDS

The following numbers can be used to report and stop lost or stolen bank and credit cards:

▶ **American Express**
Tel. +44 1273 696 933

▶ **MasterCard**
Tel. +44 20 7557 5000

▶ **Visa**
Tel. +1 410 581 9994

▶ **Diners Club**
Tel. +44 1252 513 500

▶ **HSBC**
Tel. +44 1442 422 929

▶ **Barclaycard**
Tel. +44 1604 230 230

▶ **NatWest**
Tel. +44 142 370 0545

▶ **Lloyds TSB**
Tel. +44 1702 278 270

The standard international credit cards such as Mastercard, American Express, Visa and Diners Club are accepted almost all over Norway. Travellers' cheques can normally be used without problems. Occasionally, however, transaction fees are imposed. ATM machines at all the important tourist destinations allow cash withdrawals using a bank card in conjunction with the PIN.

Credit cards

If bank cards or cheque and credit cards should get lost, you should call your own bank or credit card organization to make sure they are immediately stopped. It is a good idea to make a note of the telephone number on the back of the card.

Loss of bank cards and credit cards

Norwegian banks are open at the following times: Mon–Fri 8.15am–3.30pm, some also Thu 8.15am–5pm.

Bank opening times

National Parks

The national parks are large areas of countryside under nature preservation orders and managed by the state. The natural environment and its native flora and fauna are to remain as **untouched as possible** is these areas. There are numerous national parks in Norway and in

Great destinations

many there are wonderful opportunities for hiking, with huts for overnight stays. During winter, there are also opportunities for ski touring and snow-shoe hiking in the fjell (highland) regions. In northern Norway, autumn usually begins in the second week of September.

All plants including trees and animals are **protected.** Fishing is allowed according to certain rules. Mushrooms and berries can be picked, depending on local regulations. Motorized traffic is prohibited. Walkers should stick to marked footpaths and in the period between 15 April and 15 September it is strictly prohibited to light fires in the open.

The main section of this guide (► Sights from A to Z) describes the following national parks: Ånderdalen (see Senja), ► Dovrefjell-Sunndalsfjella, Femunden (see Femundsmarka), ► Hardangervidda, ► Jotunheimen, ► Jostedalsbreen, Ormtjernkampen (see Gudbrands-

National parks are an important refuge for endangered species, such as the arctic fox.

dal), Øvre Dividal (see Troms), Øvre Pasvik (see Finnmark), Rago National Park (see Bodø), Rondane (see Gudbrandsdal), Saltfjellet–Svartisen (see Saltfjellet), and on ► Spitsbergen the national parks Nordvest Spitsbergen, Forlandet and Sør Spitsbergen.

Post and Communications

Stamps and postage Stamps can be purchased in all post offices, from machines, from many kiosks and in numerous stationary shops. Letters and cards up to 20g for destinations within Europe cost 9.50 NOK, for destinations outside Europe 10.5 NOK.

Telephone All phone numbers in Norway have eight digits and there are **no local codes**. Coin operated telephones work with 1, 5, 10, and also 20 krone coins. Telephone cards (telekort) can be bought at kiosks and in post offices.

TELEPHONING

National: tel. 180
International: tel. 181

INTERNATIONAL
DIALLING CODES

► **Dialling codes to Norway**
from the UK and Republic of
Ireland:
Tel. 00 47
from the USA, Canada and
Australia: tel. 00 11 47

► **Dialling codes from Norway**
to the UK:
Tel. 00 44
to the Republic of Ireland:
Tel. 00 353
to the USA and Canada
Tel. 00 1
to Australia:
Tel. 00 61

The 0 that precedes the subsequent local area code is omitted.

Even remote areas of Norway have good mobile phone coverage. Owners of mobile phones will automatically be redirected to Norwegian service providers via their roaming facility. In contrast to landlines, there is no need to input the first double zero for international codes. As in other countries, car drivers in Norway are only allowed to telephone with hands-free equipment while driving.

Mobile telephones

Prices and Discounts

Norway is an expensive country. Here more than anywhere it pays to be on the look out for discounts. With Color Line's **Norway Card**, available at a cost of 5 euros to those who book a return journey with the ferry company, holidaymakers get up to 60% disount at more than 90 Norwegian tour companies. Oslo and Bergen offer a City Card with which parking is cheaper and entrance to museums and is free or reduced (for more information see the relevant sections on ►Bergen and ►Oslo).

Norway Card and City Card

Accommodation is expensive in Norway, but many hotels offer weekend discounts. To take advantage of the hotels' **special offers**, it is often necessary to buy a hotel pass or a hotel cheque which gives discounts on accommodation, usually with breakfast included. Many discount cards, such as the Fjordpass, the Nordic Hotel Pass, the ProScandinavia Cheque or the Scandic Holiday Card, are valid in all Scandinavian countries. The hotel cheques have to be bought prior to your journey.

Hotels

WHAT DOES IT COST?

| **One-course meal** from £8 | **0.5l/1pt beer** from £3–7.50 | **Double room** from £32 | **1l/0.26gal petr** 98 octane £1.3 95 octane £1.1 Diesel £1.20 |

DNT Card The Norwegian Trekking Association, the DNT (De Norske Turist-forenig), maintains 450 cabins in Norway and those with a DNT Card can stay the night at much reduced rates. More information at www.turistforeningen.no.

Railway Travelling by rail is a pleasure that doesn't come cheap in Norway. Discounts of 25% are available for groups of at least ten people (15% from June to August) and discounts of 50% are available for seniors from age 67. The ScanRail pass was discontinued at the end of 2007, meaning that European nationals must use the Interrail pass to get cheap rail travel in Scandinavia (www.interrailnet.com), while non-Europeans can purchase the Eurail Scandinavia pass, which is almost identical to the old ScanRail pass (www.eurail.com).

By air Substantial discounts on domestic Scandinavian flight routes are available for those who use the **SAS Visit Scandinavia Air Pass**. Travel agents and SAS representative offices can supply the latest conditions. Travellers from the age of 18 have the option of taking part in the **SAS EuroBonus Programme** which offers air miles for multiple flights. Furthermore, participants gain discounts or air miles when checking into SAS hotels, as well as when hiring cars with Avis and Hertz. The Norwegian airline company Widerøe, which serves over 35 airports in the country, offers a **Norway Discovery Ticket** for €490 (2008 price), which offers unlimited flights within Norway during a period of 14 days. Extension weeks are available. Carriers of the Braathens SAFE airline operate from Kristinsand in the south as far as Tromsø and Spitsbergen in the north of the country, and serve 15 airports. For travellers resident outside Norway, discounts are available via the **Visit Norway Pass**, which is valid for one month.

Road Traffic

Road network Even though Norway is almost entirely mountainous, the road network is very well developed. In the south and on the major tourist routes during the holiday season, motor traffic is on a par with other

▶ BREAKDOWN ASSISTANCE

Car drivers in the high north must expect snow right into the summer.

Tel. 22 34 14 00, fax 22 33 13 72
www.naf.no

▶ **Breakdown service of NAF**
Tel. 81 00 05 05

▶ **Vegmeldingstjenesten**
(Road maintenance)
Tel. 175 (within Norway) or
81 54 89 91 (from overseas)

▶ **Statens vegvesen /
Vegdirektoratet**
Tel. 22 07 35 00, fax 22 07 37 68
www.vegvesen.no

▶ **Norges Automobil Forbund
(NAF)**
Østensjøveien 14
N-0609 Oslo

European countries. However, the in part rather narrow **mountain roads**, often with limited visibility, require driving skill and a relatively disciplined attitude. Drivers heading uphill always have priority on difficult tight bends or on narrow stretches. Some mountain roads are only passable in one direction at a time. Travellers with mobile homes and camper vans would do well to make enquiries with an automobile club or at the »Vegdirektoratet« in Oslo before choosing routes. Certain stretches of road in the southern Norwegian mountains and in northern Norway are only passable from June to mid-October, due to the long winter season. Many bridges, tunnels and private roads charge tolls (»bompenger«). Some **minor roads** are unpaved gravel or sand roads. In those cases, it is recommendable to keep your distance from the driver ahead to avoid stones flying onto the windscreen.

In 2007, Norway's new national tourist routes received the Norwegian Prize for Cultural Heritage. There are five such routes: along the the coast of Helgeland; along the Sognefjell Road high in the Jotunheimen mountains; along the Strynefjell Road, which is more than a hundred years old; the route through Lofoten; and the route through Hardanger. A particularly popular route is the »**Adventure Road**« (Eventyrveien; www.eventyrveien.no). Stretching 500km/310mi from Oslo to Bergen, the route passes through some of the most spectacular landscapes of the north, including the Hallingdal valley, Hardangervidda, Europe's largest mountain plateau, and the world famous fjords of western Norway, as well as the country's two largest metro-

National tourist routes

polises. By 2018 there will be a total of 18 national tourist routes, including one along the over 100-year-old Trollstigen pass to the famous Geirangerfjord.

Kilometres or miles? As a rule, distances are indicated in kilometres (km). Locals, if asked about distances, however, often still respond with an account of distances in Norwegian miles (mil). One Norwegian mile equals 11.3km or 7 British miles.

Main roads The major routes are divided into European roads, state roads (»riksveg«, RV for short), rapid transit roads (»motorveg«) and, around major cities, motorway style highways. All important county roads (»fylkesveg«) also have numbers.

Road signs International road signage applies in Norway. In addition though, there are signs that are unknown elsewhere. For example, a white M on a blue background signifies a passing place; »Innkjøring forbudt« means access prohibited. A stylized castle in a blue frame indicates a cultural heritage site (such as a castle or rock art).

Petrol The network of petrol stations in the densely populated areas comes up to European standards. While planning routes, it is a good idea to remember that the number of petrol stations in Norway declines as you move further north; carrying a reserve canister of petrol is a good idea. **Petrol prices** are somewhat above the European average, but it is difficult to give a reliable guide to prices. The following fuel is sold: 97 octane leaded, 98 octane leaded, premium unleaded (Super blyfri, 95 octane), Super Plus, unleaded (blyfri, 98 octane), and diesel.

Traffic regulations Rules concerning right of way are the same as standard European rules. Trams always have priority. Seatbelts are obligatory both on the front and back seats. The **alcohol limit** for drivers is presently set at 0.2%. Those caught behind the wheel with more than 1.5% alcohol in their blood can expect a prison sentence.

Parking is prohibited on all main roads. Parking within larger urbanized areas is only permitted at signed and (normally) fee-paying sites. **Dimmed headlights** are also **obligatory during the day**.

Chains are officially required to be carried and mounted in good time during winter and spring in the mountains. **Spiked winter tyres** are permitted from 1 November to 1st Sunday after Easter (in northern Norway from 15 October to 30 April).

Speed limits In urbanized areas: 31mph/50kmh.
Outside urbanized areas: 50mph/80kmh.
On motorway style roads: 56mph/90kmh, sometimes 62mph/100kmh.
Buses: 50mph/80kmh.
Vehicles with non-breaking trailers or caravans: 37mph/60kmh.

There are frequent speed traps and traffic controls all over Norway. Speeding is very expensive! By particularly grave offences, driving licences can be confiscated or even a prison sentence passed without possibility of parole or remission.

On-the-spot fines are issued by the police who have the right to impound vehicles until the full fine has been paid.

All over Norway there is a heightened **risk of collisions with wandering game**, especially during dusk and in particular on wide roads, as the animals prefer them for the light breeze that keeps the insects off. **Elk** may have thin legs, but they are very large and can weigh up to 800kg/1764lbs. During a collision between a car and an elk, the heavy body usually smashes the windscreen.

If an animal is hit on the road, the accident site must be clearly marked and the **police contacted**. They will contact the agency responsible for wild game (Viltnemnda), who will ensure the animal is killed. Even animals that are already dead have to be reported to the Viltnemnda and it is absolutely prohibited for the driver to remove the animal from the scene: as reindeer always have an owner, it is even possible to be accused of theft. The police simply make a record of the accident. Damages are not payable by the driver; the reindeer's owner can apply to the state for payment. Fleeing the site of an accident generally carries very serious consequences and is highly inadvisable.

Shopping

Opening Hours

There are no standard official opening hours for commercial businesses in Norway. Usually, though, shops are open Mon–Fri, 9am/10am–4pm/5pm; Thu 9am/10am–6pm/8pm; Sat 9am–1pm/3pm.
Many supermarkets are open in the evenings until 8pm. On Saturdays they remain open till 6pm.

Wine and spirits can be bought at the Vinmonopolet shops Mon–Wed 10am–4pm; Thu 10am–5pm; Fri 9am–4pm, Sat 9am–1pm (15 May–31 Aug 8.15am–3pm).
Banks in Norway are open Mon–Fri 8.15am–3.30pm; sometimes also Thu till 5pm. Post offices open Mon–Fri 8am/8.30am–5pm; Sat 8am–1pm.
As in the UK, increasing numbers of Norway's local post offices are closing down in favour of postal counters in supermarkets, which have the same opening hours as the shops.

eed traps

nirs

n arts and crafts make popular souvenirs, especially domes-
made of wood such as spoons and forks. Glass, tin, enamel,
d silver jewellery is another favourite, especially from Tele-
ndmade dolls in national costume also make pretty souvenirs, as do woven wall-hangings and embroidered tapestries. **Norwegian jumpers** with their beautiful patterns are world famous and the
colourful knitted hats and even socks and stockings made of pure
wool go down well with the folks back home. The regions of Setesdalen, Seibu and Fana are famous for their embroideries. **Trolls**, rooted
in Norwegian mythology, are offered for sale both as beautiful wood
carvings and as cheap plastic kitsh. Those travelling by car through
Telemark and in the Hallingdal valley can also stock up on
Norwegian **decorative painting**, furniture decorated with rose motifs
and other goods made of wood.

Jewellery

Semi-precious stones, such as thulite, mylonite, peridotite and ama-
zonite, are popular souvenirs, as are valuable items made of gold, silver and tin. Gold jewellery made in the Norse style copied from original Viking jewellery is an absolute hit with many.

*Some of the most precious souvenirs are silver jewellery,
such as that in this display in Kongsberg.*

Norwegian glassmakers have been bringing their beautiful works to market since the 18th century, and there is great demand for the various crystal figures (especially animals). Norwegian pottery, especially porcelain, is very popular. Norwegian porcelain is exported all around the world.

Glass and porcelain

Goods made by Norwegian tanners and **furriers** are considered the best of their kind in the world, though these high-quality products certainly do not come cheap. Those who prefer a cheaper and more rustic style can bring a little of Norway home in the shape of a **reindeer hide** or carvings made of reindeer horn.

Norwegian sportswear shops offer top quality **outdoor clothing**, shoes and equipment for various sports (fishing, skiing, hiking, cycling) at good prices.

If making purchases worth 310 NOK or more, advantage should be taken of the tax free shopping system, which benefits the foreign tourist on a shopping spree. Show your passport proving residency outside Scandinavia at the time of purchase, and you will be given a tax-free form, which should ideally be filled out in the shop. The goods are then packed and sealed and are only allowed to be unpacked outside Scandinavia. On leaving Norway, the sealed goods along with passport must be presented to the Norway tax-free shopping representative (not the customs officials), along with the tax-free shopping form issued by the relevant shop. In this way, the value added tax (VAT) of 11–18.7% will be refunded (minus a fee). This system does not apply to foodstuffs, chocolate, tobacco or services. For more information see www.globalrefund.com.

Tax free shopping

Sport and Outdoors

Please also see ►Hiking, ►water sports and ►winter sports.

Fishing

One of the most popular leisure activities for locals and tourists alike is fishing. The many fjords and bays along the Atlantic coast, as well as the many thousands of inland waters offer more or less ideal conditions for passionate anglers. Furthermore, Norwegian waters are some of the least crowded you will find. Fishermen need a **fishing card** (fiskekort), available for purchase at local tourist offices, at hotel receptions, at campsites, in sports shops and at post offices. The price depends on the period of validity required, as well as on the dimensions of the fishing territory. As a rule, there are waiting lists for

Paradise for fishermen

Is the salmon jumping yet? Two of St Peter's disciples check their hunting grounds.

the salmon rivers known to insiders. All fishermen over the age of 16 also have to aquire a **state fishing licence** (fiskeravsgiftskort), available at post offices with the special payment card.

Information The Norwegian tourist board publishes a free brochure entitled *The Official Fishing Brochure* that contains detailed information. Additional information is also supplied by the Norwegian hunting and fishing association.

Fjord fishing and fishing at sea Fishing **without a licence** is permitted at sea and along the fjords as long as the intended catch is not salmon or trout. Fishing huts and boats can be hired all along the coast. Tours to the high seas on fishing boats are also organized locally and it is possible to catch mackerel (makrell), shellfish (hyse), cod (torsk), halibut (kveite), coley (sei) and herring (sild) all year round.

Freshwater fishing Spawning time is the closed season. This varies according to region and fish species, and is regulated by the relevant municipalities or counties. The ideal fishing seasons also vary from region to region. May and June can be successful months in low-lying areas, whereas late summer is best for fishing in the highland regions. Good catches are also made by ice fishermen who drill approx. 25cm/0.8ft holes in the pack ice to fish on frozen lakes. **Good fishing grounds** can be found at Glomma (Hedmark), around Kongsvinger, in Sørland (pike, perch, whitefish, eel), Mandalselva, Audneselva, Aust-Agder, Finnmark and eastern Norway (pike, char, grayling, trout); and also in the region of Kristiansand, north of Røros, in Østerdalen, Gudbrandsdalen, Hallingdal, Valdres, and the rivers of the Hardangervidda (especially trout).

Those who want to fish for salmon (laks), trout (brown trout; **Salmon fishing** sjøørret) and char (sjørøye) must pay an increased fee for their fishing card and fishing licence. There are also varying limits set on the minimum and maximum weight permitted for salmon catches. Be aware that in many places there are waiting lists for salmon fishing, so timely enquiries are very worthwhile. Sea fishing for salmon is only allowed during the months of

i **The best salmon rivers …**

■   … are the Alta, Drammenselva, Gaula, Målselva, Namsen, Neiden, Numedalslågen, Orkla, Størdalselva and Tana, as well as the Årøyelv, which flows into the Sogndalsfjord.

June and July; in rivers only from the beginning of June to mid-August. There is good salmon fishing in all the fjords, including in the northern regions. These days, travel agents also offer all-inclusive salmon fishing tours.

Cycling

Cycling is booming in Norway too, though the country does not of-   **Good fitness** fer ideal conditions for cyclists. There are only a few dedicated cycle   **needed** paths and cyclists must compete on the roads with cars and mobile homes, especially during high summer. Furthermore, the many tunnels that save on exhausting mountain traverses are closed to cyclists. Transporting bicycles on public transport has not yet been developed particularly well, so that a great deal of initiative is needed. For fit and well equipped cyclists, though, Norway is quite an experience. The natural surroundings can be fully appreciated on minor roads, and cycle tours along the fjords in Trøndelag and Lofoten are most rewarding.

Information on carrying cycles on public transport and bicycles hire,   **Information** as well as other touring tips, is provided by local tourist offices and   **sources** by Sykkelturisme i Norge, who also offer excellent suggestions for tours along with all the necessary background information at www.bike-norway.com.

Mountain biking is very popular. Enthusiasts should remember,   **Mountain biking** though, that the use of footpaths, as well as cross-country cycling in protected areas, is strictly prohibited. The thin and very delicate layer of vegetation only recovers very slowly when damaged and it often takes many years for gashes through moorland and moss to grow together again.

SPORT AND OUTDOORS INFORMATION

FISHING

▶ **Norges Jeger- og Fiskerforbund**
Postboks 94, Hvalstadåsen 5
N-1378 Nesbru
Tel. 66 79 22 00, fax 66 90 15 87
www.njff.no

CYCLING

▶ **Sykkelturisme i Norge**
Postboks 3132 Handelstorget
N-3707 Skien
Tel. 35 90 00 21
www.bike-norway.com

FLYING

▶ **Norsk Aero Klubb / Norges Luftsportsforbund**
Radhusgaten 5B, N-0102 Oslo
Tel. 23 01 04 50
www.nak.no

GOLF

▶ **Norges Golfforbund**
Postboks 163 Lilleaker
N-0216 Oslo
Tel. 22 73 66 20, fax 22 73 66 21
www.ngf.golf.no

HORSE RIDING

▶ **Norges Rytterforbund**
Ullevål Stadion
N-0840 Oslo
Tel. 21 02 69 50, fax 21 02 96 51
www.rytter.no

TENNIS

▶ **Norges Tennisforbund**
Postboks 287
N-0511 Oslo
Tel. 22 72 70 00
Fax 22 72 70 01
www.tennis.no

Other sports

Flying   The regional operators of the Norsk Aero Klubb offer all imaginable flying sports, including gliding, parachute jumping, hang-gliding, parapenting and ballon trips.

Gold panning   Gold panning is possible in various places. This is hardly a chance to get rich, mind you, but it is quite good fun. More precise information on gold safaris or goldpanning camps and tours is supplied by the local tourist office at ▶Karasjok.

Golf   There are 80 golf courses in Norway, of which 20 are 18-hole courses, such as those at Oslo, Stavanger, Tønsberg and Drammen. The world's northernmost 18-hole golf course is in Tromsø. Further north, there is the smaller North Cape Golf Club at Lakselv. The so-called Midnight Sun Tournament takes place at the golf course in Trondheim at the end of June, beginning of July. The **golfing season** lasts from May to the end of September/beginning of October.

Hunting   In the southern regions of Norway, the animals available for hunting are the same as those known in the UK and other parts of Europe:

deer and small game, as well as wild fowl. The hunting season for **elk** is usually limited to a few weeks of the year and the services of a local hunter with elk hounds must be used. The **kill fees** are substantial. More information is supplied by the local tourist offices.

Orienteering is quite popular in Norway. They take place on around 200 routes, from spring to autumn, all over Norway. The tourist information offices have details.

Orienteering runs

In Norway's rural farming areas, horse riding has a long tradition. The Norwegian fjord horses (▶Tip p.292) are known for their comfortable riding and are very popular. Many country estates and farms rent out horses and offer riding lessons. So-called trail riding is becoming ever more fashionable too.

Horse riding

The Birkebeinerrennet, which takes place in March, is a real classic: the ski race from Rena to the Birkebeiner Skistadium, Lillehammer has been taking place for over 70 years. In 2008 over 12,000 skiers entered; 10,426 crossed the finish line. The fastest athletes cover the 54km/33.5mi stretch in only 2–3hrs (www. birkebeiner.no).

Ski race

Summer skiing is a typical Norwegian experience and it is possible to enjoy skiing on many névés and glaciers during high summer. See also ▶winter sports.

Summer skiing

Many towns and hotels have tennis courts installed. Bring your own tennis equipment.

Tennis

Leisure Parks

Most parks are only open daily between June and mid-August; during the early and late season (May, mid August to end of September), they are often open only at weekends.

▶ LEISURE PARKS

BØ I TELEMARK
▶ **Bø Sommarland**
www.sommarland.no
Norway's largest aqua park with giant slides, pools and surf installations

HARDANGER
▶ **Holiday park at Kinsarvik**
www.hardangertu.no
Aqua park with giant slide, mini zoo, open-air stage and viewing tower

KRISTIANSAND
▶ **Kristiansand Dyrepark**
Open all year round
11km/7mi east of Kristiansand
www.dyreparken.com
The main attractions include the zoo with its monkey jungle, the Nordic animals and a pirate ship.

► **Hunderfossen**
Fåberg (near Lillehammer)
www.hunderfossen.no
One of the country's most beautiful parks with fairytale grotto, giant trolls, Ivo Caprino's Super Videograph and a fascinating energy centre

► **Lilleputthammer**
Approx. 20km/12mi north of Lillehammer
www.lillehammer.no
Toy town of old Lillehammer on a scale of 1:4, with model workshops and various play installations

OSLO

► **Tusenfryd**
Approx. 30km/19mi south of Oslo at Mosseveien near Vinterbro
www.tusenfryd.no
Attracts visitors especially for its new cable car, the Thunder

Coaster, as well as for the Space Shot, carousels and aqua park.

SKARNES

► **Lekeland**
Aquapark with giant slide, playground and mini-golf

STAVANGER

► **Havanna Badeland**
Open all year round
www.havanna.no
10km/6mi south of Stavanger
Wave pool, water cannons, giant slide, large sauna installation, solarium

► **Kongeparken**
30km/19mi south of Stavanger, located in Ålgård
www.kongeparken.no
Family park offering one of Norway's longest bobsleigh runs, a mine train, a western town and a traditional Norwegian farm. The big dipper is a new attraction.

Time

Winter and summer time
Central European Time (CET; GMT + 1hr) applies in Norway. From the end of March to the end of October the Central European Summer Time applies (CEST; British Summer Time + 1hr).

Transport

For information on driving see ►Road Traffic.

Hire Cars

High costs
Local car hire firms offer their services alongside the international car hire firms, but their fees are no lower. Those wishing to rent a vehicle must be 21 or over (in some places even 25) and hold a valid EU/EEA driving licence. Those without a credit card have to leave a hefty deposit.

HIRE CARS, RAIL AND BUS TRAVEL

HIRE CARS

► **Avis**
Reservations in UK:
Tel. 0844 581 0147, www.avis.com

► **Budget**
Reservations in UK:
Tel. 0844 581 2231
www.budget.co.uk

► **Europcar**
Reservations in UK:
Tel. 0845 758 5375
www.europcar.com

► **Hertz**
Reservations in UK:
Tel. 08708 44 88 44, www.hertz.com

► **Bodø Bobilutleie**
Armbakken 2, N-8023 Bodø
Tel. 75 56 01 68, fax 75 56 00 26

TRAIN INFORMATION

► **Norges Statsbaner (NSB)**
Prinsensgt. 7 – 9, N-0048 Oslo
Tel. 81 50 08 88, www.nsb.no

ATTRACTIVE RAIL ROUTES

► **Bergen route**
Oslo – Bergen
Journey time around 6.5hrs

► **Dovre route**
Oslo – Trondheim
via the Dovrefjell (6.5hrs)

► **Flåm route**
Myrdal – Flåm (just under one hour)

► **Northern lands route**
Trondheim – Bodø (approx. 11hrs)

► **Ofot route / Lappland route**
Narvik – Kiruna (Sweden)

► **Rauma route**
Dombås – Åndalsnes
Journey time: 1hr 20min

► **Sørland route**
Oslo – Kristiansund –
Stavanger
Journey time approx. 7.5hrs

VINTAGE TRAINS

► **U.H.B.**
Urskog – Høland train
(»Tertitten«); Sørumsand station
(40km/25mi west of Oslo)

► **Krøder Line**
Vikersund – Krøderen
(Midt-Buskerud)

► **Thamshavn Railway**
Thamshavn – Løkken; stations at
Løkken, Svorkmo, Fannrem

► **Setesdal Railway**
from Grovane or Beihølen

► **Voss Railway**
Garnes – Midttun (Nesttun);
stations at Garnes or Midttun

► **Rjukan Railway**
Rjukan – Mæl and Tinnoset –
Notodden
along with rail and steamship ferry
Ammonia (Rjukan station)

► **Rauma Railway**
Åndalsnes – Bjorli (Trolltindane);
station at Åndalsnes

BUS INFORMATION

► **NOR-WAY Bussekspress**
Schweigaardsgata 8 – 10
N-0185 Oslo
Tel. 00 47 / 81 54 44 44
www.nor-way.no

Mobile home rental ▶ Unfortunately there is no central address for the rental of mobile homes and camper vans in Norway. One firm, Bodø Bobilutleie, in the north of the country offers this service.

Rail Travel

Slow progress The rail network of the Norwegian state railway (NSB Norges Stats-baner) is relatively limited. The main routes lead from Oslo to Stavanger (via Kristiansand), Bergen, Åndalsnes, Trondheim (via Dombås or Røros) and Bodø (the NSB's most northerly station with connections for the Norway Bus to Kirkenes).

Travel on the express trains is relatively comfortable, though slow, as three quarters of the network is along tracks with high gradients. A journey from Oslo to Bergen during summer takes just under seven hours. During the winter there can be delays of many hours. Reservations must be made on Norwegian night trains, but on other services it is no longer necessary to reserve a seat, though this is strongly recommended for long-distance routes. Rail Europe's Norway Pass allows unlimited train travel on 3–8 days within any given month Vintage trains ▶ (www.raileurope.com). A large number of vintage trains are lovingly maintained – a selection of the most attractive vintage rail routes is given on p.119.

Bus or Coach Travel

The long-distance bus network is quite extensive in Norway. The various bus companies are very well coordinated with each other, so that rapid headway can be made. Here, too, there is a broad range of discounts and special offers.

Travelling by Ferry

The inland ferry connections play a vital role in the national transport network. In Norway the car ferries servicing the numerous fjords complement the road network. Coastal and fjord cruises are also popular. From Bergen, the **Hurtigruten** (▶ Baedeker Special p.237) postal boats service the Norwegian west coast as far as Kirkenes, travelling there and back in eleven days. During June and July the ice breaker *Kapitan Dranitsyn* travels **from Kirkenes to Spitsbergen** and to the islands of Franz Joseph Land, which are surrounded by thick pack ice (see address box).

Domestic Air Travel

In a country with about 50 airports and airstrips, the aeroplane is a good way to cover long distances in a short time, and to reach even remote destinations. Norway's hub for air traffic is Oslo, while signif-

❯ FERRY COMPANY AND AIRLINE ADDRESSES

FERRY COMPANIES

▶ **Bornholm Ferries**
Service Center Havnen
DK-3700 Rønne
Tel. 56 95 18 66, fax 56 95 57 66
www.bornholmferries.dk

▶ **Color Line**
PO Box 1422, Vika
N-0115 Oslo
Tel. +47 22 94 42 00
Fax +47 22 83 04 30
www.colorline.com

▶ **DFDS Seaways**
Scandinavia House
Refinery Road
Parkeston
Essex CO12 4QG
Tel. 0871 522 9955
Fax 0191 293 6245
www.dfdsseaways.co.uk

▶ **Fjord Line**
Skoltegrunnskaien
N-5003 Bergen
Tel. +47 55 54 87 00
Fax +47 55 54 87 01
www.fjordline.com

▶ **Scandlines**
Hochhaus am Fährhafen
D-18119 Rostock
Tel. +49 1805 11 66 88
Fax +49 381 5435 678
www.scandlines.com

▶ **Silja Line**
Jernbanetorget 4A
N-0154 Oslo
Tel. +47 23 355750
Fax +47 73 884136
www.tallinksilja.com

The express boat Flagruten connects
Bergen with Stavanger.

▶ **TT-Line**
Zum Hafenplatz 1
D-23750 Lübeck-Travemünde
Tel. +49 4502 801 81
Fax +49 4502 801 407
www.ttline.com

▶ **Viking Line**
Lönnrotinkatu 2
FIN-00100 Helsinki
Tel. +358 9 12 351, fax +358 9 647
075
www.vikingline.fi

OSLO AIRPORT

▶ **Oslo Lufthavn AS**
P.O. Box 100
N-2061 Gardermoen
Tel. 64 81 20 00
Fax 64 81 20 01
www.osl.no

DOMESTIC AIRLINES

▶ **SAS Norway Hotline**
Tel. 81 52 04 00 (in Norway)
Hotline tel. (00 45) 32 32 68 00
(international)

▶ **Norwegian Air Shuttle**
Reservations and enquiries:
Tel. 815 21 815
www.norwegian.no

▶ **Widerøe's Flyveselskap ASA**
Vereide, 6823 Sandane
Tel. 81 00 12 00
www.wideroe.no

icant regional airports are at Bergen, Trondheim, Stavanger, Kristiansund, Bodø, Tromsø and Alta (for Nordkapp tourists). The national airlines are SAS (Scandinavian Airlines System), Norwegian, Coastair and Widerøe.

Travellers with Disabilities

Norway is exemplary in its provision for disabled travellers. Many hotels offer specially adapted rooms. All public facilites have disabled toilets. Pavements and street corners are often adapted for wheelchair access and wheelchair lifts are common. Traffic lights give sound signals for those with impaired vision or hearing. Rapid and express trains have disabled access. Campsites also have appropriate sanitary facilities.

 ADRESSES

INFORMATION IN UK

▸ **RADAR**
12 City Forum, 250 City Road,
London EC1V 8AF
Tel. (020) 72 50 32 22
www.radar.org.uk

INFORMATION IN USA

▸ **SATH (Society for the Advancement of Travel for the Handicapped)**
347 5th Ave., no. 610

New York, NY 10016:
Tel. (21) 4 47 72 84
www.sath.org

INFORMATION IN NORWAY

▸ **Norges Handikapforbund**
Schweigaardsgt. 12
Postboks 9217, Grønland
N-0134 Oslo
Tel. 24 10 24 00
Fax 24 10 24 99
www.nhf.no

Water Sports

Bathing
During high summer, long sandy beaches, remote protected coves and thousands of little islands and ice-smoothed cliffs (holms and skerries) await, and not only for the hardy. Swimming is possible in Norway, especially along the southern coast where the water reaches temperatures of at least 18ºC/64ºF, and in protected bays and coves after sustained periods of sunny weather up to 20ºC/68ºF. It is also possible to take a cool dip at one of the country's many inland lakes. When there is hot and sunny weather for some time, the shallower of the inland lakes reach quite pleasant temperatures. At the same time, though, the plague of mosquitoes can become unbearable.

Nude bathing is not generally prohibited, but should be avoided at popular bathing spots and near private property. More information is available from the Norwegian Nudist Association.

A special natural experience is gliding peacefully across one of Norway's many lakes in a **canoe or kajak**. There are beautiful tours possible in the Sørlandet. The waters east of Lake Femund are also among southern Norway's most popular paddling regions; **white water paddlers** can find all grades of rapids here. Guided white water rafting tours are available at Voss and Dagali, both sides of Hardangervidda, or on the Sjoa river in the Heidal valley. A famous paddling tour runs along the **Telemark Canal**. A great variation on paddling is **sea kajaking**, which takes place all the way up to Mo i Rana.

Fun in the water at Grimstad

Sailing Few countries possess a coast that is better suited to the sport of sailing than Norway. Around 120 very well-equipped marinas await their visiting yachts in the summer months. The waters of the Oslofjord are especially popular with sailors, as is the region of the Norwegian south coast as well as the west, south and central Norwegian coastline (including the fjords). Experienced sailors head all the way up to the Lofoten islands and even further north. **Surfboards** can be hired at numerous beaches.

Diving There are excellent opportunities for diving among the coastal skerries. The water is very clear but cold.

► WATERSPROTS ADDRESSES

NATURISM

► **Norsk Naturistforbund (NNF)**
Postboks 189 Sentrum
N-0102 Oslo
Tel. 95 96 46 89

CANOE, KAJAK

► **Norges Padleforbund**
Serviceboks 1
N-0840 Oslo
Tel. 21 02 98 35
Fax 21 02 98 36

When to Go

RAFTING

▶ **Norwegian Wildlife & Rafting A/S**
Randsverk, N-2680 Vågå
Tel. 61 23 87 27
Fax 61 23 87 60
nwr@nwr.no

SAILING

▶ **Kongelig Norsk Seilforening (KNS)**
Huk Aveny 1, N-0287 Oslo
Tel. 23 27 56 00, fax 23 27 56 10
www.kns.no

DIVING

▶ **Norges Dykkeforbund**
Postboks 1
N-0840 Oslo
Tel. 21 02 97 42, fax 21 02 97 41
www.ndf.no

WATERSKIING

▶ **Norges Vannskiforbund**
Sognsveien 75L
N-0855 Oslo
Tel. 21 02 98 70
Fax 21 02 90 03
www.vannski.no

When to Go

The ideal time

The best times to travel to southern Norway are the months of May to June; for northern Norway, mid-June to mid-August is best. After those months, the weather gets noticeably worse all over the country. Those who put a high premium on warm **summer weather** with lots of sunshine and little rain are best served by the southeast of the country, between Kristiansand and Oslo, or the eastern interior. The latter is also attractive for winter sports enthusiasts because of guaranteed snow. During the drive up to Nordkapp, winter driving conditions can still be expected in Lapland in June. For cruise journeys, the months of April to June are recommended for the best chance of clear views and lots of sunshine. The best opportunity for experiencing the fjords in sunshine occurs during April and May. March and April are especially suitable for **winter sports**, because the days get longer then. There is more information on climate in the Facts and Figures section.

Winter Sports

Cradle of winter sports

Guaranteed snow, low temperatures from December to the end of April and ideal natural terrain have allowed Norway to become the cradle of modern winter sports. Skiing was first practiced as a sport in the regions of Telemark, Gudbrandsdal, Oslo and the Holmenkollen hill, and around Lillehammer. The same goes for sports on the ice and Norwegian sportsmen and women have played a major role in championships for skiing and ski jumping, as well as in speed skating, figure skating and ice hockey.

As yet there are no crowds on Norway's highlands.

Numerous sporting competitions are organized each winter throughout the land, from the Oslofjord all the way to Nordkapp. Every year, thousands of fit Norwegian skiing fans meet for the traditional Birkebeiner race (a Nordic ski marathon between Rena and Lillehammer). Additionally, countless spectators are always drawn to the world famous ski jumping at the **Holmenkollen** hill near Oslo, as well as to the World Cup downhill and slalom races in Hamar and Lillehammer. Recently back in vogue are also the Nordic ski combinations of cross-country skiing and jumping, as well as the traditional Telemark style.

Ice skating has at least as long a tradition as skiing in Norway. In Viking times, skating blades were made from reindeer horn, and by the 15th century they were made from metal. Competitive skating championships began at the latest in the 19th century, and in 1823 several thousand people participated in an ice skating race on the frozen Oslofjord. Norway quickly rose to become a leading ice skating nation and has produced a continuous stream of champions, such as the five-times world speed skating champion Oscar Mathisen, or the skaters Hjalmar Andersen, Geir Karlstad and Johan Olav Koss. There are skating rinks in all the larger towns and at the winter sports resorts. A historic venue for championships of Norwegian skating is the Bislett Stadium in Oslo. Figure skating is also very popular in Norway, though the unchallenged queen of Norwegian figure skating remains Sonja Henie, who first brought home Olympic Gold in 1928, aged just 15.

Numbers of huski racing fans, both actively involved and passive, are on the increase. Setting off with a dog sled with snow-heavy clouds hovering above the track is a very special adventure. Information is available from the DNT (►Hiking) and the tourist office at ►Karasjok. Riding snowmobiles is another way to explore the Norwegian winter landscape during the cold season).

▶ WINTER SPORTS CENTRES

▶ **Oslo and surroundings**
Oslo, Eggedal, Hurdal, Norefjell, Ringerike, Vikersund-Modum (ski jump)

▶ **Kongsberg and Numedal**
Kongsberg, Flesberg and eastern Blefjell, and Numedal to Dagali, Uvdal

▶ **Telemark**
Bolkesjø and Blefjell, Gautefall, Haukelifjell, Lifjell, Morgedal, Rauland, Vinje, Rjukan

▶ **Setesdalen**
Byglandsfjord, Hovden, Vråliosen, Vrådal-Kviteseid, Åserdal

▶ **Hallingdal and Bergen**
Dagli-Skurdalen, Geilo (family-friendly resort with 32 runs, 18 lifts and 200km/125mi of maintained cross-country routes). Ustaoset, Gol, Golsfjell; Hemsedal (30 runs, major snowboarding centre)

▶ **Valdres, Fagernes area**
Aurdal-Tonsåsen, Fagernes, Fjellstølen, Hovda – Sanderstølen, Vaset – Nøsen

▶ **Beitostølen Region**
Beitostølen and surroundings

▶ **Vang / Filefjell area**
Tyin, Eidsbugarden – Tyinholmen – Jotunheimen

▶ **Western Norway**
Finse, Mjølfjell, Vatnahalsen, Voss, Oppheim, Seljestad, Stranda, Sykkylven, Ørsta, Utvikfjell

Dog sleds: a totally different travelling experience

▶ **Vestoppland – Gjøvik**
Gjøvik, Toten, Lygnaseter,
Synnfjell

▶ **Lillehammer and Around**
Excellent terrain for cross-country
skiing tours with over 500km/
313mi of tracks, Nordseter, Sjusjøen, Øyerfjell, Tretten; Hamar

Hafjell alpine centre 15km/9mi
north of Lillehammer: 9 lifts,
23km/14mi easy to medium level
runs; greatest difference in elevation 850m/280ft; 20km/12mi alpine touring routes

▶ **Central Gudbrandsdal**
Espedal, Kvam, Gausdal,
Vinstra
Kvitfjell: Olympic run 50km/31mi
north of Lillehammer, near Ring-
ebu

▶ **Northern Gudbrandsdal
and Jotunheimen**
Bøverdalen, Sjodalen, Vågå

▶ **Rondane**
Høvringen, Mysuseter, Otta

▶ **Dovrefjell**
Bjorli, Dombås, Hjerkinn

▶ **Østerdal**
Atna, Engerdal, Elverum, Folldal,
Os, Rendalen, Tynset

▶ **Trysilfjell**
Norway's largest interconnected
ski region, with 70km/44mi of
downhill pistes and 24 lifts, lies to
the northwest of Lillehammer.
Early risers can take part in
»tidligski« on Wed and Sat.
Breakfast on the summit between
7 and 9am is part of the fun.

▶ **Skeikampen**
A traditional destination in the
Gausdal valley with snow park, 17
pistes, 12 lifts, a 200km/125mi
cross-country ski run, evening
skiing and spa.

Tours

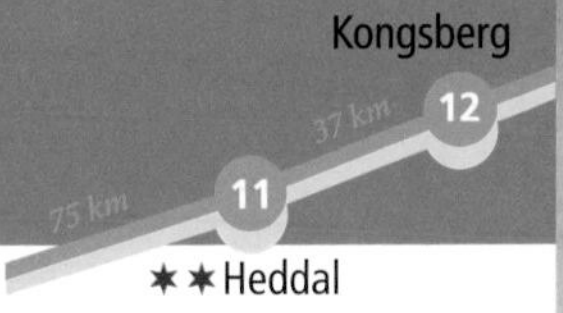

Kongsberg

37 km

75 km

12

11

**Heddal

THE SUN-DRENCHED BEACHES ON THE SOUTH COAST, OR THE ICY WORLD OF SHIMMERING BLUE GLACIERS? UP TO NORDKAPP, THROUGH FJORD COUNTRY, OR A TRIP TO SEE THE MOST FAMOUS STAVE CHURCHES? WE'LL SHOW YOU NORWAY AT ITS MOST BEAUTIFUL.

TOURS THROUGH NORWAY

These tours reflect the many faces of Norway. Whether you would like to explore interesting towns and cities to enjoy their art and culture, explore fjord landscapes, or set off on the lonely journey beyond the Arctic Circle – we will take you there.

TOUR 1 **From the South Coast to Telemark**
This round trip begins with some of Norway's most beautiful beaches and coastal towns before heading into the hinterland, where extensive forests, small villages and farms characterize the Setesdal valley (Norwegian: Setesdalen) and the county of Telemark. ► **page 134**

TOUR 2 **Into the Wild Heartland**
A spectacular tour around southern Norway to the highest Jotunheimen mountains, the icy world of the Jostedal Glacier or Jostedalsbreen, the narrow Geirangerfjord and on to the king of fjords: the Sognefjord. ► **page 136**

TOUR 3 **Always in Sight of the Sea**
Keeping to the coast, heading north from Norway's southernmost point, this is no tour for those in a hurry. The jagged coast with its many fjords only allows for narrow, winding roads, and the numerous ferries further ensure sedate progress. ► **page 139**

TOUR 4 **Off to Nordkapp**
It is a long way to Nordkapp (North Cape), but the majestic cliffs in the middle of a bare arctic landscape exert a magical fascination. Consequently there is no shortage of hubbub here. ► **page 142**

Stavanger
Discover all you ever wanted to know about oil here; a good supply of sardines also awaits.

Ålesund
Fish-watching up close in Atlantic Sea World

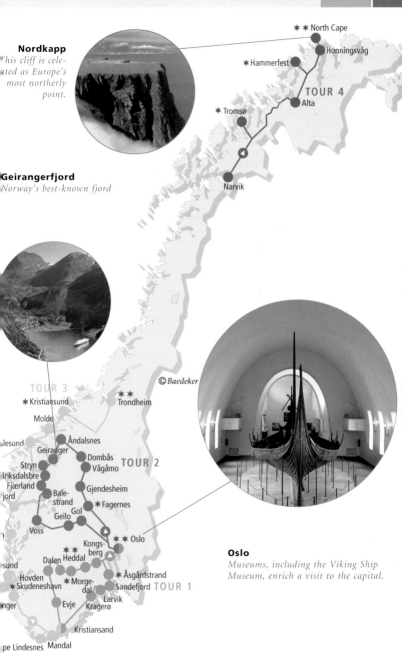

Nordkapp
*This cliff is cele-
brated as Europe's
most northerly
point.*

Geirangerfjord
Norway's best-known fjord

** ** North Cape
● Honningsvåg
* Hammerfest
TOUR 4
● Alta
* Tromsø
◁
● Narvik

© Baedeker

TOUR 3
* Kristiansund
** ** Trondheim
Molde
Ålesund
Åndalsnes
Geiranger
Stryn
Dombås
Briksdalsbre
Vågåmo
Fjærland
TOUR 2
fjord
Bale-
Gjendesheim
strand
* Fagernes
Gol
Geilo
Voss
Kongs-
berg
** ** Oslo
** ** ◁
Dalen Heddal
sund
Hovden
* Morge-
* Åsgårdstrand
Skudeneshavn
dal
Sandefjord   TOUR 1
Larvik
Evje
Kragerø
nger
Kristiansand
pe Lindesnes Mandal

Oslo
*Museums, including the Viking Ship
Museum, enrich a visit to the capital.*

Travelling in Norway

Slow progress Norway is a large and particularly long country. Those standing at its southernmost point, Lindesnes, are exactly 2518km/1574mi from Nordkapp; and if you also want to continue on to Kirkenes from Europe's most northerly point, you still have another good 500km/312mi to go. The many **valleys, fjords, mountains** and glaciers have been **mighty obstacles** since time immemorial. Direct road connections, motorways and express highways are therefore the exception, despite major investment, and that means travel in Norway is predominantly via winding country roads. In addition, the extremely disciplined driving habits of the Norwegians and the hefty fines for speeding also guarantee an unusually sedate travelling tempo. For these reasons it is a good idea to **choose your route carefully** prior to the journey and to plan enough time and resources for detours and hikes, as well as for the occasional day of bad weather. Those heading for **Nordkapp** should allow at least four weeks, otherwise there will hardly be time for sights beyond the E 6. It is by no means cheap travelling around Norway by car: petrol is extremely expensive and the cost of **road tolls and ferry tickets** is an additional expense.

Choosing a mode of transport Of course Norway can also be explored by public transport. However, the **car** does offer considerably more options for detours to the more remote sights. An essential item in your luggage should be **hiking boots**, as there are many places where there are opportunities to undertake short or indeed longer tours during which the magnificent natural environment can be fully experienced. Cycle touring is also becoming more and more popular, though the heavily segmented landscape makes careful planning essential. A paradise for **cyclists** is provided by the Lofoten and Vesterålen islands, where the imposing mountain panorama can be enjoyed in the light of the midnight sun on routes almost completely free of inclines.

i **Tolls**

■ The use of tunnels, bridges and some motorways incurs toll charges. Toll booths are installed without cashiers but with automatic payment machines. Sometimes cash is thrown into a basket, but it is also always possible to pay by credit card.

Rather optimistically known as the »Norwegian Riviera«, the **south coast** nevertheless offers the **most beautiful sandy beaches**, small bays and the sheer cliffs of skerries. This is a serpentine water world where a boat grants untold opportunities. Places like Risør, Tvedestrand, Arendal or Mandal fill up with holidaymakers at the drop of a hat during the Norwegian summer vacations. Yet the hurly-burly never gets out of hand and it is almost always possible to find a quiet spot by the sea. The country's interior awaits with a dream holiday for travellers seeking solitude, for this is where it truly exists: a cabin right on a lake, with nothing but nature as far as the eye can see. The water in these small lakes is often warmer than the sea and the swimming is wonderful!

Mountain ranges lie across southern Norway like a pearl necklace: Setesdalsheiene, then Hardangervidda, Jotunheimen, Dovrefjell and Rondane. Scandinavia's highest mountains can be found here, as well as wild jagged peaks and glaciers, and barren and **treeless high plateaus**. The Norwegian fjells (mountains) begin to impress even when still approaching in the car. A crossing of the Hardangervidda plateau on the RV 7 between Eidfjord and Geilo, or a drive through the Jotunheimen mountains via the Valdresflya (RV 51), or touring on the RV 55 between Skjolden and Lom and over Sognefjell count among the most beautiful extended panoramic routes through Norway. There comes a point, though, when the visitor should do as the Norwegians do: leave the car behind and **set off on foot**.

The **west** of the country is cut by countless fjords and driving becomes a trial of patience, because the roads are often narrow and interspersed by tunnels. Caravan trailers and mobile homes can expect painfully slow progress. One of the most attractive times of year for holidays in western Norway is the **spring**, for this is when the fruit trees are already blossoming along the fjords, while the mountains are still covered by snow. A warning: swimming in the fjords at that time of year is only for the hardy!

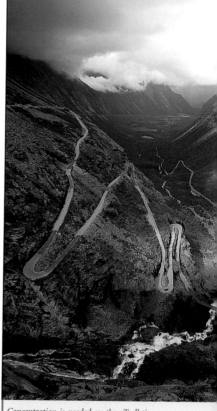

Concentration is needed on the »Trollstigen«.

During summer, the north is illuminated by the light of the midnight sun. The countryside glows in warm colours and the visitor is often alone in a mighty **primeval landscape** in these sparsely populated northern lands, able to stroll along wild coasts, try their luck in the salmon-rich rivers, or explore the desolate highland plateaus of Finnmarksvidda.

The north

Tour 1 From the South Coast to Telemark

Length: 873km/546mi   **Duration:** 6 days

During summer, the south coast is among the most popular holiday regions in all of Norway because of its beautiful beaches. Even those who don't particularly want to swim can experience the country from its sunniest side here. The starting point is Oslo, and visits to interesting museums are followed by opportunities for rafting and collecting minerals, as well as calling in at Heddal's famous stave church.

Oslo for starters After the exploration of Norway's capital, ❶ ✶✶ **Oslo**, for which two to three days should be planned, the tour heads off on the E 18 (developed into a motorway) to Drammen – which can happily be left by the wayside – before reaching small and quiet ❷ ✶ **Åsgårdstrand**, which does merit a stop because of its location on the Oslofjord and for its decorative white wooden houses and the many mementos of the painter Edvard Munch. For those with a little more time, the former whaling town of ❸ **Sandefjord** has an interesting whaling and seafaring museum. The ferries for Denmark depart several times a day from ❹ **Larvik**, while the seaside resort of Stavern to the south is worth a small detour to see the fortress of Fredriksvern with its mighty ramparts. After Larvik the E 18 traverses inland for a time and passes the industrial town of Porsgrunn, famous for its porcelain manufactory.

DON'T MISS
- The cathedral in Kristiansand
- Minerals in Evje
- Stave church in Heddal
- Baroque church of Kongsberg

Pack your bathing costume! ❺ **Kragerø**, the next destination, lies somewhat off the main road and marks the beginning of the sun-drenched southern coast that is one of Norway's most popular holiday destinations thanks to its beautiful beaches, jutting skerries and immaculate settlements with their numerous white wooden houses. It is therefore worth making repeated detours off the E 18 to small coastal towns, such as Risør, Tvedestrand, Lyngør, Arendal or Grimstad, before reaching ❻ ✶ **Kristiansand**, which is one of the country's most important ferry ports and offers a quick connection to northern Denmark. A visit to the cathedral and the historic wooden houses of the Posebyen quarter should definitely be on the Kristiansand itinerary.

Up into the mountains The RV 9 leads north from Kristiansand through the Setesdal valley and along the Otra river, which forms several lakes. The richly for-

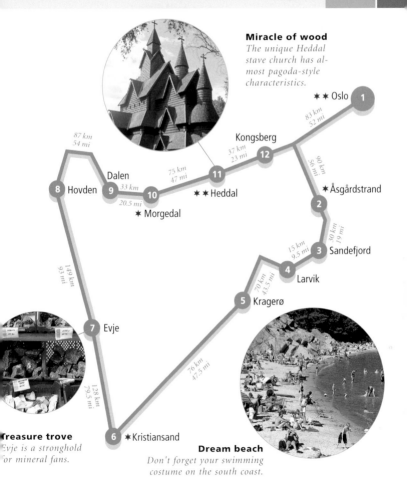

Miracle of wood
The unique Heddal stave church has almost pagoda-style characteristics.

★★ Oslo **1**

Kongsberg

87 km
54 mi

Dalen

8 Hovden **9** 33 km

75 km
47 mi

11

37 km
23 mi

12

90 km
56 mi

83 km
52 mi

20.5 mi

10

★ Morgedal

★★ Heddal

★ Åsgårdstrand

2

149 km
93 mi

7 Evje

4

15 km
9.5 mi

3 Sandefjord

30 km
19 mi

Larvik

70 km
43.5 mi

5 Kragerø

128 km
79.5 mi

76 km
47.5 mi

6 ★ Kristiansand

Treasure trove
Evje is a stronghold for mineral fans.

Dream beach
Don't forget your swimming costume on the south coast.

ested valley surrounded by high mountains remained remote for many centuries, but has now become a popular holiday destination. **7 Evje** is of particular interest to mineral hunters and rafting fans. **8 Hovden**, one of Norway's best-known winter sports destinations, is reached along a steadily ascending road heading north along the length of the Byglandsfjord, a long lake with several attractive bathing spots. Several miles north of Hovden, the road reaches Sessvatn (917m/3009ft), this highest point offering a panoramic view of the barren, high alpine landscape here. Soon afterwards the descent to Haukeligrend and the E 134 is marked by tight serpentine bends. From there a widened road leads to the little town of Åmot before turning into the RV 38 in the direction of **9 Dalen**.

A visit to Heddal Dalen, on the banks of the long, narrow Lake Bandak, is the end-point of the Telemark Canal. The Dalen Hotel – a historic wood construction in the dragon style – and the nearby stave church of Eidsborg are worth taking a look at here. The main road is reached again via the RV 45, which soon leads on to ⑩ ✳ **Morgedal**. Another highlight awaits shortly before the small town of Notodden, in ⑪ ✳✳ **Heddal**, where Norway's largest stave church can be viewed. The old mining town of ⑫ **Kongsberg**, which owes its foundation to the surrounding silver mines, is today known as a centre for jazz and also for the marvellous interior of its Baroque church. Finally, Oslo and this round tour's starting point are reached once more via Hokksund and Drammen.

Tour 2 Into the Wild Heartland

Length: 1335km/835mi   **Duration:** 8 days

This panoramic tour on adventurous serpentine roads leads to the craggy Jotunheimen mountains and through the narrow Romsdal valley. Experience the Geirangerfjord and the Sognefjord, as well as the icy world of the Jostedal Glacier (Jostedalsbreen) and the austere Hardangervidda highland plateau.

Straight through Jotunheimen Hønefoss is reached from ❶ ✳✳ **Oslo** via the E 16, where a worthwhile detour can be made to the ✳ **Hadeland Glassverk**, Norway's most renowned glassworks at the southern end of the Randsfjord. After Hønefoss, the E 16 follows the river Begna (which soon widens into Lake Sperillen) all the way to ❷ ✳ **Fagernes**, the most important town in the Valdres region. Fagernes is a significant tourist centre at the southern edge of the Jotunheimen range and has an open-air museum worth visiting. Steadily climbing, the RV 51 now leads in the direction of the Jotunheimen mountains, reaching the tree line at the winter sports resort

DON'T MISS

- Shopping at the Hadeland Glassverk
- View of the Trollstigen
- Hike to Briksdalsbreen
- Rest stop at the Vøringfoss

of Beitostølen. A beautiful view of Lake Bygdin surrounded by imposing mountains can be enjoyed at the town of the same name. The road reaches its highest point at the Valdresflya mountain pass, and then leads on to ❸ **Gjendesheim**, which lies on the long, narrow Lake Gjende and is one of the most important bases for hikes into the Jotunheimen mountains. The crossing of the Jotunheimen ends shortly before ❹ **Vågåmo**, which boasts a stave church that is worth taking a look at.

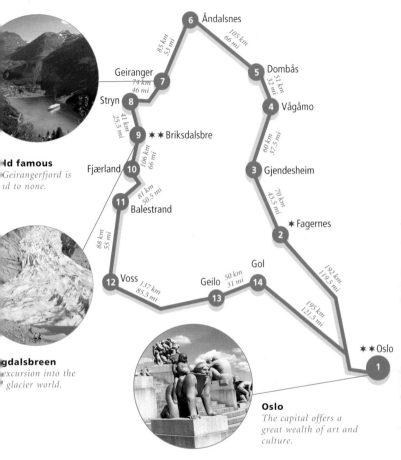

6 Åndalsnes

85 km
53 mi

105 km
66 mi

Geiranger
7
74 km
46 mi

5 Dombås

51 km
32 mi

Stryn
8

4 Vågåmo

41 km
25.5 mi

60 km
37.5 mi

9 ✳✳ Briksdalsbre

106 km
66 mi

Fjærland 10

3 Gjendesheim

81 km
50.5 mi

70 km
43.5 mi

11

Balestrand

✳ Fagernes

88 km
55 mi

2

Gol

192 km
119.5 mi

Voss
12
137 km
85.5 mi

Geilo

50 km
31 mi

14

13

195 km
121.5 mi

✳✳ Oslo

1

...ld famous
*Geirangerfjord is
...d to none.*

...gdalsbreen
*...excursion into the
... glacier world.*

Oslo
*The capital offers a
great wealth of art and
culture.*

The sparsely populated ✳ **Romsdal** is finally reached via ❺**Dombås**, **To Trollwand and** a route whose highlights are the 1000m/3280ft-high, vertical ✳ **Romsdalhorn** **Trollveggen** (»troll wall«), reached shortly before ❻**Åndalsnes**, and the no less imposing Romsdalshorn. Shortly afterwards, the serpentine road leads up to the ✳✳ **Trollstigen** (»troll ladder«), which is one of Norway's most impressive roads. The viewing point at the pass is not to be missed. The spectacular road continues through the Meirdal valley down to the fjord, which is crossed by a ferry, before turning back into the mountains on the winding ✳ **Eagle Road** followed by the descent into ❼**Geiranger** on the ✳✳ **Geirangerfjord**. The road from Geiranger past Dalsnibba mountain to ❽**Stryn** is also a worthy fjell-and-fjord panorama tour. From Stryn, the road follows the banks of the fjord to Olden, where it turns off for ❾✳✳ **Briks-**

dalsbreen glacier, which numbers among the most beautiful arms of Jostedalsbreen and is roughly an hour's walk from the car park.

It is well worth paying a visit to the Norwegian Glacier Museum in ⑩**Fjærland** located at the southern end of Jostedalsbreen and reached via Olden, Byrkjelo and Skei. From there the route follows the E 5 to Sogndal and continues on the RV 55 to Hella and the ferry, from which ⑪✳ **Balestrand** is reached via Dragsvik. Take a look at the Swiss-style wooden villas on the sunny Sognefjord here as well as the magnificent Kvikne Hotel. From Balestrand return to the ferry at Dragsvik and take the boat to Vangsnes before heading for ⑫**Voss** on the RV 13 via Viksøyri. Voss boasts an impressive location on Lake Vangsvatn, but the townscape is modern. During summer a cable car takes hikers directly into the mountains, and during winter it is the ski slopes that attract people to Voss. The drive to ⑬**Geilo** leads through Måbødal, where it is worth stopping at one of Norway's best-known waterfalls, Vøringfoss. Afterwards the RV 7 traverses the austere Hardangervidda before finally reaching Geilo, a popular winter sports resort because of its excellent alpine sports facilities. ⑭**Gol** is reached via Hol, Ål and Torpo, after which the RV 7 leads through the Hallingdal valley to Noresund via Nesbyen. Oslo and the starting point of this tour is then reached once more via Hønefoss.

From the Sognefjord to Hardangervidda

Tour 3 Always in Sight of the Sea

Length: 1268km/792mi   **Duration:** 10 days

Plenty of time is a real boon for this route, as at many fjords the only way forward is to take the ferry. Some of the country's most important towns are on the itinerary: oil-boom town Stavanger, atmospheric Bergen, Ålesund with its art nouveau buildings, and Trondheim, once the glittering capital of the kingdom.

Starting point ①✳ **Kristiansand** is one of Norway's most important ferry ports and maintains regular routes to northern Denmark. After visiting the district of wooden houses in Posebyen and the imposing cathedral, leave town in a westerly direction on the well maintained E 39. The route soon reaches ②**Mandal**, the southernmost town of the »Norwegian Riv-

✔ **DON'T MISS**

■ Stavanger: Oil Museum
■ Bergen: Bryggen quarter
■ Trondheim: Nidaros Cathedral

← *Visitors just need to pause; the action is courtesy of Norwegian nature.*

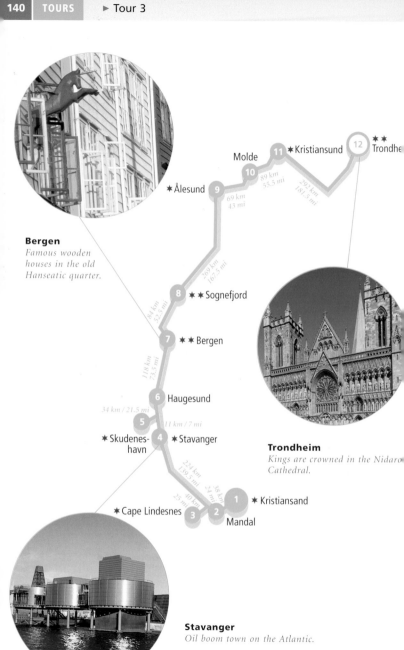

Bergen
Famous wooden houses in the old Hanseatic quarter.

Trondheim
Kings are crowned in the Nidaros Cathedral.

Stavanger
Oil boom town on the Atlantic.

12 ** Trondhe

11 *Kristiansund

Molde

10

89 km
55.5 mi

293 km
181.5 mi

*Ålesund **9**

69 km
43 mi

269 km
167.5 mi

8 ** Sognefjord

84 km
52.5 mi

7 ** Bergen

118 km
73.5 mi

6 Haugesund

34 km / 21.5 mi
5
11 km / 7 mi

*Skudenes-
havn **4** *Stavanger

224 km
139.5 mi

38 km
24 mi

*Cape Lindesnes **3**
40 km
25 mi **2** **1** *Kristiansand

Mandal

The Hanseatic Museum in Bergen illustrates how people slept in the olden days.

iera«. A draw here is the long sandy beach of Sjøsanden, right by the centre, and the nearby recreational area of Furulunden, which also boasts attractive beaches. From Mandal, the southernmost point of the Norwegian mainland is reached at ❸ ✱ **Lindesnes**. A sweeping view of the austere skerry landscape can be enjoyed from the small lighthouse.

On the way to ❹ ✱ **Stavanger** it is worth making stops at the nearby Flekkefjord – the »Dutch town« – with its narrow lanes and restored white wood houses, and also at Orresanden, a long, sandy beach to the south of the oil town. Stavanger itself is Norway's modern boom town: expensive, lively and open to the world. The ferry can take you to the island of Karmøy, to the north, and to the small fishing village of ❹ ✱ **Skudeneshavn**, which feels a lot like an open-air museum. In ❻ **Haugesund**, the largest town between Stavanger and Bergen, there is an opportunity to stroll along the water on the promenade and visit the pink town hall. The E 39 then continues in a northerly direction, very often along the water's edge and, after several breaks for ferry trips, eventually reaches ❼ ✱ ✱ **Bergen**, capital of fjord country. It is easy to spend several days here: strolling around the fish market, enjoying the view from Fløyen, and exploring the Hanseatic Museum.

Stavanger and Bergen

Several ferries, including those that cross the broad ❽ ✱ ✱ **Sognefjord,** ensure there are repeated breaks along the way to the art nouveau town of ❾ ✱ **Ålesund**. The jazz town of ❿ **Molde** can also only

Road to Trondheim

be reached after a wait for the ferry at the Romsdalsfjord. ⑪ ✳ **Kristiansund**, on the other hand, has been connected to the mainland since the elaborate bridge and tunnel construction of 1992. From here there are two routes to ⑫ ✳✳ **Trondheim**: the shortest in terms of distance, but a considerably slower option due to the numerous ferries, is the route via small serpentine roads along the coast; alternatively there is the inland route via Sunndalsøra and Oppdal.

Tour 4 Off to Nordkapp

Length: 1017km/636mi   **Duration:** 4 days

At the latest from Narvik onwards, there is no alternative but the E 6 for those who are heading north. Many at this point are in a hurry to reach Nordkapp (North Cape) at last, but travellers who leave themselves a little more time and who are lucky with the weather will fall in love with the solitude of these northern lands bathed in the midnight sun. It is an overwhelming wilderness that has no equal in Europe.

Towns beyond the Arctic Circle
The route follows the E 6 north from the iron ore mining town of ❶**Narvik** on the Ofotfjord, through the sparsely populated county of Troms and passing the small town of Andselv, until it reaches a junction at Nordkjosbotn. This is where the E 8 turns off and runs 73km/46mi to the port of ❷ ✳ **Tromsø**. The city lies on a small island connected to the mainland by a daringly arched bridge. Tromsø likes to refer to itself as the »Paris of the North« and its emblem is the modern Arctic Cathedral. Returning to the E 6 after this detour, the route continues on its way to Nordkapp. Next stop is ❸ **Alta**, where northern Europe's largest collection of Bronze Age rock paintings can be found to the south of the town, at Hjemmeluft.

DON'T MISS

- Alta: Stone Age rock paintings
- Honningsvåg: North Cape Museum
- Nordkapp: breathtaking views from the Nordkapp cliffs and sending cards with special postmark

The next destination is ❹ ✳ **Hammerfest**, which lies 57km/36mi off the main road and is a significant fishing and trading centre due to its year-round ice-free port.

Hubbub at the cape
To reach ❺**Honningsvåg**, it is necessary to return to the E 6 and follow it to the turn-off for the E 69, where the route leads to Kåfjord. A toll tunnel and bridge has connected Kåfjord with the island of Magerøy since 1999, where ❻ ✳✳ **Nordkapp** is located. The most expensive part of the road is made up by the roughly 7km/4mi of the

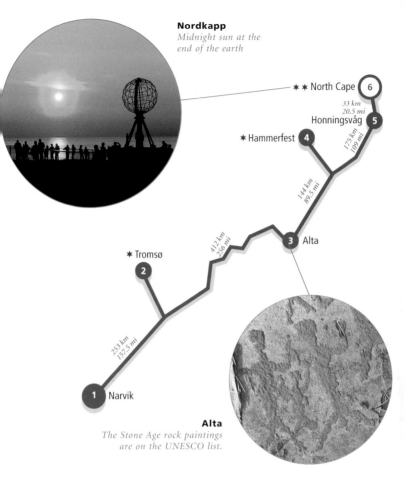

Nordkapp
*Midnight sun at the
end of the earth*

★★ North Cape ⑥

33 km
20.5 mi

Honningsvåg ⑤

175 km
109 mi

★ Hammerfest ④

144 km
89.5 mi

③ Alta

412 km
256 mi

★ Tromsø
②

253 km
157.5 mi

① Narvik

Alta
*The Stone Age rock paintings
are on the UNESCO list.*

North Cape Tunnel (Nordkapptunnelen) between Kåfjord and Honningsvåg. In good weather, there is a beautiful view of the neighbouring disjointed peninsulas and the Polar Sea from the flattened summit of the Nordkapp cliffs, which are a good 300m/984ft high. However, you will never be alone at Nordkapp: indeed the tourist hubbub here reaches unsuspected extremes. Those enraptured by the north can now set off for the 544km/340mi two-day journey to Kirkenes, following the E 69 along the Porsangerfjord back to the E 6 and then driving almost to the Russian border, through the barren and almost entirely uninhabited landscape of the Finnmark. In contrast to Nordkapp, only very few tourists find their way to this town at the end of the world.

Sights from A to Z

FROM THE STREETS OF OSLO UP TO THE HIGH FJELLS; ONWARDS TO THE FJORDS AND NORTH TO THE LOFOTEN ISLANDS AND NORDKAPP – THERE IS MUCH TO DISCOVER IN NORWAY.

★ Ålesund

E 3

Region: West Norway

Population: 39,000

Ålesund is one of Norway's most beautiful towns: the location alone makes it worth a visit, situated on several islands in the midst of fjords and skerries, but the art nouveau buildings turn it into a veritable jewel.

Islands and klippfisk
Looking down onto Ålesund's sea of houses from the local hill of Aksla, this lively market town and port appears to spread itself over numerous islands. The largest part of town reaches across the islands of Heissa (4 sq km/2 sq mi), Nørvøya (7 sq km/3 sq mi) and Aspøya (0.5 sq km/0.2 sq mi). Several of these islands are connected by road, though 12km/8mi is via underwater tunnels. Home to Norway's largest and most up-to-date fishing fleet, Ålesund has become one of the country's most important fishing ports and, globally, one of the largest export bases for dried salt cod or »klippfisk«. 80% of the world's requirement for this product is met from Ålesund, with the largest customer being Portugal. Furthermore, Ålesund's clothes and furniture factories are renowned well beyond the region.

Waterways run through Ålesund's town centre.

▶ VISITING ÅLESUND

INFORMATION

Ålesund Reiselivslag
Rådhuset, 6025 Ålesund
Tel. 70 15 76 00, fax 70 15 76 01
www.visitalesund.no

WHERE TO EAT

▶ Expensive

Brasserie Normandie
Storgata 16
Tel. 70 13 23 00
Expensive, yes, but good: the gourmet restaurant in the Rica Parken Hotel prepares fine fish dishes, such as porbeagle (håbrann), mini salmon (pjakk) and grenadier fish (skoklest). The fish platter is recommended.

Sjøbua Restaurant
Brunholmgata 1a
Tel. 70 12 71 00
A popular fish restaurant located in a former warehouse where the raw materials are delivered directly from the fishing boat. The interior décor is maritime, the view over Brosund very beautiful. Dried salt cod au gratin is recommended.

▶ Moderate

Café Brosundet
Rasmus Rønnebergsgate 4
Tel. 70 12 91 00
Ålesund's best pastries from their in-house bakery are served at the café in the First Hotel Atlantica. They also do lunch and evening meals.

▶ Inexpensive

Apoteker'n Café
Apotekergt. 16
Tel. 70 10 49 70
Charming café in the art nouveau town centre and an ideal place for a snack and an espresso. The speciality is »Queen Maud's cake«.

WHERE TO STAY

▶ Luxury

Scandic Ålesund
Molovn. 6, tel. 21 61 45 00
118 rooms; www.scandic-hotels.com
Modern hotel with all the comforts; most rooms have views onto the water and the island world of Ålesund.

▶ Budget

Goksøyr Camping
Runde, tel. 70 08 59 05
Meeting place for ornithologists and nature photographers at the foot of the cliffs that are home to hundreds of thousands of nesting birds. Knut Asle Goksøyr ensures there is well-informed service staff, and there are also cabins and rooms.

Baedeker recommendation

▶ Live like Robinson Crusoe

Since 2004, it has been possible to stay in the restored pilot house on the island of Runde. The facilities of this small place are simple, but the exposed location on a spit of land really does make you feel like Robinson Crusoe, especially out of season when the wind howls around the building. Tel. 70 08 59 05

EXCURSIONS

Motor boats and high-speed ferries connect to the outer islands and into the smaller fjords to the south of the city. There are also sightseeing helicopter flights departing from the airport.

FESTIVALS

Mid-June: Dragon Boat Festival (www.dragebat.no); around the 10th July: boat festival; end of August: gourmet festival with a championship for master chefs (www.matfestivalen.no).

What to See in Ålesund

Art nouveau town

Ålesund is famous for its art nouveau architecture, which is a style that hardly exists elsewhere in Norway. Numerous houses in the town centre were rebuilt in this style with the help of international aid after a massive fire in 1904, during which 10,000 people were made homeless. Among the donors was German Emperor Wilhelm II, who was an enthusiastic Norway fan. A tour of the town centre reveals colourful embellishments on the façades and countless turrets and towers.

Aspøya, Nørvøya

The centre of Ålesund is on the two main islands. Ålesund's church (1909), with its remarkable frescoes and wonderful painted glass (some a gift from the German emperor), stands on Aspøya. A patrician house on Nørvøya contains the **municipal museum**, with an extensive section devoted to art nouveau architecture and historic craftsmanship, as well as an interesting section on fishing, complete with old ships.Ålesund's most magnificent buildings in the art nouveau style with colourful façades line Hellesundet, the inner harbour between the two islands. The houses on Kongensgata on Nørvøya and Apotekergata on Aspøya are especially worth seeing. The **Art Nouveau Centre** is housed in one of the most beautiful buildings in the city, at Apotekergata 16, right on the sound (Norwegian: sund). The museum in the former Svane pharmacy was opened by Queen

✳
Art nouveau houses ▶

Experience the wonders of the ocean in Atlantic Sea World, one of Norway's largest aquariums.

Sonja in 2003, and provides information on the fire in the town as well as telling the story of art nouveau (opening times: June–Aug Mon–Fri 10am–7pm, Sat 10am–5pm, Sun noon–5pm, otherwise Tue–Fri 11am–5pm, Sat 11am–4pm, Sun noon–4pm.)

Harbour

The quays lie to the south and north of the islands of Aspøya and Nørvøya. Fresh fish and shellfish are sold at the harbour on Skanse-gata.

Park

East of the city centre, lies the municipal park (Norwegian: bypark) with its 7m/23ft Bauta stone with a relief portrait of Emperor Wilhelm II, recalling German assistance after the great city fire of 1904. There is also a statue of the Viking Rollo (Gange-Rolv), who allegedly came from Ålesund and who founded the Duchy of Normandy in 911.

★
View from Aksla

East of the park, 418 steps lead up to the 189m/620ft-high hill of Aksla, from which there is a wonderful view onto the city, the sea and the islands around, as well as of the Sunnmøre mountains to the southeast. The view from the cafeteria »Fjellstua« (135m/443ft), which can also be reached by car via Fjelltunvei east of the city, presents an especially popular photo opportunity at sunset.

Atlantic aquarium

On a spit of land known as Tueneset, about 3km/2mi west of the city centre, lies one of Norway's largest aquariums. It is discretely incorporated into the otherwise untouched coastal landscape. The giant acrylic tanks of the Atlantic Ocean Park (Atlanterhavspark) contain fish and marine animals from the North Sea (opening times: June–Aug daily 10am–7pm, Sat till 4pm, otherwise daily 11am–4pm, Oct–April closed on Mon).

Around Ålesund

Borgund

Not to be confused with the home of the famous stave church (► Borgund stave church), Borgund is located around 4km/2mi east of the city centre. The oldest part of the church here was built in 1130. It burnt down in 1904, but it was then reconstructed true to the original. The interior contains beautiful wood carvings in the old style. Right next to the church, the **Sunnmøre Museum** attracts visitors to its open air exhibition of around 50 historic houses. There is also an interesting fishing exhibition with 30 old boats and the *Borgund-Knarren*, a historic merchant ship from the year 1000 (opening times: daily 11am–4pm/5pm, Sun from noon).

! Baedeker TIP

Take to the waves in a Viking ship
The *Borgund-Knarren* Viking ship departs from the Sunnmøre Museum for a one-hour tour every Wednesday during the summer.

Runde

Norway's southernmost **nesting cliffs**, the »Rundebranden«, are on the island of Runde, southwest of Ålesund. So far, over 200 different species of birds and around 170,000 breeding pairs have been observed here, especially puffins, guillemots and gannets. Hundreds of ornithologists and nature photographers come to the island's only settlement of **Goksøyr** every year. However, it is also possible to view the lower sections of the cliffs' guano speckled rocks from on board a small fishing boat that makes daily **sightseeing trips**. In 1725, the Dutch merchant ship *Akerendam* sank off the coast here. Divers found over 60,000 gold and silver coins in the old wreck in 1972, and divers can still go treasure hunting in the area.

Ivar Aasen Museum

The Ivar Aasen Museum is located near the E 39 road, between Ørsta and Volda. Aasen formulated the basis for Nynorsk, which is one of the two Norwegian official languages. The museum was designed by one of the country's foremost architects, Sverre Fehn, and provides ☉ exhaustive information on language and literature (opening times: Mon–Fri 10am–4pm, Sun 1pm–6pm).

✳
Stordal church

Stordal is around 50km/31mi east of Ålesund, and its church really is worth a visit. The entire interior of this Rosekyrkja (rose church) rebuilt in 1789 to replace an earlier one is covered in paintings. Large parts of the interior furnishings still originate from the first medieval ☉ church (opening times: 20 June–20 Aug, daily 10am–4pm).

Magnificent: the interior of the Stordal rose church near Ålesund

✳ Alta

Region: North Norway   **Population:** 17,000

People lived in the region around the Altafjord as early as the Stone Age, leaving thousands of rock paintings now famous. Today the Sami settlement of Alta in the far north is an ideal base for tours in the direction of Nordkapp and Finnmark.

The largest town in the sparsely populated county of ►Finnmark lies at the point where the Alta river – Norway's best known river for salmon – flows into the Altafjord. The excellent tourist infrastructure of the town make it very suitable as a base for tours to ►Nordkapp, ►Hammerfest, and the Sami towns of ►Karasjok and ►Kautokeino. Even though the town is on the 70th northern latitude, the mild climate softened by the Gulf Stream creates ideal conditions for agriculture and forestry.

Mild climate in the far north

Humans inhabited the area around Alta more than 10,000 years ago. This fact is proven by the rock paintings of Hjemmeluft and by excavations on the Komsa mountain (Komsa culture). The Sami settlement of Alta developed into an administrative centre early on, after increasing numbers of Norwegians moved here in the 17th century to trade in reindeer meat and other goods. Immigrants from southern Norway and Finland also arrived with the beginning of copper mining in Kåfjord. Alta was totally destroyed by German occupying troops towards the end of the Second World War. With the exception of the churches of Alta and Kåfjord, therefore, the entire townscape dates from the post-war era.

! *Baedeker* TIP

A thousand barking dogs

Visiting Alta is especially worthwhile at the beginning of March, when the whole town is gripped by the thrill of the forthcoming Finnmarksløpet. There is tremendous excitement surrounding the event. 70 mushers competing in Europe's longest and most northerly dog sled race arrive with around one thousand huski dogs. After 12 stages, racing 1000km/625mi across the deeply snowed-in north, they cross the finishing line at Alta (information at www.finnmarkslopet.no).

What to See in Alta

The area around the Altafjord is one of the most ancient population centres in the county of Finnmark, as proved by the giant fields with close to 3000 rock paintings discovered in 1973 immediately south of Alta, on the E 6. It is the largest collection of its kind in northern Europe and listed among the UNESCO World Heritage Sites. The oldest of the paintings, which have been coloured in by archaeologists, go back to the Stone Age and are 6200 years old; the most re-

✳ *Rock paintings*

cent are 2500 years old. The question of how humans survived the Ice Age here remains unanswered to this day. Hunting scenes, dancers, circles and fertility symbols can be discovered by following a 5km/3mi educational route.

Access to the rock paintings is via the prize-winning **Alta Museum** next door, which has been designed on the latest pedagogic principles for museums. The museum gives an interesting overview on slate extraction, river and fjord fishing, the craftsmanship of the Finnmark Sami, and the Stone Age culture of Sørøya Island. A special exhibition also recalls the Sami's bitter campaign (1978–82) against the development of a hydro-electric dam on the Alta river. The Sami lost the battle, though they won politically: as a result of this conflict, a Sami parliament was set up by the Norwegian government and Sami culture was incorporated into the national constitution, officially recognized as worthy of preservation (▶ Finnmark and ▶ Baedeker Special p.36). (Opening times: daily 8am–8pm, mid-June–mid-August till 11pm.)

Slate extraction and its associated working methods can be experienced close up near **Peska** (15km/9mi south of the centre of town, 5km/3mi off the RV 93).

The roughly 3000 rock paintings at Alta are part of our global heritage.

Alta's main attraction is the rich choice of leisure activities and excursion options on the Alta river. With a length of 6km/4mi and a depth of 300–400m/980–1300ft, the **Sautso Canyon** (or Alta Canyon) is the largest in Europe and provides a fascinating insight into the power of nature. Just under 30km/19mi from Alta, the canyon is reached via the old road passing Gargia on the way to the Baskades highlands. From there a signposted path leads to the gorge, a two-hour walk from the Gargia hut. This natural wonder can also be reached via the Alta river, though every boat should have a guide.

▶ VISITING ALTA

INFORMATION

Destinasjon Alta
Parksenteret
9504 Alta
Tel. 78 44 95 55
Fax 78 43 65 08
www.destinasjonalta.no

GETTING THERE

There are direct flights from Oslo.

WHERE TO STAY

▶ Luxury
Rica Hotel Alta
Løkkeveien 61
Tel. 78 48 27 00, fax 78 43 65 08
155 rooms, www.rica.no
Luxury in the far north. The largest hotel in town is ultra modern, with two restaurants, a bar and nightclub.

▶ Mid-range
Hotel Aurora
Saga
Tel. 78 45 78 00
Fax 78 45 78 01
30 rooms, www.hotelaurora.no
Boasting views across the Altafjord, the Hotel Aurora is located in a quiet spot 3km/2mi from Alta's airport, and yet it is only 200m/219yd from the E 6 road. There is a sauna, bar and restaurant with attentive service and assistance in planning excursions is on offer.

Alta Igloo Hotel
Alta Friluftspark AS
Tel. 78 43 33 78, www.ice-alta.no
Located 15km/9mi from the town centre, the most northerly ice hotel in the world offers 20 rooms in which guests sleep in sleeping bags on reindeer skins.

MIDNIGHT SUN

The midnight sun can be seen in Alta between 16 May and 26 July; from 24 November to 18 January the sun does not appear at all.

Beginning each 22 June, salmon fishing is the most popular leisure activity on the Alta river. At this time anglers come to Alta from all over the world and, with their highly-prized fishing card in their pockets and their fly fishing rod in hand, they go after the salmon.

Salmon fishing

Around Alta

Kåfjord, once the largest community in the Finnmark during the mid 19th century, is reached by driving west along the coast from Alta. Travelling further to Isnestoften (also known as Toften) via Talvik, it is possible to find both old German fortifications and the remains of four Stone Age settlements. The Langfjord cuts deep into the countryside here. From Langfjordbotn it is possible to make a beautiful excursion on minor roads to the large Øksfjordjøkulen glacier – the only glacier on the European mainland that empties into the sea (►Troms).

Kåfjord

◄ Øksfjordjøkulen

✳ Arendal

Region: South Norway   **Population:** 39,000

Arendal is the largest town on the country's southern coast, a stretch known as the »Norwegian Riviera«. The busy town once had numerous canals. Today it enchants the visitor with its attractive wooden houses. Pleasant holidays can also be enjoyed in nearby Gimstad, where the 15-year-old Henrik Ibsen once embarked on his pharmacy apprenticeship.

The white pearl

The picturesque port of Arendal is spread over seven islands and was originally cut through by many canals, a fact that earned it the name »Venice of the North«. After repeated fires, however, most recently in the 1960s, the canals were filled in. The last relic of the canal system is the lively Pollen marina, were numerous yachts and motorboats bob in the water. Arendal is the largest town of those known as the »white pearls« (named for their white wooden houses) on the Norwegian Riviera, stretching between Kragerø to the north and Lillesand to the south. Arendal was one of Scandinavia's most important seafaring towns up to the end of the 19th century. In addition to wood exports to the Netherlands (particularly during the heyday of the East India Company), shipbuilding and the port, the economic life of the town was defined by the mining of iron ore for 400 years.

! *Baedeker* TIP

Sun, sea and car-free

For the locals, the most popular destination during the summer is the car-free island of Merdø. The ferry from Arendal takes 25mins. There are several old Sørlands houses, the Merdøgaard Museum and, of course, the beaches – partly sandy and partly rocky – that all make a visit worthwhile. Those little hunger pangs can be satisfied with a light lunch at the island café.

What to See in and around Arendal

Town centre

To the west of the harbour basin of Pollen, in the crooked lanes of the Tyholmen district, well preserved wooden houses in the styles of Baroque, Rococo, Empire and Biedermeier recall the age of sail, before steam shipping was invented.

Town hall ►

The four storeys of the mighty town hall building stand right by the harbour basin. It was built as a private home for the Kallevig shipping family in 1815, and is the country's second largest wooden building after the Stiftsgården in ►Trondheim.

The Aust Agder Museum is located in several buildings on the northern edge of town, and displays furniture, costumes, dolls, minerals and ship utensils (Parkveien 16; opening times: end of June–mid-Aug Mon–Fri 9am–5pm, Sun noon–5pm, otherwise Mon–Fri

► VISITING ARENDAL

INFORMATION
Arendal Turistkontor
Langbrygga
4803 Arendal
Tel. 37 00 55 44
Fax 37 00 55 40
www.arendal.com

WHERE TO EAT
► Moderate
Frøken Bang
Nedre Tyholmsvei 9 E
Tel. 37 02 12 22
Pleasant fish restaurant in the middle
of the Tyholmen district, the historic
centre of Arendal.

► Inexpensive
Fiskebrygga
Nedre Tyholmsvei 1
Tel. 37 02 31 13
You can buy freshly caught fish and
seafood here, sit on the terrace by the
harbour, and enjoy fish soup or the
typically Norwegian »Fiskekaker«
(fish cakes).

WHERE TO STAY
► Mid-range
Scandic Hotel Arendal
Friergangen
Tel. 37 05 21 50
Fax 37 05 21 51
84 rooms, www.scandic-arendal.no
This modern hotel is ideally located to
explore the town, right by the lovingly
restored historic centre, on the former
yacht marina. The wine tavern and
the restaurant »1711«, with probably
the best fish dishes in town, are both
very popular. The nightclub is a
meeting place for the young. During
summer, it is also possible to eat
outside and watch the comings and
goings of the port.

Clarion Hotel Tyholmen
Teaterplassen 2
Tel. 37 07 68 00
Fax 37 07 68 01
60 rooms, www.tyholmenhotel.no
This comfortable hotel on a famous
spit of land is built in the style of
the 19th century. Its bar and
terrace restaurant are also very
popular.

► Budget
Hove Camping
Hove, Tromøy
Tel. 37 08 54 79
www.hove-camping.no
A generously laid out camp site in a
forested area and with a nice beach,
about 15mins from Arendal on
Tromøy. There are also 21 huts for
4–5 people available for rent.

D/S Surabaya
Port entrance of Arendal
Tel. 97 08 20 56
www.ds-surabaya.com
Those who like something a little
different can sleep on the »Surabaya«.
Until it was remodelled into a floating
guesthouse in 1999, this 1938 ship
spent many years carrying stone along
the Norwegian coast. It is predominantly favoured as a base for divers,
but bunks are also available for other
guests. A value-for-money alternative
to a hotel or cabin, with lots of
maritime flair.

EXCURSIONS
The nearby islands of Hisøy and
Tromøy can be reached by ferry or
bridges. The latter island has very
attractive sandy beaches and a viewing
point on the Vardåsen hill.

Charming wooden houses provide the backdrop for a visit to Grimstad.

9am–3pm, Sun noon–3pm). The **Bomuld factory** is also worth a visit, with its permanent exhibition of contemporary art in an area of 2500 sq m/26,910 sq ft featuring works by 40 Norwegian artists; there are also temporary exhibitions (Oddenveien 5; opening times: Tue–Sun noon–4pm).

Fevik

Fevik lies on the way from Arendal to Grimstad and its sandy beaches are considered to number among the best in Norway.

✳ Grimstad

The holiday resort of Grimstad (pop. 18,000) lies around 20km/ 12mi away on the E 18 in the direction of ►Kristiansand. It is especially popular for the wonderful sandy beaches located to the east of the town. The skerries just off-shore make for an idyllic backdrop. The town itself is also an excellent place to relax, enhanced not least by the picturesque old wooden houses by the harbour.

Near the landing quay, on Østregate, the former pharmacy of **Ibsenhuset** can be found, where the famous dramatist began his apprenticeship in 1843, aged 15. He wrote his first play, *Catilina*, during that time, publishing it under a pseudonym in 1850. The authentically decorated rooms containing manuscripts and pictures painted by Ibsen while in Grimstad can be viewed (opening times: May–Sept Mon–Sat 11am–5pm, Sun from 1pm).

The literary Nobel Prize winner Knut Hamsun also lived near Grimstad for some time, on the Nørholm estate about 6km/4mi away.

★ Bergen

Region: West Norway   **Population:** 236,000

Many Bergen locals consider their home to be Norway's true capital. There is indeed some justification for this view, as Bergen is the country's most historic city. It is the old houses along Vågen harbour and the fish market that draw the most visitors, and the view of the city from Fløyen, the local hill, is magnificent, though only when the sun is shining – a somewhat rare occurrence in Bergen.

Nestling in a crown of partly forested hills (up to 643m/2110ft), the city is surrounded by the slopes amphitheatre style, making Bergen one of Norway's most beautiful places. A breathtaking view of the city, the coastal landscape with the islands of Askøy and Sotra, and all the way out to the open sea is offered from 319m/1047ft-high Fløyen – especially in the mornings and at sunset – which can either be reached in 8mins (every half hour) by the Fløibanen cable car or via a 3km/2mi footpath.

Jewel of the north

Until the building of the Bergen railway line from Oslo in 1908 (► Baedeker Special p.407), it was very hard to reach the city overland. Countless tunnels were blasted into the rock in order to connect the city to the road network that for centuries was focused exclusively on the sea. Norway's second city is the most important port along the west coast, with an impressive merchant fleet and several large dockyards, as well as being home to the country's second-largest university with 12,000 students. Thanks to the moist and unusually mild climate, almost all central European deciduous trees and a richly varied flora survive here despite the location at 60° northern latitude. The flipside of this, however, is that Bergen is renowned for its persistent heavy rain (2000mm annually, compared with approx. 750mm in Oslo). The city is the starting point for the ►Hurtigruten shipping route (Baedeker Special p.237).

Renowned for constant rain

The oldest quarters of the city form a semicircle around Vågen harbour, busy with shipping traffic, and also stretch along the northeastern slopes of Fløyen. As with most Nordic towns, Bergen was repeatedly destroyed by devastating fires that few of the original buildings survived. Stone buildings and wide roads characterize the city centre today. Nordnes quarter and those on Fløyen hill, where wooden houses and narrow lanes (called »smug« by the locals) predominate, are popular destinations for city walks. In the northern quarter of Sandviken in a park directly on the fjord, more than 50 17th–19th-century wooden houses have been grouped together to form the

Historic buildings a rarity

★

◄ Gamle Bergen

VISITING BERGEN

INFORMATION
Bergen Turistinformasjon
Vågsallmenningen 1
Tel. 55 55 20 00
Fax 55 55 20 01
www.visitbergen.com

WHERE TO EAT
▶ Expensive
② Lucullus Restaurant
Valkendorfsgt. 8
Tel. 55 30 68 20
Excellent restaurant in the Neptun Hotel, with French-inspired cuisine and a large selection of wines. The artworks in the restaurant make for an elegant atmosphere.

④ Enhjørningen Fiskerestaurant
Bryggen
Tel. 55 32 79 19
Those wishing to eat in this nice fish restaurant housed in a historic building on Bryggen should be sure to book ahead. During the summer at lunchtime diners join the feast at the somewhat expensive cold fish and seafood buffet.

▶ Moderate
③ Holbergstuen
Torgalmenningen 6
Tel. 55 55 20 55
Norwegian specialities and small dishes at acceptable prices can be found at this traditional tavern dating from 1929, decorated with richly coloured rose painting and quotes from Ludvig Holberg on the walls.

⑤ Bryggen Tracteursted
Bryggestredet 2
Tel. 55 31 40 46
Norway's oldest restaurant serves typical national dishes. The later the hour, the more people gravitate to the bar for a beer. From 11am between May and September the beer garden is also open.

▶ Inexpensive
① Café Opera
Engen 18
Tel. 55 23 03 15
The old wooden house painted white opposite the theatre is a popular haunt for both young and old, for journalists and students, and for local residents. Good coffee and unpretentious small dishes.

⑥ Fløien Folkerestaurant
Fløyfjellet 2
Tel. 55 33 69 99
Don't miss the sunset from the restaurant and café with the best view of Bergen and its surroundings. The café serves delicious snacks such as waffles, cake and soups.

WHERE TO STAY
▶ Luxury
④ Grand Hotel Terminus
Zander Kaaesgt. 6
Tel. 55 21 25 00
Fax 55 21 25 01
131 rooms
www.grand-hotel-terminus.no
The Grand Hotel was built near to the train station in 1928 and has won prizes for its architecture. The interior décor of its rooms and salons is stylish and the café is one of the best on the Norwegian fjord coast.

① Comfort Hotel Holberg
Strandgaten 190
Tel. 55 30 42 00
Fax 55 23 18 20
140 rooms
holberg@comfort.choicehotels.no
Regularly booked hotel in the second

row of houses from the port, especially popular with organized groups.

③ *Best Western Victoria Hotel*
Kong Oscars gate 29
Tel. 55 21 23 00
Fax 55 32 81 78
43 rooms
www.victoriahotel.no
This beautiful old building, centrally located near the fish market, has long been run by the same family and offers comfortable rooms. The day room, bedrooms and bar also double up as a gallery for the worthwhile art collection.

► Mid-range
② *Hotel Park Pension*
Harald Hårfagresgt. 35
Tel 55 54 44 00
Fax 55 54 44 44
33 rooms
www.parkhotel.no
Erected in the neo-Gothic style in 1890, this small hotel is not far from the university and continues to reflect the pride of the Bergen citizenry.

⑤ *Sandviken Brygge*
Sandviksveien 94
Tel. 55 39 61 00
Fax 55 39 61 50
45 rooms
www.sandvikenbrygge.no
New hotel with a highly modern interior of pleasant, light colours, situated on the fjord, just 2km/1.2mi from the city centre. The hotel also has a good spa.

► Budget
⑥ *Lone Camping*
Hardangerv. 697
Haukeland
Tel. 55 39 29 60
Fax 55 39 29 79
www.lonecamping.no

The largest and most attractive camp site in the area around Bergen, on route 580, 19km/12mi from the city centre. Direct access to a lake, with the Liafjell as a backdrop. Facilities include tents, mobile homes, 18 cabins of varying sizes, motel with 18 apartments, restaurant and canoe rental.

SHOPPING
Fish market
Market square: June–Aug daily from 7am–5pm, Sat till 4pm, otherwise Mon–Sat 7am–4pm

Shopping
There are numerous shops to the southwest of the market square, including the Galleriet shopping centre. Attractive little shops and arts and crafts places can also be found in Lille Øvergate.

> **!** *Baedeker* TIP
>
> **Bergen Card**
> Parking is only permitted in Bergen for a fee, and then only in marked spaces. The Bergen Card, valid for 24 or 48 hours (adults 190/250 NOK, children 75/100 NOK), allows free travel on local public transport, reduced admission into the town's attractions, discounts on theatre and cinema tickets as well as a 30% reduction at the Bygarasjen car park.

FESTIVALS
Mid-May–early June: Night Jazz Festival (www.nattjazz.no)
Mid-July–mid-Sept: medieval plays by the Hanseatic Theatre (www.bergen-byspill.no)
Beginning of September: Bergen Food Festival (www.matfest.no).

Pretty as a picture: Bergen in the sun as seen from »Fløyen«.

🕐 open-air Old Bergen Museum (opening times: houses May–Sept 10am–5pm, site accessible all year round, Nyhavnsveien 4, www. bymuseet.no).

History Olav Kyrre elevated the already important harbour settlement of Bjørgvin (»hillside meadow«) to **town** status in around 1070, after which the occasional **royal residence** developed quickly. In 1233, Håkon Håkonsson's right to the throne was recognized during a national assembly here. Germans had already settled in Bergen by 1236, and the town's real heyday was thanks to the **Hanseatic Bureau** first mentioned in 1343. A codicil issued by the Danish kings had ensured that no trade in fish was permitted north of Bergen. Thus all northern fishermen had to transport their catches down to Bergen on dangerous sea journeys and the German merchants were able to dominate the entire Norwegian trade. Cereals, salt and beer were traded against stockfish (dried fish with no salt) from the Lofoten Islands and dried salt cod from Kristiansund.

The Hanseatic Germans lived in a separate district near the German bridge, where 16 long and narrow »courtyards« stretched out to serve as both homes and warehouses. Each courtyard was run by a »byggherre« and had several quarters (»stuer«) that each belonged to a different individual. The might of the Hanseatic League was broken in 1559, though the accounting bureau continued for around another 200 years, until the last »stuer« was sold to a Norwegian in 1764.

Bergen also suffered considerable losses during the **Second World War**, including the old theatre on Sverres gate – Norway's first stage – which had been inaugurated by the famous violinist Ole Bull in 1851. Ibsen was the director there from 1851–57, and his successor was Bjørnson, in the position from 1858–60 (►Famous People).

Highlights Bergen

What to See around Vågen Harbour

Bergen's wealth has always been founded on seafaring and the trade in fish. Even in the 17th century, Bergen was significantly more important as a trading location than Copenhagen and by the beginning of the 19th century the city still had more inhabitants than Kristiania (now Oslo). Bergen was to remain Norway's most important fish trading centre until modern times, even if today the large fishing multinationals and canning factories nearer the fishing grounds have allowed other fish trading centres to flourish.

Fish!

The heart of the city is the **market square** (Torget) in the middle of the main Vågen harbour area, at whose landing stages the fishing boats land their catches each morning. The large selection of various types of seafood, freshly cooked shrimps, red lobsters, salmon and caviar is a joy for the eyes and palate – though the prices charged at the picturesque fish market are impressive too.

✳ **Fish market**

A statue by John Börjeson of the local Bergen poet **Ludvig Holberg** (1684–1754),creator of Danish-Norwegian comedy theatre, stands at the southeastern side of the market square. The former **stock market** lies behind the statue, today home to the tourist information office. At the upper end of the Vetrlidsallmenning, which leads off the market in a northeasterly direction, the **base station of the Fløibahn cable car service** can be found.

At the northern side of Vågen harbour, beginning at the market, stands the Bryggen (formerly also known as the Tyskebryggen =

✳✳ **Bryggen**

»German Bridge«). It got its name because the wooden houses used for loading and unloading ships stood directly at the harbour basin. This is where the »courts« of the German merchants once stood, later to be replaced by the stone warehouses whose architecture recalls the era of the Hanseatic League. The merchant houses and warehouses were rebuilt after the great fire of 1702. Today these colourfully painted wooden houses are on the **UNESCO World Heritage List** of cultural sites worthy of preservation (see photo p.144–145).

Hanseatic Museum

Only the first trading hall (the Finnegården) at the front on the square or »torg« survives in its original form, and this building has housed the Hanseatic Museum since 1872. Even though it was rebuilt after the fire of 1708, the Finnegården is an outstanding example of the traditional architecture of the early Hanseatic era. The squat, dark rooms with their small windows recall a ship's hull. The museum gives a good idea of the Hanseatic court interiors. The exhibits include weapons, household goods and pieces of equipment, mostly from the 18th century. The ground floor was once the warehouse and the first floor contained the manager's office, as well as the dining room and bedroom. The second floor contains the »klever«, the dormitories for the apprentices and market helpers. Take a look at the collection of the Hanseatic city seals, whose independence was confirmed by these official markings. Many seals contain images of ships that reflect the art of shipbuilding at that time (opening times: June–Aug daily 9am–5pm, otherwise 11am–2pm).

Bryggens Museum

The Bryggens Museum displays archaeological finds from medieval Bergen. The basement floor contains the oldest fragments of urban settlement from the 12th century. The **Bryggen Ship**, originally a 30m/33yd-long and 10m/11yd-wide merchant ship, can be seen in the cultural historical exhibition entitled »The Medieval City – Bergen around the year 1300«. Furthermore, traditional trades are illustrated, including those of cobblers, comb makers, coopers and goldsmiths (opening times: May–Aug daily 10am–5pm, otherwise noon–3pm).

? DID YOU KNOW ...?

■ ... that the Bryggens Museum contains the world's largest collection of rune scripts carved in wood? Around 500 examples were unearthed during excavations in the city around 40 years ago.

St Mary's Church

Close to the Bryggens Museum stands the twin-spired Romanesque-Gothic St Mary's Church (Mariakirken), which dates from 12th and 13th centuries and is the city's oldest building. It is very well preserved and has been in continuous service since the early Middle Ages. The church belonged to the Hanseatic League between 1408 and 1766 and sermons were held in German until 1868. Tombs in the choir recall the German merchants, seamen and priests laid to rest here between the 15th and 17th centuries. Much about this par-

Bergen Map

Where to eat
① Café Opera
② Lucullus Restaurant
③ Holbergstuen
④ Enhjørningen Fiskerestaurant
⑤ Bryggen Tracteursted
⑥ Fløien Folkerestaurant

Where to stay
① Comfort Hotel Holberg
② Hotel Park Pension
③ Best Western Victoria Hotel
④ Grand Hotel Terminus
⑤ Sandviken Brygge
⑥ Lone Camping

ish church resembles a cathedral, and the architectural style is that of a basilica.

The impressive, colourful **interior** dates predominantly from the 17th century. The winged altar in the choir is the oldest piece in the church and was built by north German masters in the 15th century, and repainted in the 17th century. The magnificent pulpit is unique in Norway and was probably a gift from German merchants at the end of the 17th century. The canopy with its twelve astrological signs is topped by a Christ figure. The pulpit itself displays eight female statues with a variety of adjuncts that illustrate **fundamental Christian virtues**: repentance (with pelican), wisdom (with snake), the bare truth, chastity (with two doves), patience (with lamb), hope (with dove and parts of an anchor), faith (with the book and cross) and love (with two children).

✳
◄ Pulpit

Schøtstuene Opposite the church, at Øvregate 50, are the Schøtstuene. These were the Bryggen's only heated rooms during the winter and therefore meeting rooms of the German merchants, for no fire or candlelight was permitted in the merchant houses due to the risk of fire.

Bergenhus fortress The northwestern continuation of the Bryggen is the Festnings quay with the old **Bergenhus fortress**. King Øystein Magnusson moved his royal court (built of wood) onto »Holmen« (»island«) as early as the 12th century. King Håkon Håkonsson then had the wood structures gradually replaced by solid stone buildings and had the entire royal residence encircled by a protective wall from the 13th century onwards.

✳
Rosenkrantz Tower At the southern end of the fortress, directly by the quay, stands the Rosenkrantz Tower named after the castle captain Erik Rosenkrantz, who combined two older installations into one and gave it a Renaissance façade between 1562 and 1567. The most historic core of the building was King Magnus's square residential fortified tower (1273) known as the »Fortress by the Sea«. The king's bedroom and the chapel with a soapstone altar date from that time. The tower was restored around 1520 by the castle captain Jørgen Hanssøn, who added a barbican. The Rosenkrantz Tower was extensively damaged during the explosion of a German munitions ship in 1944, and later rebuilt. The tower exhibition rooms display a model of the fortress Bergenhus, swords and uniforms, and there is also a nice view of the entire city from here (opening times: May–Aug daily 10am–4pm, otherwise Sun noon–3pm).

Håkon Hall Behind the Rosenkrantz Tower stands Håkon Hall, which was built by King Håkon Håkonsson between 1247 and 1261 to commemorate the wedding and coronation of his son Magnus Lagabøte. It was modelled on English Gothic stone halls. It is **Norway's largest medieval secular building**. After the royal court moved away from Bergen

Elk sausage or reindeer schnitzel? The choice in Bergen's shopping centres is overwhelming.

in the late Middle Ages, the hall increasingly fell into ruin and was used as a warehouse. It was restored at the end of the 19th century, but during the explosion of the German munitions ship in the harbour in 1944, the hall burnt down to its foundations. It was opened to the public in 1961, the seven hundredth jubilee of King Magnus' coronation. Concerts, state receptions and other official festive events take place in the large festival hall whose beautiful wood vaulting recalls a Viking ship.

A good overview of the Norwegian fishing industry can be obtained at the Fishery Museum (Fiskerimuseet) at the Bontelabo, near the landing quay for ferries from Iceland and the Faroe Islands. **Fishing Museum**

Nordnes Park (good views) lies in the northwest of the city, at the tip of the Nordnes spit between Vågen and Puddefjord. In the park is Bergen Aquarium, one of **northern Europe's largest aquariums** and definitely worth a visit. A particular attraction is the feeding of the seals and penguins that swim in the giant pool in the museum courtyard (noon, 3pm and 6pm) (opening times: May–Aug daily 9am–7pm, otherwise 10am–6pm). **★ Aquarium**

South of the Market

Many day trippers restrict themselves to the sights along Vågen harbour, but a stroll around the streets to the southwest of the market, where most shops, including the attractive **Galleriet shopping centre** **City centre** are located, is also worthwhile. Beyond lies the municipal park with a statue by Ingebrigt Vik of the composer **Edvard Grieg** (1843–1907), who was born in Bergen. Another **memorial** for a famous citizen of Bergen can be found on the long Ole Bulls Plass, namely the statue of the »violin king« Ole Bull (▶ Around Bergen) created by Stephan Sinding in 1901. Norway's oldest theatre stands on the western side of the square. It is called the Nasjonale Scene, and was built in the art nouveau style between 1906 and 1909.

Theatre ▶

Cathedral

Kong Oscars gate leads southeast from the northern end of the market, past the Korskirke, originally dating from the 12th century and rebuilt in the Renaissance style in 1593, to the cathedral, which was originally built in 1248 as a monastery church in Romanesque style. It was given a 60m/66yd-long Gothic choir in 1537. The beautiful Gothic windows and the altar that recalls a medieval reliquary shrine are considered the cathedral's most noteworthy features.

Leprosy Museum

Following Kong Oscars gate further out of the city, one of Bergen's most beautiful wooden buildings is reached, the Danckert Krohns Stiftelse, built in the style of an 18th century Danish mansion. Opposite stands the small Leprosy Museum, which gives an insight into Norway's contribution to the international leprosy research programme (opening times: during summer daily 11am–3pm).

Art collections

The architecturally interesting **Grieg Hall**, in which concerts, operas and ballets are performed, stands to the south of the Lille Lungegårdsvann lake, on Strømgate. Nearby, at Rasmus Meyers Allé 7, is the **art collection** donated by the businessman **Rasmus Meyer** with paintings by Norwegian artists from between 1814 and 1914, such as J. C. Dahl, H. Gude, E. Munch, and G. Munthe. Next door, at Rasmus Meyers Allé 3, the **City Art Museum** exhibits Norwegian painting (J. C. Dahl, E. Munch) and European art. The building also houses the Bergen Art Society which presents temporary exhibitions of contemporary art and the **Stenersen Collection**, with works by Munch, Picasso and Klee (opening times: mid-May–mid-Sept daily 11am–5pm).

Arts and Crafts Museum

Rare ceramics, Bergen gold jewellery and modern Norwegian arts and crafts are shown at the Vestlandske Kunstindustrimuseum (»Permanenten«), located around 200m/220yd further on at the southern edge of the municipal park.

University collections

University collections on the subject of natural history can be reached by following Christies gate south, past the Catholic Church of St Paul and up Sydneshaugen hill, where the university buildings can be found by the Botanical Garden. Right next door is the **Seafaring Museum** with curiosities and illustrations of life on the ocean wave.

The composer Edvard Grieg lived and worked in Troldhaugen.

Around Bergen

A road (30mins on foot) leads from the base station for the Fløyen **Hiking on Fløyen** cable cars via the increasingly barren mountain plateau to the foot of Blåmann (551m/1808ft) to the northeast. From there a footpath can be followed to the peak, which offers an attractive panoramic view, especially with evening lights. The ascent of the somewhat higher peak behind is frankly not worth the effort. The road also continues on to the radio station on Rundemann (556m/1824ft). There are nice views along Fjellvei half way up the side of Fløyen, and a rest stop can be made at the Bellevue restaurant at the southeastern end of the footpath, about 25mins from the Fløyen cable car station.

En route to Troldhaugen, 6km/4mi south of the city centre in a small **Fantoft stave church** forest, stands the Fantoft stave church, which can be reached by buses 19, 20 and 21 from the terminal. Originally constructed in Fortun on the Sognefjord in 1150, the church was moved to Fantoft in 1883. It was rebuilt after being totally destroyed by fire in 1992 🕐 (opening times: daily 10.30am–6pm).

Follow the sign for Troldhaugen, Edvard Grieg's home (▶ Famous ✱ People) after another 2km/1.2mi. In the house, the foundation of **Troldhaugen** Bergen's claim to being Norway's cultural capital, the life and work of the world famous composer can be explored. Edvard and Nina Grieg only managed to realize their dream of having their own home after eighteen years of marriage. They moved into the villa in 1885, which was built in the style of a Victorian mansion, though its bare interior wood walls recall Norwegian farmhouses. Troldhaugen (Troll's Hill) was named after a small ravine not far from the house that is known to locals as »Troll's Valley«. The original interior can still be found in the dining room and the living room. Among the numerous presents that Grieg received is the Steinway grand piano, given to the couple on the occasion of their silver wedding anniversary by Bergen fans of his music. Grieg practiced undisturbed in the **»composer's cabin«** down the slope (opening times: May to Sept daily 9am–6pm).

The 1.52m/5ft tall composer's final resting place is in a rock face at the lake. Grieg concerts are presented in the new Troldsalen concert hall during the summer (Wed 7.30pm, Sat and Sun 2pm and 7.30pm).

Ulriken

A wide panoramic view can be enjoyed from the highest of Bergen's seven hills, the Ulriken (643m/2110ft), which stands to the southeast of the outskirts of the city. The base station of the Ulriksbanen cable car can be reached in a few minutes via the double decker buses departing from the city centre every half an hour. The ascent to the summit takes two hours on foot.

Lysøen

Another famous Norwegian lived just under 30km/19mi south of Bergen, on the little island of Lysøen: namely the **eccentric violinist and composer Ole Bornemann Bull**. He was born in Bergen in 1810 and died here in 1880, a deeply revered figure. He had his villa built between 1872 and 1873 which, with its onion domes and Moorish style elements, evokes a small »fairy tale castle«. The eccentric style of the owner is also reflected in the castle's unusual interior. The villa can only be reached by boat: from Sørstraumen every hour on the hour (opening times: May–Aug Mon–Sat noon–4pm, Sun 11am–5pm, Sept Sun noon–4pm).

? DID YOU KNOW ...?

■ ... that though the world famous violin virtuoso and composer Ole Bornemann Bull never received systematic violin tuition, he gave his debut performance at the age of nine? A life changing event occurred when he went to Paris in 1930 and met Paganini, on whose style he based his own playing. He achieved international success and his fellow Norwegians celebrated him as a national hero.

The ruins of Norway's first Cistercian monastery, founded by monks from York in 1146, can be found nearby. Lyse monastery was Norway's largest until the Reformation. The ruins were excavated between 1822 and 1838, and today they provide an insight into monastic life during the Middle Ages.

Lyse monastery

Hardangerfjord ►Hardangerfjord

Bodø

K 11

Region: North Norway   **Population:** 42,000

Bodø makes a good base for visits to the Lofoten Islands, though due to the devastation wreaked during the Second World War the city itself is hardly idyllic. Nearby, the historic market town of Kjerringøy is worth a detour – and not only for fans of Knut Hamsun – while the tidal river of Saltstraumen is an impressive natural phenomenon.

Most tourists only make the 60km/37mi detour from the main E 6 in the direction of Nordkapp to the port of Bodø if they want to catch a ferry to the Lofoten Islands. NATO jets continuously fly over the city, since northern Norway's most important military air force base is located here. Bodø is also an important traffic hub and the final destination for the Nordland rail route from Trondheim. The town gained its municipal charter in 1816, but it was only herring fishing during the second half of the 19th century that accelerated development. Today Bodø is a lively trading town with a busy harbour. Ferries to the Lofoten Islands and the ►Hurtigruten boats land here, and an airport offers connections to the Scandinavian airline network. Thanks to numerous music festivals, Bodø is not short on culture, and is considered to be the **»music capital of northern Norway«**.

Military base

Idyllic port at Bødo with an impressive mountain backdrop

What to See in and around Bodø

Town centre
The town hall was completed in 1959, and there is a fine view from its tower. It stands on the town hall square (Rådhusplassen). The nearby **cathedral** (1956) is impressive, particularly its interior of beautiful painted glass by Aage Storstein. Finds from prehistoric and medieval times, as well as exhibitions on agriculture, fishing and arts and crafts are shown at the **Nordland County Museum** (Nordland fylkesmuseum), to the south of the cathedral (opening times: Mon–Fri 9am–3pm, during summer also Sat, Sun 10am–3pm).

Norwegian Flight Centre ►
The city's most interesting sight is the Norwegian Flight Centre, opened in 1996, which offers an overview of the history of Norwegian and international airborne transport. Among the attractions are the only JU 52 water aeroplane in the world, and an American U 2 spy plane. The museum also has a **flight simulator** (opening times: June–Aug daily 10am–7pm, Sat till 5pm, otherwise till 4pm).

► VISITING BODØ

INFORMATION

Destinasjon Bodø
Sjøgt. 3, 8006 Bodø
Tel. 75 54 80 00
Fax 75 54 80 01
www.bodoe.com

WHERE TO EAT

► Inexpensive
Kafé Kafka
Sandgt. 5 B
Tel. 75 52 35 50
An institution in Bodø since 1998. An original cultural and literary café with a cosy interior. The kitchen offers a good cross section of the world's delicacies, as well as tasty homemade cakes.

WHERE TO STAY

► Luxury
Radisson SAS Hotel Bodø
Bodø, Storgt. 2
Tel. 75 51 90 00
Fax 75 51 90 01
190 rooms
www.bodo.radissonsas.com

Hotel tower with panoramic views, especially from the top floor bar, in the town centre. The rooms are comfortable and pleasingly decorated in various styles.

► Mid-range
Kjerringøy Rorbusenter
Tårnvik
(20km/12mi north of Kjerringøy)
Tel. 75 58 50 07
Fax 75 58 50 08
These fishermen's cabins in a wonderful off-the-beaten-track location are very comfortable and right on the water. Large sauna and open-air swimming, good fishing and hiking opportunities too.

► Budget
Kjerringøy Parish House
Amtmann Worsøes gt. 28 A
Tel. 75 50 77 10
Fax 75 50 77 33, 8 rooms
The listed old parish building in Kjerringøy, dating from 1889, has been a simple hostel for the past 25 years.

A broad panoramic view can be enjoyed from Rønvikfjell (155m/508ft; tourist cabin), around 4km/3mi north of Bodø. From there, it is about another two hours by marked footpath to the summit of Løpsfjell (603m/1978ft), from which there is a good view towards the 100km/62mi distant mountain chain of the Lofoten Isalnds; to the

east, glacier-covered Sulitjelma (1913m/6276ft) is visible, which is around 90km/56mi away near the Swedish border. To the left is Blåmannsis, with its névé fields (expanses of compacted snow) reaching a height of 1571m/5154ft.

The coastal road north leads to Geitvågen, the most beautiful sandy beach north of the Arctic Circle. The midnight sun in Geitvågen is one of the annual highlights for many inhabitants of Bodø.   **Geitvågen**

The old trading centre of Kjerringøy and one of northern Norway's most important commercial centres in the 19th century, is 40km/25mi north of Bodø. An interesting overview of life and trading habits along the Norwegian coast is offered by the **open-air museum**. There are 15 buildings, including a domestic house in Empire style, a general store, a post office and a pub. The beautiful film *Dina – My Story* by Ole Bornedal was partly filmed here at the open-air museum of Kjerringøy. Based on a novel by Herbjørg Wassmo, the film tells the dramatic story of Dina, a young woman in the Norway of 1860. The main roles are played by Gérard Depardieu, Maria Bonnevie and Christopher Eccleston.   **✶✶ Kjerringøy**

The shopkeeper K. Zahl had his shop in Kjerringøy, where a certain Knud Pedersen from the island of Hamarøy began his apprenticeship. The apprentice later called himself Knut Hamsun (► Famous People), after his parents' farm on the Hamsund farming estate. Born in Gudbrandsdal, he came to Nordland when he was three years old. The impressions he gathered here during his childhood and youth are recorded in his novel entitled *Benoni and Rosa* (1908). Kjerringøy is called »Sirilund« in Knut Hamsun's writings, and Zahl the shopkeeper is portrayed in the main character of Mack in his novel entitled *Pan* (1894). Several of his novels have been filmed on location here.   ◄ **Apprentice Knut Hamsun**

Near the open-air museum is the Zahlfjøsen **cultural centre**, where visitors can view a weaving workshop, a boat-building workshop, a gallery and various arts and crafts. Excerpts from around 20 films inspired by Hamsun's work can be seen on the first floor.

It is worthwhile taking an excursion 35km/22mi east to the Saltstraumen **tidal waters**. 2km/1mi long, about 150m/164yd wide   **✶ Saltstraumen** and up to 50m/164ft deep, the Saltstraumen connects the Saltfjord with the Skjerstadfjord between the islands of Straumen and Straumøy. Each time the tide turns, around 370 million cubic metres of water is squeezed through the narrow gap, creating **rapids and whirlpools** (tide tables are available from the tourist information office). Numerous fishermen try their luck here. In 1998, a leisure park was opened complete with restaurants, a camp site, a hotel and souvenir shops, so it gets pretty busy. The Saltstraumen Experience Centre illustrates the region's 10,000-year old cultural history and includes a multimedia show. It is also possible to see the largest fish ever caught here: a 32.7kg/72.1lb cod.

Fauske

Renowned for its marble, Fauske lies about 65km/41mi from Bodø on the E 6. The red marble from here was used for the buildings of the UN in New York, as well as for Oslo city hall. The bus to Nordkapp (2 days) and Kirkenes (3–4 days) departs from Fauske. Those travelling by train will have to change onto buses here, as Bodø is the end of the line.

Rago National Park

Small, but special

Located north of Bodø between the E 6 and the Swedish border, the Rago National Park covers an area of only 171 sq km/66 sq mi. On the other side of the border lie the Swedish parks of Padjelanta and Sarek. By car the park is reached by leaving the E 6 at Nordfjord to the north of Fauske and parking at Lakshola village. Rago is a typical hiking region with very few accommodation options, and the damp climate makes appropriate clothing and equipment essential. The beauty of this park's landscape makes a visit worthwhile, though: no other region of Norway exhibits such variety on such a small scale. It is especially nice to stay at the Øvereng camp site (tel. 75 69 65 40), at the end of the byroad to Lakshola.

Storskog valley

The main artery through the park is the Storskog valley, with the Trolldals river and the impressive Trollfoss. Waterfalls tumble through moist, green pine forests that climb several hundered metres up the slopes of the mountains. Snow and ice fields begin at elevations as low as 1000m/3281ft, while the forested valley is home to elk, beaver and wolverines.

Hiking in the national park

The hiking tour from Lakshola leads east, initially through the valley and then slowly upwards into the sparse vegetation of the mountains. Past the park's only cabin (accommodation free), the path follows the old route to Sweden that was once used by the Sami to herd reindeer from their summer pastures to their winter ones. To the right rises the barren Rago mountain (1300m/4265ft). Silver and lead were discovered here before the First World War, but the seam was too small and extraction too expensive to make mining worthwhile.

* Borgund Stave Church

D 4

Region: Central Norway

Borgund stave church at the entrance to the Lærdal valley is one of the most interesting and beautiful in the country. The dragon heads of the upper gables are especially noteworthy, as are the two doorways elaborately decorated with carvings and the almost windowless interior.

This rather small stave church, blackened with tar, was probably constructed as early as 1150. It has been sensitively restored and still exhibits its original design today, baring one window that was cut in at a later date. The roof rises in six levels covered in wooden shingles. Roaring dragon heads reach up into the air from the upper gables, recalling ancient heathen traditions. The two doorways are embellished with beautiful ornamentation. The **wood carvings** of the west doorway is especially magnificent, displaying fighting dragon-like creatures along with leaf motifs. Only the 16th-century pulpit and the altar from the early 17th century survive from the original interior, which appears very dark and sombre. Mighty wooden pillars support the artful roof construction and separate the nave from the lower aisles. The pillars are supported by connecting crossbeams that display carved masks of humans and imaginary animals at their ends. To the south of the stave church between the new and old church stands the **bell tower**; it was rebuilt in the original style around 1660.

By the way, this church is among-**Norway's main tourist attractions** and long waiting periods for permission to enter are sometimes necessary due to overcrowding (opening times: May–Sept daily 10am–5pm, mid-June–mid-Aug daily 8am–8pm). A visitor centre opened in May 2005 provides information on everything there is to know about Norway's stave churches.

Always popular with visitors: the stave church of Borgund

Around Borgund

Lærdal

Leaving Borgund, the road leads through the picturesque Svartegjel gorge, which the Lærdalselv, **one of Norway's best-known salmon rivers**, has cut through the rockface of the Vindhella. Another imposing gorge is traversed beyond Husum (316m/1037ft), before finally reaching the sleepy little town of **Lærdalsøyri**. The place was an important fjord port for centuries and British aristocrats came here to fish for salmon from the middle of the 19th century. The historic 17th-century town centre with its countless wooden houses is on Norway's national heritage preservation list.

Villakssenter

A few years ago, the largest and most impressive of the many **salmon aquariums** opened on the banks of the Lærdalselv. Visitors here discover all they ever wanted to know about salmon: their habitats, migration patterns, and the history of salmon fishing (in films and exhibitions). Large display windows in the observatory also offer views of wild salmon and sea trout, while a workshop runs exhibitions on the practicalities of the art of fly fishing (opening times: June–Aug 10am–7pm, Sept 11am–5pm).

To Aurland or Sognefjord

To enjoy the breathtaking passage through the Nærøyfjord, those with time should avoid the tunnel in the direction of Aurland and instead take the ferry operating between Kaupanger (► Sognefjord) and Gudvangen.

 VISITING BORGUND

INFORMATION

Lærdal Tourist Information
Lærdalsøry centre
Tel. 57 64 12 07, fax 57 66 64 22
www.alr.no

GETTING THERE

The famous Borgund stave church is reached via the E 16 coming from Valdres. The ideal base for exploring the region around Borgund, especially the Lærdal valley, is the main settlement of Lærdalsøry. Since 2000, the world's longest road tunnel (24km/15mi) connects Lærdal with Aurland (in a southerly direction), which cuts the journey time along the E 16 to Bergen by several hours.

WHERE TO STAY AND EAT

► **Mid-range**
Lindstrøm Hotel
Lærdal
Tel. 57 66 69 00, fax 57 66 66 81
86 rooms, www.lindstroemhotel.no
Hotel with an interesting mixture of traditional romance and modern elements. It is also possible to eat well here – albeit expensively.

► **Budget**
Lærdal Ferie- og Fritidspark
Lærdal, Grandavegen 5
Tel. 57 66 66 95, fax 57 66 87 81
www.laerdalferiepark.com
Camp site with comfortable cabins, a café and restaurant at the end of the Lærdalfjord.

The stave church of Gol today stands in Oslo's open-air museum.

MASTERPIECES IN WOOD

The wooden stave churches (»stavkirker« in Norwegian) are the most famous and original testaments of medieval architectural art in Norway. Of an original number of around 600 of these wooden churches, only 31 have survived the ravages of time to the present day. These architectural treasures are now jealously guarded.

Stave churches are wooden churches with either a single nave or a nave and two aisles, and steep roofs over several levels. They owe their name to the **stave building method** which, in contrast to a block building with horizontal pillars, utilizes posts anchored into the ground or fixed to an open fixed frame that supports the saddleback roof. Similar to **ship construction methods from Viking times**, the succession of frames, cleats, and diagonal crosses strengthen the building to such a degree that it can well resist the Nordic storms. Massive round corner posts stabilize the outer wall, which is separate from the church interior. In between the pillars and posts of the interior, built without the use of a single iron nail or iron component, rounded arches ensure the necessary elasticity. The stave

church was documented as early as the 9th century, but its **heyday** was between the 12th and 13th centuries – a period when the emergence of Christianity had also already resulted in the building of stone churches in Scandinavia.

Viking heritage

Romanesque forms combined with the ancient techniques of building with wood, though ornamentation initially remained entirely bound to the traditions of the Vikings. Artful stylized animal and vine carvings date from this era, whose decorative compositions with motifs from the **pre-Christian Edda sagas** create a fantastical, almost spooky impression. However, with the emergence of Christianity, this figural sculpture art, considered heathen, was replaced

A love of detail also shows itself in the carvings of the stave church at Lom.

Borgund Stave Church

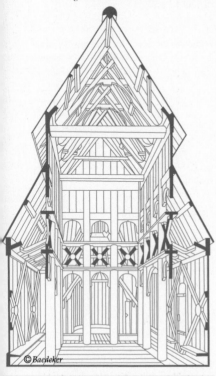

©Baedeker

by the more sombre ornamentation of the Norman-style epoch which took contemporary stone buildings as its models.

At the same time, the older single-nave design of the main body of churches was supplanted by the **basilica style** which had an excessively high central nave separated from the aisles by mast-style pillars. While the Roman basilica established itself as the pre-eminent architectural style, the first bishoprics were also established in Norway, where once there had only been missionizing itinerant bishops. Gradually, the wealth of forms of figural sculpture decoration revived, and the Viking tradition experienced a Renaissance. The heathen ornamentation of the past was exchanged for symbols influenced by European Christianity. Thus the famous »**Dragon style**« emerged, named after the fear-inspiring dragon heads mounted at the crowns of buildings. Large wall paintings were relatively rare, due to the inadequate lighting conditions.

Stave churches today

Around 1300, there are believed to have been over 600 stave churches in Norway. After the **plague** decimated the Norwegian population by more than half, most of these sacred buildings fell into disrepair and, from the 17th to the 19th century, many churches had become too small for their communities and were demolished, so that only 31 stave churches survive (more or less unchanged) to this day. Most of these wooden churches still stand in their original locations, though some have been moved to other places and rebuilt as museum pieces (see map p.57). A **renewed interest** in these sacred buildings developed in the mid-19th century, largely because of the Norwegian painter Johann Christian Dahl, who was a professor at the art academy in Dresden from 1824 onwards and who, after many journeys to his Norwegian homeland,

initiated the battle to preserve these unique cultural monuments. He persuaded the Prussian King Friedrich Wilhelm IV to buy the stave church of Vang in Valdres that was first rebuilt on Peacock Island near Berlin, and later in the Karkonosze mountains (also known as the Giant Mountains, bordering Poland and Czech Republic). He thus brought the Norwegian stave church into the limelight.

From then on, work began to preserve the remaining sacred buildings, although some restoration efforts resulted in a **loss of authenticity**: for example, **windows** were installed where once there would only have been dim lighting provided by small openings high up.

Today's surviving stave churches are found in the southern region of Norway, an area that extends from Oslo to Bergen and Trondheim to the north.

✳ Dovrefjell

E 6

Region: East Norway   **Height:** 982m–2286m/3222ft–7500ft

The highest mountain of the Dovrefjell range, the imposing Snøhetta, is already easily recongizable from the E 6, which cuts through the Dovrefjell-Sunndalsfjella National Park. Around 100 musk oxen have made themselves at home in this barren mountain landscape carved out during the Ice Age. Rivers, such as the Driva, are suitable for rafting as well as swimming.

King's road

The change in vegetation on the way to the fjell is remarkable. An initially homogenous pine forest becomes ever lighter as it transforms into a birch forest before giving way to the barren highlands. One of the country's main transport routes was established here during the time of the Vikings.

Pilgrims and kings alike – the former visiting the tomb of St Olaf in Nidaros (later Trondheim), the latter on their way to coronations there – had to brave the challenges of crossing the Dovrefjell mountains, which is why this route is also known as the Kongevegen (king's road).

Fokstumyra

Fokstua (982m/3221ft) can be reached after 10km/6mi on the E 6 from Dombås, crossing Dovrefjell. To the left of the road spreads the bird-rich moorland of Fokstumyra, a nature reserve. To the right, there is a view of the Fokstuhø mountain (1716m/5630ft), which can be climbed in just under three hours. The E 6 follows Lake Vålåsjø, at the end of which a minor track leads to Dovregubbens Hall (pub and accommodation).

Hjerkinn

Then Avsjøen follows to the right, before Hjerkinn(956m/3137ft), 10km/6mi further on. Located in a broad highland valley of Dovrefjell, this is the driest place in Norway, with an average rainfall of just 217mm per annum. A restricted military shooting range extends to the west. A memorial plaque marks the **Kongevegen** (king's road), along which 41 ruling monarchs travelled; the road's highest point (1026m/3366ft) is less than a mile further north. To the west, on Tverrfjell, lie the Folldal mines for iron ore, pyrite and copper. Those who head northeast on foot, climbing Hjerkinnhø (1282m/4206ft), which takes about 1.5hrs, are rewarded with wonderful views of Snøhetta and the mountain chains of the ►Rondane and ►Jotunheimen ranges.

The wonderful waters of the Driva →
tempt visitors to genuine leaps of courage.

Dovrefjell-Sunndalsfjella National Park

After the E 6 has reached its highest point to the north of Hjerkinn, the route descends through the Driva valley to the national park and its alpine plants, musk oxen and wild reindeer. The **Kongsvold Fjell-stue** (887m/2910ft) is reached after 12km/7mi, by the railway station of the same name. The University of Trondheim maintains a **biological research station** here, and the university also established the small botanical garden with alpine plants, which is situated 700m/770yd behind the mountain hotel. Kongsvold is the starting point for the ascent of Søndre Knutshø (1690m/5545ft; 3–5hrs) towering up-

▶ VISITING DOVREFJELL

INFORMATION
Oppdal Turistkontor
7340 Oppdal, Postboks 50
(In the centre by the E 6)
Tel. 72 40 04 70, fax 72 40 04 80
www.oppdal.com

Dombås Turistkontor
2660 Dombås, Postboks 172
Tel. 61 24 14 44, fax 61 24 11 90
www.dovrenett.no

WHERE TO STAY
▶ Luxury
Dombås Hotel
Dombås
Tel. 61 24 10 01, fax 61 24 14 61
78 rooms, www.rica.no
The best and most expensive hotel locally is housed in a large imposing wooden house with modern extensions. Tip: the simple holiday houses behind the hotel are cheaper.

▶ Mid-range
Quality Hotel Oppdal
Oppdal. Skasliensvei 8
Tel. 72 40 07 00, fax 72 40 07 01
75 rooms, www.choicehotels.no
This traditional hotel primarily attracts mountain walkers. The »Perrongen« restaurant's house speciality: steaks cooked on the wood-fired grill. Round off the meal with a visit to the hotel's English-style pub.

Vangslia cabins
Oppdal, 3km/2mi west of the centre
Tel. 72 40 08 00 fax 72 40 08 01
Large comfortable wood cabins with fireplaces, a sauna for up to 12 people, and wonderful views.

Baedeker recommendation

▶ Tavern steeped in tradition
Kongsvold Fjellstue
Dovrefjell (south of Oppdal, by the E 6 / Kongsvold railway station)
Tel. 72 40 43 40, fax 72 40 43 41
32 rooms, www.kongsvold.no
A former stagecoach post dating back to 1720, the Kongsvold Fjellstue is a cosy tavern in the middle of the national park offering simple dishes during the day, including waffles and »smørbrød«. In the evenings, diners can spoil themselves with outstanding elk dishes and an imaginative menu, while the rooms all have their own unmistakable charm.

WATER SPORTS
The Driva river offers many opportunities for kayak trips, from family-friendly tours to white water adventures. Trained guides also conduct rafting tours; for information contact the tourist office.

wards to the east, and for hiking paths (4–5hrs) to the Reinheim hut (key kept in Kongsvold), from which it is possible to ascend Snøhetta (2286m/7500ft) in about four hours.

Further down the Driva valley, the road is partly blasted from the rock. 9km/6mi further on, a section of the old Kongsvegen begins to the east of Vårstigen. Today a footpath, this route was first mentioned in 1182 and offers wonderful views. About 5km/3mi further on, to the right, the Drivstua hut, a former mountain cabin (accommodation option), lies at 680m/2231ft; further on to the left, Åmotsdal valley can be glimpsed. The sparse birch stands give way to pine forest once more, and around 10km/6mi behind Drivstua, the Driva foams through the Magalaupet flume for 100m/109yd. Shortly afterwards, Iron Age burial mounds are reached at Rise. Smedgarden camp site and Driva railway station are within close reach. To the right, a toll-road leads into the beautiful Loseter (1100m/3609ft) mountain landscape. To the northeast stands the 1621m/5318ft-high Sissihø mountain, which can be climbed from Oppdal in about five hours.

✱
Vårstigen

The valley broadens out again and to the right, the steep Ålmenberg (1340m/4396ft) can be ascended from Oppdal in three hours. Skiers are attracted to the Oppdal area: along with Trysil, this is Norway's largest interconnected ski area, with 55km/34mi of downhill pistes. The E 6 continues northeast to ►Trondheim (122km/76mi).

Oppdal

Hiking in the Footsteps of Kings

The ideal starting point for hiking trips is Kongsvoll stasjon on the rail route between Oslo and Trondheim, reached by car on the E 6 coming from Dombås and travelling in the direction of Oppdal. Hjerkinn station is less suitable, because of the necessity to negotiate a military shooting range.

Getting there

Arrangements for accommodation and getting the key for the Reinheim hut (provisions supplied) should be made in Kongsvoll prior to setting off on this walking tour. The sign-posted track goes directly from the railway station, and heads west through **Stroplsjøda-len**. This section of the national park features the typical fjell vegetation. After around two hours, the track passes Hestgjeterhytta, where horses are grazed during summer. After a further three hours, the day's final destination is reached at Reinheim.
The second day begins with an ascent of **Snøhetta**, the highest mountain of Dovrefjell. This day tour ends at the Reinheim hut once more, so only a light pack is required. The marked route follows the eastern flank of the mountain to its southern peak. The view of Dovrefjell in its entirety is impressive, though somewhat spoilt by the military helicopter landing pad. During the descent across the north-

Three-day hike

Mountains of fur on the fjell: around 100 musk oxen now live in the national park once more.

ern flank, snow fields can be expected, even during summer. The route heads in a northwesterly direction, directly to the main hiking path, marked by a red »T«, that connects Reinheim with Åmotdalshytta. At the junction, a right turn should be taken for the return to Reinheim and the night's accommodation. The return leg from Reinheim to Kongsvoll is the same as the first day in reverse. Experienced and fit hikers can also do this tour of 42km/26mi in two days, or extend it by heading northeast in the direction of Driva from Åmotdalshytta. Camping is possible along the entire route.

Primeval inhabitants of the arctic tundra

Encounters with the archaic looking musk ox that sometimes cross the hiker's path are unforgettable, though you should always keep at a safe distance.

One of the world's largest herds of musk oxen, native to the area since prehistoric times, lives in the 200 sq km/77 sq mi once covered by the Dovrefjell National Park (now part of the much larger Dovrefjell-Sunndalsfjella National Park), though the species was only reintroduced to the area with animals from Greenland in 1932, and boosted by more in the 1950s. The original herd of 15 has now expanded to around 100 animals.

! Baedeker TIP

Musk ox safari

Those who don't want to leave encounters with musk oxen to chance can join a guided walking tour. During the high season, there are daily departures from Kongsvold Fjellstue (tel. 72 40 43 41), which can also be booked through Oppdal Booking (tel. 92 60 19 37, www.moskus-safari.no) or at the Dombås tourist information office.

✱ Femundsmarka

Region: East Norway

The Femundsmarka region is a thinly populated wilderness near the Swedish border. It is very beautiful here, though lonely – precisely the conditions valued by certain hikers and canoeists.

Norway's third largest lake, Lake Femund, is 60km/37mi long north–south. It is 150m/492ft deep, and the water temperature is a chilly 12°C/54°F. Most of the region between the eastern banks of the lake and the Swedish border was declared a national park in 1971. The Femundsmarka National Park (573 sq km/221 sq mi) is a wilderness of mighty spruce trees, boulders, rivers and lakes – and not a single road.

Wilderness without roads

The Femundsmarka region is the southernmost settlement area of the Sami people. The Blokkodden Wilderness Museum near Drevsjø explores their lifestyle as nomads and hunters.

Blokkodden open-air museum

The starting point for a walking tour that offers insight into the primal environment of the Norwegian fjells is the small settlement of Elgå. Initially, a path marked with the familiar red »T« is followed from the local bus stop, turning off to the right onto a narrow path at the signpost for Revlingkletten. This route soon breaks through the tree line, crossing several little streams, and ascends to the highland plateau where superb views await. Towards the end of the long fjell the path disappears and from this point it is advisable to follow a dried-out river bed in a strictly easterly direction. The route then leads left past a smallish lake. From the lake, the route descends to a transverse valley in which two electrical pylons can be spotted from afar. Here, rejoin the main hiking path that comes from the Svukuriset DNT hut belonging to the Norwegian hiking association. Marked with the red »T«, the main path bears right and there are beautiful camping opportunities all along here.

Three-day mountain tour

The route continues east past Mount Storslåga (1344m/4410ft) in the direction of Valdalen, where it is possible to stay the night in simple cabins or get a meal. The path from Valdalen leads onwards to Småsjøvollen. The road is crossed here before the path leads along a wire fence and directly into a marshy area that should only be crossed on the tracks marked by red sticks. After about 1.5hrs there is a low-lying lake to the left of the path, at the foot of the Sorkvola Mountain (1011m/3317ft), which offers ideal camping opportunities. After a steep incline up Sorkvola, the route then continues in the direction of Tolgevollenseter, where a barrier is passed (stop on the left). A gravel road then leads to the main tarmac road that runs be-

◄ Valdalen

tween Sorken and Røstvollen. Turn right here and follow the road for around 300m/330yd before turning left onto the sign-posted hiking path into the forest. The path now passes several smaller lakes and crosses a reindeer enclosure – used only in September – before finally reaching the banks of Lake Femund.

There is affordable accommodation in cosy cabins as well as on a well-maintained camp site at **Femundsvika**. From here there are also buses that connect with the tour's starting point back at Elgå.

✳
Lake Femund

The wealth of lakes in the Femundsmarka region make an almost unlimited number of different **canoe tours** possible. Lake Femund itself is especially attractive for its numerous small islands, especially in the central portion south of Elgå. Sudden winds causing high waves can often crop up, so extreme caution is necessary here. It is especially inadvisable to enter the lake when there is a **north wind**. **Lake Isteren** to the west of Lake Femund is much safer. Isteren is only 18km/11mi long, but experience with the use of compasses and maps is necessary because its many beautiful islands turn the lake into a **labyrinth**.

▶ **VISITING FEMUNDSMARKA**

GETTING THERE

There is no road leading into the national park, but the *Fæmund II* ferry offers a convenient way in. Alternatively, a tour can start off from Elgå or Valdalen on the Norwegian side or from Sylen/Grøvelsjøen on the Swedish side. The *Faemund II* ferry travels daily during summer (timetable available at tel. 72 41 37 14 or www.femund.no).

WHERE TO EAT

▶ **Moderate**
Bryggeloftet Villmarks Restaurant
Elgå
Tel. 62 45 95 43
There is a nice view of the lake from this wooden house with a grassed roof. The menu includes elk, reindeer, trout and whitefish, with delicious berries for dessert. The shop also sells freshly caught fish.

WHERE TO STAY

▶ **Mid-range**
Femund Fjellstue
Elgå
Tel. 62 45 95 41
12 rooms, www.femundfjellstue.no
This camp site with a comfortable fjellstue is centrally located on the eastern banks of Lake Femund. The Eriksen family ensures a comfortable stay and provides excellent food in the restaurant, where a great deal of game, fish, poultry and berry dishes are served.

BOAT HIRE

Femund Canoe Camp
Drevsjø, Sorken
Tel. 62 45 90 19
Fax 62 45 92 39
Boats and equipment can be hired at the southern end of the lake, in Femundsenden. The camp also offers four small cabins for accommodation.

Another recommended area is the lake district to the east of the southern end of Lake Femund. Fishermen's huts can be found by driving from Sorken in the direction of Storknallen and turning off right after 7km/4mi onto an unpaved track, which ends at the huts around 6km/4mi away. From here, the entire region around the Gunnarsjøen and the Storgyltingen lakes can be toured by boat. Most of the small lakes here are connected by rivers, so that when water levels are high enough, portage can be avoided. **Very rare animals and plant species** can still be found in this highly remote part of Femundsmarka.

✴ Gunnarsjøen, Storgyltingen

South of Femundsmarka, right by the Swedish border, lies the **Gutulia National Park**, a veritable paradise for all tree lovers. The Norwegian spruce trees here are up to 300 years old, and many pine trees have been standing for 500 years. The forest in the national park is allowed to evolve without the interference of mankind so that scientists can study its development over several generations of trees. A car park can be found at the end of a signposted track leading off road number 654. A cabin offering coffee and waffles during July is half an hour's walk away along the banks of Gutulisjøen.

Paradise for tree lovers

Magical colours enliven the autumnal Femundsmarka.

✶ Finnmark

M/N 19-27

Region: North Norway	**Population:** 76,000

Finnmark, the land of the Sami people, is the largest and most sparsely populated province of Norway: a giant wilderness area, the like of which can rarely be found in Europe today. The coast is characterized by broad, open fjords, and the interior by a flat highland plateau that is typical of the Finnmarksvidda region.

Lakes, fjords and tundra

Although it is characterized by Arctic tundra vegetation, the several thousand lakes of Finnmark recall the Finnish lake district. Broad, open fjords that are up to 120km/75mi long characterize the Finnmark coastline. The interior consists of a flat highland plateau that lies at an elevation of 300m/984ft–600m/1968ft above sea level, known as Finnmarksvidda.It encompasses 36% of the region, yet it is only inhabited by 7% of the provincial population, mostly Sami people.

Rough climate

Even though extensions of the Gulf Stream keep the ports free of ice, a cold and stormy climate prevails. Summer temperatures normally struggle to reach 10°C/50°F in sheltered areas, such as valleys and fjords, while a record-breaking –52°C/–62°F was once reached during winter in Karasjok.

 VISITING FINNMARK

INFORMATION

For addresses for tourist information, hotels and restaurants, see the sections on Alta, Hammerfest, Katasjok, Kautokeino, Kirkenes, Nordkapp and Vardø.

GETTING THERE

All larger settlements have their own airstrip. Ferries and speed boats, as well as numerous bus routes, connect the northern Norwegian settlements, as well as heading into Sweden and Finland. The most important ports are also serviced by the Hurtigruten shipping line.

FISHING

A good time is during the ocean fishing festival at Sørvær, on the island of Sørøya, to the west of Hammerfest. Worthwhile fishing grounds can be found at Straumen under the Langfjord bridge (15km/9mi off Kirkenes), and the salmon catch is especially good along the Alta river and at Tanaelva.

Baedeker recommendation

Pasvik taiga

Tel. 78 99 54 44, fax 78 99 54 99
One of Norway's most unusual gourmet restaurants stands in the western half of the Pasvik valley, in the very midst of the wilderness. In this wooden house with view onto the Russian border, marinaded elk meat, reindeer tartar, bear meat, sea lion, seabirds and Kamkatcha shrimps are all on the menu. Accommodation is also availabl

The Formula One of the high north? Reindeer races are very popular among the Sami people.

This is »Sápmi« – the land of the Sami (►Baedeker Special p.36). **Land of the Sami**
The county of ►Troms, whose coast is also deeply fissured by fjords,
is part of Norwegian Lapland (Norwegian: Sameland). But, while
agriculture is still possible in Troms, and fertile pastures do exist, the
region becomes ever more barren and hostile to the northeast. The
high mountain groups to the west give way to low plateaus to the
east, where just occasional bare hills stand out. Centres of Norwegian
Sami populations are at ► Karasjok (administrative centre) and
►Kautokeino (cultural centre).

Reindeer are the Sami's most important possession. In this cold-lov- ◄ **Reindeer herding**
ing game animal, both males and females grow a set of antlers. An
individual Sami must have at least 100–200 animals to maintain him
or herself, though a person rarely owns more than 500. Since a region grazed out by reindeer takes many years to recover, the herds
need extensive territories. The former nomads have become modern
reindeer breeders, who herd their animals with motorized snowmobiles and even on occasion do their counting from a helicopter. In
addition to reindeer breeding, the Sami also often carry out other
animal husbandry and a small amount of arable farming.

History
The present day borders of Finnmark date from 1751 and 1826. Prior to that, the countryside was the communal region of Norwegian, Swedish and Russian Sami people. Between 1920 and 1944, the area of the former Soviet Union that now borders Finnmark was Finnish territory. The border near Troms has existed since 1866.

Trade with the Pomor ►
For centuries, the **Russian Pomor people** were welcome traders in Finnmark. They exchanged flour, cereals, rope, tar and wood beams for coffee, sugar, herring, cod and halibut. Not least because of the long Russian winters and the high demand for fish, the so-called Pomor trade achieved great significance.

German destruction ►
When the occupying German forces attempted to cut off Allied supply routes to Murmansk at the end of the **Second World War**, they eliminated northern Norway's entire infrastructure. The scorched earth policy of the retreating troops in November 1944 resulted in the destruction of most houses and only a few places, such as Hamningberg and Bugøynes, survived the devastation.

After 1945 ►
For a long time after 1945, northern Norway was considered a **developing country**. Thousands of fishing families were close to ruin because their incomes had become too small. Nowadays, fishing stocks have recovered and tourist numbers have been growing for years. The exploitation of gas and oil reserves in the Baring Sea is also destined to improve standards of living here. ► Kirkenes, final destination of the ►Hurtigruten shipping line, has evolved into the gateway to the east. Day trips to the Russian town of Murmansk – the world's largest city north of the Arctic Circle – are organized from here.

✸
Øvre Pasvik Nasjonalpark
The Øvre Pasvik National Park at the end of the 120km/75mi-long forested Pasvik valley between Finland and Russia is, as it were, the westernmost extension of the Siberian taiga. The primeval pine forests here are very impressive. The highest point is Steinfjell, which barely reaches 202m/663ft above sea level. A quarter of the national park is covered by water. A single cohesive water labyrinth is formed by the lakes of Ellenvatnet, Parvatnet, Skinnposevatnet, Grenseparvatnet and Dagvatnet. **Lynx, bears and wolverines** still survive in the national park and it is also possible to spot birds that are normally residents of Siberia, such as the great grey owl. **Wood grouse, fish eagle and whooper swan** are also seen here. This pristine national park is best explored by canoe. There is only one hiking cabin at the Ellenvatnet, which can be reached by a path leaving from the car park. In the meantime, however, organized canoe and husky tours have also been made available within the Øvre Pasvik National Park.

! *Baedeker* TIP

Arctic wilderness

Untouched Arctic wilderness can be experienced on the Nordkyn peninsula 40km/25mi east of Nordkapp. This huge tundra region, set with lakes and moors, is one of Scandinavia's most important bird breeding colonies. Among many other types of bird there are nesting snow grouse and numerous duck and seagull species, including the Arctic tern.

✱ Fredrikstad

B 7

Region: South Norway   **Population:** 70,000

The former fortress town on the Oslofjord has survived completely intact. Lovingly restored 17th-century houses line the streets, and the lanes of the charming Old Town are wonderful for strolls along ramparts, past bastions and over drawbridges.

Scandinavia's best preserved fortress town is located where Norway's longest river, the Glomma, flows into the ►Oslofjord. It was founded on the orders of the Swedish King Fredrik II in 1567, and redeveloped into **Norway's most impenetrable fortress** in 1660. The town was only released from military control in 1903, and 60 of the original 130 cannons are still to be seen on the bastions of the fortified walls. A statue on the main square recalls Fredrik II, after whom the town was named. This now modern industrial town and port extends along the western bank of the Glomma river and can be reached by boat, or via the 40m/131ft-high Fredrikstadbrua. The neo-Gothic **cathedral** here dates from 1880, and contains one of the largest church organs in Norway, with 4000 pipes, as well as glass paintings by Emanuel Vigeland, the brother of Gustav Vigeland (►Oslo).

Founded by Sweden

First he gave the town his name, now he stands on the market square: Swedish King Frederik II.

What to See in and around Fredrikstad

Old Town ✳ A walking tour around the Old Town leads along narrow streets paved with rough cobble stones. Several of the old buildings now house the workshops of craftsmen. It is worth looking in at the **provisions store** dating from 1687 and the **municipal museum** opposite, in the old »slaveriet« (slave house) dating from 1731, which documents the time when Fredrikstad was still a fortification (opening times: May–Aug Mon–Sat 11am–5pm, Sun from noon, Sept Sat/Sun only.)

Kongsten fort, which was built on the occasion of a visit by King Christian V in 1685, is one of the exterior constructions of the fortified town and lies 500m/550yd beyond the Old Town. Underground rooms and passages in the fort give insight into the military thinking of the period. Another satellite of the town lies on the island of Isegran. Norway's last »jarl« (a royal governor) had his castle there around the end of the 12th century.

Oldtidsvei ✳ A drive along the Oldtidsvei (ancient history route) between Fredrikstad and Skjeberg on the RV 110 is a journey through several thousand years of European history. At **Begby**, there is a sign for »Helleristninger«, the **3000-year-old rock paintings** with images from agriculture and seafaring that prove this route was already in use during the Bronze Age (1800-600 BC). Representations of ships, fishing nets, the sun (a fertility symbol), a dancer, cult items and footprints

▶ VISITING FREDRIKSTAD

INFORMATION

Opplev Fredrikstad
Tøhusgata 41
1632 Gamle Fredrikstad
Tel. 69 30 46 00
Fax 69 30 46 01
www.fredrikstad.no

WHERE TO EAT

▶ **Expensive**
Balaklava Gjestgiveri
Færgeport gate 78b (Gamlebyen)
Tel. 69 32 30 40
This tavern with a gourmet restaurant has existed since 1803. Fine fish dishes dominate the menu. The atmospheric wine cellar is a popular meeting place for a glass of wine – albeit an expensive one.

WHERE TO STAY

▶ **Mid-range**
Hotel Valhalla
17 rooms, Valhallsgate 3
Tel. 69 36 89 50, fax 69 36 89 60
www.hotelvalhalla.no
Guests are housed on the »roof of the town« at the Valhalla, where the view over Fredrikstad is fantastic.

Baedeker recommendation

▶ **A pleasant boat tour**
The eight-hour boat tour on the Halde canal is a real pleasure. Boats set off from Strömsfoss to Tistedal from June to Aug, Wed, Fri, Sat & Sun at 11am.

typify the imagination and technology of that era. The Hornnes rock paintings, with numerous magnificent images of ships decorated with animal heads at the bow, can be viewed shortly before Skjeberg. Also along the Oldtidsvei is the church of Borge dating from 1861, ◄ Borge though the foundations indicate there was an older church here dating from the early Middle Ages. The famous polar explorer **Roald Amundsen** (►Famous People) was born in Borge in 1872. He spent his childhood in the »Tomta« house that contains numerous mementos of his life.

✱ Halden
Halden, which was known as Fredrikshald from 1665 to 1927, enjoys an attractive location on the Iddefjord and is surrounded by numerous idyllic lakes. High above the town towers the **Fredriksten fortress**, which Fredrik III had built as protection against the Swedes in 1661–71 and 1682–1701. There is a wonderful view of the town and the skerry coastal landscape from up here. The fortress was constructed on the ridges of two hills and today accommodates a restaurant and a camp site. The walls run from west to east on the northern hill, with the Queen's Bastion at the western end and the Prince Christian Bastion at the eastern end. The Prince Georg Bastion stands to the south, while the main bastion of Overkongen is located at the highest point. The citadel stands between the two elevations, with fortifications on the western slope facing the town (guided ⏲ tours mid-June–mid-August daily noon, 1.30pm and 3pm). A muse-

Maritime expedition of 3000 years ago? The riddles of the rock paintings of Begby

um devoted to war and cultural history documents the history of the fortress, which is a popular venue for cultural events of all kinds these days.

✳ Halden canal

One of the country's most beautiful technical cultural monuments is the Halden canal, which winds through the region and connects five lakes and rivers. It is not only an important shipping route, but also popular with **canoeists**. There are several locks along the canal. The Brekke lock has four compartments that cover a water height difference of 39m/128ft, which is a record in Europe.

Svinesund Bridge

Svinesund Bridge was opened on 10 June 2005 in a joint ceremony with Norway's King Harald and Sweden's King Carl Gustaf. Spanning 247m/270yd, this filigree construction is the **largest single-arched bridge in the world**, connecting Norway with Sweden via the road that goes between Oslo and Göteborg. Four lanes on the new bridge, instead of the two available before, are intended to ease the long and frequent traffic jams on this stretch. The border crossing is especially popular with the Norwegians themselves, who stock up on meat, cigarettes and alcohol in the cheaper supermarkets across the border.

✳ ✳ Geirangerfjord

E 3/4

Region: West Norway

Tourists have been streaming to the Geirangerfjord since the middle of the 19th century. An area of great natural beauty, it is among the most beautiful places in Norway. The mountains rise almost vertically out of the water, waterfalls with poetic names thunder into the depths, cruise ships sparkle brilliant white on the deep waters and serpentine roads wind up the slopes – all combining to form a scene that can truly be described as breathtaking.

Seven Sisters

The famous Geirangerfjord forms the eastern end of the Sunnylvsfjord that itself branches off the Storfjord. The car ferry sails the 16km/10mi across the fjord travelling between Hellesylt and Geiranger, passing imposing waterfalls: »The Seven Sisters«, »The Suitor« and the »Bride's Veil«. Several abandoned farms cling precariously on rock promontories. Impressive, too, are the views from the eleven hairpin bends of the Eagle Road (Ørneveien), and from the viewing point of the 1495m/4905ft Dalsnibba mountain, both accessible from Geiranger. Over 100 cruise ships weigh anchor in Geiranger annually and even the Hurtigruten line does not pass up the chance to make a detour to this picturesque fjord during the summer months.

Norway's most famous postcard motif is the narrow Geirangerfjord.

What to See around the Geirangerfjord

The narrow, winding RV 63 road to Geiranger branches off to the north from the E15, to the west of Grotli. Initially it runs along Lake Breidalsvatnet, at whose western end stands the Djupvasshytta hotel. The so-called Nibbevei road, open from June to September, which branches off to the right near the Djupvasshytta hotel, leads up to the summit of the 1495m/4905ft-high Dalsnibba, climbing the 5km/3mi up to the top via many hairpin bends (toll payable; up to 12.5% incline). The summit offers a magnificent view over the mountains and down to the Geirangerfjord lying far below.

An impressive alpine road to Geiranger begins shortly after Djup-vasshytta – a distance of just 7km/4mi as the crow flies, but 17km/11mi on the ground. The road was completed in 1885 and sur-mounts a difference in elevation of 1000m/3281ft in 20 occasionally very sharp bends, with gradients of up to 8%. There are also several bridges. During the journey, the sudden transformation from rough alpine climate to the gentler mild climate of the protected valley can be experienced. 2km/1.2mi along the road, **Blåfjell** can be seen rising up to the left with an ice field known as the »Jettegryte« (giant pot), an glaciated area about 2m/2yd wide and 10m/33ft deep at the top of the mountain.

Narrow access road

✶ ✶

◀ Side trip to Dalsnibba

✶

Road to Geiranger

▶ VISITING GEIRANGERFJORD

INFORMATION
Geiranger Turistkontor
6216 Geiranger
Gamle Fergekai
Tel. 70 26 30 99, fax 70 26 57 20
www.geiranger.no

WHERE TO EAT
▶ Expensive
Union Hotel
(on the RV 63, above the centre of
Geiranger)
Tel. 70 26 83 00
Diners here have the choice between
spoiling themselves with the à la carte
menu at the excellent restaurant or
stilling those hunger pangs with a visit
to the hotel buffet.

▶ Moderate
Westeräs Hytteutleige
4km/2.5mi outside Geiranger
Tel. 92 64 95 37
Fax 70 26 32 14
www.geiranger.no/westeras
Iris and Arnfinn Westerås's rustic and
nicely furnished restaurant is also
popular with the locals. Those who
wish to stay the night can do so in the
huts and holiday homes in the courtyard. Children will love the Shetland
ponies and goats.

WHERE TO STAY
▶ Luxury
Union Hotel
On the RV 63, see above
Tel. 70 26 83 00, fax 70 26 83 51
168 rooms, www.union-hotel.no
This hotel is equipped with every
comfort and also boats an indoor
swimming pool with attached outdoor
pool, a sauna, a Turkish bath and a
much frequented nightclub – not to
mention an overwhelming view over
the Geirangerfjord.

▶ Mid-range
Villa Utsikten
Tel. 70 26 96 60
Fax 70 26 91 61
31 rooms, www.villautsikten.no
Traditional establishment that goes back
over a century. The name of »Utsikten«
(view) is entirely appropriate, since the
Geirangerfjord is nearly always in sight,
whether from the Aida restaurant, the
lobby, or from many of the rooms.

Euro Pollfoss Gjestehus
Nordberg (60km/37mi from Geiranger)
Tel. 61 21 47 00, fax 61 21 48 46
This striking black guesthouse with
white window frames in the Swiss style
lies right next to the road. The rustic
atmosphere of the interior recalls the
old stagecoach post of 1889 that the
place was once home to.

Baedeker recommendation

▶ Grotli Høyfjellshotel
Grotli
Tel. 61 21 74 74
Fax 61 21 74 75
53 rooms, www.grotli.no
Several national ski teams have used this ho
as a base to train at the Stryn summer ski
centre. Guests enjoy the cosy evening atm
phere of a Scandinavian wooden house an
the generous portions of Norwegian food.

▶ Budget
Fossen Camping
Tel. 70 26 32 00
www.fossencamping.no
The site offers several huts with shower,
bath and kitchen for 2–6 people, as well
as a beautiful location with views of the
Geirangerfjord.

FERRIES

► Sightseeing

A cruise on the Geirangerfjord is one of to the highlights of any visit to Norway. The *MS Geirangerfjord* sets off daily from the old ferry quay near the tourist office for the 90-minute fjord tour between June and August. Departures at 8am, 9.30am, 11.30am, 2pm and 5pm. Demand is often high so expect queues.

► Transport

The car ferry between Geiranger and Hellesylt operates between May and September; during the high season it departs up to eight times a day, but queues must still be expected. From 15 June to 15 August, the ferry travels between Geiranger and Valldal, with departures from Valldal at 10.30am and 3.30pm, and from Geiranger at 1pm and 6pm.

LEISURE AND SPORT

Sea kayaks are rented out for excursions from near the camp site at the end of the fjord (tel. 91 11 80 62). The rafting centre in Valldal offers two four-hour tours daily during summer (tel. 90 01 40 35; 11am and 3pm, Sun 1pm). The meeting point is the tourist office.

Beyond the **Øvre Blåfjellbro** bridge, there is a wonderful view of the »Eagle Road« winding its way up from Geiranger to Eidsdal: to the left stands the Flydalshorn, to the right the Vindåshorn, and beyond the 1779m/5837ft high Såthorn. Further on, the route leads over the Nedre Blåfjellbro and past the Kvandalselv waterfalls before descending initially to the first ledge of the valley and then down to the second, the Flydal.

Flydal

Flydalsjuvet (300m/984ft; car park) can be found beyond Ørjeseter, from where there are good views to be had. Shortly afterwards by Hole, it is worth making a detour to **Vesterås**. A signposted footpath leads to the Storseterfoss, a 30m/98ft high waterfall. Back on the main road, the Hotel Utsikten Bellevue appears beyond Hole, and to the left of a bridge after that a stone memorial records the establishment of the Norwegian constitution in 1814.

✱
◄ Flydalsjuvet, Storseterfoss

Finally, Geiranger is reached, the much-visited little port and often overcrowded tourist resort with a lovely location at the eastern end of the Geirangerfjord. Geiranger's Fjord Centre, opened in 2002, gives a good idea of living conditions along the fjords: visitors are guided through a historic fjord settlement as well as seeing typical fjord landscapes. The RV 63 follows the northern bank of the Geirangerfjord out of Geiranger, reaching Møllgårdene after 3km/2mi, where there are several houses over 200 years old. This is also where the Eagle Road begins.

Geiranger

To the west, the Geirangerfjord flows into the Sunnylvsfjord which has two settlements: Hellesylt to the south and Stranda to the north. There is a ferry connection between Hellesylt and Geiranger.

✱
Sunnylvsfjord

Eagle Road

The Eagle Road connects the Geirangerfjord with the Norddalsfjord. Initially the road winds its way to Korsmyra (624m/2047ft) – the route's highest point – in eleven loops offering beautiful views onto the Geirangerfjord and the waterfalls. Afterwards it leads past Lake Eidsvatnet before descending all the way to **Eidsdal** on the Norddalsfjord. The octagonal church there, which dates from 1782, is worth taking a look at. A ferry travels to Linge on the north bank of the fjord. Åndalsnes (►Romsdal) is east of Linge, while heading west the route leads to ►Ålesund.

✦✦ Gudbrandsdal

D 6/7

Region: South Norway

Gudbrandsdal is one of the most popular tourist destinations in Norway. And not without reason: the climate is mild and the valley full of charm, with forested hillsides and blossoming meadows. The mountains nearby are ideal for every kind of sporting holiday.

The Gudbrandsdal valley (Nowergian: Gudbrandsdalen, meaning »the valley/dale of Gudbrand«) extends northwards along the 200km/125mi-long Lågen river, from Lillehammer to Dombås. Old farms line the green hillsides, almost like a pearl necklace. The Norwegians call this region the »valley of valleys«, and it has been the most important north-south axis for travelling inland for centuries, and is also the most densely populated valley in Norway. Its inhabitants, the Gudbrandsdøler, are known to be very fond of their traditions and live predominantly from farming and woodworking.

What to See in Gudbrandsdal

Hunderfossen

Leaving ►Lillehammer (180m/590ft), the E 6 follows the Lågen upriver through the Gudbrandsdal valley. North of Lillehammer lies the **Hunderfossen power station**, which is fed by a 7km/4mi-long reservoir. There is a fish ladder and a trout farm producing 20,000 fish annually. A camp site with cabins can be reached via the dam.

On the same side, about 3km/2mi further on, is the **Hunderfossen Family Leisure Park**, whose 37m/121ft-high troll is an easily spotted landmark. This leisure park, whose style is distinctly non-Disney, is especially popular with the little ones

! **Baedeker TIP**

Marvels of technology

Those interested in tunnel and road construction from medieval pilgrim routes to contemporary high-tech projects would do well to visit the Norwegian Road Museum (Norske Vegmuseum) near the Hunderfossen Family Leisure Park (opening times: daily 10am–3pm, May–Aug till 6pm).

► VISITING GUDBRANDSDAL

INFORMATION

Otta Turistkontor
Ola Dahlsgt. 1
2670 Otta
Tel. 61 23 66 50, fax 61 23 09 60
www.visitrondane.com

Vinstra Turistinformasjon
Peer Gynt Arrangement
2640 Vinstra
Tel.61 29 47 70, fax 61 29 47 71
www.peergynt.no

WHERE TO EAT

► Moderate
Kornhaug Gjestegård
Follebu
(17km/11mi north of Lillehammer)
Tel. 61 22 92 50
This imposing 100-year-old wooden
building in the Dragon style is the
perfect setting for an excellent five-
course game menu. The à la carte
menu is certainly affordable and the
»Lunsmeny« is a fairly priced dish
(daily except Sun, noon to 6pm).

► Inexpensive
Sinclair Vertshuset
Kvam (on the E 6)
Tel. 61 29 54 50
Cosy cafeteria serving snacks and
good waffles.

WHERE TO STAY

► Luxury
Euro Gudbrandsdal Hotel
Ringebu
Tel. 61 28 40 00, fax 62 28 40 01
www.gudbrandsdal-hotel.com
A top class hotel in the midst of the
mountain landscape of Ringebufjell.
Exclusive spa and numerous sporting
opportunities, such as ice-hole fishing
and hiking.

Rondane Spa Høyfjellshotell
Otta, Mysæster
Tel. 61 23 39 33
Fax 61 23 39 52
65 rooms, www.spa.no
Mountain hotel picturesquely located
in the Rondane National Park with a
large spa and swimming facility.

Rondablikk Høyfjellshotell
Kvam
Tel. 61 29 49 40, fax 61 29 49 50
82 rooms, www.rondablikk.no
This popular mountain hotel lies in a
wonderful location very close to the
Rondane National Park. It has a pool,
sauna, fitness centre and nightclub.
The price difference between full
board and bed and breakfast is
minimal, so go for the former.

► Mid-range
Sygard Grytting
Sør-Fron
Tel. 61 29 85 88
www.grytting.com
The estate by Harpefoss (70km/44mi
north of Lillehammer) was a pilgrim
hostel 700 years ago. Today it is an
excellently restored historic hotel and
the three-course evening meal is
served in a wonderful atmosphere
harking back to bygone days.

► Budget
Rondvassbu Turisthytta
Mysuseter, Sel
Tel. 61 23 18 66
www.rondvassbu.com
Basic hut belonging to the Norwegian
hiking association (DNT) in the
Rondane National Park. Travel by car
or bus (from Otta) as far as Mysuseter, after which another 1.5hrs' walk
is necessary.

Fun for kids: the miniature houses at Lilleputhammer

and also includes a swimming facility and a museum on energy production (opening times: June–mid-Aug daily 10am–5pm, July till 8pm). Not far from the Hunderfossen leisure park is the **world's most northern ski bob and toboggan rink**, where all the races for the 1994 Winter Olympics took place. Now anyone can take part in a hair-raising race down the track – in the company of an experienced rider.

Øyer   Around 6km/4mi beyond Hunderfossen, the Øyer church (1725) stands to the right, whose interior is in the rustic Baroque style of the region. In Øyer itself there are several ski lifts and 20 pistes of the **Hafjell Olympic Grounds**. An attraction for children awaits at the **Lilleputhammer** by the Øyer Gjestegård (inn): a reconstruction of the Storgata district of Lillehammer in miniature, complete with workshops and all kinds of attractions for children (opening times end of June–mid-Aug daily 10am–7pm).

Tretten   Tretten lies at the southern end of the 17km/11mi-long Lake Losna with its rich stock of fish. Losna is actually a widening of the Lågen river. Take a look at the ceiling fresco inside the church of 1728. To the west, the RV 254 branches off to lead into the Peer Gynt Road (see later).

Stave churches   The E 6 continues along the eastern bank of the Lake Losna. 4km/2mi before reaching Fåvang, the **Fåvang church** stands at the Kirkestuen crossroads. Originally a stave church, it was converted into a cross-shaped church in the 17th century and restored in 1951. After

★

Ringebu stave church ▶   7km/4mi a short road turns off right at Elstad and leads to the Ringebu stave church (approx. 1200). The old main road through the valley (the »king's road« to Trondheim; ►Dovrefjell) used to run past here. The church was extended around its choir, transept and aisles in around 1630, and then restored in 1921. The colourful interior originated from the 17th–18th century, including the altar painting from 1688 and the pulpit from 1703.

Hundorp

The Gudbrandsdal high school was once located in the village of Hundorp (193m/633ft), in an old house dating from 1850. In its courtyard there are **burial mounds** and Bauta stones (memorial or tomb stones) from **the Viking era**, as well as beautiful arts and crafts to be seen. One of the burial mounds can even be entered. The octagonal **stone church of Sør Fron** (1787) is also known as »Gudbrandsdal Cathedral«. It was built in the style predominant in the reign of the French King Louis XVI, although the interior vaulting and altar displays Baroque characteristics. The church also has an electronic glockenspiel.

Vinstra

The Sødorp **wooden church** (1752) and the **Peer Gyntgården** with its 18 old houses (private) are worth seeing in Vinstra (241m/791ft). Peder Olsen Hågå, who lived on Nordgardhågå farm from 1732 to 1785, was the inspiration for Henrik Ibsen's play *Peer Gynt*. The Peer Gynt Stugu dating from 1743 documents various versions of Ibsen's drama with photos, dolls, costumes and posters (opening times: mid-June–mid-Aug 10am–5pm). The play is also performed annually on the open-air stage by the lake.

Kvam

The valley becomes narrower behyond Vinstra. A decisive battle for the Gudbrandsdal occurred in Kvam in 1940, and a military war museum recalls the events. The1027m/3369ft Teigkamp mountain rises south of Kvam and, on the continuing drive to Sjoa (285m935ft), the Torgeirkamp (1186m/3891ft) can be seen.

Heidal

A road branches off left into the Heidal valley. 15km/9mi beyond Heidal itself – complete with many listed houses and farms – the village church is reached, a reproduction from 1938 of the original church dating from 1752, which was burnt down in 1933. Adjacent, on the attractive Bjølstad farm, stands a chapel (approx. 1600) with 11th-century portal sections from a stave church. The crucifix dates from around 1200.

Kringen is reached via the E 6. A monument recalls the farmers' victory over the Scottish army that was on its way to Sweden in 1612.

To the northwest stands the 849m/2785ft-high Pillarguritoppen from which, legend has it, a man named Pillarguritoppen is said to have warned the farmers of the advancing Scottish army.

Otta

Otta is an important traffic junction at the mouth of the Otta into the Lågen, as well as the most important base for hikes in the ►Rondane mountains. It is possible to get just short of the summit of Pillarguritoppen by car, from where there is a panoramic view. To the northeast, the Rondanevegen offers the easiest access to the Rondane National Park.

Side trip to Mysuseter

Those who enjoy geological phenomena or bizarre photo opportunities should make a short detour and take the road to Mysuseter at Sel/Selsverket. After 3km/2mi, a short, relatively steep footpath leads to the extraordinary »Kvitskriuprestinn«: 6m/20ft-high gravelstone **pyramids**, also known as »priests« because of their shape. From Mysuseter, it is another 10km/6mi on foot to the Rondvassbu tourist hut on the edge of the 570 sq km/220 sq mi ►Rondane National Park, a veritable hiking paradise.

The bizarre »Priests« at Mysuseter testify to the power of erosion.

The three farms of **Romundgård,** Laurgård and Jørundgård in northern Sel play a significant role in the literary trilogy *Kristin Lavransdatter* by **Sigrid Undset** (► Famous People). The 14th-century Jørundgård farm was reconstructed on the occasion of **filming** for the *Kristin Lavransdatter* movie. Today it is possible to experience the everyday life of a medieval farm here.

The valley becomes narrower and the landscape wilder during the next 14km/9mi stretch. In Rosten, a narrow road (10km/6mi) leads off to the right for the popular **holiday cabin region of Høvringen** (960m/3150ft). It is possible to take a hiking tour from Høvringen to Peer Gynthytta (see below).

The E 6 continues as far as Brennhaug (449m/1473ft). To the north-east, there is a view onto the Storkuven (1452m/4764ft), and to the south, the Jetta mountain chain with Mount Blåhø (1618m/5308ft) can be seen, from which there are good views. From here there is a road that cuts through to Vågåmo.

Brennhaug

Dombås is the central settlement of the ► Dovrefjell region. The E 136 road now follows the Lågen valley to the northwest, to Åndalsnes (►Romsdal).

Dombås

Peer Gynt Trail

Traces of the legendary figure of Peer Gynt, who is supposed to have lived in this region, are regularly encountered on the highland tracks and hiking routes to the west and east of Gudbrandsdal. The ambitious young man set off into the world full of vigour, survived the wildest adventures with mountain spirits and trolls, only to discover peace and happiness when he returned home, a broken and old man. Henrik Ibsen (► Famous People) was inspired to write his drama *Peer Gynt*, for which Edvard Grieg (►Famous People) wrote the music, by P. Ch. Asbjørnsen's story *Rondane Reindeer Hunt*, whose main character was the farmer and hunter Peder Olsen Hågå (1732–85). The visitor can get an idea of what inspired the two different artists by following the Peer Gynt Trail, which is also possible by car.

Trolls and mountain spirits

The 91km/57mi long, narrow and very winding Peer Gynt Trail (tolls payable along some stretches) forms an alternative route to the E 6 through the Gudbrandsdal, between ►Lillehammer and Vinstra. This scenic route is around 7km/4mi longer, but worth it for the forests and deep blue lakes, as well as the marvellous views onto the Rondane Mountains. Setting off from Lillehammer, take the E 6 as far as Fåberg (6km/4mi) and turn left onto the RV 255, following the Gausdal valley with the river of the same name as far as **Follebu**. The large farm of **Aulestad** is located here, where the poet Bjørnstjerne Bjørnson (►Famous People) lived from 1875 onwards. Today the estate is a museum (opening times: May, Sept 11am–2.30pm, June–Aug 10am–3.30pm, July till 5.30pm). ⏲

Setting off on the Peer Gynt Trail

The route that now leads further west to Vestre Gausdal and on to the ► Espedal Road is left behind at Segalstad. Instead follow the signs for the Peer Gynt Trail, which winds ever higher. Skeikampen is passed at the foot of the bizarrely shaped mountain of Skeikampen (1123m/3684m; 11 ski lifts and great views), as well as Frøysehøgda (views over the Gausdal) and Fagerhøy. At Rauhagen, the highest point of the road is reached, an altitude of 1053m/3454ft, and there is a magnificent view: to the north lie the mountain chains of ►Rondane and ► Dovrefjell with Snøhetta; to the northwest, the ► Jotun-

Highest point at Rauhagen

heimen range can be seen. Skjærvangen is reached after another 8km/5mi, where a private road turns off right to Hundorp on the E 6. It is then another 5km/3mi to the tourist resort of **Gålå** and to Wadahl, which lies 930m/3051ft above Lake Gålåvann and has a very attractive viewing platform. Henrik Ibsen's *Peer Gynt* is performed with the help of 130 actors on the lakeside each year.

In Vollsdammen it is worth making a detour west as far as **Dalseter** (21km/13mi). At Fefor lies the lake of the same name and those who dare to attempt the 45-minute walk to the summit of Feforkampen (1175m/3855ft) are rewarded with a panoramic view onto the peaks of the Rondane and the Jotunheimen mountains. At Vinstra, the road rejoins the E 6.

! *Baedeker* TIP

Delicious cheese!

Those who wish to visit the home of the famous Gudbrandsdal caramelized goat's cheese (Norwegian: geitost or brunost) that the farmer Anne Hov created by chance in 1863 should turn off towards »Solbråseter« farm shortly after Gålå. This sweet, brown cheese is an essential part of any breakfast buffet. The traditional dairy is still in operation and open to the public in July and August, Wed and Sat, 11am–3pm.

Espedal Road

This worthwhile alternative route to the E 6 through the Gudrandsdal leads through a wild mountain landscape with numerous lakes and rivers. A well developed area for tourism, and a good hiking and cross-country skiing region is found around Lake Espedal. From Lillehammer to **Segelstad**, the Espedal Road (R 255) follows the same route as the Peer Gynt Trail, before turning west to Vestre Gausdal. The Espedal Road now follows the Svatsumdal valley for the 22km/14mi to **Svatsum** (octagonal wooden church dating from 1860). It is then another 3km/2mi to the **Fjellstue Strand**, from where there is a beautiful view onto the long, idyllic Lake Espedal. There are good fishing opportunities at Espedalen Fjellstue. Beyond is **Dalseter**, where the Peer Gynt Trail is rejoined. During winter, Espedal counts as one of Norway's best regions for guaranteed snow and there is an extensive network of cross-country routes.

Go to »hell« »Helvete« (hell) can be found at the southern end of Lake Espedal, around 13km/8mi beyond Svatsum, in the form of two giant cracks in the landscape that were created by glacial erosion during the Ice Age. With depths of up to 100m/328ft and a width of up to 50m/164ft, they are the largest examples of this geological phenomenon in Norway. The largest cavern measures around 100m/109yd by 40m/44yd.

Ormtjernkampen National Park A mountain landscape with numerous rivers and lakes extends to the west of the Espedal Road, which is also suitable as a hiking region for families with children. Only those who wish to explore the summit area of Ormtjernkampen (1127m/3697ft) need mountaineering experience. At 19 sq km/7 sq mi, the Ormtjernkampen National Park is Norway's smallest national park, famous for its pristine landscape. To reach the northwestern sector of the hiking region, a road heading southwest off the main route through **Vestre Gausdal** should be followed to **Fagernes**. The road is only open during summer, has many bends and beautiful viewing points (up to 1000m/3281ft), and is 84km/52mi long. There are plenty of huts providing food in Fagernes that also offer accommodation. The hiking region can be reached via the RV 51 from Fagernes, heading in a northwesterly direction.

✳ Rondane National Park

The Rondane mountain range stretches between Gudbrandsdal to the west and Atnedalen to the east. 572 sq km/223 sq mi of this area was turned into a national park in 1962 and, even though there are **ten summits over 2000m/6562ft**, the range is a popular and relatively easy hiking region. A high alpine dry climate with sparse vegetation is typical for the Rondane mountains: grey-yellow lichen covers the

Wonderful hiking region

Heaven and earth touch in a very special way in the Rondane National Park.

In the Rondane National Park, the Sjoa, Lågen and Otta rivers are especially suitable for adventurous rafting tours.

chalky sandstone that predominates here. During the Middle Ages, the Rondane range formed a natural obstacle for farmers and merchants who wanted to reach the important markets of the copper town of ►Røros. Derelict stone huts recall that ancient journey route and also the Rondane region's significance as a **hunting ground** for English aristocrats in the 19th century. Despite their limited numbers here, reindeer were hunted in the area from ancient times and walkers can find numerous **Viking trapping pits** built of stone.

The heart of the national park

At the heart of the national park stands the Rondvassbu tourist hut, where all walking paths through the mountains converge. The hut is at the western border of the park and can be reached on foot in about 1.5hrs from Mysuseter. The long, narrow Lake Rondevatn, at an altitude of 1100m/3609ft, extends north, squeezing itself through the high mountains. To the left and right lie the highest mountain summits. Hikers of average fitness will manage the ascent of **Rondslott** (»Ronde Castle«), whose summit is at 2178m/7146ft, in less than five hours. The walk through the Rondane mountains that continues into the adjacent ►Dovrefjell to the north is very popular with Norwegians.

The entire region is dotted with a network of huts belonging to the Norwegian hiking association (DNT ► Practicalities: Hiking), so comfortable day walks on well signposted paths are possible.

The Rondane massif boasts numerous rivers and lakes that are ideal for paddling tours. A river tour on the **Atna** is a very special experience. The river flows through impressive natural landscapes and is also suitable for inexperienced paddlers, with only class one and two rapids. During a 2–3-day river tour, several sandbanks are passed that make for excellent camping. Embedded in the mountains of the Rondane range, the river winds its way between primary forests and a wild, completely isolated meadow landscape. A little excitement is provided by the rapids near Staumbu bridge.

Exploring by canoe

On the other hand, crossing the 9km/6mi-long **Atnasjø** requires strong paddling muscles, and beware the high waves in windy conditions! At its southern end the lake flows back into a river that runs alongside the road. Progress should be made carefully along the right bank from here and early preparations made for landing, as there is a life-threatening stretch full of boulders in the river after the bridge that **must be avoided by portage**. Once back in the water, it is not far to the **Skogli Camp**, where making land is made easier by means of a wooden jetty on the right river bank. Beyond this point, only **experienced paddlers** should continue along the Atna, as the rapids ahead are difficult to judge.

It is also possible to follow in Peer Gynt's footsteps through the Rondane National Park on well signposted paths, for example during a one-day hike from Høvringen to Peer Gynthytta. **Hiking maps** are available from the tourist information office at **Otta**. Høvringen is reached by continuing to follow the E 6 in the direction of Dombås. A steep secondary road to **Høvringen** turns off to the right shortly after Laurgård, from where the very pleasant three-hour walk to the **Peer Gynt hut** begins.

Hiking in Peer Gynt's world

The famous Laurgårdseter Fjellstue lies on the way to the Peer Gynt hut. This alpine cabin is where writer and winner of the Nobel Prize in Literature Sigrid Undset gathered material for her novel *Kristin Lavransdatter* (► Jørundgård p.200; guided walking tours from Otta). The waterfalls, lakes and moraine landscape combine to make this walk a first-rate experience of Norwegian nature. A hanging bridge leads over the Imbertglupen ravine. The high path to Høvringen between the east and west summits of the Skorutberget requires sure-footedness for the section from the southern slope of Baksidevassberget as far as the Rondane Haukeliseter Fjellhotell and is definitely not recommended for vertigo-sufferers.

Laurgårdseter Fjellstue

It is also possible to do the route in the **opposite direction** by catching a **morning bus** at 9am from Otta to ► Haukeliseter, and walking to the Peer Gynt hut from there. The route onwards to the Smukksjøseter Fjellstue takes around one hour, and a bus returns to Otta via Høvringen. Those who want to extend the experience can spend the night at the Smukksjøter Fjellstue and hike to Høvringen the next day.

Take the bus

✳ Hallingdal

Region: South Norway

The valley of Hallingdal is lined with tourist resorts like pearls on a string. During summer it is possible to do first-class walking tours here, as well as climbing and cycling, and to get refreshment at the many alpine huts. During winter, Geilo and Hemsedal are considered to be world-class ski resorts.

The richly forested, broad Hallingdal valley spreads from the northern end of Lake Krøderen in a northwesterly direction to ►Hardangervidda, along the gently flowing waters of the Hallingdalselv. Only the adjacent heights are barren, with smoothly weathered, lone boulders. The valley is an ancient settlement area, but in recent centuries many left the area. Only with the completion of the mountain railway at the beginning of the 20th century and the subsequent emergence of tourism did people return to Hallingdal.

Adventure Tour through Hallingdal

Gulsvik
In Gulsvik, the »Gateway to Hallingdal« at the northern tip of Lake Krøderen, the R 7 passes through the Hallingporten tunnel, the actual entrance into the valley. To the right is the Hallingdalselv river. Continuing on, there are several camp sites and accommodation options (at Stavn, at an island in the river at Kolsrud, at Bromma and at Roløkken).

Nesbyen
After 33km/21mi, the settlement of Nesbyen is reached, located on the broad cone of a hill. A good idea of local Hallingdal nature and culture is provided by the **Hallingdal Folkemuseum**. Most of the 25 farmhouses display beautiful examples of rose painting, an art with a long tradition in this valley. Traditional arts and crafts are demonstrated on Wednesdays (opening times: May–Sept 10am–5pm). Excursions to beautifully located alpine dairies (be aware of the charges for accommodation and road tolls) can be made from Nesbyen, as well as trips onto the ►Hardangervidda mountain plateau. 650 million years ago a meteorite hit an area close to Nesbyn.
Gardnos Meteorite Park arranges tours of the 5 sq km/2 sq mi crater created by the impact (June–9 Sept daily 10am–5pm, www.gardnos. no).

Gol
With more than 200km/125mi of maintained tracks and seven ski lifts, including the chairlift at an altitude of 1600m/5249ft that climbs 450m/1476ft, Gol is especially popular as a winter sports resort. The view from the mountain top is beautiful.

▶ VISITING HALLINGDAL

INFORMATION

Geilo Turistinfo Reiselivssenteret
Postboks 68 (information in the shopping centre)
3581 Geilo
Tel. 32 09 59 00, fax 32 09 59 01
www.geilo.no

Gol Turistkontor
Skysstasjonen, Sentrumsv. 93
3550 Gol
Tel. 32 02 97 00, fax 32 02 97 01
www.golinfo.no

Hemsedal Turistkontor
Postboks 3 (Info in the Hemsedal Center)
3561 Hemsedal
Tel. 32 05 50 30, fax 32 05 50 31
hemsedal@hemsedal.net
www.hemsedal.com

WHERE TO EAT AND STAY

▶ **Expensive**

Dr. Holms Hotel
Geilo, Timrehaugveien 2
Tel. 32 09 57 00, fax 32 09 16 20
www.drholms.com

This is one of the best hotels in all of Scandinavia. Tastefully decorated dining rooms, wine from the house cellar, a delicious cold buffet in the summer, a dance floor and numerous fishing and sporting options ensure that stays here are an absolute pleasure.

WHERE TO STAY

▶ **Mid-range**

Norlandia Skogstad Hotell
Hemsedal
Tel. 32 06 03 33, fax 32 06 05 71
83 rooms, www.norlandia.no
This very pleasant hotel is located in the centre of the mountain village of Hemsedal, and is very popular with alpine skiers. It has a swimming pool and several restaurants and bars.

Ustedalen Hotel
Geilo
Tel. 32 09 01 11, fax 32 09 18 20
85 rooms, www.ustedalen.no
This comfortable, recently renovated hotel is just 700m/770yd from the town centre and offers wonderful views over the Ustedalsfjord. Good prices are offered for surplus rooms.

SPORT

Hiking, fishing and outdoor activities
A great deal of outdoor action is on offer in Hallingdal alongside the traditional classics of hiking and fishing: canoeing and elk tours are two examples. Tour companies can be contacted through the tourist information office.

Ski hang-gliding
Ski hang-gliding enthusiasts consider Hardangervidda to be the best place in the world for this new sport. The constant wind ensures that even tours from hut to hut are possible. Courses costing around 100 euros can be booked through the tourist information office in Geilo (www.geilo.no).

Wolves still range in the Langedrag Nature Park, though in enclosures.

✱

Side trip into Hemsedal

About 2km/1mi beyond Gol, the Heslabru leads from the Hallingdal valley past the Hemsila waterfall, which flows into the Hallingdalselv river. The RV 52 turns off right towards Hemsedal. Initially, this road passes the new church at Gol (the old stave church was moved to the Ethnological Museum in Oslo) and then the valley of Hemsedal gradually opens up at **Robru**. The journey continues to Ulsåk, passing the **Hjelmen bru** power station to the left. There are views of Veslehorn (1300m/4265ft high) on whose eastern flank the Hydnefoss waterfall cascades down from a height of 140m/459ft. Behind Veslehorn rises the 1478m/4849ft-high Storhorn.

From **Ulsåk**, a high alpine road turns off to the right to **Lykkja** (toll payable). It passes Skogshorn (1728m/5669ft) whose summit can be reached in two to three hours on foot. From Lykkja, it is either possible to continue on to Røn (48km/30mi) and Fagernes, or to head south to Fjellheim and Gol. From Ulsåk it is another 3km/2mi to the winter sports resort of **Hemsedal** (609m/1998ft), one of Scandinavia's largest alpine centres that can certainly compete with the European Alps. The stable winter climate guarantees snow from November to the beginning of May and the large choice of runs – including 13 green, 8 blue, 10 red and 8 black

! *Baedeker* TIP

Howling with wolves

Langedrag Nature Park is located along the elongated Runhovdfjord between Hallingdal and Uvdal. Wolves, lynx, Artic foxes and reindeer run wild in these extensive grounds, which attract many visitors during summer. There are numerous activities laid on for children and nourishment is provided in the restaurant (tel. 32 74 25 50; daily 10am–6pm).

– enchants good skiers. During the summer visitors can don wetsuits, diving masks, and snorkel and, from June to mid-October, embark on a trout safari in the Hemsil river.

The section of road from Hemsedal down to Borlaug, where the road rejoins the E 16, **is among Norway's most beautiful high mountain routes**. There are hardly any people in this barren and wildly romantic landscape dotted with several small lakes.

Torpo

From Gol onwards, the journey continues through the Hallingdal valley in a southwesterly direction, the R 7 road mostly following the wild Hallingdalsev and its many waterfalls. At Torpo, after 13km/8mi, stands the **stave church**, with beautiful dragon ornamentation on the doorways and a well preserved painted ceiling from the 13th century. The church looks more like a tower than anything, because only the central nave with its high pillars and boxed capitals and painted masks survives.

Ål

The tourist resort of Ål also has a small **village museum** with rose paintings. Art lovers should not pass up the opportunity to visit the Rolf Nesch Museum. Fleeing the Nazis, **Rolf Nesch** (1893–1975) came from Germany to Norway in 1933 and lived in Ål until 1951. The museum displays drawings, oil paintings and sculptures by the internationally acclaimed artist (opening times: Mon–Fri noon–7pm, ⊙ Sat till 3pm).

Beyond Ål the Hallingsdalselv opens into the Satrandefjord and the road follows the northern bank. A power station is located at the end of the fjord at Kleivi.

Aurland Road

From Hagafoss, it is possible to take in the impressive landscape along the **Aurlandsvei** (RV 50) to the Aurlandsfjord, 97km/61mi away. Thanks to numerous tunnels, this road is also passable during winter. After a short distance, the **13th century stave church of Hol** is reached, which however has been extensively modernized.

Geilo

Lillehammer excepted, Geilo (pronounced »Yeilo«) is entitled to call itself Norway's most famous winter sports resort. It sits at around 800m/2624ft in a broad valley and also offers excellent conditions for hikers, cyclists and horse-riders during summer, with many sign-posted footpaths and hiking huts. Fishing, canoeing and white water rafting are also possible.

Those who want a magnificent view without the exertion can take the chairlift up to the 1056m/3465ft-high **Geilohøgda**. From there, it is also possible to follow a footpath to Geilo's »local« mountain, **Hallingskarv** (1933m/6342ft), which even in summer is partly covered in snow. An easier ascent is possible from Ustaoset, on the northern bank of Lake Ustevatn (11km/7mi beyond Geilo), though it takes six to eight hours. To the south rises Ustetind at 1376m/4515ft, whose ascent takes 3–4hrs.

★ Hamar

C 8

Region: South Norway   **Population:** 27,000

Hamar is beautifully located on the eastern shore of Lake Mjøsa, which flows into the Furnesfjord here. The most interesting sights are the »Vikingskipet« events hall, built on the occasion of the 1994 Olympic Games, as well as the Open-air Hedmark Museum and Norway's largest railway museum.

Important industrial town

The town, originally founded as a bishopric in 1152, was an important trading centre during the Middle Ages. The cathedral was destroyed during the Danish-Swedish War in 1567 and only steam shipping on Lake Mjøsa in the 19th century, as well as the opening of the railway line in 1880, brought new impetus. The skyline of this important industrial and commercial town is not very attractive, however. Hamar was chosen, along with Lillehammer and Gjøvik, to host competitions in various sports disciplines during the 1994 Winter Olympics.

What to See in Hamar

★ Open-air museum

The impressive ruins of the 12th century cathedral that lie next to the remains of a Romanesque episcopal castle can be viewed on the grounds of the Hedmark Museum on the southwestern edge of town, which also includes 50 buildings from the Hedmark region, the oldest dating from 1583. The renowned Norwegian architect Sverre Fehn designed a museum for the castle restored in 1979. Clev-

▶ VISITING HAMAR

INFORMATION

Hamar Turistinformasjon
Vikingskipet
2317 Hamar
Tel. 62 51 02 03
Fax 62 51 02 51
www.inlandshovedstaden.no

WHERE TO EAT

▶ **Inexpensive**
Elgstua
Elverum, Trondheimsveien 9
(junction of the RV 3 and RV 25)
Tel. 62 41 01 22
Norwegians travelling in the region are

willing to make a detour to savour the delicious elk dishes in this small tavern. Self-service.

WHERE TO STAY

▶ **Budget**
Eidet Gård
Engerdal
Tel. 62 45 69 43
Fax 62 45 69 11
A farm dating from 1699, located 27km/17mi north of Trysil. Margit and Ingjald Eidet make sure guests feel at home in their two comfortable apartments that contain a total of 15 beds.

er wood constructions, protective glass roofs, ramps, walkways and steps combine to create an atmospheric setting for the museum displays. One section of the building contains the folklore museum (opening times: mid-May–mid-Sept daily 10am–4pm, mid-June–mid-Aug till 6pm).

A modern sporting city, Hamar's emblem is the Olympic Hall that is also known as the »Vikingskipet« (Viking Ship) due to its striking roof construction (96m/315ft x 110m/361ft), designed by the architectural firm of Biong & Biong/Niels Torp A.S. The roof was designed to look as if it was light and floating, so the roof area was sectioned with glass slits. Among the city's other sporting venues, the Northern Light Hall on Knut Alysons gate is notable for being one of the largest wooden buildings in the world.

Olympic Hall

Hamar deals only in superlatives when it comes to railways: the town is home to Norway's oldest railway station, Scandinavia's largest and oldest railway museum (Jernbanemuseet), as well as Norway's largest steam engine, the Dovregubben. With 2200 horsepower, it once managed the ascent onto Dovrefjell at a speed of 70kmh/44mph.

Railway Museum

Not a UFO, but the Olympic Hall at Hamar

Norway's largest railway museum is in Hamar.

The museum collection includes numerous engines, sumptuous saloon coaches and historic railway fittings. During summer, the Tertitten narrow gauge museum train travels the 2km/1mi distance to Killingmo (opening times: see Hedmark Museum).

Emigration Museum

The history of Norwegian emigration to America is documented in the Utvandrermuseet by the pier for the historic Skibladner steamboat that crosses Lake Mjøsa.

Around Hamar

Elverum

Elverum (pop. 18,000) lies around 28km/18mi to the east of Hamar and is known as Norway's »forest capital« thanks to its 972 sq km/ 375 sq mi of forested area. An important road and railway junction, Elverum forms the southern gateway to Østerdalen. The Glomma river flows right through the middle of the town and is popular with fishermen for its abundance of fish; it is also surrounded by wonderful wilderness that offers good hunting opportunities. The open-air **Glomdalsmuseum** is especially interesting and worth visiting for its 89 old farmhouses from the Østerdal valley. A very lively impression of forest, hunting and fishing is presented in the **Norwegian Forest Museum**, named Norway's »Museum of the Year« in 2002. Among other things, it contains a collection of hunting weapons, particularly knives, as well as Norway's only fresh water aquarium, where the section entitled »From the Mountains to the Sea« contains around 40 species of freshwater fish from the highlands, lakes, and estuaries (opening times: July–Aug daily 10am–6pm, otherwise till 4pm).

Winter sports fans are recommended to make a detour into the Trysil-Femund-Engerdal region. Trysilfjell is **Norway's largest ski region** and offers all levels of difficulty on its 70km/44mi of pistes. It offers 24 lifts and 93km/58mi of cross country skiing routes, as well as several half pipes for snowboarders. Night skiing is ensured by illuminated runs. During summer and autumn, it is also possible to go rafting, riverboat fishing and even panning for gold.

Trysilfjell

★ Hammerfest

N 20

Region: North Norway   **Population:** 9000

The skyline of Hammerfest is characterized by bijou houses, its port is ice free all year round and in the immediate vicinity is the world's northernmost forest. Yet many tourists pass up visiting the friendly town, seeing it merely as a stop-over on the way to Nordkapp.

Located on the west side of the island of Kvaløy, Hammerfest has always been a **significant commercial and fishing settlement** due to its protected ice-free port. It received its municipal charter in 1789 and Hammerfest continues to be the base for fishing in the North Polar Sea. Its status as the world's most northerly town has been challenged lately, however, as Honningsvåg, further to the north, has recently been granted its municipal charter. Hammerfest was bombed by the British in 1809, destroyed by fire in 1890, and razed

Home of the polar fishermen

Hammerfest Map

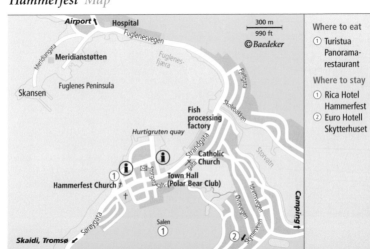

Airport   Hospital
Fuglenesvegen
Meridianstøtten   Fuglenes-fjæra
Skansen   Fuglenes Peninsula
300 m
990 ft
© Baedeker

Fish processing factory
Hurtigruten quay
Catholic Church
Town Hall (Polar Bear Club)
Hammerfest Church
①
Salen ①
②
Camping
Skaidi, Tromsø

Where to eat
① Turistua Panorama-restaurant

Where to stay
① Rica Hotel Hammerfest
② Euro Hotell Skytterhuset

to the ground after a forced evacuation by the Germans in 1944. Only the cemetery chapel remained standing. The inhabitants rebuilt their town from the ashes on the narrow strip of land between Salen, a ridge of hills on the south side of the town, and the sea, and the **colourful façades of the houses** really catch the eye. In recent times, the town has profited from the oil boom and with approx. 200,000 visitors to Nordkapp passing through each year, **tourism traffic** has now become so heavy during the summer months that the little town centre can hardly cope.

What to See in Hammerfest

Society of Polar Bears ⊙

Directly next to the jetty used by the ferries it is possible to become a member of the »Royal and Ancient Society of Polar Bears« (opening times: summer 9am–5pm, winter till 3pm, Havnegata 3, www.isbjornklubben.no). A small museum shows Arctic exhibits, including a 3m/10ft-long polar bear pelt, which recall the time when the town was the metropolis of the North Polar Sea and a centre of whaling. A statue of the composer **Ole Olsen** (1850–1927), who was born here, can be seen on the market square. To the north, the pier for the Hurtigruten ships is reached via the Storgata quarter. A footpath leads up onto the Varden hill behind the town hall, a vantage point from which the entire town can be viewed.

Stop-over on the way to Nordkapp: Hammerfest

▶ VISITING HAMMERFEST

INFORMATION

Hammerfest Turist AS
Rådhusplassen
9615 Hammerfest
Tel. 78 41 21 85
Fax 78 41 19 00
www.hammerfest-turist.no

WHERE TO EAT

▶ Moderate
① **Turistua Panoramarestaurant**
Am Berg Varden
Tel. 78 41 46 11
The meals are simple and basic, but people come here for the view onto town and the surrounding country-side.

WHERE TO STAY

▶ Mid-range
① **Rica Hotel Hammerfest**
Sørøygt. 15
Tel. 78 41 13 33
Fax 78 41 13 11
86 rooms, www.rica.no
The exterior of this hotel should not put you off. Inside it is modern and the décor is appealing, with an atrium that reaches over two floors. There is a nice view from the hotel and in the new restaurant it is possible to enjoy the midnight sun through the large panoramic windows.

② **Euro Hotel Skytterhuset**
Skytterveien 24
Tel. 78 41 15 11
Fax 78 41 19 26
75 rooms, www.skytterhuset.no
The hotel is open all year, surrounded by a large garden, and located near the stadium. Its name comes from the shooting club that erected the main building in 1952. Later it was used as accommodation for the 100 female workers of the Findus fish factory.

Today, after complete renovation, it is one of the best value for money hotels in Hammerfest, offering rooms of a good standard.

GETTING THERE

Hammerfest can easily be reached by air via Tromsø and Oslo, as well as by bus from Oslo via Sweden. The ships of the Hurtigruten line weigh anchor here daily, and faster boats also connect the town with Tromsø, as well as Honningsvåg on Magerøya island, a stop-off on the route for Nordkapp.

EXCURSIONS TO NORDKAPP

The postal ships of the Hurtigurte line depart from Hammerfest daily at 7.45am and reach Honningsvåg at around 12.45pm. From there the journey to Nordkapp is by bus (one hour). After a short stay, the return journey is to Honningsvåg, where the evening bus for Hammerfest awaits. The Hurtigruten ship heading south

does not set off from Honningsvåg before 6.45am in the morning, but when the light conditions are good an opportunity to experience the mid-night sun is an excellent reason to stay awake all night.

MIDNIGHT SUN

The midnight sun shines from 17 May to 28 July.

Hammerfest church To the west of the market, the architecture of Hammerfest church (1961) on Kirkegata is worth taking a look at. The church is reminiscent of the Arctic Cathedral of Tromsø. The missing altar was replaced by a large section of painted glass by Jardar Lunde (1962), inserted into the tent-shaped gable. There are church concerts here every night during summer. Next door stands the wooden chapel that survived the last war.

Following Strandgata to the northeast from the market square, pass the **Catholic church** (1958) that was almost entirely built by volunteers. The cross was carved by Georg Wimmer, who remained imprisoned in Narvik after the war.

✳ Meridianstøtten The road then follows the bay around to the Fuglenes spit and the »Meridianstøtten«: a bronze atlas on a granite pillar. The monument is intended to recall the joint survey of the earth's shape and form undertaken by Norwegians, Swedes and Russians between 1816 and 1852. Its southern counterpart was a point near Ismail at the mouth of the Danube, 2872km/1795mi away. The concrete lump next to the monument dates from 1929, and indicates a subsequent measurement, which was at variance to the first by only slightly. There is a nice view of town from here. At the end of the Fuglenes peninsular stand the fortifications known as the **Skansen**, which were built in 1810 during the Napoleonic Wars.

Around Hammerfest

Salen A footpath (20mins) runs from the market square up Salen (»Saddle«; 86m/282ft), a ridge of hills at the southern end of the town. Salen can also be reached via a road that passes the small lake of Storvatn to the east of town.

An extensive view over the open sea is offered from the western slopes (stone indicator). At the southern edge of town to the left lies the Jansvatn open-air swimming pool, and the **world's northernmost forest** is a little further on. Early risers who have watched the Hurtigruten ship come in can often see **reindeer** heading towards town at the foot of Salen.

Skaidi The road leads onwards to Skaidi. Take a look at Tyven (419m/1374ft; ascent from Hammerfest takes 1.5hrs) towering up to the left. From its summit, the island and many small lakes to the east can be seen, while to the south and west the partly snow and ice-bound mountains can be seen. To the north the view is onto the endless Polar Sea.

✳ Hardangerfjord

B 2 - C 2/3

Region: West Norway

There is still snow on the mountain peaks in May when 500,000 fruit trees begin to blossom and the banks of the Hardangerfjord are smothered in a sea of delicate colours and scents. Norway's second largest fjord penetrates into the interior via dozens of inlets and twists and turns, a wealth of spectacular landscapes along its banks.

Due to the mild climate influenced by the warm Gulf Stream along the west coast, sweet plums, juicy apples and morello cherries ripen in the wind-protected valleys during the short summer season with its long and light nights. The fruit is sold all along the road. **Over one fifth of the country's fruit trees** thrive here. It was probably Cistercian monks who first introduced fruit farming to Hardangerfjord at the beginning of the 13th century, but it was the photographer **Knud Knudsen** (► Famous People), born in Odda in 1832, who really made decisive progress in fruit growing. Even the German Emperor Wilhelm II regularly stopped by with samples from the imperial fruit orchards for Knudsen's trees on the Hardangerfjord.

Norway's garden paradise

Thanks to Knud Knudsen, thousands of fruit trees blossom by the Hardangerfjord.

▶ VISITING HARDANGERFJORD

INFORMATION

Destination Hardanger Fjord
Sandvenvegen
5600 Norheimsund
Tel. 56 55 38 70
Fax 56 55 38 71
www.hardangerfjord.com

Turistkontor Odda
Postboks 114
(office in Odda town centre)
5751 Odda
Tel. 53 65 40 05
Fax 53 65 40 01
www.visitodda.com

Eidfjord
Eidfjord Reiselivslag
Postboks 132
5786 Eidfjord
Tel. 53 67 34 00
Fax 53 67 34 01
www.eidfjordinfo.com

WHERE TO STAY

▶ Mid-range
Rica Brakanes Hotel
Ulvik i Hardanger
Tel. 56 52 61 05
Fax 56 52 64 10
143 rooms, www.brakanes-hotel.no
This outstanding hotel has been popular with tourists for decades. The
hotel also has boat jetties and a bathing
beach.

Sauda Fjord Hotel
Saudasjøen
Tel. 52 78 12 11
Fax 52 78 15 58
59 beds, www.saudafjordhotel.no
This hotel in a former mansion has
been restored with a loving eye for
detail and lies in the wildly romantic
Saudafjord region (Ryfylke, Røldal).
The fjord's good fish stocks have

long made it popular with passionate
and wealthy salmon fishing enthusiasts.

Strandebarm Fjord Hotel
near Norheimsund
Tel. 56 55 91 50
Fax 56 55 93 05
26 rooms, www.eurohotels.no/stran-
debarm
Small, cosy hotel with friendly service,
far from any hustle and bustle and
with many regular guests who enjoy
the comforts offered here. Wonderful
location on the Hardangerfjord, with
views onto the mountains and private
bathing beach.

Baedeker recommendation

Utne Hotel
Utne
Tel. 53 66 10 88
There was already an inn here in 1722 and
the old furniture and antiques in the guest
room alone make a visit worthwhile. The
good home-cooking is lovingly prepared and
meals are served at one long table so guests
may get to know each other better. There are
no radios or TVs in the rooms, adding to the
atmosphere of the past created by the décor.

▶ Budget
Vik Pensjonat
Eidfjord town centre
Tel. 53 66 51 62
Fax 53 66 51 51
www.vikpensjonat.com
Comfortable cabins and rooms in the
centre of Eidfjord for 4–6 people. The
café serves breakfast, lunch and dinner, and there is pleasant seating
outside in good weather.

Several attractive villages are located on the banks of the main fjord and along its side arms, but there is also a hydro-electric power station and significant industrial settlements, too. East of Eidfjord in the interior of the fjord, ► Hardangervidda, Europe's largest mountain plateau begins, which offers an unforgettable experience in good weather and clear visibility.

What to See around the Hardangerfjord

The starting point is the attractive tourist resort of ► Voss, which is on the Bergen railway route (► Baedeker Special p.407). Just a few miles from Voss the RV 13 starts to wind its way through a varied landscape, looping around breathtaking mountain scenery and traversing narrow valleys with wild waterfalls hemmed in by high cliffs. Once past the highest point of the route at 262m/860ft, the **Skjerve-foss** waterfall can be seen crashing down from the heights.

From Voss to Bergen

Shortly before Granvin church (1720), which contains what are probably Norway's oldest bells, the RV 572 turns off towards the Osafjord, an arm of the Hardangerfjord where the idyllic tourist resort of Ulvikis located. The impressive panoramic road – whose several narrow sections will present a challenge to drivers of mobile homes – winds past green meadows, small farms and orchards before reaching Ulvik. The views of the resort and the up to 1600m/5250ft-high mountains surrounding the fjord are superb. Ulvik is also home to Norway's oldest state school for fruit-growing, founded in 1765 by **Kristofer Sjursen Hjeltnes** who was also the first to cultivate potatoes in Norway. The small, white, wooden church (1858) contains a pretty altar panel dating from 1630 and beautiful leaf motifs painted by local artist Lars Osa (1860–1958). A real experience is a tour over the fjord and the Hardangerjøkulen glacier by waterplane.

✶ ✶
Ulvik

The RV 7 turns off into the 7511m/24643ft long Vallavik tunnel heading for the **Bruravik** ferry port at Granvin, at the northern tip of the Granvinfjord. The port can also be reached from Ulvik and the idyllic Osafjord. The ferry to **Brimnes** (10mins) leads to the other side of the fjord heading east. Before the tunnel was built, it was often necessary to wait several hours in **Kvanndal** (14km/9mi south of Granvin), for the 50-minute ferry journey to Kinsarvik. In fact, this ferry trip is still worth a detour, especially for those who want to visit Utne (20mins, see below).

Ferry ports

A **smelting works** for ferrosilicium and ferrochrome can be seen on the western side of the Hardangerfjord at Ålvik. Above the works the system of pipes belonging to the power station that uses the 880m/2888ft-high Bjølvefoss waterfall is visible. The warmed water is then also used in the fjord for **salmon farming**, which is an important economic sector in the Hardanger region.

Ålvik

Hardanger Akvasenter

At Fykesund it is possible to have a peek behind the scenes at a typical Norwegian fish farm – from the rearing of the young fish to the production of the seafood speciality ready for the table. An expert takes visitors out on the fjord to the salmon farm, and an underwater camera provides live pictures of the life of the salmon (Ligavegen 206, Strandebarm; opening times: only in summer Tue–Sun 11am–6pm, www.akvasenter.no).

After 12km/8mi, the **Fyksesund bru** comes into view, a narrow suspension bridge, built in 1939, crossing the mouth of Fyksesund. To the east of the bridge the road is narrow and has limited visibility, which often leads to traffic jams.

Passing strawberry fields and fruit plantations, the RV 7 reaches the village of **Øystese**, which is beautifully located on the bay of the same name. Opposite the church, there is a **museum** containing the 150 works by the sculptor **Ingebrigt Vik** (1867–1927), whose most famous piece is a statue of Edvard Grieg in Bergen.

✶ Norheimsund

An ideal place for an interim stop is Norheimsund (pop.1500), a picturesque holiday resort with a pretty little harbour and the renowned Sandven Hotel, a Swiss style white painted wooden palais dating from 1857. In clear weather, it is possible to spot the ice fields of the Folgefonna glacier on the other side of the fjord. A tunnel over 11km/7mi-long was built underneath the glacier in June 2001, and connects Odda on the Sørfjord with Rosendal (see below). In Norheimsund it is possible to watch tradesmen at their traditional work at the **museum dockyard**. A short tour on the fjord is also heartily recommended.

✶ Steinsdalsfoss

The RV 7 now leaves the fjord, heading west towards Bergen (85km/53mi). After 2km/1mi, the wild Steinsdalsfossen waterfall formed by the Fosselva river comes into view to the right, in the midst of lovely countryside. During the summer months tourists virtually step on each other's toes on their way to the waterfall. A curious fact: it is possible to walk behind the thundering 30m/98ft wall of water without getting wet.

Tokagjelet

The road now inclines upwards, winding along an astounding 3km/2mi stretch through the impressive Tokagjelet gorge. While drivers must enter four cleverly hewn tunnels cut into the rock, cyclists and pedestrians have to brave the old path on the outside of the tunnels, directly above the abyss. The road then leads onwards to the Veafjord where it joins the E 16 to Bergen, passing the lively recreational region of **Kvamskogen** and its numerous holiday cabins, going along the Samnangerfjord, and crossing the ski and hiking region of Gullbotn.

Alternative routes to Bergen

It is possible to follow the Hardangerfjord from Norheimsund to Mundheim on the RV 49 and then drive to Bergen via Eikelandsosen

Neither ocean nor lake, but the Hardangerfjord that widens substantially at Strandebarm

and Tysse (detour of 56km/35mi). Alternatively, there is a route from Eikelandsosen to Fusa, on to Hattvik by ferry (20mins) and via Osøyro and Søfteland to Bergen – a detour of 20km/13mi.

Vikøy

The RV 49 winds its way along the west bank of the fjord from Norheimsund to the little church village of Vikøy, where Norway's well-known painter Adolph Tidemand (1814–76) painted many of his pictures. Several miles beyond Vikøy, at the foot of the Salthammaren cliff in the village of Vangdal, there is 3500-year old rock art to be found, largely with images of ships. High up the hill there are also 5000-year old images of herds of animals, especially elk and deer. These, however, are hard to reach.

Summer skiing

13km/8mi south of Norheimsund, in the village of Tørvikbygd, the **car ferry to Jondal** sets out on its 20-minute journey. From there, ski enthusiasts can reach the popular **Folgefonn summer ski resort** (1200m/3937ft) located at the northern end of the Folgefonn glacier which, at 34km/21mi long and up to 16km/10mi wide, is Norway's third largest. Skis can be used here from June to October, either to head downhill alongside **Norway's longest glacier lift** (1100m/1203yd) or to go cross country skiing and glacier hiking on routes of varying degrees of difficulty. The 36km/22mi-long stretch between Jondal and Utne is extremely narrow but a very rewarding way to experience nature in all its glory.

From Strandebarm to Holdhus

Once there was a flourishing boat-building industry in the church village of Strandebarm (on the RV 49 south of Nordheimsund) on the Strandebarm bay. Few now build the traditional wooden boats

The Rosendal barony is a popular excursion destination thanks to its rose garden and its fine interiors.

known as the »Strandebarmer«, though the beautiful bathing beach remains. Mundheim is reached 15km/9mi after Oma, where aluminium catamarans are built for customers from around the world. From there the RV 48 can be followed north in the direction of Holdhus and Eiklandsosen (17km/11mi). The interior of the **wooden church at Holdhus** is decorated with wonderful vines and friezes. The pulpit dates from 1570 and is possibly the oldest west Norwegian ulpit from the time of the Reformation. Shortly outside **Eiklandsosen**, the Koldalsfossen waterfall crashes down into the depths.

★ ★
Rosendal Barony

The Hardangerfjord intersects the RV 48 at its southern end and at the southern continuation of the road lies the Rosendal Barony. It can either be reached from the north via the 11km/7mi-long Folgefonn tunnel, or by means of the ferry from Gjermundshavn (25mins, 13km/8mi south of Mundheim) to Løfallstrand; or from the south via the E 134 and Skånevik. Karen Mowat, one of Norway's wealthiest heiresses, and the poor Danish aristocrat Ludvig Rosenkrantz were given the Hattenberg estate in Rosendal as a wedding gift in 1658. Rosenkrantz had the estate remodelled into a small Nordic Renaissance-style palace by 1665, and King Christian V elevated it to a barony 13 years later. Today it is one of the region's most visited sights. Since the 19th century, it has also been surrounded by a **picturesque, landscaped park** which provides wonderful views onto the

Hardangerfjord and its mountain backdrop with several waterfalls. The **rose garden** is especially worth seeing. The palace is now a **museum** offering guided tours and also serves as a venue for concerts played on its Pleyel grand piano dating from 1860, theatrical performances in the courtyard and art exhibitions in the wine cellar ⊙ (opening times: July–mid-August daily 10am–6pm, May–mid-Sept till 3pm).

Not far from here is one of Norway's oldest medieval stone churches, **Kvinnherad church** dating from 1255, which has Romanesque and Gothic style elements. For a long period it was the private property and burial ground of the barony.

What to See around the Sørfjord and the Eidsfjord

Small fjord villages dot the shores of the northern end of the narrow, 45km/28mi-long Sørfjord – the longest branch of the Hardangerfjord. Pleasant banks give way to more dramatic high mountains and the mighty Folgefonn glacier lies above the western shore, whereas the steep slopes of the ►Hardangervidda mountains on the eastern side make excellent hiking country. **Sørfjord**

The industrial town of Odda, a place of great economic significance **Odda** for Norway in the past century, lies at the southern end of the fjord surrounded by high mountains. Workers from all over Scandinavia flocked here at the beginning of the 20th century, when several smelting works, industrial outfits and the Tyssedal hydro-electric power station opened in the interior of the fjord. Daily life during those times is recalled in three worker's apartments on Folgefonngata that have been turned into a **museum**.

The Tyssedal hydro-electric power station stands majestically to the **Tyssedal** north of Odda, right on the Sørfjord. It is possible to relive the days between 1906 and 1918 when the great turbines here produced energy for the industrial plants in Odda and Tyssedal. The high pillars of the turbine hall, which was one of the first high pressure plants in Europe, are somewhat reminiscent of a cathedral. Meanwhile, the former administrative building in Tyssedal today houses the **Norwegian Hydro-power and Industry Museum**, which recounts the history of the two industrial settlements and the lives of the workers who once lived here (opening times: June–Aug daily 10am–5pm, other- ⊙ wise Tue–Fri 10am–3pm). The 33m/108ft-high and 529m/1735ft-long **Ringedal Dam**, a masterpiece built by hand out of granite between 1910 and 1918, lies above Tyssedal, in the barren landscape of the Hardangervidda mountain plateau near Skjeggedal.

To the south of Odda, it is worth making a detour to the formerly **Side trip to** important industrial town of Sauda. Just a short distance after leav- **Sauda** ing Odda, the **Låtefoss** waterfall appears to the left, its mass of water tumbles down a 400m/1312ft-long series of steps descending from the Hardangervidda mountains. The final 165m/541ft section is especially spectacular and covers the road in a **haze of spray**. Crossing the barren Røldalsfjell and passing through the Ekkjeskaret ravine (closed in winter), the RV 520 finally reaches its highest point at 900m/2952ft. Driving along the Eld ravine, there is then a wonderful view of the imposing mountain landscape before reaching Sauda, where **Europe's largest ferrous alloy works** (Eramet Norway) is located (tours July–mid-Aug, weekdays at noon, reservations at the tourist office; tel: 52 78 39 88). From July to mid-August daily at 2pm, it is possible to take a two-hour tour of the nearby **zinc mine**. A visit to the settlement built for the miners at Åbøbyen and the industrial workers museum housed in two restored apartments dating from 1920 and 1960 provide a fascinating insight into the workers' lives.

»Agatunet«

Leaving Odda, the narrow RV 550 winds its way along the west bank of the Sørfjord, beginning underneath the snow fields of the Folgefonn and continuing between numerous fruit orchards to Aga (28km/18mi) and »Agatunet«, a really beautiful hamlet of around 30 to 40 buildings among narrow lanes, all listed buildings under a preservation order, and complete with a medieval smoke house, the Lagmannstova (»judge's chamber«). The oldest letter held at the University of Bergen's library is from Aga and dated 1293, proving that people were already living here at the end of the 13th century (tours during summer daily 10am–4pm).

✳
Utne

About 17km/11mi further to the north, on the west side of the mouth of the Sørfjord, lies one of this region's most romantic fjord villages: Utne is especially worth visiting for its **view over the Hardangerfjord**. Those arriving by ferry, either from Kvanndal or Kinsarvik, can spot the small church from 1895 and an English-style little wooden palace painted white (the Utne Hotel) from a good way off.

The **Hardanger Folkemuseum** is not far from the pier, whose oldest building dates back to the 13th century. Old boat houses with boats and fishing equipment stand right by the water. Above the main building containing tools and folk arts and crafts, it is also possible to take a stroll in the orchard where historic fruit varieties are cultivated (opening times: July, Aug Mon–Fri 10am–6pm, Sat & Sun from noon, otherwise 10am–3pm).

Lofthus

After leaving Tyssedal and Odda, the RV 13 winds its way along the eastern bank of the Sørfjord, through orchards and blossoming

The Låtefoss foams madly as it descends from Hardangervidda and →
cascades down a 400m/1312ft-long series of steps into the Hardangerfjord.

meadows, until it reaches the pretty tourist resort of Lofthus 30km/ 19mi away. South of the settlement stands the **stone church of Ullensvang**, which dates from the 13th century and contains a medieval font and bells. New strains of fruit and berries are constantly being cultivated at the national experimental orchards here and, in Ullensvang alone, 80% of the country's sweet cherries are harvested. The largest farm in the Hardanger region is the Opedal estate, where the monks from the Lyse monastery at Bergen maintained a chapel during the Middle Ages. They also cultivated a fertile orchard and built the **monks' steps** that lead up to the 900m/2953ft Hardangervidda highland plateau: a steep ascent that takes around three hours. At the top there is a unique view over the Hardangerfjord. The composer Edvard Grieg's (1843–1907) hut stands in the garden of the deeply traditional Ullensvang Hotel in Lofthus, a place to which he withdrew, in his early life especially, to compose on the shores of the Hardangerfjord.

! Baedeker TIP

Four in one

Four spectacular waterfalls can be passed during a hike through the Kinso valley, walking from Kinsarvik up to Hardangervidda. The valley is one of Norway's loveliest natural landscapes and offers many beautiful views onto the fjord. The spray from the waterfalls encourages an explosion of green vegetation along the path and the rocks are covered in a thick carpet of moss, while many trees sport long beards of moss and lichen.

Eidfjord
Beyond **Kinsarvik**, the centre of the parish of Ullensvang and home to the Brimnes ferry port (ferries to Utne 25mins; Kvanndal 50mins; Bruravik 10mins), sections of the road now follow directly along the bare rock along the steep banks of the Eidsfjord, the eastern branch of the Hardangerfjord, until reaching the small settlement of Eidfjord after around 40km/25mi.

Simadalen
North of Eidfjord, at the beginning of the Simadal, the Kjeåsen track leads through a 2km/1mi-long tunnel to reach the remote **Kjeåsen farmhouse**, from which there are wonderfully beautiful views onto the Hardangervidda summits as well as down onto the fjord. A more interesting alternative to the route through the tunnel is taking the old climbing track that ascends the almost vertical cliff face to reach Kjeåsen farm. In the old days, this was the only way up to the summer pastures that lie 600m/1967ft above the fjord. The ascent can be made in around 1.5hrs by those with a good level of fitness.

✳ Hardangervidda Natursenter
The Hardangervidda Nature Centre is a major attraction about 6km/ 4mi south of Eidfjord that presents the history, geology, flora, fauna and wonders of nature of the ►Hardangervidda mountains and fjord country in an impressive way with the help of dioramas, aquariums and films (opening times: April to Oct daily 10am–6pm, June to Aug 9am–8pm).

✶✶ Hardangervidda

Region: South Norway   **Height:** 1200–1600m/3937–5250ft

The Hardangervidda highland plateau is the largest in Europe – an austere, treeless expanse dotted with numerous lakes and broad areas of moorland. For an even more intense experience of the colours and shapes of this light-flooded country, the visitor should strike out on foot rather than touring by car on the RV 7.

 VISITING HARDANGERVIDDA

INFORMATION
Tourist offices at Odda, Eidfjord (see Hardangerfjord for both) and Geilo (see Hallingdal).

WHERE TO EAT
► Inexpensive
Finsehytta
Finse
Tel. 56 52 67 32
Fax 56 52 67 60
Close to Finse railway station, there are value for money meals offered at the comfortable mountain hut. Definitely try the »rømmegrøt«, a delicious porridge (open from beginning of July to mid-Sep and from approx. 20 Feb to approx. 20 May).

WHERE TO STAY
► Luxury
Finse 1222
Finse
Tel. 56 52 71 00, fax 56 52 71 10
44 rooms, www.finse1222.no
This alpine hotel is right next to Norway's highest railway station and therefore an ideal base for hiking and ski tours in the Hardangerjøkulen region. The only option is full board which is expensive, though guests do enjoy the excellent cuisine.

► Mid-range
Fossli Hotel
Vøringfoss
Tel. 53 66 57 77
Fax 53 66 50 34
30 rooms, www.fossli-hotel.com
The hotel offers great views onto the waterfall and the Måbø valley. The list of famous guests is long and includes Edvard Grieg, who took inspiration here.

► Budget
Halne Fjellstova
Tel. 53 66 57 12, fax 53 66 50 83
10 rooms, 9 huts, halnefj@online.no
The mountain lodge lies on the RV 7 in the barren Hardangervidda landscape 44km/28mi from Geilo; open from Easter to mid-Oct.

SPORT
Ski race
The »Skarve Nordic Ski Race« is held in April, a 36km/23mi-long race from Finse to Ustaoset (www.geiloil.no/skarverennet/pamelding).

Glacier tours
Glacier tours onto Hardangerjøkulen are offered out of Finse (information from the DNT, see p.92).

Not much distraction, but a lot of nature:
Hardangervidda is a place for contemplation.

In the land of wild reindeer 3400 sq km/1313 sq mi of Hardangervidda's 9000 sq km/3475 sq mi form Norway's largest national park, while additional areas are also officially protected. It is an impressive landscape characterized by large expanses of moorland, an enormous number of lakes, and rivers rich in fish, as well as the typical Norwegian fjell vegetation, such as mosses, lichen and dwarf birch. To the southwest, the Hardangervidda mountains present a different character. Here a rough alpine landscape predominates, where the highest peak in the region is **Sandfloeggi** at 1719m/5640ft. Reindeer graze on the bare mountain pastures; these are the largest **reindeer herds living in the wild** anywhere in Europe. This landscape above the tree line is rough and uncomfortable, yet also very impressive, so the Hardangervidda region is renowned for hiking, fishing and hunting and popular among skiers during winter.

Access The best access to the region is offered by the RV 7 from Geilo (► Hallingdal) to Eidfjord, which divides Hardangervidda from the area around Hardangerjøkulen, a snowfield covering 120 sq km/46 sq mi to the north at an elevation of 1862m/6109ft. The RV 7 climbs up from Haugastøl (990m/3248ft) to reach its highest point at the Dyranut turisthytte (1246m/4088ft), before descending into the Bjoreia valley.

✳ Rallarvegen The famous Rallarvegen construction and supply route for the Bergen railway line begins in Haugastøl, winding its way through the rugged mountain world of Hardangervidda – mostly above the tree line – all the way to Norway's highest railway station at Finse (1222m/4009ft), before descending down to the Flåmtal valley at sea

level. The 90km/56mi-long gravel road was built in the most mountainous section of the Bergen line at the end of the 19th century and
today makes for one of Europe's most beautiful cycle tracks. Accommodation options, such as DNT hiking huts ►Practicalities: Hiking)
can be found at Finse, Hallingskeid and Myrdal. The last 20km/13mi
stretch of the road from Myrdal down to Flåm (►Voss) is the most
adventurous.

A small toll road branches off to the Fossli Hotel about 20km/13mi
beyond Dyranut. It lies just a short distance from the main road
above the edge of the Måbødal, at a height of 729m/2392ft, and offers a beautiful view onto the Vøringfoss waterfall. The Bjoreia
waterfall cascades 182m/597ft in an unbroken vertical drop into the
narrow abyss below, from which a dense haze of water spray continuously rises to the upper rim, producing wonderful rainbow effects
that are especially beautiful in the afternoon sun. There are also magnificent views down into Måbødal and its almost vertical cliff faces
from the falls above, as well as from a viewing point directly on the
road. The Vøringfoss has lost much of its drama these days because
of the large amount of water siphoned off for energy production in
the nearby power station; the
construction of the tunnel didn't
help either. But the old railway
track has been converted into a
wonderful footpath that leads
downwards after the turning into the wild Måbødal valley. Passing the almost vertical cliffs in
five large loops, the route leads
down to Måbø (250m/820ft).
Cyclists are fortunate to be directed to the old track that has
also been turned into a wonderful footpath and it takes one

★ ★
Måbødal,
Vøringfoss

> ! *Baedeker* TIP
>
> **Travelling on the Troll Train**
> An attraction for children: from June to August, the
> Troll Train travels through the Måbødal valley
> between the Vøringfoss waterfall and the Måbø
> Gård Museum. Departures from Vøringfoss are
> every hour on the hour between 10am and 6pm;
> from the Måbø Gård Museum departures are at 30
> minutes past the hour from 10.30am onwards.

hour to get from the lower end of the old road up to the Vøringfoss.
The original track here consisted of 124 bends and 1300 steps, and
some remains of these can still be seen in the rock. To the west, the
Hardangervidda uplands descend steeply to the Sørfjord (►Hardan-
gerfjord), the RV 13 following along its east bank. To the south, the
picturesque ►Haukeli Road gets closest to this region.

Hiking in Hardangervidda

Since the footpaths mostly run at an elevation between 1200m/
3281ft and 1400m/4593ft and there are almost no differences in
height levels to overcome, this »moon landscape« is a paradise for
families hiking with younger children. Several of the roughly 35 huts
(usually overcrowded between mid-July and mid-August) are located

Suitable for
families too

just a few hours' walk from each other and connected by clearly sign-posted paths maintained by the Norwegian hiking association (DNT). For experienced hikers, meanwhile, the Hardangerjøkulen glacier (1876m/6155ft) is an absolute highlight.

Always pack a map – despite the good signposting.

The Fossli Hotel makes a good base for several beautiful walking tours. A highly recommended route is the path (13–14.5hrs) along the western edge of the Hardangerjøkulen glacier via the Demmevass hut located at 1280m/4100ft, which leads on to Finse (1222m/4009ft). However, the immediate environs of Finse are pretty overrun most of the time.

From Geilo the route continues in the direction of Bergen, to **Halne Fjellstova** (approx. 42km/26mi; accommodation available), where there is the opportunity to do a one-day walking tour setting off from the **Vegmannsbu Turistsenter**. At first the narrow footpath heads northwest alongside **Halnekollen** (1358m/4455ft), then joining the main hiking route marked with the red »T« coming in from the left. After a short distance a small land-bridge is crossed between the Dragøyfjord in the northwest and the Storekrækkja in the southeast, from which in good weather walkers can enjoy a tremendous view.

Next, the route passes the **Krækkja hut** that offers food and also accommodation. At this point walkers have a choice: either to make a large loop east via the **Fagerheim Fjellstue** and return along the southern banks of the Ørteren, or to follow the path that leads **directly to Haugastøl**. The latter goes past several small lakes on the western flank of Flånuten (1248m/4095ft) and then follows the banks of the **Nedre** and the **Øvre Trestiklan**. Care should be taken when crossing the small rivers on stepping stones. A stony highland plateau is then traversed before descending to the Sløtfjord, where Haugastøl comes into view, which is very close to the Vegmannsbu Turistsenter.

Harstad

Region: North Norway   **Population:** 23,000

Harstad is a modern and rather sober town that most travellers use as a stop-off point on the way to the Lofoten or the Vesterålen islands. The medieval Trondenes church is worth a visit.

Located 120km/75mi northwest of Narvik, this industrial town on the northern coast of Hinnøy island has no particular sights to offer, other than its beautiful location on the Vågsfjord. During the 19th century, herring fishing was of great significance for the local economy. Today, oil and gas industries have settled here and several oil companies have their head offices here. Harstad is included on the **Hurtigruten** shipping route, but it is also connected by buses from Fauske and Bodø, as well as having an airport at Evenes. The town is also **a base for whale safaris** that set off from Andenes (► Baedeker Special p.400).

! *Baedeker* TIP

A Hurtigruten highlight
Among those in the know, the coastal section between Harstad and Tromsø is considered one of the most beautiful on the long Hurtigruten route between Bergen and Kirkenes, so a boat journey along this stretch is a worthwhile taster.

What to See in and around Harstad

An impressive set of buildings that houses the **Cultural Centre**, opened in 1992, stands out at the port. It has a concert hall and a hotel. In front of Harstad's church, which dates from 1958, stands a statue in honour of local man **Hans Egede** (1686–1758), who is also known as »Greenland's Apostle« for his missionary work among the Eskimos there. His name, with its three Es, often features in crossword puzzles.

City centre

Most of Harstad's sights are to be found on the Trondenes peninsula, about 3km/2mi north of the city centre. North Norway's best preserved medieval sacred building is here: Trondenes church, built as early as 1250. Later, this Romanesque stone church with its almost 2m/7ft thick walls was used for defensive purposes. The view of the Vågsfjord from the church is breathtaking.

★
Trondenes church

To the south of Trondenes church stands the wood building of the Trondenes Historical Centre, where exhibitions on the history of the Vikings and the Christianization of North Norway are held. Located in a historical landscape, the building was designed especially to harmonize with its surroundings. (opening times: mid-May–mid-August daily 10am–7pm).

Historske Senter
⊙

Adolf Cannon
The »Adolf Cannon« can be discovered in the German fortifications built by the occupying forces during the Second World War, to the north of Trondenes church. It was intended to guard the access route to Narvik and Tromsø and its 42cm/16in calibre is said to make it the largest land-based cannon in the world.

Bjarkøy Island
Leaving Harstad by boat, several islands are passed before reaching Bjarkøy Island about one hour away, famous throughout Norway for the **Viking chieftains** of the Bjarkøy family, who lived here in the 9th century and feature in numerous sagas. Their best-known representative was probably **Tore Hund**, a canny merchant who amassed riches trading with Finns and Russians. In 1026, Tore raided Russian tombs for their gold, and was probably also the killer of King Olav

 VISITING HARSTADT

INFORMATION

Harstad og Omland Arrangement
Torvet 8
9479 Harstad
Tel. 77 01 89 89, fax 77 01 89 80
www.destinationharstad.com,
www.harstad.commune.no

WHERE TO EAT

▶ **Expensive**
De 4 Roser
Richard Kaarbøspl. 4
Tel. 77 06 61 54
A mecca for gourmets in the far north, closed Sundays.

▶ **Inexpensive**
Kaffistova
Richard Kaarbøsgt. 6
Tel. 77 06 12 57
Rich in tradition, this café on the Hurtigruten quay also serves good local dishes.

WHERE TO STAY

▶ **Luxury**
Hotel Arcticus
Havnegata 3
Tel. 77 04 08 00
Fax 77 04 08 01

75 rooms, www.choicehotels.com
This luxurious hotel is located right by the water's edge and offers a beautiful view across Harstad and the Vågsfjord. Significantly cheaper prices for holders of a hotel pass.

▶ **Budget**
Centrum Gjestehus
Magnus gt. 5
Tel. 77 06 29 38
Fax 77 06 52 44
15 rooms, post@centrumgjestehus.no
Simple but value for money accommodation near the Hurtigruten quay and the Cultural Centre.

FJORD TOURS

The historic sailing boat *Anna Rogde*, built in 1868 and probably the oldest schooner in the world, is moored at the quay in front of the Cultural Centre. Every day at noon it sets off for a tour around the fjord.

FESTIVALS

Sober Harstad bursts into a frenzy of activity twice a year: at the end of June for the summer cultural festival and during the fishing festival in July.

the Holy during the Battle of Stiklestad (► Steinkjer) in 1030. It seems that after these events his conscience nagged him, as he then set off on a journey to the Holy Land from which he was not to return.

The roughly 700 inhabitants of the island have traditionally not only lived from fishing, but also – until recently – from the protected species of **Eider geese**, whose down is considered among the softest in the world.

★ Haukeli Road

B 2-4

Region: South and West Norway

The Haukeli Road is barely 200km/125mi long. Full of surprises, it begins in Telemark and winds up the bare Haukelifjell, visits the dramatic Åkrafjord, and ends at the coastal resort of Haugesund.

The Haukeli Road (Haukelivegen: E 134, 184km/115mi) was opened in 1886, and has since become one of the most important and beautiful connecting roads between east and west Norway. Rich in contrasts, the Haukelivegen initially passes through a naked highland landscape with its deep blue lakes and sheep and goat herds that occasionally stray onto the road, as well as mountain passes that can easily hold their own with the European Alpine passes for sheer magnificence. It then enters a wild fjord landscape along the narrow Åkrafjord, with walls of rock that rise almost vertically out of the water and wild waterfalls. Last but not least, the journey ends with the broad, flat countryside around Haugesund and views onto the open sea.

Road of contrasts

Along the Haukeli Road

Leaving Haukeligrend, the beginning of the Haukeli Road at the junction of the E 134 and RV 9, the route passes small mountain lakes in which trout can be fished (fishing permits are available at the hotels and mountain cabins). Beyond the Vågslid tunnel at the southeastern end of the deep blue Lake Ståvatnet, the mountain cabin known as **Haukeliseter** (986m/3235ft) comes into view, which has been in service since 1870. **Delicious creamy porridge known as rømmegrøt** can be enjoyed here, and there is also accommodation. This alpine cabin serves as a good base for hiking tours, as well as cross-country skiing tours to the ► Hardangervidda National Park further to the north.

Heading west from Haukeligrend

A short distance further on, the glowing ice fields of the steep slopes of Store Nupsfonn (1661m/5450ft) can be spotted to the north. The

★ **Haukeli Pass**

▶ VISITING HAUKELI ROAD

INFORMATION
Haugesund Turistinformasjon
Smedasundet 77
5528 Haugesund
Tel. 52 72 45 25, fax 52 71 14 70
www.haugesund.no

Karmøy Tourist Information
Rådhuset
4250 Kopervik
Tel. 52 85 19 45, fax 52 85 22 32
www.karmoy.kommune.no

WHERE TO EAT
▶ **Moderate**
Big Horn Steak House
Haugesund
Tel. 52 72 90 00
Restaurant chain that specializes in steaks. A modern place with views over the water.

Lanternen
Skudeneshavn, Torvet
Tel. 52 82 82 00
Café, restaurant and pub in a central location by the market. The water babbles under the diners' chairs on the »Sjøhus« terrace.

WHERE TO STAY
▶ **Luxury**
Comfort Hotel Amanda
Haugesund, Smedasundet 93
Tel. 52 80 82 00, fax 52 72 86 21
102 rooms, www.choice.no
Hotel right on the water in the heart of Haugesund.

▶ **Mid-range**
Haukeliseter Fjellstue
Edland
Tel. 35 07 05 15
Fax 35 07 05 19
Cabin village in the highlands maintained by the Stavanger hiking club, located above the tree line, right on the lake. The artfully decorated cabins are over 100 years old and exude an air of cosiness.

Norneshuset
Skudeneshavn, Nornes 7
Tel. 52 82 72 62
5 rooms, www.norneshuset.no
This venerable, bright white wooden house built in 1830 is the oldest and largest of the row of buildings set on the water. The narrow jetty to the water is the ideal place for a comfortable breakfast. Per and Berit Nornes have decorated the rooms with a great deal of taste and provide good service at a decent price.

▶ **Budget**
Vikholmen Lighthouse
Skudeneshavn
Tel./fax 52 82 85 97
Built in 1875, the lighthouse is located at the port entrance of Skudeneshavn. Included in the price of this unusual holiday apartment is a boat, with which the lighthouse can be reached in just five minutes. The three bedrooms offer ample room for six people.

EXCURSIONS
Recommended only for those who have found their sea legs, this day trip from Haugesund goes to the small wild island of Utsira, home to a great wealth of bird species. The island is located in the middle of the frequently stormy North Sea (crossing takes 1.5hrs 2–3 times daily).

CULTURE
Norway's largest film festival is held in Haugesund annually in September.

old pass over the **Haukelifjell** that begins right before the eastern end of the 5682m/18643ft long Haukeli tunnel is an absolute must for tourists. This incredibly beautiful highland route following the watershed between the Atlantic and the Skagerrak reaches its highest point at the 1145m/3757ft **Dyrskar**, set in the midst of mighty rock-strewn mountains.

Traversing an impressive desert-like expanse of snow and rock and passing through several tunnels, the road leads down to Røldal and the lake of the same name. Here too, it is possible to choose the old road, which was constructed in 1880 as an impressive serpentine route made up of seven large loops, which has memorable views. The 13th-century **stave church** in Røldal contains a pretty Renaissance altarpiece and a pulpit dating from 1627. The RV 520 branches off to Sauda southwest of Røldal.

Røldal

To the west of Røldal, the E 134 gradually winds its way up to the opening of the 4650m/5087yd-long **Røldal tunnel**. To the west, the white snow fields of the up to 1660m/5446ft-high Folgefon (► Hardangerfjord) appear. Here, too, there are choices to be made: to the southeast of the tunnel, an old road leads up to the **Hordabrek-kene**, a masterpiece of road build-

ing with a total of 16 hairpin bends and a spectacular view over Lake Røldalvatn (only passable during summer). An equally impressive road, built in 1896, is the steep route lined by imposing walls of rock that follows the imposing **Seljestad gorge**, where it is still possible to discover remains of the original historic transport path.

The narrow Åkrafjord, surrounded by almost vertical smooth cliffs rising from the water, begins 15km/9mi after the Jøsendal junction (RV 13 to Odda). The old, narrow road running along steep mountain slopes has now been replaced by a modern road with several tunnels, including the 7406m/8102yd Åkrafjord tunnel (toll), at whose southwestern end there is a pretty rest stop with views onto the fjord.

★ Åkrafjord

The E 134 now winds its way through gentle countryside with picturesque fjords and lakes that contrasts markedly with the dramatic natural landscapes further to the north. The road terminates in Haugesund (pop. 30,000). Snorre Sturlasson, author of sagas, mentioned the town as early as 1217, though today the initial impression created

Haugesund

A clear mirror: Skudeneshavn

by its offshore rigs and the Hydro aluminium giant is not particularly inviting. Down by the **port**, however, the lanes and streets on the Smeda sound lined with pretty white painted houses are inviting for a pleasant stroll.

Around 2km/1mi north of Haugesund, Crown Prince Oscar – later King Oscar II – had the magnificent tomb of **Haraldshaugen** built over the presumed grave of **Harald Fairhair**, who after a naval victory on the Harfrsfjord near Stavanger united Norway into one empire a thousand years ago. The monument consists of a 17m/56ft-high obelisk and 29 stones that represent the 29 Norwegian tribes that were united at the time. A stone cross dating from AD 1000 stands to the south of this monument.

Avaldnes, **Norway's oldest royal residence**, lies shortly beyond the Karmsund bridge on the long stretched out island of Karmøy, and was once home to Harald Fairhair in the 9th century. Next to the former royal chapel (around 1250) stands Norway's highest Bauta stone (7m/23ft), known as the Virgin Mary's Needle. West of Avaldnes lie the seven grave mounds of Rehaugene dating from the Bronze Age.

Skudeneshavn

Follow the RV 47 along the hilly western coast, with its occasionally superb views onto the open sea, to reach the small town of Skudeneshavn in an idyllic setting. Its picturesque, narrow lanes and prettily restored white wooden houses make it a veritable El Dorado for photographers. Those with time should take the ferry to Mekjarvik, north of Stavanger, as an alternative to the main E 39 route that leads to Stavanger via numerous tunnels. The lovingly designed musem in the old Mælandsgården tells all about Skudeneshavn's golden age during the herring fishing era (opening times: June–Aug Mon–Sat 11am–5pm, Sun from 1pm).

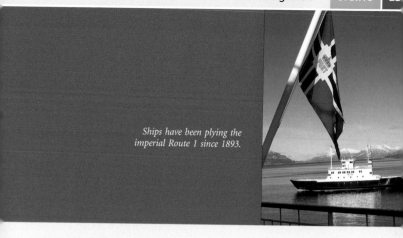

Ships have been plying the imperial Route 1 since 1893.

THE WORLDS MOST BEAUTIFUL VOYAGE

Do you know route 1? You will not find it on any map, although for many Norwegians it is the country's most important transport route. It is »Hurtigruten«, the shipping route that is plied daily to all ports along the coast between western and northern Norway.

Eleven ships connect 34 ports along the 2300km/1437mi-long route from Bergen to Kirkenes on the Russian border in Norway's high north. Until a few decades ago, some of the stops en route were only accessible on the postal ships of the Hurtigruten Line. The coastal express transports locals who have business in neighbouring ports, along with commuters and travellers, and mail, commercial goods and cars. The latter are heaved on board by means of a rather bizarre method using loading nets. The **Gulf Stream** ensures that all of Norway's ports remain ice free throughout the year. This northern journey has long since become a tourist attraction, not least because the ships travel within sight of the coast almost the whole time, ensuring **grandiose panoramic views**. Travellers can feast their eyes on fjords, mountains, glaciers, islands and sub-arctic vegetation during the journey, not to mention such sensational natural phenomena as the midnight sun and the aurora borealis. In short, the Norwegian highlights can be experienced on this comfortable journey, an ideal and restful option for all those who would find a car touring holiday in this great land too strenuous. The journey takes six days. There and back takes eleven days, and the ports that were visited at night on the way up are visited during the day on the way down, so nothing is missed.

Escaping isolation

In 1891, the bureaucrat responsible for Norwegian steam shipping, A.K. Gran, authorized the Vesterålens Dampskibsselskap shipping company

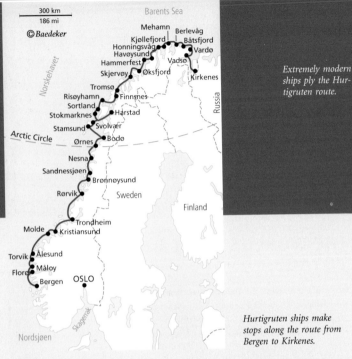

300 km
186 mi
© Baedeker

Extremely modern ships ply the Hurtigruten route.

Hurtigruten ships make stops along the route from Bergen to Kirkenes.

of Stockmarkens to establish a maritime route between Trondheim and Hammerfest. Sections of the route were already being traversed, but due to the **darkness of the northern winter**, many bays and islands were only visited as long as ships' captains could see the countless skerries and islets. For remote settlements this meant isolation for many months of the year. The Vesterålen ship owner Richard With was inspired to connect the Norwegian coastal settlements all year round, an idea that contemporaries considered too dangerous. With, however, had precise **navigational charts** drawn up so that captains could still keep to their course with the help of a watch and compass, even during the darkness of storm-battered polar nights. With's ship *Vesterålen* left

Trondheim for Hammerfest for the first time on 2 July 1893. Today's ships of between 6000 and 11,000 registered tons (the newest ships weigh up to 15,000 tons) have capacity for 550 to 1000 passengers, of which 312 to 674 can have cabins. Those without cabins can make do with a day trip on deck travelling to the next port.

Luxury and work

The only accident that has occurred in over a century of service happened in 1964, when a ship went down with 64 people on board. The Hurtigruten ships are **modern and safe**, the latest models are even equipped with saunas, fitness rooms, gourmet restaurants and bars that give cruise ships a run for their money. The **glamour** of larger cruise ships is totally missing in

the older ships though, and it is very obvious that they are workhorses. There are neither dinner parties nor other luxuries on board. Instead passengers can watch the crew at work and join in the everyday routine of the locals till the next port is reached, just as if travelling by bus.

Towards the end of the 1970s, the Oslo government had plans to cut **subsidies** for the Hurtigruten shipping line, but the howls of protest could be heard along the entire coast and the project was shelved. A **compromise** has established that the two shipping companies running vessels along the Hurtigruten route will receive around 1.9 billion NOK from the state between 2005 and 2012, in return for continued service all year round to all 34 ports, including the less commercially profitable ones between Tromsø and Kirkenes.

Pure pleasure

As prosaic as the Hurtigruten route may seem to Norwegian passengers, foreign travellers find it spectacular. The clocks move to a different rhythm during this, »the world's most beautiful voyage«. The ship glides smoothly between the skerries, occasionally entering the lively open sea. Holidaymakers spend almost every minute on deck to enjoy the changing coastal landscapes: the rock faces of **Lofoten** rising out of the sea, the entrances into narrow fjords, such as the Trollfjord, and the barren tundra of Finnmark, to name but a few.

Several tour operators combine the calls at port with a bus tour to sights inland. Crossing the Arctic Circle at 66.5° northern latitude is just one of the highlights of a Hurtigruten journey, and is usually accompanied by a small celebration.

All-inclusive tours with arrival by plane or by railway can be arranged by the Norwegian shipping agent (www.hurtigruten.com). Since the ships are first and foremost working ships, braver or less wealthy souls can still travel during winter in order to enjoy the icy beauty of the north, the rough seas and the dusky polar light.

★★ Jostedalsbreen

D 3/4

Region: West Norway   **Height:** up to 2038m/6687ft

No matter which side you approach Jostedalsbreen from, the icy mass of the largest glacier on the European mainland is impressive. On no account should an excursion to the ice tongues of Nigardsbreen and Briksdalsbreen be missed, and the same applies to the Glacier Centre in the Jostedal valley.

Europe's largest glacier

The Jostedal Glacier or Jostedalsbreen is located between the Sognefjord and the Nordfjord. It measures almost 100km/62mi in length and encompasses an area of over 1200 sq km/463 sq mi if the adjoining ice fields are included. In geographical terms the glacier, which has been designated a national park, is a kind of »inland ice« or ice sheet, as found in Greenland. Just a few low rocks peek through the body of ice, whose depth is estimated to be around 500m/1640ft. The surrounding valleys are filled with 26 large glacier tongues, of which 15km/9mi-long Tunsbergdalsbreen is only outdone by the Aletsch Glacier in Switerland for size (in Europe). In the 1990s some

The Jostedalsbreen glacier is as high as a house.

glacier arms of Jostedalsbreen grew again, due to above-average winter precipitation several years in a row – growth rates of 50–80m/165–260ft per year were observed. However, because of several years with low winter precipitation and hot summers (2002 and 2003), the glacier arms have been significantly shrinking again since 2000.

What to See around Jostedalsbreen

These days tourists can comfortably explore the glacier tongues at several places. A decade ago, the rugged Jostedal valley to the east – a gash in the mighty mountain plateau, running north-south – still lay in a Sleeping Beauty slumber; today the RV 604 leads through the long valley flanked by steep walls of rock, through which the wild Jostedalselv river also flows. The road branches off from the RV 55 at **Gaupne**, on the northern shore of the Lustrafjord. The RV 604 leads on over Høgebru. At **Gjerde**, a small road to the left turns off into the Krundal valley, which can be followed as far as **Bergset**. To the south, the valley is crowned by Høgenipa (1535m/5036ft).

Jostedal

> ! **Baedeker TIP**
>
> ### To the glacier by boat
>
> The glacier tongue of Nigardsbreen can be reached very comfortably and quickly on the small Jostedalsrypa boat that constantly ferries back and forth from the quay at the car park between 10 July and the end of August (10am–6pm).

A magnificent, though tough, three-hour guided hike leads from Bergset along Bergsetbreen to the ice field of **Jostedalsbreen**, ascending the glacier to Høgste Breakulen (1953m/6408ft). Continuing in a northwesterly direction, an impressive view of the mountains on the ► Nordfjord opens up after about an hour. This is followed by the occasionally challenging descent through the Kjenndal valley down to **Nesdal**, which lies at the southern end of Lake Loenvatn.

✱
From the glacier to the Nesdal

At the previously mentioned junction near Gjerde, the RV 604 leads onwards to the north. To the left at Elvekrok (340m/1115ft) spreads Nigardsbreen. The last section (toll payable) of the road leads through a moraine field that has been created by the retreat of the Nigard Glacier over the past 200 years. It is possible to hike right up to the edge of the glacier (good walking shoes needed) along a stony path that starts at the car park at the end of the road.

✱
Nigardsbreen

The very popular Jostedal Glacier Centre (Breheimsenter Jostedalen) at the beginning of the toll-charging road illustrates the 20,000-year-old natural and cultural history of the Jostedalsbreen area with the help of a model of the national park, an impressive video show and a replica Stone Age settlement. The architecturally interesting building, shaped like two ice towers split from each other by a crevasse, offers a beautiful panoramic view onto the shimmering blue Nigardsbreen

✱
Glacier Centre

○

(opening times: May–Sept 10am–5pm, mid-June–mid-August 9am–7pm). **Tours** onto the glacier are also organized from the Glacier Centre.

Oldenvatnet

There are also numerous glacier arms on the northwestern side of Jostedalsbreen, the best-known being Briksdalsbreen. The starting point for a visit is the small settlement of Olden on the Innvikfjord. Here, a road branches off south into the beautiful Olderdal valley. After passing the 11km/7mi-long Lake Oldenvatnet and numerous

► VISITING JOSTEDALSBREEN

INFORMATION
Glacier Centre/Breheimsenteret
6871 Jostedal
Tel. 57 68 32 50, fax 57 68 32 40
www.jostedal.com

GLACIER HIKING TOURS
The Glacier Centre (see tel. above) arranges tours at all levels of difficulty, ranging from 2hrs to 4hrs in duration. Prices include the hire of complete sets of glacier equipment, including glacier boots. No more than average fitness is required for walking tours in the lower part of Nigardsbreen.

WHERE TO EAT
► Moderate
Briksdalsbre Fjellstove
Tel. 57 87 68 00
Cafeteria and restaurant at the end of the road into the Briksdal, above the car park. Those looking for peace and quiet should visit in the late afternoons.

► Inexpensive
Lustrafjorden Kro
By route 55
Tel. 57 68 18 80
Restaurant with terrace right on the Lustrafjord with views to the Feigumfoss waterfall on the opposite shore. Home cooking and snacks.

WHERE TO STAY
► Luxury
Walaker Hotel
Gjesgivargarden, Solvorn
Tel. 57 68 20 80, fax 57 68 20 81
24 rooms, www.walaker.com
The setting on the Lustrafjord alone is stunning. One of the most beautiful hotels in Norway, whose rooms with historic atmosphere, quiet garden and excellent restaurant will appeal to lovers of tradition.

► Budget
Olden Camping
Tel. 57 87 59 34, fax 57 87 65 50
post@oldencamping.com
Small and friendly campsite for mobile homes and tents, including a few simple and well-priced cabins. Unique location right on the lake, with views of Jostedalsbreen. Around 13km/8mi from Olden.

Urnes Gard
Urnes on the Lustrafjord, near Urnes stave church
Tel. 57 68 39 44, fax 57 68 37 19
2 rooms, 3 cabins,
urnes-gard@urnes.no
Historic farm where the nobility enjoyed a hospitable reception back in the Middle Ages. Britt and Odd John Bugge also cultivate rasberries, blueberries, strawberries, cherries and apples.

waterfalls, Briksdal (150m/492ft) is reached.Brikdalsbreen, an arm of
Jostedalsbreen, is reached along a footpath after about one hour,
where the gigantic blue body of ice can be seen rising above the forest (►Nordfjord).

✱ ✱
◄ Briksdalsbreen

An additional access route to Jostedalsbreen, only opened in 1994, is
the toll-charging RV 5 – known as the Fjærlandsveg – which runs
through a outstandingly beautiful
landscape to **Fjærland**. The interesting Norwegian Glacier Museum
there is a good source of information on the secrets of the eternal
ice. It is possible to experiment with
ice here and answer such questions
as why ice is blue and fjords are
green. A model hydroelectric power
station also shows how meltwater
from a glacier produces electricity
(www.bre.museum.no, opening
times: April–October 10am–4pm,
June–August 9am–7pm).

Fjærland

> ! **Baedeker** TIP
>
> **A village full of books**
> Fjærland is worth a detour for its beautiful
> wooden houses and idyllic setting on the fjord
> alone. For book lovers, the village is a positive
> must, as about twelve antiquarian bookshops
> have about 200,000 books for sale here between
> May and September. The vast majority are
> Norwegian paperbacks, but those with time to
> hunt around a bit will also find something in
> English.

✦ Jotunheimen

D 4/5

Region: West and East Norway   **Height:** up to 2468m/8097ft

**The Jotunheimen mountains constitute the most alpine landscape
in Norway, containing Scandinavia's highest peaks: a range of
magnificent summits and glaciers cut into by clear streams and
lakes. The Norwegians reverentially call their favourite hiking region the »Home of Giants«, and dig out their walking boots to pay
homage every summer.**

Inspired by the wild landscape and Nordic mythology, it was the
writer Aasmund Olavsson Vinje who christened the region »Jøtun-
heimen«, meaning land of giants. For him, this was the obvious
home of the Jøten, the giant trolls. This predominantly untouched
fjell landscape is characterized by majestic mountains and glaciers,
but also by several extensive lakes, barren valleys and treeless plateaus, and extends between Oppland in the east and Sogn og Fjordane in the west.

In the Jotunheimen National Park

At the heart of the Jotunheimen mountain range lies the national
park of the same name. The largest part of the park area is at eleva-

Above the
tree line

tions of 1000m/3281ft and higher, and is therefore above the tree line. Norway's highest mountains lie here: Galdhøppigen (2469m/ 8100ft) and Glittertind (2452m/8045ft). Galdhøppigen is among the most climbed summits in the country, not only because it is the highest, but also because the ascent is not difficult.

Hurrungane

The southwestern part of the national park is formed by the Hurrungane range, which is largely cut off from the rest of the Jotunheimen mountains by the deep Utladal valley. Six of Norway's highest peaks

▶ VISITING JOTUNHEIMEN

INFORMATION

Beitostølen
On the main road
Tel. 61 35 22 00, fax 61 35 22 01
www.beitostolen.com

Lom
In the Fjell Museum
Tel. 61 21 29 90
Fax 61 21 29 95
www.visitlom.com

GETTING THERE

One of Norway's most beautiful roads leads through the Jotunheimen mountains: route 51 runs from Fagernes via Valdresflya as far as the E 15 near the small settlement of Vågåmo, and ends on the E 15 near Lom. During winter the high mountain sections of the road are closed.

WHERE TO EAT AND STAY

▶ Expensive
Fossheim Turisthotel
Lom
Tel. 61 21 95 00
Norway's master chef Arne Brimi magically creates delicacies from »nature's kitchen« at this historic restaurant. The menu available in the cosy »Gaukstad-stugu« is both exclusive and expensive. More affordable prices during the summer season are charged for the »lunsjbord«, or a

pizza in the herb garden. Accommodation here is also very luxurious.

WHERE TO STAY

Baedeker recommendation

Elveseter Hotel
Elveseter
Tel. 61 21 20 00
Fax 61 21 21 01).
The buildings of the Elveseter Hotel next the Saga Pillar recall a typical country esta from a bygone era. The entrance hall, tastefully decorated with antiques, creates special atmosphere. Paintings, by Adolf Tidemandt among others, and antique furniture with rose painting add to the hotel's museum-style character.

▶ Budget
Valdresflya Vandrerhjem
46 beds, Beitostølen
Tel. 22 15 21 85
Fax 22 71 34 97
This youth hostel stands at the highest point of the Valdresflya pass, at 1389m/4557ft. It is the ideal base for discovering the Jotunheimen massif. Advance booking recommended.
Open during the Easter holidays, and then again from the beginning of June to the end of August.

are bunched closely together here, dominated by the most popular climbing summit, the imposing Store Skagastølstind (2405m/7891ft). The Hurrungane mountains may be paradise for rock climbers, but this bizarre mountainous world is also a worthwhile destination for hikers and walkers.

Thanks to an extensive network of signposted footpaths and cabins maintained by the Norwegian hiking association (DNT), the shipping routes over the Gjende and Bygdin lakes, and road routes 51 and 55, the Jotunheimen massif is easily explored. For this reason, though, several of the classic routes, such as over **Beseggengrat**, become **unusually crowded** by Norwegian standards during the summer holiday season. The most beautiful time for hiking here begins at the end of June and goes until September – earlier in the year the snow fields, wet ground and total absence of any greenery spoil the pleasure somewhat. During winter, the Jotunheimen mountains are an excellent and popular destination for cross-country ski tours. Easter is peak season, and at this time many Norwegians are drawn to the mountains and almost all cabins are operational.

Walking in the »Home of Giants«

Along the Sognefjellvegen

Route 55 winds its way from the Lustrafjord via Skjolden onto Sognefjell. There is a magnificent view onto the valley, fjord and the Hurrungane peaks from the **Turtagrø Hotel** (900m/2953ft). The hotel is also a good base for **hiking tours** to Skagastølstind, Dyrhaugstind or Austabotntind. Following the main road, known as the Sogenfjellvegen, the route continues steadily uphill until the highest point is reached at the **Sognefjellhytta** (cabin at 1434m/4705ft). The panorama either side of the road is impressive: a high alpine landscape with jagged peaks, snow fields that survive long into the summer months, and several smaller glaciers.

From Skjolden into the Leirdal valley

There is a small summer skiing resort on Sognefjell and it is possible to rent cross country skis from the cabins along the road. The signposted footpaths begin from the car parks and make for worthwhile one-day walks as well as longer tours. Beyond the Sognefjellhytta, the road slowly but steadily leads downwards into the **Leirdal** valley. To the right, there now follow three toll-charging secondary roads, one after the other, heading to Leirvassbu, the **Juvasshytta and Spiterstulen** respectively. At the end of each road there is a mountain hut that is ideally suited as a base for hikes into the central Jotunheimen mountains.

If **Spiterstulen** is chosen as a base, which is located in the valley between the Galdhøppigen and Glittertind peaks, Norway's two highest mountains can be climbed from the same place. Note, however, reaching the summit of Galdhøppigen requires an ascent of around 1400m/4593ft on a steep path (there and back takes around 5hrs).

★
Galdhøppigen, Glittertind

The path up Glittertind is equally strenuous and, depending on levels of fitness, at least 7–9hrs should be calculated for the hike. The best point to begin an ascent of Galdhøpiggen is the **Juvasshytta** mountain cabin. The ascent to the summit is easy and only takes around 3–4hrs. Nevertheless, it is essential to join one of the daily guided tours, becaused the path leads across the Svellnos Glacier (Svellnosbreen), which is cut by crevasses.

To the left of the Elveseter Hotel, shortly before the turn-off to the Juvasshytta, the 33m/108ft Saga Column comes into view. Offering a cross section through Norwegian history, beginning with the first unified empire in 872 and ending with the Council of 1814, the column was designed by W. Rasmussen prior to the Second World War and was originally intended to stand in front of the Storting (national assembly) in Oslo.

★
Saga Column

> ## ! Baedeker TIP
>
> ### Minerals galore
> A substantial collection of minerals can be seen at the Fossheim Steinsenter on the edge of Lom, heading out towards Vågå, and afterwards jewellery and minerals are offered for sale in the souvenir shop (tel. 61 21 14 60; opening times during summer daily 9am–9pm).

The Sogenfjellvegen finally ends in **Lom**, the main tourist centre of the northern Jotunheimen mountains. The place compares favourably with many other, more austere, settlements due to its numerous dark wooden houses. The greatest sight is the 800-year-old basilica style **stave church**, whose choir arch and pulpit (1793) are by the wood carver Jakob Sæterdalen. Just a few steps further away stands the **Norwegian Mountain Museum** (Norsk Fjellmuseum), which provides a useful overview of the Norwegian fjells (opening times: mid-June–mid-August daily 9am–9pm, Sat, Sun 10am–8pm, otherwise shorter, www.fjell.museum.no).

Over the Valdresflya Plateau

From Fagernes, route 51 climbs slowly but surely northwards until it reaches the tree line and the southern edge of the Jotunheimen mountains near Beitostølen. The large cabin and lodge settlement of Beitostølen makes for a good summer base for walks in the mountains, while in the winter it is known as a winter sports resort with family-friendly pistes. Cross-country skiers will find a unique area here, several of whose well maintained tracks lead deep into the high mountains. Bitihorn (1608m/5276ft) is a striking peak that can already be spotted from the village, and its summit can be reached in 3–4hrs via a footpath that begins right by the road a short drive to the north of Beitostølen.

Beitostølen

← *Norway's most famous and most visited hiking region is the Jotunheimen. Camping wild in the open enhances the experience of nature.*

Valdresflya

After Beitostølen, the road continues its ascent, passing the Bygdin and Vinstri lakes and reaching its highest point on Valdresflya. Unlike the alpine summits of the surrounding area, Valdresflya is a flat and very barren highland plateau. Before reaching Lake Gjende, there is the option of making a half-day tour up Knutshø, beginning near Vargbakken a short distance south of Maurvangen. Whether or not Knutshø is more exposed than Besseggen is debatable, but its ridge is certainly narrower and the view from the top is simply stupendous. Some even believe that Peer Gynt made his journey on the back of a reindeer not over Besseggen but over the Knutshø ridge.

✱
Lake Gjende

Lake Gjende, which is around 20km/12mi long but only 1km/0.6mi wide, numbers among Norway's most beautiful lakes. Carved out by the glaciers of the last Ice Age, the lake enchants with its intensely blue-green waters and the steep mountainsides that rise up to 1300m/4265ft above it. The three **mountain lodges** on its shore at Gjendesheim, Memurubu and Gjendebu, as well as the campsite at Maurvangen on route 51 are some of the most visited destinations in the Jotunheimen mountains.

✱
Besseggen

Many Norwegians return year on year to climb the Besseggen ridge, following in the footsteps of the mythical Peer Gynt. Henrik Ibsen took the liberty of turning the Besseggen into a hellish ride, but in fact it is not so daunting. In fact, this panoramic tour requires no more than good fitness, firm shoes, a little surefootedness and a lack of vertigo. The changeable weather, however, should never be underestimated. The starting point for this spectacular **six-hour tour** offering breath-taking views is **Gjendesheim**. The day begins with a 35-minute crossing by **boat** of Lake Gjende to reach the catered cabin at **Memurubu**. The steep ascent then begins immediately next to the jetty. Shortly after the turn-off for **Glitterheim**, the path continues along the southern shore of a small pond before reaching Lake Bjørnbøltjørna (»Bear's Den Puddle«). A short descent via a narrow path follows, leading to **Lake Bessvatnet**. The just 50m/55yd-wide land bridge between the almost black Lake Bessvatnet and the blue-green Lake Gjende several hundred metres below, at 984m/3228ft, is called Bandet.

The steep ascent of Besseggen then begins over the first ridge (where walkers even occasionally need to use their hands to remain steady) until the highest point is reached, where the giant stone man stands. Before then making the relatively easy descent to Gjendesheim, it is still necessary to walk a good distance across the broad **Veslefjell** mountainside.

Vågåmo

Route 51 continues above the tree line for some distance after Gjendesheim before the first trees come into view once more at Sjodal and the green hues become deeper again. The E 15 is finally reached at Randen, and Vågåmo is just a short distance further on.

Karasjok

M 22

Region: North Norway   **Population:** 2800

For the Sami people, Karasjok is one of the most important cultural centres, where they have their own newspaper, a radio station and their parliament. Tourists can get a good idea of Sami life in the high north in the Sápmi Theme Park.

The secret capital of the Sami people lies along the Karasjohka river on the E 6 east of ►Alta (145km/91mi), 14km/9mi from the Finnish border. In addition to tourism, the economic foundation of the town is based on the traditional Sami activities of reindeer keeping, hunting and fishing. Due to the inland location, the temperature differentials are extreme here, so that during winter the thermometer can sometimes sink to –50°C/–58ºF, while on warm summer days, it can rise as high as 30°C/86ºF. The bus to Rovaniemi in Finland stops in Karasjok, as does the once daily »Nord-Norge« bus.

Sami town

What to See in Karasjok

The Sami Centre at the junction of the E 6 and RV 92 not only houses the tourist information office, but also has a sales centre with

Sami Centre

VISITING KARASJOK

INFORMATION
Karasjok Opplevelser AS
In the Sápmi Theme Park /
Postboks 192, 9735 Karasjok
Tel. 78 46 88 10, fax 78 46 88 11
www.koas.no

WHERE TO EAT
► **Expensive**
Stor Gammen
In the Rica Hotel Karasjok
(Porsangervn. 3)
Tel. 78 46 74 00
The restaurant is inside an authentic copy of a Sami earth hut complete with open fire. Dishes are prepared according to ancient Sami recipes. Seated on reindeer furs, diners are treated to reindeer casserole (bidos) and smoked reindeer hearts.

WHERE TO STAY
► **Budget**
Karasjok Camping and Vandrerhjem
Kautokeinoveien, tel. 78 46 61 35
20 huts of varying standard offering a range of accommodation options are available at this youth hostel. The site is a mere 1km/0.6mi from the centre of town.

EXCURSIONS AND COURSES
The tourist information office can arrange boat trips on the Karasjohka river or excursions to Sami settlements, as well as dog sleigh and ski bob tours during winter, gold panning courses, and fishing tours to the world famous salmon fishing grounds at the confluence of the Karasjohka and the Anarjohka.

Delicate colours and a mild light embrace the land of the Sami near Karasjok.

outstanding Sami craftwork and a restaurant where Sami dishes can be tried.

Church Karasjok church dating from 1807 stands opposite. It is the oldest Protestant church in Finnmark and was the town's only building to survive intact after the retreat of German forces during the Second World War.

Sami collections The museum, called Samiid Vuorka Davvirat, offers a good insight into the culture and history of Scandinavia's native population, displaying costumes, domestic interiors, Sami domestic tools and arts and crafts from the metal workshop and the silver workshop (opening times: June–August Mon–Sat 9am–6pm, Sun from 10am).

Sápmi Theme Park The Sápmi Theme Park (or Land of the Sami) opened in July 2000, is also dedicated to the history and culture of Scandinavia's indigenous people. A Sami family going about their daily chores can be observed in a traditional summer and winter campsite. An entertaining performance in the magical Stálubákti theatre carries spectators off into Sami mythology, while a large earth hut is available for trying Sami food specialities (opening times: June–Aug 9am–10pm, or by arrangement tel. 78 48 27 00).

Around Karasjok

The E 6 follows the western shore of the Tanaelv, past several miles of Ailestrykene rapids. The Tana valley was initially exclusively inhabited by Sami, and it was not until between 1730 and 1740, that the first Finnish settlers appeared. Norwegian settlements did not appear until the end of the 18th century. Beyond the Tana bru, the only bridge over the Tanaelv, the E 6 becomes known as the RV 98, should you wish to continue in the direction of Lakselv. An exhibition by the **local museum** of the Tana district can be visited in **Rustefjelbma**, but the main museum on the topic of salmon fishing on the Tanaelv is in Polmak.

Tanaelv

> ! **Baedeker TIP**
>
> ### Among the mushers and the huskis
>
> Musher Sven Engholm has won Europe's longest dog sleigh race eleven times and completed the legendary Alaskan »Iditarod« among the top ten. Around 50 huskies live on his farm, where guests live in authentic wooden block huts and can take dog sleigh tours. Located 6km/4mi from Karasjok, tel. 78 46 71 66, www.engholm.no).

Øvre Anarjåkka National Park, on the Finnish border to the southeast of Karasjok, is the largest natural protected area in northern Norway (1290 sq km/498 sq mi). Because of its extensive moorlands, it is only really suitable for hiking, but there is a **superb view** to be had across the endless landscape of Finmarksvidda from one of its peaks (none higher than 600m/1969ft).

✴ Kautokeino

M 20

Region: North Norway

Population: 3000

Kautokeino in the county of Finnmark is a traditional Sami strong-hold where, with a bit of luck, Sami costume can still be seen worn as everyday clothing. During Easter, it is also possible to take part in the festivities whose highlight is the Sami Grand Prix.

Norway's largest Sami community lies in Finnmarksvidda, about 120km/75mi south of Alta and 130km/81mi southwest of Karasjok (daily bus connections from both places). Kautokeino is the only Norwegian settlement which also has an official Sami name – **Guovdageaidnu** – and an interpreter is indeed occasionally necessary in this bilingual town. The cultural centre of the Sami (►Baedeker Special p.36 and ►Finnmark), Kautokeino is the seat of numerous Sami institutions. In existence since the 16th century, this Sami community belonged to Swedish Lapland until 1751, after which it came to Norway under the Danish Crown. For centuries, the survival of the

More reindeer than people

▶ VISITING KAUTOKEINO

INFORMATION

Kautokeino Turistinformasjon
9520 Kautokeino
Bredbuktnesveien 6
Tel. 78 48 65 00
www.kautokeinokommune.no

LEISURE

Kautokeino not only offers a large range of leisure activities for hikers, canoeists and horse-riders in summer, but also attracts visitors during winter, when rides with reindeer, dog sleighs, or on snow mobiles are on offer. Trips in a traditional river boat on the Kautokeino river are also an unforgettable experience (details from the tourist office).

WHERE TO EAT & STAY

Baedeker recommendation

▶ **Madame Bongo's Fjellstue**

Madame Bongo alias Karen Anna Bongo is legend in Kautokeino. She receives visitor in one of her »lavvus«, a traditional Sami tent, where she dishes up »bidos« by the open fireside – once the feasting dish of the Sami for special occasions, consisting of a beef and potato casserole. It is also possibl to spend the night in a lavvu for a reasonable sum. To add this to their list o experiences visitors need only a reservatio and their own sleeping bag (Madame Bongo's Fjellstue, Cunovuoppe, 11km/7m northwest of Kautokeino, tel. 78 48 61 60

indigenous people here was ensured by the hunting of wild reindeer, which were either caught in pits or herded into enclosures.

With an area of 9687 sq km/3740 sq mi, Kautokeino is the largest municipality in Norway, although population density is very low. Only **1500 people** live in the place itself – the majority of the population are indigenous Sami – but there are around **100,000 reindeer**, traditional reindeer breeding still being an important source of income in the village today. Tourism also plays an key role all year round, since most visitors to Finnmark stop off here.

What to See in Kautokeino

Open-air museum The open-air museum (Guovdageainnu Gilisillju) is especially worth seeing. A traditional Sami settlement of older buildings conveys an impression of Sami lifestyle a century ago. The exhibits show just how much skill the Sami have traditionally commanded in the creation of their daily tools and jewellery (opening times: mid-June–mid-August Mon–Fri 9am–7pm, Sat and Sun from noon, otherwise daily 9am–3pm).

! *Baedeker* TIP

Jewels at Juhl's

Probably the best traditional jewellery to be found in Finnmark can be purchased at Juhl's silver workshop 2km/1mi from Kautokeino. Open daily in summer, 8.30am–10pm, otherwise 9am–8pm.

A Sami herder travels through the arctic landscape near Kautokeino with his reindeer.

The Nordic Sami Institute (Nordisk Samisk Institutt), including a library and theatre, is housed in the architecturally interesting cultural centre whose shape is reminiscent of a Sami tent. Information on Sami culture can be found here, and there is also an indigenous teacher training college and a technical school teaching reindeer husbandry.

★
Sami cultural centre

Kirkenes

Region: North Norway   **Population:** 6000

Kirkenes is journey's end. The Hurtigruten ships turn around after a short stop here and even route E 6 goes no further. A trickle of border traffic with Russia has however brought more life into this small town in the far north of Europe.

The Norwegian port and industrial town of Kirkenes lies on the south side of the Varangerfjord, on a spit of land between the Lang-fjord and the broad mouth of the Pasvikelv river – only 150km/90mi from Murmansk, Russia's only harbour not under German control during the Second World War. The Russians retaliated against repeated attempts to capture Murmansk: more than 1000 air raid warnings and 328 Soviet bombing raids made Kirkenes Norway's most bombed town of the war. What stood up to the bombs was burned down by the Germans as they retreated – in the end, only 20 buildings were left standing.

Oil instead of iron ore

Originally, Kirkenes served as a port for shipping out the iron ore found at Lake Bjørnevatn, 11km/7mi to the south. Once upon a time the mining and processing of iron ore were significant, but streamlining measures resulted in the loss of over 1000 jobs and the Bjørnevatn pits were closed in 1996. Meanwhile, the town is hoping that a revival of trade with Russia, as well as oil exploitation in the Barent Sea, will revive its economy. The local Norwegian dockyard is predominantly kept busy servicing Russian ships.

»Russian market«

The Russian border at Storskog is just a short drive from the town centre and since the opening of the eastern border, a **»Russian market«** has established itself close to the port area. What the local authorities are hoping to achieve in terms of improved economic relationships on a wider scale is already functioning perfectly on a smaller scale: the Russians supply the population with cheap cigarettes and vodka and receive Western consumer goods in return.

▶ VISITING KIRKENES

INFORMATION

Kirkenes Turistinformasjon
Presteveien 1
9915 Kirkenes
Tel. 78 99 25 01
Fax 78 99 25 25
www.kirkenesinfo.no

WHERE TO EAT

► Expensive

② *Direktørboligen*
Kr. Nygaardsgt. 37
Tel. 78 99 18 09
A small, exclusive hotel and restaurant has been established in the pit director's former house. The menu offers choice fish and meat specialities, though the culinary delights do not come cheap. Table reservations are essential.

► Moderate

① *Arctic Restaurant*
Kongensgaten 1–3,
Tel. 78 99 29 29
The hotel restaurant is good, especially for fish dishes.

WHERE TO STAY

► Mid-range

① *Pasvikdalen Villmarkssenter*
Tel. 78 99 50 01, fax 78 99 53 25
This wildlife centre is located right in the heart of bear country on the Norwegian-Russian border. 40 modern rooms, shared kitchen facilites and a sauna, all in the middle of the wilderness. Guests can also book a night in a Sami tent.

MIDNIGHT SUN

Shines from 20 May until 20 July

Kirkenes Map

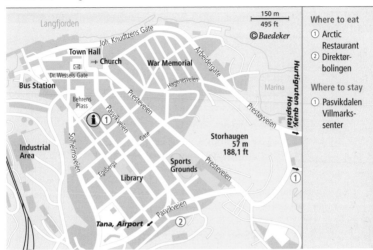

Where to eat
① Arctic Restaurant
② Direktør-bolingen

Where to stay
① Pasvikdalen Villmarks-senter

150 m
495 ft
© Baedeker

Langfjorden
Joh. Knudtzens Gate
Town Hall
→ Church
War Memorial
Arbeidergate
Dr. Wessels Gate
Bus Station
Hagenesveien
Marina
Behrens Plass
Presteveien
Hurtigruten quay / Hospital
Pasvikveien
Presteøyveien
Solheimsveien
Gate
Industrial Area
Egebergs
Storhaugen
57 m
188,1 ft
Library
Sports Grounds
Presteveien
①
Pasvikveien
Tana, Airport ✈
②

What to See in and around Kirkenes

The few tourists that end up in Kirkenes are passengers on the Hurtigruten ships and rarely stay more than a couple of hours. Visitors with more time could visit the former Andersgrotta mine right underneath the town centre. In the dripping wet catacombs, where most of the town's residents survived the Second World War, a film is shown conveying the horrors of the war. Guided tours are available by request from the tourist office.

Andersgrotta

The Kirkenes area offers opportunities for white water fishing in the Karpelva, Klokkerelva, Munkelva and Neidenelva rivers, and there is also the possibility to go deep sea fishing and canoeing. Another option is an excursion through the Pasvik valley in the Øvre Pasvik National Park, whose transitional habitat close to the northern Russian tundra boasts a wealth of flora and fauna.

Fishing and canoeing

Day trips by boat or overland to Murmansk and the Kola Peninsula in Russia can be booked via the tourist information centre. A passport, passport photo and a reservation are needed at least two days ahead of time. During the week, a visa can be requested on the day of travel, though it is cheaper to request it two weeks in advance. Buses to Murmansk depart from Kirkenes Mon–Fri at 2pm and 3pm, Sun at 3pm and 4pm (journey time around 4hrs; Grenseland, tel. 78 99 25 01, www.grenseland.no). It is also possible to travel to Russia by car, for which a car stamp is necessary as part of the visa. The border crossing at Storskog is open daily 7am–9pm.

Excursion to Murmansk

✳ Kongsberg

B 6

Region: South Norway   **Height:** 170m/558ft
Population: 22,000

Life in Kongsberg is tranquil. Stress is unknown in the old silver town with its magnificent Baroque church. Visits to the Mining Museum and the decommissioned silver mine in Saggrenda should definitely be on the itinerary.

Silver town   The old mining town of Kongsberg, set on either side of the Lågen in the southern part of the Numedal valley, owes its foundation to the silver mines that were established in 1624 a few miles south. Up to 4000 people were employed in the mines during the second half of the 18th century. Today Kongsberg is also known for its jazz festival (www.kongsberg-jazzfestival.no).

What to See in and around Kongsberg

Museums   On the banks of the foaming rapids of the Lågen, the **Mining Museum** is housed in the former works buildings. Among other things, it exhibits the collection of the Royal Norwegian Mint, which traces
⊙   the production of silver coins since 1686 (opening times: May–Sept

▶ VISITING KONGSBERG

INFORMATION
Karschesgt. 3
Tel. 32 29 90 50, fax 32 29 90 51
www.visitkongsberg.no

WHERE TO EAT
▶ Expensive
Opsahlgården
Kirkegaten 10
Tel. 32 76 45 01
The building is located in the old part of Kongsberg near the church and its restaurant is considered one of the best in town. Reindeer filet, duck breast, rack of lamb or the changing 3-course menus are all prepared with the freshest high-quality ingredients – which come at a price. Beautiful seating in the tranquil courtyard during summer.

▶ Moderate
Peckels Resept
Peckelsgate 12
Tel. 32 73 25 25
Named after the apothecary Franz Peckel's recipes, this restaurant is a great place to eat. Pictures on the walls tell the story of the town.

WHERE TO STAY
▶ Budget
Kongsberg Vandrerhjem Bergmannen
Vinjesgt. 1
Tel. 32 73 20 24
Fax 32 72 05 34
www.kongsberg-vandrerhjem.no
Modern youth hostel in the town centre with comfortable rooms.

noon–4pm, during high season from 10am). Furthermore, the small Ski Museum contains the skis of the world famous Kongsberg sportsman Birger Ruud. The **silver mine**, shut down in 1957, can be visited on a small pit railway that travels 2.3km/1.4mi through dark passages into the mountain (not suitable for small children). Its destination is the royal pit, which never reaches a temperature of more than 6°C/43°F. Adventurous visitors can also book a 3hr 5km/3mi pit walk (information from the tourist office).

The mighty red brick Kongsberg church (1741–61) stands imposingly south of the rapids. A Baroque church, its unusual interior includes 2400 seats distributed across several levels, some at giddy heights. Before they began work in the mines, workers had to assemble here each morning at 5am – those who failed to attend service were not paid.

★ **Kongsberg church**

By Norwegian standards, the unique complex of organ, pulpit and altar are excessively opulent, embellished with gold and Baroque figures. The loges or boxes stand out, especially the royal box concealed behind a beautifully decorated window façade reminiscent of a townhouse in northern Germany. No wonder perhaps: the architects came from Germany.

In **Modum**, about 50km/31mi northeast of Kongsberg in the direction of Gol, it is worth making a detour to the **Pigment Production Works** of Blaafarveværket. The works were established in 1776 for the extraction and processing of cobalt, and produced 80% of the world's requirements for this blue pigment during the 19th century. At one of Norway's most visited exhibitions, beautiful cobalt blue **glass and porcelain products** are shown in the former works buildings below the churning Haugefossen waters. During summer, works by famous Norwegian and foreign artists are shown in changing exhibitions (opening times: May–Sept daily 10am–5pm/6pm, pit from noon).

Stalls in the Kongsberg Church

Two of southern Norway's most beautiful rock engravings are located around 5km/3mi south of the centre of Drammen: one (at Nordbyveien 49) is of an elk that is estimated to have been created around 6000 years ago; there is also a variety of such figures at Skogerveien 8.

Rock art

★★
Heddal stave church
Norway's largest stave church (see p.372), the beautiful 13th-century Heddal church, stands right next to the E 134 to the west of Kongsberg and Notodden.

Numedal
If the southern part of the Numedal valley from Kongsberg as far as Geilo on the RV 40 in the ►Hallingdal region has little to offer, the northern part enchants all the more. The road winds its way along the Lågen which rises on the edge of the ►Hardangervidda plateau, passing narrow gorges and continuing onwards to **Rødberg**, where the neo-classical works building of the hydroplant »Nore I« is a striking sight in the centre of the town. The route first passes the pretty **stave church at Uvdal** (north of the road, not the one right next to it), and there are roads branching up onto Immingfjell (heading for Telemark) and the idyllically located mountain lodge of Solheimstulen, on the edge of Hardangervidda – from both there are good hiking opportunities to the catered mountain cabin of Mårbu. Eventually the road reaches the 1100m/3609ft-high **mountain hotel of Vasstulan**, from which there is a fantastic view onto the Numedal valley and the Hardangervidda mountain plateau. After traversing two further passes, it is possible to make out the tracks of the Geilo ski lifts on the opposite side of the valley. The jagged **Hallingskarvet** ridge towers high above the popular winter sports resort, where the 1933m/6342ft-high Folarskarnut forms the highest peak of this range.

★ Kristiansand

A 4/5

Region: South Norway   **Population:** 75,000

With its numerous stone houses, Kristiansand, Norway's fifth largest town, is not particularly representative of the country. Though for many it is just a place to be passed through on arrival from Denmark, the sandy beaches of the surrounding area are very pretty and there is no shortage of opportunity to indulge in water sports.

Second largest port
Surrounded by large dockyards, off-shore installations and industrial complexes, the town with the country's second largest port does not initially seem inviting to visitors. Nevertheless, as the regional administrative centre for the Vest-Agder region, Kristiansand has quite a bit to offer. Loated right by the mouth of the Otra river where it opens into the Byfjord, for example, the pretty quarter of **Posebyen** is a good place to stroll among historic wooden houses, in which galleries and artisan workshops have been set up. To the right and left of the **Christiansholm fortress** (1672), which hosts summer art exhibitions, there are several marinas swarming with fancy yachts and boats during the summer months. It is popular to sail the Skagerrak in the direction of Risør along the »Riviera of the North«.

► VISITING KRISTIANSAND

INFORMATION

Destinasjon Sørlandet
Vestre Strandgt. 32
4612 Kristiansand
Tel. 38 12 13 14, fax 38 02 52 55
www.sørlandet.com

WHERE TO EAT

► Expensive
② **Bakgården Restaurant**
Tollbugate 5, tel. 38 02 99 55
Excellent restaurant that really lives
up to the highest expectations. Once
the entrance in the back courtyard of
the Bakgården has been found, a
rustic interior with dark wood furniture and white-washed walls is re-
vealed. The delicious marinated
dishes are recommended, as well as
the tuna, which looks a lot like meat
on the plate.

► Moderate
③ **Restaurant Sjøhuset**
Østre Strandgt. 12 A
Tel. 38 02 62 60
Very good though expensive fish
dishes in a maritime atmosphere. The
Sjøhuset's popularity over the past 20
years has been enhanced by its outdoor seating, where diners listen to
the waves and watch the sun go down.
The lunchtime fish platter is certainly
affordable.

► Inexpensive
① **Café Generalen**
Ravnedalen
Tel. 97 08 66 61
This small café surrounded by greenery serves tasty snacks such as ham-
burgers, waffles and cake. Cultural
evenings and live concerts are held on
Thursdays and Fridays.

WHERE TO STAY

► Luxury
① **Clarion Hotel Ernst**
Rådhusgaten 2
Tel. 38 12 86 00
Fax 38 02 03 07
67 rooms, booking@ernst.no
The top hotel in town, whose rooms
have tasteful interiors and whose
atmospheric lobby is huge. Kristiansand locals also appreciate the good
restaurant and the bistro.

► Mid-range
② **Sjøgløtt – Det Lille Hotel**
Østre Strandgt. 25
Tel. 38 02 21 20
Fax 38 02 21 20
12 rooms, www.sjoglott.no
This small family hotel lies in the
town centre, near the old fortress. No
frills, convenient and good value for
money.

BOAT TOURS

Tour boats depart from the port in
Kristiansand for trips among the
skerries to the idyllic island of Ny-
Hellesund and its Second World War
fortress. Tours to the picturesque little
town of Lillesand, with its pretty
white mansions and harbour are also
interesting (tickets from the tourist
office).

What to See in and around Kristiansand

Kvadraturen The strictly square design of Kristiansand's town centre – known as the Kvadraturen – is thanks to its founder and namesake Christian IV. The Danish-Norwegian king designed the network of streets in a chess board pattern according to strict Renaissance style in 1641. Today, the town's thriving economic and cultural heart pulsates in these right-angled streets, where there is a pretty pedestrian zone (Markensgate) with attractive restored houses.

Cathedral The neo-Gothic cathedral stands out at the market square in the town centre (Torget), where fresh fruit and vegetables are sold during summer. It was rebuilt between 1882 and 1885 after a fire, and its interior is worth seeing for the altar with its *Christ at Emmaus* painting and the collection of Baroque wood carvings of the Evangelists (opening times: 9am–2pm).

Next to the church stands a monument by Vigeland to the poet Henrik Wergeland (1808–45; ▶ Art and Culture: Literature), one of the town's famous sons.

Kristiansand Map

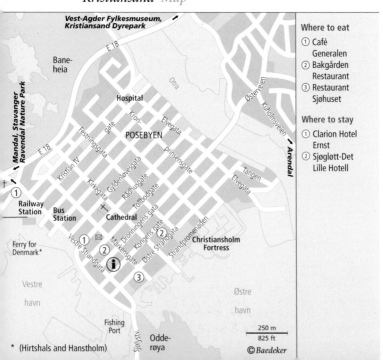

Vest-Agder Fylkesmuseum, Kristiansand Dyrepark

E 18

Baneheia

Otra

Østerveien

Kuholmsveien

Mandal, Stavanger Ravendal Nature Park

Hospital

Kron-

Elvegata

POSEBYEN

Festningsgata

Kristian IV

Prinsensgate

Arendal

Tangen

Elvegata

Kirkegata

Gyldenløvesgata

Rådhusgate

Tollbodgate

Kongensgate

Dronningensgata

Østre Strandgata

Strandpromenaden

Railway Station

Bus Station

Cathedral

Markensgate

Christiansholm Fortress

Ferry for Denmark*

Vestre Strandgata

Vestre havn

Østre havn

Fishing Port

Odderøya

250 m
825 ft

© Baedeker

* (Hirtshals and Hanstholm)

Where to eat
① Café Generalen
② Bakgården Restaurant
③ Restaurant Sjøhuset

Where to stay
① Clarion Hotel Ernst
② Sjøgløtt-Det Lille Hotell

Northeast of the town, hiding behind high trees in the middle of an attractive English garden, stands the white **Gimle Gård** mansion built around 1800 – a historic cultural treasure trove with a beautiful interior.

To the northwest of the town centre, in the Ravnedalen Nature Park, it is possible to climb the 200 steps to the viewing platform on the Ravneheia boulder, from where there is a wonderful view over the town, its nearby islands, and the sea. Designed around 1875, the park also contains several small bathing lakes, pretty nature walkways and a small café.

A dead straight street branching off from the »Kvadraturen«, known as the »Bygaden«, comprises around 40 old buildings and various cultural history exhibitions. Complete with furnished houses, workshops and junkshops, it has been recreated in the attractive open-air **Vest Agder Fylkesmuseum**, 4km/2mi east of Kristiansand near the E 18. The Setesdaltunet farm, with its smokeroom dating from the 17th century, is also worth seeing (opening times during summer Mon–Sat 10am–6pm, Sun from noon).

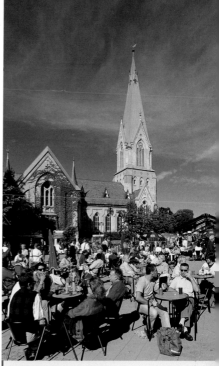

A good atmosphere outside the cathedral

Kristiansand Dyrepark ✱

Every Norwegian has to have been to the Kristiansand Animal and Leisure Park at least once during their childhood. The park is also located on the E 18, 12km/7mi east of town. Unbeatable favourites are the town of the »Thieves of Kardemomme« and Captain Sabretooth's Castle with its secret passages. The large Nordic beast of prey enclosure and the monkey jungle are also impressive (opening times: mid-June–mid-Aug 10am–7pm, otherwise till 4pm).

Skerry experience

The best way to experience the coastal skerries of the southern Norwegian Riviera is by paddlling a kayak or canoe through the labyrinth of little rocky islands, narrow fjords and silent, sandy bays. A good base for such activities is offered by the **Skottevig holiday park** (Skottevig = Scottish bay) about 20km/12mi east of Kristiansand.

✴ Kristiansund

F 4

Region: West Norway   **Population:** 17,000

Kristiansund was only joined to the mainland in 1992, with the construction of a 300-million-euro bridge. For centuries, the town was oriented towards the sea and its inhabitants lived almost exclusively from cod and herring fishing. Today, the source of most of the town's income is North Sea oil.

Town on three islands
Located southwest of Trondheim, Kristiansund's urban area spreads over three islands in the sea, connected to each other by bridges. The protected harbour was already being used over 8000 years ago and is still used by the Hurtigruten ships today. Up to 60% of Kristiansund was destroyed during an air raid during the Second World War in 1940, and the town lost much of its original natural character during the modern reconstruction. Collectively known as the Krifast (Kristiansund og Freis fastlandsforbindelse), the transport connection that links Kristiansund's islands consists of the world's only swimming bridge without side anchors, the longest underwater road tunnel and Norway's longest suspension bridge.

»Klippfisk«
Kristiansund's history is inextricably linked to fish (cod and herring). Almost all of the town's inhabitants lived from dried salt cod or »klippfisk« between 1750 and 1950, and the »Salt Cod Woman« at the harbour recalls that time. A hint of Portugal can be savoured in the many klippfisk restaurants in town; once upon a time, dried salt cod was exported to Portugal as »bacalao«. Indeed Kristiansund dried fish is prepared in a very Mediterranean way, with olive oil, olives, peppers and tomatoes.

Klippfisk Museum
A warehouse on the Vågen harbour basin where dried salt cod was once stored, today serves as the Klippfisk Museum. A tour and photos illustrate the various processes involved and impress the visitor with just how tough the work to produce this product was. Every fish, usually cod, had to be cleaned, salted and laid out on the cliffs to dry – a process that took from four to six weeks and involved the salt cod women turning the fish several times daily. The dried salt cod produced at the end could last for years (opening times: mid-June–early Aug Mon to Sat 1pm–5pm, Sun 1pm–4pm).

What to see in town
A substantial part of the town is characterized by parks and green spaces. The oldest buildings can be found on the southern island of Innlandet, such as the first **toll house** (1660–1748). Large sections of the town have been renovated and a walk around the Vågen harbour basin gives a good impression of the architectural style of the old

warehouses. Unfortunately, several of the beautiful historic buildings right by the port burnt down in November 2001.

The **Mellomværftet dockyard**, founded in 1865 and over on the western shore of the harbour, is of particular interest and still carries out contract work today as part of the Nordmøre Museum. The modern town church (1964) and the late 18th-century Lossiusgården townhouse are more sights worth adding to the itinerary. A fantastic view of the harbour entrance and the Grip Islands on the horizon can be enjoyed from the old **Varden lookout tower** – turn 180° and you can cast an eye over the mighty Nordmøre mountain range.

 VISITING KRISTIANSUND

INFORMATION
Kristiansund Reiselivslag
Vågeveien 5
6501 Kristiansund N
Tel. 71 58 54 54, fax 71 58 54 55
www.kristiansund.no

WHERE TO EAT
► **Moderate**
Ytterbrygga Restaurant
Håholmen Havstuer
Håholmen island
Tel. 71 51 72 50
The crossing from Gjetøy to Håholmen Island (during summer hourly between 11am and 9pm) is worth making, and not just for the restaurant housed in an 18th-century warehouse. Here at the old dried salt cod quay, you naturally also find genuine salt cod on the menu and a delicious lunch buffet is served in the afternoons.

Smia
Fosnagt. 30 b
Tel. 71 67 11 70
Award-winning restaurant housed in a former smithy dating from 1787. The bacalao, dried salt cod or the mixed fish platter made from the catch of the day are all highly recommended.

Baedeker recommendation

Sjøstjerna Fiskerestaurant
Skolegata 8
Tel. 71 67 87 78
To savour typical Kristiansund dried salt cod dishes head for this cosy little restaurant right in the middle of the town centre. The maritime atmosphere is underlined by fishing nets and other fishing utensils used as decoration.

WHERE TO STAY
► **Mid-range**
Quality Hotel Grand
Bernstorffstredet 1
Tel. 71 57 13 00
Fax 71 57 13 01
www.choicehotels.no
Traditional hotel in the town centre run with flair and to a high standard. The upper rooms offer a nice view of the harbour.

ISLAND HOPPING
The best way to get from island to island is on the boats travelling the sound that commute back and forth every 30 minutes.

Around Kristiansund

Grip Islands

The Grip Islands, 14km/9mi northwest of Kristiansund, consist of over 80 different islets and skerries. For centuries only up to 400 people lived here, predominantly fishermen and maritime pilots. Today the islands are only inhabited during the summer. Of particular note are the pier and **stave church** (late 15th century) with its altar painting from 1520. A tourist ferry operates during summer.

✳
Smøla Island

The island of Smøla, about 30km/19mi northeast of Kristiansund, is a paradise for anglers, ornithologists, hunters and divers. The island has a wealth of bird and animal species, including deer, mink, grey geese, herons and willow grouse – to name but a few.

✳ Atlantic Road · Atlanterhavsveien

Right along the sea

Between Kristiansund and ►Molde – or rather, between Vevang and Kårvåg 28km/17mi southwest of Kristiansund – lie countless islands that were only accessible by ferry until just a couple of decades ago. The 8km/5mi-long Atlanterhavsveien runs directly along the sea shore and is a vital lifeline for the rugged skerry landscape, as well as drawing in anglers, divers and visitors who want to experience the sea up close.

The islands and islets along this road are connected by an impressive system of a total of **twelve bridges** and several dams. It is probably one of **Europe's most interesting coastal stretches** and offers up a veritable paradise, especially for divers. In calm weather, the views across the open sea are wonderful; when the wild northwesterly wind blows the elements provide a fascinating spectacle.

Life in a fishing village

There are several fishing villages (»fiskevær«) along the Atlantic Road whose houses are rented out to visitors these days. At the turn of the last century, 120 people still lived exclusively from fishing on the countless little islands here. Today, water sports enthusiasts and holidaymakers predominate from spring to autumn. There is an hourly ferry connection during the summer from **Gjetøy** on the Atlantic Road out to the fishing village of **Håholmen**. Salt cod was once dried here, too.

Bud

In the Fræna parish south of the Atlantic Road lies the small fishing village of Bud, where Norway's last archbishop convened the Norwegian state council, farmers and burghers in 1553, in an attempt to free the country from its Danish yoke. The attempt failed and four years later the archbishop was forced to flee Norway. The wooden church at Bud dates from 1717.

✳
Trollkirka (Troll church)

Inland, in the direction of Molde on the RV 64, the Trollkirka is located near Eide, the largest and most imposing of the local **chalk-**

stone grottoes (70m/76yd long and up to 7m/8yd high), complete with waterfall (good shoes and a torch are required). The 4km/2.5mi-long path leading from the car park through pine forest is sometimes steep and it requires some effort to reach the Troll church.

✳ Lillehammer

D 7

Region: South Norway
Population: 25,000

Height: 180m/590ft

The Olympic town of Lillehammer is beautifully located on the upper reaches of Lake Mjøsa, at the exit of the Gudbrandsdal valley. Its biggest attractions are its charming pedestrian zone, good sporting opportunities and the Maihaugen Open-Air Museum.

A very popular holiday destination among Norwegians themselves, Lillehammer has been internationally famous since the 1994 Winter Olympics. Its beautiful location and mild climate attract thousands of visitors, who annually enliven the picturesque Storgata shopping street and its colourful wooden houses, as well as populating the restaurant terraces along the Mesna river that splits the town in two.

High rises? Not along the Storgata, Lillehammer's main shopping street.

▶ VISITING LILLEHAMMER

INFORMATION
Lillehammer
Jernbanetorget 2
2601 Lillehammer
Tel. 61 28 98 00, fax 61 28 98 01
www.lillehammerturist.no

WHERE TO EAT
► Moderate
Egon Lillehammer
Elvegaten 12, tel. 61 25 23 40
A restaurant from the Egon chain set in an old mill; there is always something suitable for children on the menu.

Bryggeriet Bar & Bifhus
Elvegt. 19
Tel. 61 27 06 60
Good, large steaks can be found in this restaurant and bar in a beer cellar. The same building is also home to the Brenneriet nightclub.

WHERE TO STAY
► Mid-range
Rustad Hotel og Fjellstue
Sjusjøn
Tel. 62 36 34 08, fax 62 36 35 74
89 beds, www.rustadhotel.com
This rustic hotel, especially popular with fishermen, hikers and winter sports enthusiasts, lies on a lake in a wonderful mountain landscape.

Mølla Hotel
Elvegaten 12
Tel. 61 26 92 94
Fax 61 26 92 95
www.mollahotell.no
This mill in the centre of town on the Mesnelva river had been grinding corn for 130 years before it was converted into an unusual hotel in 1991. All the rooms are installed with rustic pine furniture. The best view of town can be enjoyed from the hotel bar on the top floor, in the former grain barn, where the atmosphere and cocktails also draw great praise.

► Budget
Øvergaard
Jernbanegt. 24
Tel. 61 25 99 99
Fax 61 26 02 26
Located in a quiet and family-friendly location within easy walking distance of the town centre, this 150-year-old building offers practical, value for money rooms.

What to See in Lillehammer

Art Museum and artists

The architecturally interesting **Art Museum** on the Stortorget market place is worth a visit. It contains works by the Norwegian painters J. C. Dahl, A. Tidemand, Erik Werenskiold, Christian Krohg and Edvard Munch.

Transport Museum (Norsk Kjøretøyhistorisk

⊙

A special attraction is the Transport Museum, Norway's first, located on the Lilletorget. The exhibits illustrate the development from sleighs to horse-drawn carriages to the car (opening times: mid-June–mid-Aug daily 10am–6pm, otherwise 11am–3pm).

Lillehammer *Map*

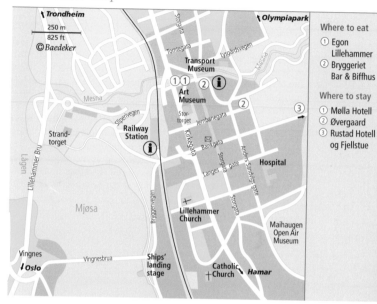

The Olympic sports facilities and village are located just a few blocks from the pedestrian zone. Standing above the town, the first part is Lund Hangem's **Olympic village** displaying traditional Norwegian architecture, and then the **Håkon Stadium** (Stampesletta) with its light roof and façade construction designed by the architectural office of Østgård AS. Originally the ice-hockey stadium, it is now used for general sporting events, trade fairs, conferences and concerts. The **Olympic Museum** was installed here in 1998, and gives an overview of all the Olympic Games, from 1896 to the present day (opening times: mid-June–mid-Sept daily 10am–6pm).

★

Olympic Park

The ascent to the Lysgårdbakkene (Kantvegen) **ski jump installation**, with its extra high 120m/394ft ramp as well as its standard 90m/295ft ramp, is a little more strenuous. It is possible to ride up to the top of the ramp's tower by chairlift (daily between 11am and 4pm), from where there is a commanding view across the town and Lake Mjøsa. The more energetic visitor can also climb up the tower's 954 steps instead.

Right on top of the hill lies the **Birkebeiner Ski Stadium**, with its 55km/34mi-long tracks that were once used by cross-country competitors and are now ideal for long walks and Nordic skiing. The name of Birkebeiner goes back to 13th-century skiers, who used birch tree bark for their boots. A memorial in honour of the Birkebeiner stands in front of the library.

★★
Maihaugen
Open-Air
Museum

Lillehammer's main attraction, drawing annual visitor numbers of around 175,000, is the Sandvig collection spread over the 40ha of the **Maihaugen** Open-Air Museum, on the southeastern edge of town. Founded by the dentist Anders Sandig (1862–1950) in 1887, the museum contains over 175 original buildings from the Gudrandsdal valley set in a natural environment of ponds, streams and tree landscape. The historic farm houses, complete with barn yards, stables and silos, have been rebuilt here true to their original design, often complete with their original interiors.

The oldest building in the museum complex is the **Garmo stave church** dating from around 1200. Of the other buildings, it is worth mentioning the Gynts Stue, originally built around 1700, that was the supposed home of the person Ibsen used as his inspiration for the famous character in his story. In one of the other houses, thin flatbread is baked daily on the open fire: it can be tasted for free. The

Maihaugen Open Air Museum

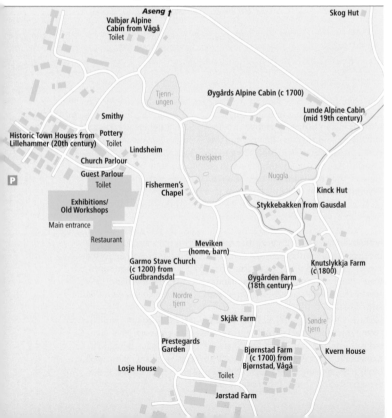

new museum building houses historic workshops with over 30 different trades represented such as wheel-makers, cobblers, blacksmiths, basket weavers, stone masons and saddlers.

The fascinating multimedia exhibition at Maihaugen entitled »How the Land Became Ours« takes the viewer on a journey from the Ice Age to the present and is really worth seeing, especially for children (opening times: mid-May–end of Sept daily 10am–5pm, beginning of Oct–mid-May 11am–4pm; www.maihaugen.no).

Around Lillehammer

Around 14km/9mi outside Lillehammer lies the modern holiday resort of Nordseter (786m/2579ft), with 350km/219mi of prepared pistes and tracks and three lifts. A worthwhile ascent to the 1086m/3563ft-high Neverfjell (just over one hour) can be made from Nordseter, where a broad panoramic view awaits. South of Nordseter, a road branches off to the ski lift by Sjusjøen (830m/2723ft), which is located on the pretty Lake Sjusjøen, which is lined by lodges, numerous holiday cabins, ski lifts and a colonial shop. The region is crisscrossed by 300km/187mi of cross country skiing routes. There is also a narrow road (toll payable) leading from here to the southern shore of the Mellsjø, 6km/4mi away.

Nordseter, Sjusjøen

∗ Lofoten

K/L 9-11

Region: Nordland
Population: 25,000

Area: 1308 sq km/505 sq mi

Mountains up to 1000m/3281ft high with strangely shaped summits rise vertically out of the sea in the Lofoten region, where small fishing villages add colour to the coves and the Nordic light is simply unique. A visit to this group of islands is an unforgettable experience.

Lofoten (Norwegians only refer to the islands in the singular, the Lofot, -en being the article) consists of an island chain almost 150km/94mi long, stretching into the ocean from the northeast to the southwest and separated from the mainland by the Vestfjord. From a distance, the four large islands of Austvågøy, Vestvågøy, Moskenesøy and Flakstadøy, along with several medium-sized islands, adjoin each other so closely that they give the impression of being just one long, jagged, mountainous ridge. A swarm of skerries surround the major islands and on some of the more alpine mountains (up to 1266m/4154ft) there is even snow.

Rugged beauty

Many places have rocks with colonies of nesting seabirds. Tree growth is sparse. Near the seashore lie swamps and lakes, meadows

Spiritual contemplation is easy in this little church on the Lofoten island of Augstvågøy.

and even a few cultivated fields. The coastal climate ensures mild winters and relatively cool summers. The main leisure activities here are fishing – either off piers or out of rowing boats – deep sea fishing, mountaineering and hunting.

Lofoten fishery The Lofoten population's main source of income is fishing and the season runs from the beginning of February to the middle of April. Significantly less boats come here than they used to, however. Once there were thousands of fishermen, and the Lofoten fishing industry attracted countless fishermen from as early as the 11th century, who would spend several weeks travelling along the coast, mostly in open rowing boats. At night, they sheltered in small wooden huts (rorbuer = rowers' huts) that stood on posts in the water, which today provide the typical holiday accommodation of the Lofoten region.

The bulk of the catch consists of cod or »torsk«, though there is also herring, sea trout, ocean perch, halibut, cusk, ling and shellfish. The predatory cod that usually inhabits the deep waters of the Atlantic Ocean migrates for spawning from the Barents Sea to these coastal waters at the beginning of each January. The depth at which the shoals of cod travel depends on the water temperature, and normally ranges in the region of 100m/328ft–300m/984ft. At one time, 20,000 fishermen took part in cod fishing; since the 1990s only between 2000 and 2500 have remained. While 140 million tons of cod were caught in 1980, today the fishing quotas that have been restricting the industry for years in an effort to replenish stocks allow a maximum of only 22,000 tons a year. In the meantime, some fishing families have moved into hunting minke whales, as well as salmon and trout farming.

Along with fishing there is some sheep and cattle farming, and more recently mink farms have also been established. Tourism plays a major role on the islands all year round, and fishing huts (»rorbuer«), some of which are very basic and old fashioned and some of which have been modernized, are rented out. In recent years around 220,000 visitors annually have been streaming onto these sparsely populated islands.

Sheep, cattle and tourists

Austvågøy

The capital and administrative centre of Lofoten is Svolvær, on the southern coast of the island of Austvågøy. The small town has around 4000 inhabitants whose number rises to over 6000 during the cod fishing season (»lofotfiske«) between February and April. Svolvær is the main port for the fish processing industry, as well as a major transport hub and the islands' most important trading centre.

Svolvær

The work of numerous artists who have sought inspiration in Lofoten can be viewed at the **»Nordnorsk Kunstneresentrum«** on Svinøya. Opposite the landing bridge, the grave of the Nordland painter Gunnar Berg Berg (born 1864 in Svolvær, † 1894 in Berlin) can be found on the little island of Gunnarholm by crossing the bridge from Svolvær. His most famous painting is the *Battle in the Trollfjord* (1890), which hangs in the Svolvær town hall. It portrays the bloody battle of 1880 between the traditionalists who used sailing boats and competing fishermen who were using »modern« steamships.
North of Svolvær, **Blåtind** (597m/1958ft) rises steeply; experienced hikers with a good level of fitness can get to the summit and back in 5hrs and are rewarded with wonderful views.

Art museum

A brilliant motorboat trip (2hrs) goes from Svolvær through the Raft sound to the southern end of Hinnøy, which is part of the ▶ Vesterålen region. A climb up Digermulkollen (just over one hour) is recommended. Today a bridge also connects Hinnøy with Austvågøy.

Ride to the island of Hinnøy

A narrow entrance through the cliffs leads west from the Raft sound into the slim Trollfjord. The snow-covered mountains of Higravstinder (1161m/3809ft) and jagged Trolltinder (up to 1045m/3429ft) rising out of the usually ice-covered 3km/2mi-long mountain lake of Trollfjordvatnet provide the backdrop beyond. The most popular day tour to the Trollfjord goes from Svolvær to Stokmarknes (via Fiskebøl) by bus, returning by Hurtigruten ship back over the Trollfjord.

**✷ ✷
Trollfjord**

▶ VISITING LOFOTEN

INFORMATION

Destinasjon Lofoten
8301 Svolvær
Torget (between the Hurtigruten quay
and the market place)
Tel. 76 06 98 00, www.lofoten-tourist.no

WHERE TO EAT

► Expensive
Fiskekrogen
Henningsvær, tel. 76 07 46 52
How about a spot of dried cod?
Diners in this cosy harbour restaurant
can be sure that the fish dishes have
been prepared in an authentically
Norwegian way.

► Moderate
Børsen Spiseri
Gunnar Bergsv. 2, Svolvær
Tel. 76 06 99 30
Once, fish were landed at the wharf,
which dating from 1828 is the oldest
harbour building still surviving here.
Today it offers a unique setting for a
good meal. In contrast to the delicate
presentation of the food, the interior
is rustic and characterized by its aged
wood. The starter »En smak av
Lofoten« is recommended for those
who wish to sample a variety of
typically local delicacies.

WHERE TO STAY

► Mid-range
Nusfjord Rorbuanlegg
Ramberg, tel. 76 09 30 20
34 rorbus huts, nusfjord@rica.no
No finer Lofoten setting can be found
than that of Nusfjord: red fishing
huts, a tiny harbour, an old merchant
shop and, in the background, magnificent mountain scenery. The fishing huts come in various standards,
from basic to comfortable, but all are
in a beautiful location.

Henningsvær Bryggehotel
Henningsvær
Tel. 76 07 47 50, fax 76 07 47 30
This hotel in the largest fishing
harbour in Lofoten was built right on
the water in 1995 and fits perfectly
into its surroundings. 31 comfortable
rooms offer spectacular views onto
the harbour and the steeply rising
mountains in the background.

► Budget
Justad Rorbuer og Vandrerhjem
Stamsund
Tel. 76 08 93 34
Fax 76 08 97 39
During the summer this youth hostel
is almost always fully booked as it lies
close to the Hurtigruten quay and is a
favoured destination for backpackers.
In addition to dormitory rooms, there
are also comfortable huts for rent.
There are good fishing opportunities
here too.

GETTING THERE

Lofoten can be reached on the
Hurtigruten ships (from Bodø to
Svolvær 6hrs); there are also shipping
connections to and from Skutvik
(2hrs) and Narvik (9hrs), and daily
flight connections from Bodø and
Evenes to Svolvær, Røst and Leknes.
Since the Lofoten Mainland Connection, otherwise known as »Lofast«,
was opened on 1 December 2007, the
group of islands in North Norway has
also been accessible without using a
ferry. The 51km/32mi-long E 10 leads
from Fiskebøl through four tunnels
and over two large and ten small
bridges to Gullesfjordbotn.

MIDNIGHT SUN

27 May to 17 July on the north and
west side of the islands

About 10km/6mi to the southwest of Svolvær (bus connection) lies Kabelvåg, with its attractively restored wooden houses, originally from the 19th century. Today, most of them are holiday homes. Kabelvåg was the main port for Lofoten before the establishment of steam shipping. A fishing museum and the **Lofot Aquarium** containing fish and sea lions from the Vestfjord are both worth seeing here. **Vågan church** is the largest wooden church north of Trondheim. The well-known Espolin Gallery displays works by the Nordland painter Kåre Espolin Johnson and the entrance ticket is valid for the gallery, the Lofot Aquarium and the Lofot Musuem in the suburb of Storvågan as well (opening times: 15 June–15 Aug daily 9am–8pm; beginning of June and end of Aug till 6pm).

✱ Kabelvåg

Festvåg lies at the southwestern end of Austvågøy island, where the 942m/3090ft Vågakallen can be climbed in 3.5hrs. A bridge there also leads to the typical fishing village of Henningsvær, where a major fishing fleet gathers each winter. The drive from Kabelvåg to Henningsvær takes about 20mins and the harbour of the so-called »Venice of the North« is one of Norway's most popular photographic motifs. Many visitors have a look around the gallery of local artist Karl Erik Harr, who also owns a gallery near ► Harstad, in the Røkenes Gård og Gjestehus (opening times: daily 10am–6pm, mid-June–mid-Aug 9am–9pm).

✱ Henningsvær

Vestvågøy

Stamsund, located on the southeastern coast of the large island of Vestvågøy (pop. 11,000), is one of the most important fishing centres in the Lofoten archipelago and transport hub for western Lofoten. Accommodation is available at the Stamsund Lofoten Hotel, various fishing huts, and the numerous holiday homes.
There are several freshwater lakes in Vestvågøy, as well as extensive **wetlands and moorlands**. On the ocean side of the island, there are veritable **dream beaches** on the Vikspollen Bay, with fine, white sand, and an imposing, lush green mountain setting as a backdrop. If only the water were not so cold! This is made up for, though, by the **midnight sun**, which can be seen very clearly from here.

Dream beaches for the hardy

The remains of the largest Viking houses known to date were found in Borg, on the E 10 road, 14km/9mi from Leknes. The chieftain's house measures an impressive 83m/90yd x 8m/9yd. Several of the utensils found are of Celtic origin, objects looted by the Vikings from France and England. The reconstructed building houses a museum since 1995 that recreates the Viking era: there is weaving, knitting, spinning and dyeing in the main living quarters, while dishes according to original recipes are served in the former guild hall where the Vikings once convened their meetings (opening times: end of May–beginning of Sept 10am–7pm, otherwise 1pm–3pm).

Borg Viking Museum

Beach near Utakleiv on the island of Vestvågøy: for many, Lofoten is a dream destination – and rightly so.

Ballstad   The fishing port of Ballstad lies at the southwestern end of the island of Vestvågøy, in the shadow of the Ballstadaksla mountain (466m/ 1529ft). The island is linked to neighbouring Flakstadøy by the 2km/ 1mi-long Nappstraumen underwater tunnel (toll payable).

Nordland Sculpture Park   In Eggum, on the northwest coast of Vestvågøy, there is art to be discovered in the green meadow landscape. A short footpath leads to the first sculpture: *The Head* by the Swiss artist Markus Raetz displays different facets depending on the viewer's position, either appearing as a classic portrait looking out to sea, or, if viewed from the mountain side, resembling an upside down head. It is one of 33 sculptures created by international artists for the Nordland Sculpture Landscape Project, of which five are in Lofoten (see Baedeker Special p.300).

Flakstadøy

Ramberg   The small settlement of Ramberg lies on the northwest coast of the island of Flakstadøy (holiday homes in Nusfjord). Not far to the east stands Flakstad church (1780), which was originally built from driftwood. Facing the open sea, Ramberg's 300 inhabitants have a wonderful view of the **white sandy beach**. There are interesting artisan and craft workshops in the village and surrounding area. Flakstadøy is connected to neighbouring Moskenesøy by a suspension bridge. It is worth paying a visit to the blacksmith at Sund, around 12km/7mi from Ramberg: he makes the handmade »King Cormorants«.

Around 10km/6mi beyond the Nappstraumen tunnel, a country road turns off for the pretty fishing village of Nusfjord. One of the most authentic surviving Lofoten villages, it has been added to the **UNESCO** World Heritage List for cultural properties worth preserving. There are many fishing huts for rent here and professional fishermen offer fishing trips – for which warm clothing is essential.

★
Nusfjord

Moskenesøy

The main settlement on the island of Moskenesøy is the fishing village of Reine (holiday homes) on the Kirkefjord – a favourite location of numerous painters and mountaineers. Around 10km/6mi to the southwest lies the little village of Å, which marks the end of the Lofoten road. The tidal Moskenstraumen between Cape Lofotodden and Mosken Island can be observed from the hills around the village. Jules Verne and Edgar Allan Poe described it as the original »Maelstrom«. Å too has its fishing village museum with a brine boiling room and a dried cod museum, housed in the former packing house by the harbour.

Reine, Å

The island of Værøy to the southwest can be reached by boat from Reine (a trip not recommended for those liable to seasickness!). Værøy is home to just 760 people. In the south, the Mostad Mountains rise sharply above the abandoned settlement of **Mostad**. The hills here are a **paradise for birds**, where over one million of them breed from May to August each year: most are puffins, but there are also guillemots, sea eagles and others. The breeding cliffs can be reached by hired boat in 20mins from Værøy. The last survivors of a strange dog species with six toes live on the island: known as puffin dogs, they were once used to hunt these birds.

Journey to Værøy

Also accessible by boat from Reine (journey time around 5hrs), as well as from Bodø (5hrs) and Værøy (just over 2hrs), is the last outpost of civilization: the **island group of Røst** lies almost 100km/62mi from the mainland. **Scandinavia's largest bird breeding colony** can be found on the high cliffs of Vedøy, Storfjell, Stavøy, Trenyken and Hernyken, where in addition to around three million puffins, there are also rare species of petrel and fulmar. Boat tours to the cliffs set out from Røstland, and there are also helicopter tours from Bodø during the peak season.

★
Bird cliffs

Norwegian stockfish is exported all the way to Portugal.

FROM COD TO STOCCAFISSO

The striking roof-shaped scaffolds used for drying fish stand all along the Lofoten coast, filled with headless and gutted fish bound together two by two. They are part of a centuries-old tradition of conserving fish by drying it in the cold air.

The trade in stockfish – named after the scaffold drying racks – is documented from Viking times, and **fish merchants from Milan** still come to Lofoten today to inspect the valuable ingredient for their »stoccafisso«. During the Middle Ages, the stockfish was Norway's most important export by far. Catholic Europe hungered for fish every Friday as well as during Lent, and due to the wealth of cod along their coast Norwegians were able to supply vast amounts. To ensure that catches did not rot in the Hanseatic boats during their long journeys, they were **preserved by drying**. Each spring, after the Lofoten fishing season, predominantly cod, but also coley, cusk and ling are cut either lengthways into two pieces (whereby half the spine is removed), or beheaded and gutted. Two fish are then tied together by their tails and hung on the scaffold, known as a »Hjeller«, where they are left to dry in the salty sea air until 12 June at the latest. The fish loses 70% of its original moisture during the drying process, but **the nutritional content is preserved**. Thus five kilos (11lbs) of fresh fish contain exactly the same amount of vitamin B, protein, iron and calcium as one kilo (2.2lbs) of stockfish, which the Norwegians generally call »tørrfisk«, meaning dried fish. It is even possible to purchase dried fish pieces in small paper bags as a healthy snack for nibbling on.

Strong odour

Norway's most famous dried fish speciality is »lutefisk«. It appears on all fish restaurant menus during the advent period before Christmas (but some claim that more lutefisk is eaten by Norwegian immigrants in North America).This marinated fish dish requires the dried fish to be soaked in a strong solution for two days, followed by one day of soaking in fresh water, after which it is cooked. When its colour turns a faint yellowish grey and the first overpowering odours appear, the dried fish can be sautéed. According to strict tradition at least, the dish should be served with mashed peas, potatoes and bacon cubes.

✳ Lyngenfjord

Region: North Norway

The Lyngenfjord is among the most majestic of Norway's fjords. Between it and the Ullsfjord, the Lyngen Peninsula reaches far out to sea. The Lyngen Alps, partly covered in glaciers, provide almost entirely undeveloped hiking and climbing territory.

The Lyngenfjord extends about 80km/50mi south from the foothills of the Lyngstuen (395m/1296ft). While the road winds along the eastern shore, past small villages and occasionally lush, green meadows below the forested hills, the snow and ice covered mountains of the Lyngen Alps (Lyngsalpene) rise directly out of the water on the western shore. From Tromsø, the Lyngenfjord can be reached on the E 8 as far as Nordkjostbotn; from the south the route is via the E 6.

Northern Norway's most beautiful fjord

Eastern Shore of the Lyngenfjord

The route to **Oteren** at the southern end of the Storfjord (the southern arm of the Lyngenfjord) goes through the valley of the Nordkjoselv, framed by mountains, with its typically north Norwegian birch forests. To the southeast tower the jagged ridge of Mannfjell (1533m/5030ft) and Otertind (1360m/4462ft), whose double pyramid is also known as the **»Arctic Matterhorn«**. 3km/2mi northeast of Oteren a road turns off into the **Signaldalen** valley, which is surrounded by mighty mountains, and a sign-posted footpath leads to the Alpine cabin of Gappohytta (4hrs), as well as connecting with the Nordkalotten hiking route in Sweden.

Storfjord

A magnificent view onto the Lyngenfjord and the glacier-topped Jiekkevarre (1833m/6014ft) opens up at Falsnes. The peak is the highest summit of the Lyngen Alps on the west side of the fjord.

The small settlement of **Skibotn** was already an important market for Swedish and Norwegian merchants and the Samis in the 17th century. The mountain Sami came with furs, reindeer meat, iron and agricultural goods and traded them for fish, schnapps and tobacco.

▶ LYNGENFJORD

INFORMATION

See Tromsø

WHERE TO STAY

▶ **Mid-range**
Euro Hotel Maritim
Strandveien 35, Skjervøy
Tel. 77 76 03 77, fax 77 76 07 16
31 rooms, www.hotell-maritim.no
Centrally located hotel with modern and practical no-frills rooms. There is often live music in the restaurant on Saturdays.

Rugged beauty: the Lyngenfjord and the mountainous Lyngen Alps

Detour to Finland
The E 8 turns off in the direction of Finland (39km/24mi) to the south of Skibotn. The Skibotn Sami's summer camp at the southern end of **Lake Galgojavvre** can be reached via the forested valley of the fish-rich Skibotnelv, past the 25m/82ft-high Rovijokfoss (where a footpath leads to a viewing point). To the south, on the other side of the Norwegian-Finnish border, it is possible to make out the 39km/24mi-long **Lake Kilpisjärvi**. At the northern end of Kilpisjärvi, a round marker stone stands at the tri-border point between Sweden, Norway and Finland. This point can be reached from Norway along a signposted footpath that leads off the E 8 in the direction of the Goldalhytta (around 6hrs) or via the Gappohytta (around 5hrs; see also under Storfjord). All walking tours in this isolated region require good fitness and equipment. Note that it can snow here even during summer.

Holy mountain
To the east, the characteristic silhouette of Saanatunturi – the **»holy mountain of the Sami people«** – catches the eye. The 1024m/3360ft mountain can be climbed in a good two hours from the Kilpisjärvi hiking hostel. The reward is a beautiful panoramic view of snow-capped peaks, mighty highland landscapes, numerous lakes and the endless forests of Finland.

Kåfjord
Passing the viewing point at Odden, the E 6 winds its way along the shore of the Kåfjord – a side arm of the Lyngenfjord. Near the mid-

dle of the fjord lies the settlement of Birtavarre (with a small **open-air museum**), which used to be where iron ore from the nearby Birtavarre mine was prepared for transport. Next to fishing and agriculture, an important source of income here is the sale of a type of hand-woven carpet known as the »radno«. The imposing **Goikegorsa Canyon** in the **Kåfjorddal** is witness to the mighty erosive power of the ice-age meltwaters.

A few miles further on to the north, cast an eye over to the southern shore where the waterfalls from the **Isfjell** fall vertically into the fjord from a height of 800–900m/2625–2950ft. The next significant place is Olderdal, municipal centre for the Kåfjord parish. From here **Olderdal** there is a choice: either continue driving in the direction of Rotsund along the scenically beautiful east shore of the Lyngenfjord, where the views are often wonderful; or take a 40-minute ferry ride to Lyngseidet, on the west shore of the fjord.

> **!** **Baedeker TIP**
>
> **A trip to bird island**
> One really worthwhile trip is taking the ferry for the 20-minute journey from Skjervøy to the island of Arnøy, and then onwards to Årviksand, at the mouth of the Lyngenfjord. There is a wonderful view onto Norway's largest bird nesting island here: Fugløya is home to 300,000 puffins and numerous sea eagles.

In **Langslett**, 34km/21mi north of Olderdalen, the RV 866 branches off to the idyllic fishing village of Skjervøy, 31km/19mi away. There is a wonderful view of the Kvænangen fjord and the mountains around the Øksfjordjøkulen glacier (1204m/3950ft) from the harbour there, where the Hurtigruten ships stop daily.

Western Shore of the Lyngenfjord

Lyngseidet, which can be reached either by ferry from Olderdalen (E 6) or from Oteren (see above) on the RV 868 along the western **Lyngen Alps** shore of the fjord, is a suitable base for ascending Goalsevárri (1280m/4200ft). Setting off from the hamlet of **Furuflaten**, it is also possible to climb Njallevárri (1525m/5003ft) in about 4–5hrs, from which there is a spectacular view onto the ice fields of Mount Jiekkevarre (1833m/6014ft) to the west, one of northern Norway's highest mountains.

North of Lyngseidet, the imposing Store Jægervasstind towers 1596m/5236ft up into the sky. This mighty mountain is a veritable **Store Jægervasstind** mountaineering paradise and, even though the Englishman William S. Slingsby climbed it as early as 1898, many mountaineers still enjoy the challenge of finding new routes to the summit. A good staring point for such ventures is the **Jægervasshytta** to the west, on Lake Jægervatnet.

✳ Mandal

A 4

Region: South Norway   **Population:** 13,000

In good weather, everyone in Mandal heads to Sjøsanden, undoubtedly one of Norway's most beautiful beaches. This pretty south coast town doesn't get really packed, however, until the annual shellfish festival in August.

Norway's most southerly town
The most southerly town on the Norwegian Riviera is characterized by narrow lanes and the numerous listed buildings in the old town. Once upon a time, wood from the region's great oak forests and sal-

 VISITING MANDAL

INFORMATION
Mandal Turistkontoret
Bryggegata 10
4514 Mandal
Tel. 38 27 83 00
Fax 38 27 83 01
www.vistiregionmandal.no

WHERE TO EAT
▶ **Moderate**
Art Café
Birkelandsvannet, Øyelsbø (about 25mins north of Mandal)
Tel. 38 28 78 00
Mirrors are an important feature of the innovative interior of this café, run by an artist.

WHERE TO STAY
▶ **Mid-range**
Kjøbmandsgaarden Hotel
12 rooms, St. Elvegate 57
Tel. 38 26 12 76, fax 38 26 33 02
www.kjb-hotel.no
Cosy little place in Mandal's old town with an outstanding restaurant.

▶ **Budget**
Lindesnes Camping og Hytteutleie
Lillehavn, Spangereid
Tel. 38 25 88 74, fax 38 25 88 92

www.lindesnescamping.no
Norway's most southerly campsite lies right by the sea on the southern tip of the Lindesnes peninsula. Two cabins in a wonderful location offer room for up to 8 people.

Baedeker recommendation

Fish galore: during the shellfish festival in August, a line of tables several hundred metres long is set up on the street and loaded with seafood delicacies. Thousands of people come to Mandal just for the festival, where everyone eats, drinks and generally has a splendid time.

LEISURE
Sjøsanden is Norway's largest beach, where regular beach volleyball championships are held.

mon from the Mandalselva river formed the basis of the town's economic wealth. During the 17th and 18th centuries, both the wood and the fish were loaded onto ships destined for foreign climes at Mandal's harbour, one of Norway's oldest. Smoked Mandal salmon was even a highly sought-after delicacy at royal courts overseas.

What to See in and around Mandal

One of Mandal's most beautiful buildings is the old merchant's house of Andorsengården (1801), today a museum with a sailing boat gallery, fishing exhibition and an art gallery showing works by Mandal painters, including Adolf Gustav Vigeland (► Famous People). The former Skrivergården house of a civil servant dating from 1766 was built from Scottish sandstone and is surrounded by an attractive park designed by the German-Danish landscape gardener Ludvig Blumenthal. Mandal's plain church in Empire style (1821) has seating for 1800, making it one of northern Europe's largest wooden churches.

Old town

!	*Baedeker* TIP

Fun in the water

If you find Sjøsanden too busy, try taking the signposted footpath – suitable for those with disabilities as well as for children's buggies – along the coast to the Sørland cliffs. Along the way there are many small coves, ideal for a dip and usually more or less empty.

Precisely 2518km/1574mi from Nordkapp and the most southerly point on the Norwegian mainland, Lindesnes, lies at a northern latitude of 57°58' 43" around 40km/25mi west of Mandal. Norway's first lighthouse was built here back in 1655 and there is a wonderful view in good weather as far as Mandal to the east and Lista to the west from the new lighthouse, whose flashing light can be seen from up to 19.4 nautical miles away. A special experience is seeing Lindesnes during a storm, when the waves can reach up to 14m/46ft.

Lindesnes

The narrow lanes and beautifully restored white wooden houses of the quarter known as »Dutch Town« were originally built in the 18th century, when the wood trade with Holland flourished in Flekkefjord (80km/50mi northwest of Mandal). One of the most appealing buildings in the old town is the Grand Hotel, its white-painted wooden façade decorated with bays and turrets. Other attractions include the several beautiful swimming beaches by the skerry landscape on Hidra Island, south of Flekkefjord. A ferry makes the crossing from Kvellandstrand every hour and the journey takes about 10mins.

Flekkefjord

For travellers with plenty of time who want to continue breathing the sea air, the Nordsjøvegen can be taken as an alternative route between Kristiansand and Stavanger. The most varied section of this beautiful coastal road runs from Flekkefjord to Stavanger.

Coastal road due north

✳ Mjøsa

C/D 7/8

Region: East Norway

Height: 124m/407ft

Lake Mjøsa, Norway's largest lake, lies in a fertile landscape with many large farms. The most comfortable way to enjoy this gentle countryside is by taking a ride on the historic »Skibladner« steamboat.

Norway's largest lake When the meltwaters from the north flow into the 362 sq km/140 sq mi of Lake Mjøsa in early summer, it takes on a very special greenish colour. The region around Hamar and Stange, »Norway's bread basket«, is characterized by large waving cereal fields and handsome farms painted red. Further to the north the lake, which reaches depths of 443m/1453ft, is only 2km/1mi wide; here it is possible to get a first taste of the Gudbrandsdal valley, fertile land surrounded by steep hillsides. The farms of the area lie in green meadows below steep, forested slopes that soon merge into a barren mountain landscape.

What to See on and around Lake Mjøsa

✳ **Eidsvoll-bygningen** Just a short drive (signposted) to the south of Lake Mjøsa and east of the E 6 stands one of Norway's national shrines: the old Eidsvoll mansion, in whose state hall 112 of the country's representatives met

▶ VISITING MJØSA

INFORMATION

Gjøvik-Toten Turistkontor
Jernbanegt. 2
2821 Gjøvik
Tel.61 14 67 10
Fax 61 14 67 01
www.turistinnlandet.no

WHERE TO STAY

▶ **Mid-range**
Quality Hotel Grand
Jernbanegt. 5, Gjøvik
Tel. 61 14 00 00, fax 61 14 00 01
82 rooms, www.choicehotels.no
This traditional hotel, regularly modernized, is situated near the subterranean Gjøvik Olympic Cavern Hall. Its American restaurant is famous far and wide.

WHERE TO EAT

▶ **Expensive**
Belvedere
Hans Mustadsgt. 14, Gjøvik
Tel. 61 18 02 58
This high-class restaurant is located in a fine villa above the town.

EXCURSIONS

The most pleasant option is a trip on the oldest steamboat still in operation, the »Skibladner«, which has been in service since 1856. Departures at 9.30am from Gjøvik mid-June–mid-Aug Tue, Thu & Sat, arriving in Lillehammer 2.45pm; departures from Lillehammer at 3pm, arriving in Gjøvik at 5.20pm
(www.skibladner.no).

The paddlesteamer »Skiblander« glides over the lake.

on 17 May 1814 to sign Norway's first constitution (opening times: mid-June–mid-Aug daily 10am–5pm, otherwise 10am–3pm).

At the southern end of Lake Mjøsa, the RV 33 branches off towards **Gjøvik**, winding its way directly along the lakeshore for the first 40km/25mi, occasionally passing below steep hillsides (there are several pretty rest stops and viewing points). North of Skreia stands **Balke church** (1200), an attractive stone church with an altar cupboard and religious sculptures dating from the 13th century. It is worth making a detour to the Stenberg country estate, which dates from 1790 and whose park has a pretty **open-air museum** (Toten Økomuseum) dedicated to the Toten region.

During the 1994 Winter Olympics, the regional centre of **Gjøvik** (pop. 27,000) had the honour of hosting all the ice hockey games in its purpose-built Olympic Cavern Hall, which was blasted out of the mountain right in the centre of town. With a ground plan spanning 5550 sq m/59,740 sq ft and seating for 5830, the venue is the largest **underground spectator hall on earth**. 170 tons of dynamite was used to create the cavern, and the rocks left over were built into the Gjøvik beach promenade. The road rejoins the E 6 17km/11mi north of Gjøvik.

✳ Gjøvik Olympic Cavern Hall

On the eastern shore, the conveniently widened E 6 initially follows a beautiful route above the lake for about 20km/12mi before leaving Lake Mjøsa and heading through birch and pine forests (watch out for elk) in Norway's most fertile **region around Stange** and ► Hamar. The **church** (1250) west of Stange is among the most important medieval churches of the Hedmark region. The stained glass windows are outstanding. Near the lakeshore there are numerous country estates (storgårder), often dating from the 18th century, which underline the historic wealth of this fertile region.

Eastern shore

Just a short drive beyond the Brummundal on the main road, there is a turn-off to the stone basilica of Ringsaker (1150). The chalk paintings in the choir portray St Olav (►Trondheim; ►Steinkjer, Stiklestad), who – occasionally by force – brought Christianity to Norway at the beginning of the 11th century. The old Flemish painted wooden altar from 1530 is a real treasure (opening times: during summer Sat 10am–4pm, Sun noon—5pm). The Prøysenhuset, a museum containing an exhibition (of interest for children too) on Alf Prøysen (1914–70), Norway's best known composer and author of folktunes, lies on the E 6, which then continues to Lillehammer via the 1420m/4659ft Mjøsa bridge (toll payable) leading over the lake

✳ Ringsaker church

⊙

to its western shore. Those who wish to remain on the eastern shore continue through Moelv on the old Europa Route, which winds idyllically above the lake as far as ▶Lillehammer.

Mo i Rana

J 11

Region: North Norway   **Population:** 25,000

Mo i Rana itself is not very spectacular and tends to be passed by. However, it is worth taking the time to visit Svartisen – which after all is Norway's second largest glacier – and the grottoes nearby.

Lively port   Mo (pronounced Mu) i Rana is the largest settlement in the Helgeland region (▶ Nordland). During the 19th century, the German L. A. Meyer and his descendants ensured that this former trading post developed into a lively industrial centre. They installed a mine, shops, and even a wine trading post. After the war, the town also gained an ironworks and a cokeworks that are now both decomissioned. This industrial adventure can be traced in the local **museum**, which in addition provides information on the Sami people (▶Baedeker Special p.36), whose culture and trade also had a strong impact on the town. A local curiosity to the west of the town centre is the 10m/33ft-high statue of the **»Havmannen«** (Man of the Sea), the water reaching up to his stone thighs at each high tide.

Around Mo i Rana

Mysterious caves   Only two of the 120 caves in this region are open to the public. The most well known is the **Grønli Cave** (Grønligrotta), a maze of wind-

 VISITING MO I RANA

INFORMATION

Mo i Rana Turistinformasjon
O. T. Olsensgt 2, 8602 Mo i Rana
Tel. 75 13 92 00, fax 75 13 92 09
www.arctic-circle.no

WHERE TO EAT

▶ **Moderate**
Meyergården Hotel
Fr. Nansensgt 28, tel. 75 13 40 80
This traditional hotel in the town centre is well known for its good restaurant. The »Dagens Middag«

offered between 1pm and 7.30pm is a good deal.

WHERE TO STAY

▶ **Budget**
Mo Gjestegård
Hans Wølnersgt. 10
Tel. 75 12 22 11, fax 75 15 23 38
This guesthouse is in a quiet location surrounded by a well-maintained garden. The 15 rooms (incl. family rooms) are newly renovated with pine-clad walls.

ing paasages with an underground stream, moulins – and lighting. Indeed it is the only cave in Northern Europe to be illuminated. In the high season from mid-June 40-minute guided tours take place hourly between 10am and 7pm. Access to Grønligrotta, which is signposted, is via a turn-off from the E 6 near Røssvoll (airstrip) 13km/8mi northeast of Mo i Rana, followed by a 20-minute walk to the cave entrance.

A visit to Setergrotta (Seter Cave) is most suitable for experienced cavers, since the two-hour tour through gigantic caverns, narrow tunnels and slippery passages requires rubber boots, helmets, waterproof clothing and headlamps (all gear can be hired out). With its 3km/2mi of mapped passages, this limestone cave is one of the largest in the district,and its formations of chalk, ice and white marble certainly make for a spooky atmosphere (June–Aug tours daily 11am, occasionally also at 3pm; for access see Grønligrotta).

★
◄ Setergrotta

Beyond the caves, the road continues to Lake Svartisvatn (huts & kiosk), where the great ice fields of Norway's second largest glacier rise up (►Saltfjell). From 20 June to the end of August it is possible to take a boat over the deep green waters of the lake every other hour between 10am and 4pm, and hike through the magnificent mountain landscape. It takes about 1.5hrs to cover the approximately 3km/2mi to the Østerdalsisen arm of the glacier; the path is often steep and very rocky underfoot (stout hiking boots needed).

★
Svartisen

The picturesque Sjøgata right on the Vefsnfjord, in the small industrial settlement of Mosjøen (pop. 13,500; 91km/57mi southwest of Mo i Rana), is northern Norway's longest and best preserved historic town road, with around 100 beautifully restored wooden houses dating from the 18th and 19th centuries.

Mosjøen

A worthwhile excursion from Mosjøen leads towards the sea at **Sandnessjøen**, which is located to the northwest of the mountain range well-known as »The Seven Sisters« (►Nordland)and is the administra-

? DID YOU KNOW …?

■ In the midst of the fjord landscape west of Mosjøen lies the small island of Tro, which can be reached by ferry from Tjøtta. The oldest representation of a skier in Norway can be found here in the rock engraving that inspired the official logo for the Winter Olympics in Lillehammer.

tive centre of Alstahaug municipality. It is kept lively by the stop of the Hurtigruten ships and as a transfer point for the oil industry. 20km/12mi further south, on the eastern shore of the Alstfjord, stands the 12th-century Romanesque church in Alstahaug with its magnificently embellished altar. On Dønna Island (25mins by ferry from Sandnessjøen), it is worth visiting the 12th-century stone church with its underground passages and burial chamber. There is a fine view of the bird island of Lovund, where around 25,000 puffins nest, from Dønnesfjell (127m/417ft). Access is by express boat.

★
◄ Dønna Island

Narvik

L 14

Region: North Norway   **Population:** 18 500

Narvik's ice-free harbour has been both a blessing and a curse. On the one hand iron ore from Swedish Kiruna is shipped out from here, but on the other the port was so fought over in the Second World War that the town was almost totally destroyed. The shipping of iron ore today is something to behold for those interested in seeing mighty industry at work.

Distributor of iron ore from Sweden

This north Norwegian town was called Victoriahavn right until 1899, but was then renamed as Narvik when the Ofot Line (Swedish Lapland Line) rail connection was built, which comes from the Swedish iron ore mining region near **Kiruna**. Thanks to its ice-free port and its position at the end of the Ofot Line, Narvik enjoys great economic importance. During the Second World War, the German occupation of the town guaranteed their supply of Swedish iron ore. Britain attempted to obstruct this, and the resulting heavy battles caused the destruction of the town.

During the reconstruction of Narvik in the 1950s, the old wooden houses were replaced with unappealing stone buildings. Most visitors to Narvik are merely passing through on their way to Nordkapp.

 VISITING NARVIK

INFORMATION

Destination Narvik
Kongensgt. 26
8505 Narvik
Tel. 76 96 56 00
Fax 76 96 56 09
www.narvikinfo.no

WHERE TO EAT

► **Moderate**

① *Astrupkjelleren*
Kinobakken 1
Tel. 76 96 04 02
Simple restaurant in one of Narvik's oldest buildings, erected in 1903. In addition to meat, game and fish dishes (incl. monkfish), there are salads, pizza and children's menus.

WHERE TO STAY & EAT

► **Mid-range**

① *Quality Grand Royal*
220 beds, Kongensgt. 64
Tel. 76 97 70 00, fax 76 97 70 07
www.grandroyal.no
Located right in the town centre, this hotel has a popular restaurant, as well as a pub and a nightclub.

EXCURSIONS

In good weather, a trip to the Swedish border on the Ofot Line is really rewarding. The train travels to and from the fjord to the high mountains in three hours, and there are superb views, but only for those sitting on the left-hand side (in the direction the train is heading). Trains leave from Narvik railway station.

What to See in Narvik

The town is sliced in two by the mighty iron ore port, which was extended in 1977. The ore arriving from Sweden by train is moved to various stores and to the Malm quay via long conveyor belts. The expansion of the port ensured that iron ore freighters with a capacity of up to 350,000 tons could be loaded and annual turnover now stands at around 14 million tons. However, since several developing countries, such as Brazil, have been able to offer iron ore at significantly lower prices, the demand for the expensive Swedish ore has declined dramatically, and the significance of Narvik's port with it. Only 300 people still find employment in the port. Tours of the Swedish company LKAB's port installations are organized by the tourist information office; schedules can also be found at www.lkab.com.

★
Iron ore port

A tank can be seen stationed in front of the entrance to the War Museum opposite the town hall. This is one of Norway's most visited war museums, and documents the events of the war with collections of uniforms, weapons, medals and pieces of wreckage (opening times: daily March–Sept 10am–4pm, June–Aug 10am–8pm).

War Museum

Narvik Map

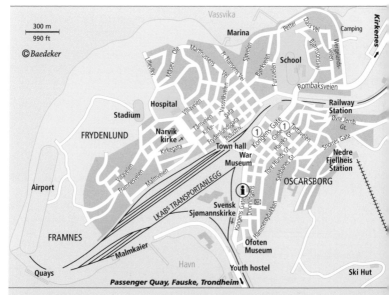

Where to eat	Where to stay
① Astrupkjelleren	① Radisson SAS Grand Royal

The Ofot railway brings iron ore and tourists over the Swedish border.

South of the market The **Swedish sailors' church**, including a library, is located at the southern end of Kongens gate. Diagonally opposite, a memorial recalls two **tank carriers**, the Norwegian ships *Norge* and *Eidsvold* that were sunk during the battles of 1940. Narvik's cultural-historic **Ofoten Museum** provides its visitors with all they need to know on the iron ore port. The **cemetery to the east** of town is the final resting place not only of Allied troops who fell here, but also of 1473 German soldiers.

Frammeåsen It is worth climbing the 102m/325ft Frammeåsen, twenty minutes west of town, from which there is a panoramic view across the Ofotfjord and over to Kongsbaktind. To the south, the famous mountain silhouette of »Den sovende Dronning« (Sleeping Queen) is also visible.

Around Narvik

To the southeast of Narvik stands the 1250m/4101ft Fagernesfjell, from which there is an extensive view. A cable car ascends to 700m/2297ft, at which point there is a restaurant. The slopes around Narvik are very well provided with alpine sports facilities, which are also regularly used for ski races.

Fagernesfjell

Driving south towards Bodø, there is a turning due northeast to Leiknes . Here, about 900m/985yd from the RV 814, around 40 animal rock paintings can be found that are up to four or five thousand years old. In Tømmernes, 47km/29mi south of Bognes, the rock paintings found near Sagelva are 5000, perhaps even 8000 years old.

**Leiknes,
Tømmernes**

At Ulvsvåg south of Narvik, route 81 turns off to the **Hamarøy** group of islands, whose rugged mountain landscape matches Lofoten in every way and is well worth a visit. Mount Hamarøyskaftet stands out in particular, jabbing into the sky like a giant green tooth. The small **Hamsun Museum**, in the house that once served as the writer's home,

> ### ! *Baedeker* TIP
>
> #### The charming Edvardas hotel
>
> The little Edvardas Hus hotel in Tranøy certainly deserved its cultural prize. The elegant wooden house has only nine rooms, all with their own delightful interiors, but what really defines the incomparable charm of this place is the service. The hotel feels like a home from home and guests are thoroughly spoiled (tel. 75 77 21 82, fax 75 77 22 21, www.edvardashus.no).

and the *Stella Maris* sculpture by Steinar Christensen that was created for the Nordland Sculpture Landscape are equally interesting. The photogenic lighthouse of Tranøy Fyr and the art galleries, including the Hamsun gallery (a small shop where Knut Hamsun once worked as a young assistant) near **Tranøy**, are also worth the trip.

✳ Nordfjord

D 2/3

Region: West Norway

A drive along the many branches of the Nordfjord shows western Norway at its most beautiful. The crowning finale is a trip to the glacier tongues of Jostedalsbreen, of which Briksdalsbreen is the most popular.

Glaciers, idyllic fjord and fishing villages, steep, high mountains, lonely beaches, narrow serpentine roads and deep, clear waters – all this is on offer at the Nordfjord which extends over 100km/62mi inland, from Måløy to Olden (at a latitude of 62º). The inner branches of the fjord have the greatest appeal, as here the wild juxtaposition of water, mighty mountains, and glaciers calving far down into the valley below create a truly unique impression.

The Fjord Interior

Strynefjell

The approach from the east is the most impressive, especially via the old unpaved Strynefjell Road that branches off the E 15 at Grotli. This route passes the Stryn summer ski resort with its chairlift up the Tystig Glacier, and makes several hairpin bends on its descent into the Videdal valley and onwards to Stryn on the northern shore of the Innvikfjord, which is an inner arm of the Nordfjord.

Lonvatn

The little holiday resort of Loen on the Innvikfjord is a good base for climbing the 1848m/6063ft Skåla, as well as for excursions to Kjenndalsbreen, a glacier that can be reached by tour boat from the eastern end of Lonvatn, a picturesque lake. In 1905, a **massive stone avalanche** crashed into the lake, causing a 6m/20ft wave that killed 50

▶ VISITING NORDFJORD

INFORMATION
Stryn
Reisemål Stryn & Nordfjord
Tinggata 3
6782 Stryn
Tel. 57 87 40 40, fax 57 87 40 41
www.nordfjord.no

WHERE TO EAT
▶ **Expensive**
Restaurant Charlotte
Loen, Hotel Alexandra,
Tel. 57 87 50 00
Visitors to this area should make sure not to miss the large cold buffet offered between 6pm and 9pm, with its delicious salmon and herring dishes, smoked fish, and divine desserts.

WHERE TO STAY
▶ **Luxury**
Gloppen Hotel
Tel. 57 86 53 33
Fax 57 86 60 02
50 beds, www.gloppenhotell.no
Wealthy salmon fishermen have been enjoying this smart hotel since 1866. Built in Swiss style, the hotel offers sterling comforts.

Hotel Selje
Tel. 57 85 88 80, fax 57 85 88 81
49 rooms, www.seljehotel.no
This rustic hotel on the wild Vestkapp (West Cape) contains Norway's first thalassotherapy facility.

▶ **Mid-range**
Stryn Hotel
Stryn, Visnesvegen 1
Tel. 57 87 07 00
Fax 57 87 07 01
63 rooms, www.strynhotel.no
Situated right on the Nordfjord, this modern and comfortable hotel makes an ideal base for trips into the Jostedal region.

EXCURSIONS
Horse-drawn carriage rides with fjord horses and glacier walking tours across Brikdalsbreen are arranged by Briksdalbre Fjellstove, tel. 57 87 38 11.

people. 74 people also died here in 1936, when large amounts of rock crashed down from the 1789m/ 5870ft-high Ravnefjell which, like Kjenndalsbreen, is a northern outcrop of ►Jostedalsbreen.

Briksdalsbreen is reached via the Innvikfjord and **Olden**, past the pretty Olden church from 1749. The narrow road then winds its way along the deep-green coloured Lake Olden and ends in the heart of the valley surrounded by waterfalls and snow-covered mountains.

The hike up to the glacial lake of **Briksdalsbreen**, a branch of the mighty ► Jostedalsbreen, is an absolute must. The occasionally steep path begins at the Brikdalsbreen

Picturesque: the Lonvatn near Stryn

mountain cabin, passes a churning waterfall that produces beautiful rainbows on sunny days, and then leads along the crystal clear glacial stream through sometimes damp terrain up to the glacial lake and the glacier tongue itself, which 80 years ago almost reached all the way down into the valley (there and back takes around 1.5hrs, see photo p.16). It is also possible to travel two thirds of the route by horse-drawn carriage or take part in a guided glacier walk. Finally, another tip: it is quietest here before 10am and in the afternoon after the cruiseships at Olden have left.

✱ ✱

◄ Briksdalsbreen

The RV 60 winds its way alongside the Innvikfjord from Olden to Utvik before travelling up to the 630m/2067ft-high Utvikfjell in broad loops that offer panoramic views across the fjord. The best scenes are near the Pension Karistova. At the top of the route there are wonderful views onto the glaciers of Geitenyken (1621m/5318ft) and Snønipa (1827m/5994ft) to the southeast.

Utvikfjell

Travelling through the fertile landscape around Byrkjelo (E 39/RV 5 to the ►Sognefjord), where agriculture has been practiced since Viking times, it is worth making a detour west to the pretty village of deep in the interior of the Gloppenfjord, yet another side arm of the Nordfjord. Here there is an open-air museum with 35 old buildings, but a special attraction is the magnificent panorama from the **Utsikten viewing point** northwest of the settlement. Along the eastern shore of this fjord visitors will also find **western Norway's largest burial mound** at Tinghøgjen. The mound is 50m/164ft wide and 7m/ 23ft high.

Sandane

From Stryn to Måløy

Nordfjordeid
One of the most beautiful stretches along the Nordfjord runs from Stryn out to the mouth of the fjord. The RV 15 heads out past **Europe's deepest lake**, the 514m/1686ft-deep Hornidalsvatn, in the direction of Nordfjordeid. A mecca for fjord horses, Nordfjordeid hosts a state-sponsored stallion show every spring.

✳
Hornelen
From now on the road winds its way directly alongside the fjord, all the way to Måløy on the island of Vågsøy, west of the mouth of the fjord. At Almenningen the eye is drawn to the 860m/2822ft cliff of the Hornelen that rises vertically out of the water.

According to legend, **Europe's highest cliff** was once a meeting place for dances between witches and the devil during Christmas Eve and Midsummer's Night.

Baedeker TIP

Fjord horse riding

They may look like overgrown ponies, but the yellow-brown fjord horses (fjording in Norwegian), with a dark stripe along their backs and their dark legs, actually resemble the world's last wild horses, Przewalski's horses of Central Asia. Once upon a time the fjord horse was a hardy working animal, but today it is used for riding out into the idyllic landscape. A good place arrange a ride is Norsk Fjordhestcenter in Nordfjordeid, tel. 57 86 13 75.

During storms, the 42m/138ft bridge to **Måløy** »sings« a high C. Those with delicate noses will quickly realize that the inhabitants of Måløy – one of Norway's most important fishing ports – live predominantly from the fishing industry. Of interest are the **hourglass shaped stone** (a strangely eroded rock right by the sea to the northwest of Måløy) and the old trading square of **Vågsberget** with its seven historic buildings.

Detour to Selje
Near Almenningen or Maurstad (8km/5mi or 21km/13mi east of Måløy respectively), it is worth making a detour to the coastal settlement of Selje where a beautiful white sandy beach awaits, perfect for swimming in good weather.

The **island of Selja** and its Selje Monastery lies just out to sea: a fascinating place, not only for its 12th-century ruins, but also for the unique play of colours ranging from the blues of the sea to the greens of the meadows. The cave above the ruins was once the hiding place of the legendary Irish **Princess Sunniva**, who fled there from the new heathen king. She is the patron saint of West Norway.

Vestkapp
From the the mainland's most westerly mountain plateau, the 496m/1627ft-high Vestkapp 33km/21mi from Selje, there is a fantastic view out onto the open North Sea. For ships heading north, this is the beginning of the unprotected open passage across the sea, notoriously exposed to storms and feared down the ages.

★ ★ Nordkapp

O 22

Region: North Norway

The view from the Nordkapp cliffs is breathtaking – though only in fair weather. But since Europe's most northerly point is generally cloudy, rainy, foggy and always icy cold, the Nordkapphallen was built. Using the services of this multi-media centre is shockingly expensive, however, as is everything else at Nordkapp.

A 30km/19mi-long tunnel and bridge connection from the mainland to the island of Magerøya, where Nordkapp is located, has been in operation since 1999 (very high toll of around 200 NOK). The most expensive section of this prestige project, known as »Fatima«, is the world's longest underwater road tunnel, which lies around 200m/656ft beneath the sea and links Kåfjord and Honningsvåg.
It is also possible to fly from Hammerfest to Honningsvåg, from where there are buses or taxis to Nordkapp. A good alternative is the six-hour journey on one of the ►Hurtigruten ships from Hammerfest to Honningsvåg.

High-cost access

The end of the earth still inspires yearning in people today.

What to See at Nordkapp

At the northern end of Europe Located at a northern latitude of 71° 10′ 21″ and an eastern longitude of 25° 47′ 40″, Nordkapp (North Cape) is the precipitous northern end of the **island of Magerøya**. The grey-green slate cliff riven by deep furrows is visited for being Europe's northernmost tip. Strictly speaking, this is untrue, since Knivskjelodden lies a little further north still, at a northern latitude of 71° 11′ 8″. Furthermore, the northernmost point of the European **mainland** is considered to be Kinnarodden (Cape Nordkinn), 68km/42mi east of Nordkapp between Laksefjord and Tanafjord (also known as Nordkyn; 234m/768ft above sea level). Average temperatures in June and July are 9–11°C/48–52°F; in January and February they hover between -2° and -4°C/28° and 25°F.

 VISITING NORDKAPP

INFORMATION
Nordkapp Reiseliv AS
Fiskeriveien 4B, 9751 Honningsvåg
Tel. 78 47 70 30, fax 78 47 70 39
www.northcape.no

WHERE TO EAT
▶ **Moderate**
Havstua
Kamøyvær, tel. 78 47 51 50
(10km/6mi from Honningsvåg)
Inside this unprepossessing fishing hut a cosy fish restaurant offering delicious meals awaits.

WHERE TO STAY
▶ **Mid-range**
Honningsvåg Brygge
Honningsvåg, Vågen 1A
Tel. 78 47 64 64, fax 78 47 64 65
27 rooms, www.brygge.no
An agreeable hotel in the port, housed in a former fish factory. The rooms are typically Norwegian, furnished with lots of wood.

Repvåg Fjord Hotel & Rorbusenter
Repvåg,
Tel. 78 47 54 40, fax 78 47 27 51
71 rooms, www.repvag-fjordhotell.no;

hotel with a stylish interior for nostalgia fans, right by the water and in the midst of a barren Arctic landscape. Located before the tunnel to Nordkapp.

▶ **Budget**
Kirkeporten Camping
Skarsvåg
Tel. 78 47 52 33, fax 78 47 52 47
kipo@kirkeporten.no
Norway's most northerly campsite lies near the Storvann, by the small settlement of Skarsvåg. There are cabins as well as several rooms in the main building. The footpath to the Kirkeporten begins here.

SPORT
Honningsvåg hosts the annual North Cape Festival in mid-June, with an orienteering race between the town and Nordkapp.

MIDNIGHT SUN
shines from 16 May to 28 July and reaches its lowest point at 23.35pm Central European Time (CET). Between 22 November and 11 January the sun never rises.

308m/1010ft above sea level, the Nordkapp cliffs were discovered as early as 1553 by the English seafarer Richard Chancellor, who was searching for the Northeast Passage (Siberia to China to America). Drivers on the road from Honningsvåg to Nordkapp (closed in winter) should beware of **reindeer**, as there are around 5000 of them on the island during summer and they are often hard to spot due to their camouflage colours – even while they are crossing the road. Drive slowly, especially in foggy conditions.

Hefty fines

Nordkapp has been a protected area since 1929. Those found picking plants, camping wild, driving off the main road or entering bird sanctuaries during breeding season can expect fines of up to £1200/US$2300!

Magerøya Island

The island of Magerøya is Scandinavia's most northerly outpost. Its mighty jagged peninsulas push into the Arctic Ocean between deep fjords, and its 300–400m/1000–1300ft-high plateaus often fall steeply into the sea. Only sparse, hardy vegetation survives in these barren surroundings.

Honningsvåg

The port of Honningsvåg on Magerøya's southeast coast is the main settlement in the municipality of Nordkapp. It is worth paying a visit to the **Nordkapp Museum** here, which offers insight into the coastal culture of ► Finnmark as well as into the development of tourism at Nordkapp. The first international tour group arrived in 1875. It is also possible to take a cruise to Norway's largest bird cliffs and to abandoned fishing villages. The economic foundation here remains, as before, fishing, fish processing and shipping. Honningsvåg became a centre for dragnet fishing at the beginning of the 20th century, because the ships working along the dangerous north coast need good pilots, and they normally boarded here. The pilot station here is still of great importance. Like Hammerfest, Honningsvåg was also destroyed during the German retreat in November 1944.

If the weather is bad, the **Nordkapphallen** (North Cape Hall) is a good place to shelter: the attractions include a panoramic

North Cape Map

© Baedeker

5 km
3.1 miles

Knivskjelodden
North Cape
Tufjord
Skarsvåg
Gjesvær
Kamøyfjord
▲ 417 m   Magerøya
1,369 ft
Kamøyvær
Vannfjord
Honningsvåg
Magerøsund
»Fatima« tunnel
Kobbfjord
Kåfjord
▲ 493 m
1,618 ft
Porsangen
Skouttanjargga
Sværholt
Halvøya
Olderfjord   Repvåg

The globe marks the »end of the earth«.

restaurant, the northernmost Champagne bar in the world, a multimedia show and an exhibition on the history of Nordkapp. The centre is built as a tunnel that ends with a grotto where a window opens onto the Arctic Sea (Nordkapp diploma, special stamps and postmarks available). An arrow indicates the direction of north and there is also a granite pillar commemorating the visit of King Oscar II in around 1873. In fair weather, the view of the Arctic Sea extends to the west, north and east. To the southwest, the islands of Hjelmsøy, Måsøy and Rolvsøy can be seen; in the distant east lies Kinnarodden; to the south, Magerøya's highlands with their snow fields, ponds and sparse vegetation (opening times: during high season daily 9am–2pm, entrance fee 185 NOK).

! Baedeker TIP

A room with a view – Nordkapp style

Quite a few have tied the knot at Nordkapp. After the wedding in the chapel and dinner in the restaurant, the happy couple can stay in the Nordkapphallen's tower suite. Of course this exclusive room with a panoramic view is available to all, not just newlyweds. Reservations: tel. 78 47 68 60.

En route from Honningsvåg to Nordkapp, a country road branches off to the fishing village of Gjesvær, 20km/12mi away in the northwest of the island. Islands and skerries protect the attractive settlement with a mere 300 souls from the rough Arctic Sea. A local nature reserve is famous among ornithologists for its bird cliffs, where great numbers of puffins and even sea eagles can be observed.

There is a signposted footpath (approx. 20mins) from the Nordkapp Turistheim to an interesting rock formation known as the Kirkeporten. The cape can be seen through this »church portal«. The peace and memorable views here at midnight are an appealing alternative for those who wish to escape the crowds on the Nordkapp plateau.

Nordland

F-N 7-19

Region: North Norway   **Population:** 238,000

The landscape of the long, narrow province of Nordland has several highlights. Along its jagged coast tremendous mountain scenery awaits, as does Svartisen, Norway's second largest glacier. Nordland's only significant towns are Bodø and Narvik, both rather plain due to their post-war architecture.

Nordland is the longest and narrowest of Norway's counties: where the Hellemofjord juts inland, it is barely 6km/4mi to the Swedish border. At five inhabitants per square kilometre (13 per sq mi), the population density is really rather low, and increasing numbers are leaving this economically deprived region. While in former times virtually every coastal community had its fishermen, many villages are now dying out. Income is increasingly dependent on tourism and its associated service sectors, though the oil and gas industry also supplies jobs.

Tourism is still very limited here, so those seeking solitude have come to the right place. The first autumnal storms in September see off the **mild summers** (12°C/54°F), and very quickly the seemingly endless polar night descends, during which the sun never climbs above the horizon. When the sun shows its face again a few weeks after Christmas, it is time for all Nordlanders to celebrate. No wonder that in many municipalities of

Mild summers, few people

 NORDLAND

INFORMATION/WHERE TO EAT WHERE TO STAY

see chapters on Bodø, Mo i Rana and Narvik

GETTING THERE

Bodø in Nordland is the end of the line for trains from Oslo. Those with little time should follow the E 6 through Nordland, though the best of the countryside can be enjoyed by driving along coastal route 17.

the Arctic Circle, **Easter** is also an opportunity to celebrate numerous other events, such as weddings and christenings.

The southern part of Nordland, known as Helgeland, awaits the visitor with many small islands and coastal villages. North of the Arctic Circle, key destinations include Svartisen, at 370 sq km/143 sq mi Norway's **second-largest glacier** (► Mo i Rana, surroundings), and the mightiest tidal waters in the world at the **Saltstraumen** (► Bodø, surroundings). A world unto itself is formed by the wildly jagged peaks of the ► Lofoten and ► Vesterålen island chains that lie off the coast between Bodø and Narvik. Whales and dolphins can be spotted from these islands.

Flora and fauna South of the Svartisen massif and ► Saltfjell in Helgeland, the landscape is green and varied, and occasionally **forested**. North of this

An elk can weigh up to 800kg/1764lbs.

area, however, an **Arctic climate** predominates and birch and pine trees only survive the short summers and long winters in a few scattered locations. In sheltered spots, flowering plants not associated with these latitudes can survive. The animal world is naturally adapted to the cold and includes stoat, fox, mink, beaver and lemming, as well as the almost ubiquitous **reindeer** and **elk**; the rivers meanwhile are alive with salmon and trout. Thanks to reduced fishing quotas, **salmon stocks** are now recovering from a period of overfishing. The sea is also (still) home to good stocks of fish, the Gulf Stream ensuring that temperatures never drop below −1°C/30°F during winter. Only catches of the ever popular cod are restricted.

Along Coastal Route 17

Mystic mountains The RV 17 coastal route, also known as the »Kystriksveien«, leads into the most beautiful corners of Nordland's island and skerry world between Steinkjer in the south and Bodø in the north. Where there are no bridges, ferries ensure a relaxed break to the journey. The tens of thousands of islands and skerries are topped by strangely shaped mountains that have always inspired the imagination of the local people. Going from south to north, the most famous are: the »Mountain with the Hole« (**Torghatten**) near Brønnøysund; the »Seven Sisters«

✳
»Seven Sisters« ► (Syv Søstre) near Sandnessjøen; the mountains of the bird islands Lovund and Træna; the »Horseman« (Hestmannen) on the island of Hestmona in the Arctic Circle; and the »Lion« on Rødøya.

According to local superstition, these are legendary saga figures turned to stone when they failed to hide before sunrise when the

Hestmannen was chasing the girl Lekamøya (mountain of the same name on the island of Leka south of Brønnøysund).

Crossing the provincial border in the south on the RV 17, the journey immediately begins with the ferry crossing from Holm to Vennesund. Further north, at **Brønnøysund**, lies the Hildurs Urterarium, where visitors can not only see numerous rare herbs and around 500 species of roses, but also hear stories from Viking times.
It is worth driving out to **Torghatten Mountain** and climbing up to its 30m/98ft high hole; pay a visit, too, to the large **island of Vega**, with its rich vegetation, footpaths, retreating glaciers, caves, **local museum** and the old trading post of Vegsteinen.

From Holm to Alstahaug

> **!** *Baedeker* TIP
>
> **Mrs Haugan's Hotel**
>
> This hotel has been under female management for the past 200 years. It is located in the centre of Mosjøen, in the middle of a picturesque quarter, and positively exudes cosiness. After its renovation in 1999, at least half of its 76 rooms were restored to their original historic state, as were the bar and living rooms. Affordable summer prices make this hotel especially attractive (Strandgt. 39, tel. 75 11 41 00, fax 75 11 41 01).

After two more ferry journeys, **Alstahaug** is reached, where the poet priest **Petter Dass** (1647–1708) once preached in the local 12th-century church. He lived in Alstahaug from 1689 until his death, and is well known in Norway as a Baroque poet. There is a museum (Petter Dass Museum) devoted to his life in the church courtyard.

There is a speedboat connection between Sandnesjøen and the **bird island of Lovund**, with its large puffin colony. The island of Dønna can also be reached from Sandnesjøen. Dønnesfjell, at 127m/417ft high, provides beautiful panoramic views onto the island world as far as the »Seven Sisters«. Additionally, there is a fertility symbol from the time of the Great Migrations (approx. AD 500–600) at **Glein** on Dønna: this **stone phallus** is the largest of its kind in Scandinavia.
Continuing on, the small island group of **Træna** can be spotted in the distance, out to sea, with its roughly 400 islands and the striking peak of Trænstaven (331m/1086ft).

From Sandnesjøen to the Arctic Circle

The Arctic Circle is crossed during the ferry crossing from Kilboghamn to Jektvik. The road then becomes a long tunnel, travelling underneath the giant **Svartisen** (►Saltfjell Mountains and ►Mo i Rana) glacier before reaching **Glomfjord**, where the Norsk Hydro company produces fertilizer for all of Norway. After passing **Ørnes**, the final highlight of the journey to Bodø is reached: the world's mightiest tidal waters, known as the **Saltstraumen** roar below the bridge of the same name (►Bodø, surroundings). By the way, this is a good spot for **salmon** fishing. Bodø is reached after traversing the wide bay.

From the Arctic Circle to Saltstraumen

»Heaven on Earth« by Inge Mahn at Ballangen

ART IN THE HIGH NORTH

Spread along the entire coast of the county of Nordland, 34 works by artists from 17 countries stand in the open air. The »Nordland Sculpture Landscape« project was begun in 1992. It is incredibly impressive to find these sometimes idiosyncratic, sometimes moving contemporary works of art in an exhibition area of 40,000 sq km/15,500 sq mi complete with the drone of the sea and wind and the unique qualities of the changing light.

The project was initiated with the three-part granite sculpture *En Ny Samtale* – a new conversation – by Kain Tapper of Finland, which was set up on the island of Vega. The title was very significant, because the project to

erect **modern artworks** in remote places was intended to inspire new impulses for art in northern Norway for many years to come. Most exhibits were placed near water, following in the tradition of rock art that Bronze Age people, with a great deal of effort, once scraped onto rocks near the coast. For all the artists the choice of location was a decisive factor in creating a clear symbiosis between their work and the magnificent landscape of the north.

The right perspectives

It is somewhat onerous finding the individual contributions to the sculpture landscape, because they often stand on small islands or in remote sections of the coast. But the effort is

worth it. What is on offer is extremely versatile: pierced stones, gold varnished steel flames and entwined ornaments of rusting steel that glow in the light of the midnight sun. There is also a more than 10m/33ft-high granite figure that stands in the water looking out to sea. With every tide it sinks a little lower into the water, only to re-emerge a few hours later. Many artworks offer very different perspectives depending from where they are viewed. Changing weather and seasons also offer continuous variations. A fascinating example is the head by **Markus Raetz** (see photo left) that changes its shape 16 times during a stroll around it: from the front it is a classic portrait, from behind it turns miraculously upside down.

Choosing locations

An overview of the entire project can be found at www.skulpturlandskap.-no. Here is a selection of locations where works of art are among the attractions:

Ballangen community, Skarstad: *Heaven on Earth* by Inge Mahn, Germany. Turn onto route 741 from the E 6 at

Efjord and drive to Skarstad.

Bø: *The Man from the Sea* by Kjell Erik Olsen, Norway. On a spit of land before the settlement of Bø on the island of Langøy.

Evenskjaer: *Seven Magic Points* by Martti Aiha, Finland. North of Evenskjaer (E10) turn off onto route 825; after about 2km/1mi, it stands on a peninsula near the road.

Flakstadøy: *Epitaph* by Toshikatsu Endo, Japan. About 2km/1mi from Ramberg on the road to Skjelford.

Hadsel: *Day and Night* by Sarkis, Turkey/France. On the bridge from Stokmarknes to Børøy.

Mosjøen: *Three Flames* by Hulda Hákon, Iceland. Near route 244 off the E 6.

Røst: *The Nest* by Luciano Fabro, Italy. On the bird island of Vedøy.

Sortland: *The Eye of the Sea* by Sigurdur Gudmundsson, Iceland. In Sortland near the E 10 on Langøya.

Vestvågøy: *The Head* by Markus Raetz, Switzerland. About 2km/1mi outside Eggum.

Vågån: *Untitled* by Dan Graham, USA. By the old quay of Lyngvaer on the E 10.

★ ★ Oslo

B 7

Region: East Norway   **Population:** 548,000

Few of the world's capitals are as blessed with beautiful natural surroundings as Oslo: lakes, forests, sand and sea, all on the doorstep. The king lives here, parliament has its seat here, and world-famous museums display their treasures here. Charming taverns, elegant restaurants and the city centre shopping district round off a visit to the Norwegian capital.

City between forest and sea Oslo, which in 2006 brought an end to Tokyo's 14-year run as the world's most expensive city, is considered Europe's greenest capital, since only a quarter of its 450 sq km/174 sq mi of urban area is built up. More than a third of all Norwegians live around the ►Oslofjord, which extends around 100km/62mi into the mainland, and at whose northern end the capital stands. The city centre is concentrated around the Pipervika harbour, an area with shops and restaurants in Aker Brygge, the city's cultural heart, as well as the Akershus fortress; along Oslo's most famous street, Karl Johansgate, at whose western end the Royal Palace stands; and, further east, around the Hotel Oslo Plaza, whose 37 floors make it northern Europe's highest building. The Akerselv river flows into the Oslofjord very close to the central railway station and has divided the city into two halves for centuries: Østkanten, to the east, is predominantly inhabited by students, older people and foreigners, while Vestkanten, to the west, is home to richly decorated historic villas. As in all of Norway's larger towns and cities, users of Oslo's access roads have to pay a **toll**.

> ! **Baedeker TIP**
>
> **Christmas magic**
> Four large markets, along with numerous smaller ones, serve to spread a typically Scandinavian Christmas mood during the festive season. Gløgg (mulled wine), Christmas beer and gifts made of wood, wool or wax, as well as designer items, are on sale at the Julenmarked on the city square, in the old Brums Verk ironworks, at Bogstad Gård (Bogstad Manor) and in the open-air Norsk Folkemuseum.

Cultural capital and centre of learning Oslo is the seat of parliament and the home of the royals, as well as the administrative centre for the districts of Oslo and Akershus. Its universities and several technical colleges make Oslo Norway's most significant centre of learning. No other city in Norway offers such a broad cultural programme and the country's only operatic ensemble is based here. Every year on 10 December, Oslo's city hall becomes the venue for the **Nobel Peace Prize** awards ceremony.

History **Scandinavia's oldest capital** was probably founded by King Harald Hårdråde in 1050, though archaeological evidence proves that a ship-

The dual towers of the town hall welcome travellers.

ping post and settlement must have existed here by AD 900 at the latest. Harald's son Olav Kyrre (1050–93) elevated the place to a bishopric and Håkon V (1277–1319) had a cathedral built, and for a long period after that Oslo remained the **the country's religious centre**, though the kings continued to reside in Bergen. Håkon V was the first to move his residence from Bergen to Oslo **around 1300**, when he also began building the **Akershus fortress**. At the same time the Hanseatic League established a base in Oslo. In 1397 Norway's period under the Danish crown began, and Oslo became less significant. After a fire in 1624, Christian IV, the Danish-Norwegian king at the time, had the city rebuilt around the Akershus fortress. The square network of streets that he designed for the area between Rådhusgata and Karl Johansgate is still recognizable today. He even changed the city's name – to his own – so that between 1624 and 1924 the capital of Norway was called **Christiania** (spelt Kristiania from 1877 onwards). Plagues and the high taxes that were imposed on the city's inhabitants during lengthy wars inhibited 18th-century Christiania's development into a merchant city based on the European model, and the capital only revived economically towards the end of the 18th century as the wood trade flourished.

When Norway was eventually ceded from Denmark after **1814**, Christiania finally became the new capital and royal residence. During the reign of Karl XIV Johan the city flourished once more and developed into Norway's most significant centre of **transport and trade**. The first railway lines were built, new roads were built, and textile and machine workshops were established. At the same time, the mid-19th century saw extensive **rural flight**. Many tried their luck in Christiania. Residential blocks up to five storeys high and with narrow back courtyards shot up all around Christiania's centre and gradually split the town into **two districts**. The typical workers and tradesmen's quarters developed in the east, while the middle class lived in spacious, elegant villas in the western districts. The city recovered its old name of **Oslo** on **1 January 1925** – a name that according to linguists could mean »plain of the gods« or »plain at the foot of a hill«.

◄ Norway's capital

▶ VISITING OSLO

INFORMATION

Turistinformasjon
Fridtjof Nansens plass 5
Entrance at Roald Amundsen gate
Tel. 24 14 77 00, fax 22 42 92 22
www.visitoslo.com
The office at the main railway station
primarily arranges accommodation.

WHERE TO EAT

▶ Expensive

② **Bagatelle**
Bygdøy allé 3
Tel. 22 12 14 40
Master Chef Eyvind Hellstrøm's fish
dishes have earned him two stars. This
is one of the best and most expensive
gourmet restaurants in the city.

⑤ **Blom**
Karl Johans gate 41
Tel. 23 13 95 00
Well known artists' restaurant in
which Knut Hamsun and Ole Bull
once made themselves at home. The
salmon and game dishes are excellent.
The walls are full of portraits donated
by the Art Association.

⑥ **Det Gamle Raadhus**
Nedre Slottgt. 1
Tel. 22 42 01 07
Oslo's oldest restaurant is housed in
the city's first town hall that was built
in 1641. Fish and game dishes are of
the highest quality. The garden seating
area in the back courtyard offers a
haven of peace.

③ **Solsiden**
Søndre Åkershus Kai
Tel. 22 33 36 30
www.solsiden.no
Possibly the city's best fish dishes are
served on the sunny side of Oslo
harbour, right underneath the
Akershus fortress and with views onto
Aker Brygge. The house speciality is
the seafood platter.

▶ Moderate

① **Bølgen & Moi Briskeby**
Løvenskioldsgate 26,
Tel. 24 11 53 53
www.bolgenogmoi.no
Bar, brasserie and restaurant under
one roof. Norway's famous Chef
Trond Moi invites guests for breakfast
and lunch at the bar, complete with
bread from the wood-fired oven.

⑦ **Engebret Café**
Bankplassen 1
Tel. 22 82 25 25
The morning Smørebrød buffet – a
typical Norwegian speciality – is
recommended.

④ **Theatercaféen**
Stortingsgaten 24–26,
Tel. 22 82 40 50
People come to this art nouveau
coffee house dating from 1901 opposite the National Theatre to see and be
seen. Good Norwegian cuisine at
decent prices.

Baedeker recommendation

Grand Café
Karl Johansgate 31 (in the Grand Hotel)
Tel. 24 12 53 00.
www.grand.no
Eat like the Bohemians at the turn of the
19th century in the historic Grand Café.
large fresco by Per Krohg conveys the
atmosphere of the epoch when Ibsen and
Bjørnson were regulars here. The menu als
offers smaller dishes suitable for lunchtim
snacks.

► Inexpensive

⑧ *Fyret*
Youngstorget 6
Tel. 22 20 51 82
Cosy café and restaurant offering a variety of small dishes and an extraordinary choice of Norwegian aquavit. Live jazz is played every Monday from 8pm.

WHERE TO STAY

► Luxury

⑧ *Grand Hotel*
289 rooms, Karl Johansgate 31
Tel. 23 21 20 00, fax 23 21 21 00
www.grand.no
The city's top hotel opened its doors in 1874 and has continuously adapted to modern requirements every since. Swimming pool with sauna and solarium; fitness and wellness programme; tasteful interior in the »Palmen« lunch restaurant.

⑥ *Hotel Continental*
Stortingsgt. 24-26
Tel. 22 82 40 00
Fax 22 42 96 89
www.hotel-continental.no
Don't be fooled by the hotel's unprepossessing façade. The hotel restaurant »Annen Étage« has earned a star. Compared to other Oslo hotels, the Continental offers very good value for money.

► Mid-range

④ *Rica Hotel Bygdøy Allé*
Bygdøy Allé 53
Tel. 23 08 58 00
Fax 23 08 58 08
57 rooms, www.rica.no
Housed in a renovated redbrick building, this is a cosy hotel between the centre and the museum island of Bygdøy. The Magma restaurant with its beautiful interior is highly recommended.

① *Gabelshus Hotel*
Gabelsgate 16
Tel. 23 27 65 00, fax 23 27 65 60
114 rooms, www.gabelshus.no
In a quiet location, just ten minutes from the Color Line quay. Amalgamated with the former Ritz and reopened in 2004, the hotel is an interesting architectural ensemble.

⑦ *Quality Hotel Savoy*
Universitetsgaten 11
Tel. 23 35 42 00, fax 23 35 42 01
80 rooms, www.choicehotels.no
This popular and well-run city hotel offers good value summer prices. It is located next to the National Gallery and just a few steps from Karl Johansgate.

Baedeker recommendation

② *Grims Grenka*
Kongensgate 5, tel. 23 10 72 00
www.grimsgrenka.no
In January 2008, Norway's first five-star design hotel opened – with 42 elegant rooms, 24 luxury suites and a spectacular rooftop lounge.

⑤ *Cochs Pensjonat*
Parkveien 25
Tel. 23 33 24 00
Fax 23 33 24 10
www.cochspensjonat.no
One of the few guesthouses established in the capital. Central location behind the palace. Rooms contain kitchenettes.

⑪ *Anker Hotel Best Western*
Storgt. 55
Tel. 22 99 75 00
Fax 22 99 75 20
137 rooms, www.anker.oslo.no
Modern hotel in a quiet location between the city centre and the student district.

⑨ *Hotel Bastion*
Skippergt. 7
Tel. 22 47 77 00, fax 22 33 11 80
99 rooms, www.hotelbastion.no
Centrally located with very pleasant atmosphere and tasteful antique furniture in all the rooms. If you prefer bright rooms, avoid those looking onto the courtyard.

► **Budget**
⑩ *Oslo Vandrerhjem Haraldsheim*
Haraldsheimvn. 4
Tel. 22 22 29 65, fax 22 22 10 25
www.haraldsheim.oslo.no
The youth hostel is not exactly comfortable, but in the expensive city of Oslo it is the best cheap accommodation available and therefore not only used by young people.

ENTERTAINMENT

The area for going out in Oslo is around the former shipyard at Aker Brygge (Bar 1 at Holmensgate 3 has an unbelievable selection of cognac), as well as the trendy Grünerlokka and Grønland districts and the West End around Bogstadveien.

SHOPPING

Popular shopping streets: Aker Brygge, Karl Johansgate
Large department stores: Steen & Strøm (Nedre Slottsgate), Glas Magasinet (Stortorvet). Oslo City with around 100 shops (near the central railway station).
Another shopping district is located west of the centre, between the palace gardens and the Frognerpark.
Paleét shopping arcade (Karl Johansgate 37–43): over 40 different shops, including Norway's largest bookshop, Tanum, which also stocks foreign language titles. Good value restaurants also found here.

OSLO PASS

Money can be saved in expensive Oslo with an Oslo Pass. It is valid for one, two or three days (220–410 NOK) and entitles the owner to use of public transport and parking spaces, as well as entry to museums. There are also discounts for sightseeing tours by ship and bus.
The pass can be purchased, among other places, at the tourist information office, the train station and the airport, as well as at hotels.

CITY TOURS

Buses depart from the city hall quay and from Trafikanten at the main railway station (3hrs including museum visit).

HARBOUR TOURS

Departures from the city hall quay every hour between mid-May and mid-August 11am–6pm; mid-June to end of July till 8pm; duration around 50mins. Other tours go to the Oslofjord islands and include a lunch buffet (2hrs), still others offer a romantic fjord tour at night. Information from Oslo Turistinformasjon.

SPORT AND LEISURE

Skiing

There is more or less guaranteed snow around Oslo between January and March. Thanks to the Holmenkoll rail route, the skiing region of Nordmarka is the easiest to reach. There are around 2200km/1375mi of prepared cross country skiing routes around Oslo, of which around 200km/125mi are illuminated at night.

For downhill skiing serviced by lifts see:
Tryvannskleiva, Rødkleiva, Wyllerløypa, Kirkerudbakken, Ingierkollen, Grefsenkleiva, Fjellstadbakken, Trollvannskleiva, Vardåsen, Varingskollen.

Swimming and surfing

The most beautiful beaches at Huk (on the Bygdøy peninsula, complete with nudist beach), Hvervenbukta, Katta, and Ingierstrand in the south of the city. The beaches of the islands of Langøyene and Hovedøya can be reached by boat from the Vippetangen quay.

Surfers prefer the waters off Rolfstangen beach. Good swimming possibilities are also offered by the 300 lakes of Oslomarka. Especially popular are Sognsvann, Svartkulp (both can be reached on the Sognsvann railway) and Bogstadvann (near Bogstad campsite).

Oslo *Underground*

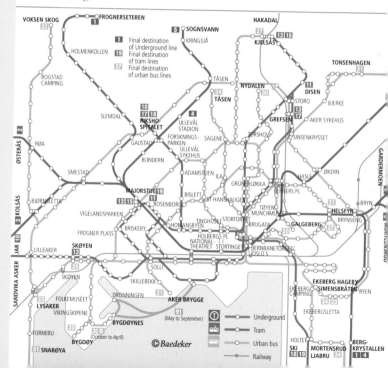

© Baedeker

...'re found
...la,

Blindern (University)

Vigeland
Exhibition
Area

Frogner
Park

Town Museum

Vigeland-
Museum

Halvdan Svartes gate

RSTUEN

Stens
Park

Fagerborg
Church

**Bislett
Stadium**

Amaldus
Nielsens
plass

Professor Dahls gate

THOMANS-
BYEN

FROGNER

Uranienborg
Church

Riddervolds
plass

Slottparken

Nobel
Institute

Solli
plass

Slottparken
Royal Palace

Carl Johan

**History
Museum**

Old
University

Henie Onstad Art Centre
Trade Fair Centre

Nobel
Institute

University
library

Observatory

Olaf
Bulls
plass

Ibsen
Museum

**National
Theatre**

Concert
Hall

Nobel
Peace
Centre

Town Hall

Rådhus-
plassen

SKILLEBEKK

Aker
Brygge

Ferry landing stage
(Color Line)

Pipervika

Akershus
Festning
(fortress)

BYGDØY

Oslofjord

Seafaring
Museum

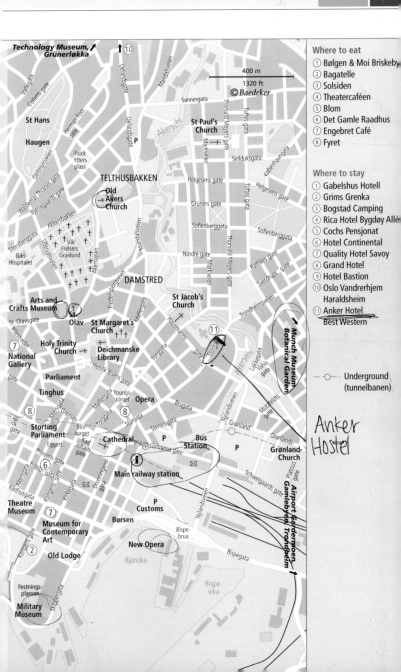

Technology Museum,
Grünerløkka

400 m
1320 ft
©Baedeker

Where to eat
① Bølgen & Moi Briskeby
② Bagatelle
③ Solsiden
④ Theatercaféen
⑤ Blom
⑥ Det Gamle Raadhus
⑦ Engebret Café
⑧ Fyret

Where to stay
① Gabelshus Hotell
② Grims Grenka
③ Bogstad Camping
④ Rica Hotel Bygdøy Allé
⑤ Cochs Pensjonat
⑥ Hotel Continental
⑦ Quality Hotel Savoy
⑧ Grand Hotel
⑨ Hotel Bastion
⑩ Oslo Vandrerhjem
   Haraldsheim
⑪ Anker Hotel
   Best Western

—○— Underground
   (tunnelbanen)

Anker
Hostel

Karl Johansgate and the Adjacent District

Railway station to Stortorget A good starting point for a stroll into the city is the **central railway station** (Sentralbanestasjonen), with its two car parks and a tourist information centre. The Oslo City shopping mall is behind the railway station. The city's main shopping street, popular for a stroll, is **Karl Johansgate**, which leads from the railway station to the Royal Palace. This magnificent road is a pedestrian zone as far as the parliament building. The large market square that has existed since the end of the 17th century is known as **Stortorget** and is overseen by a statue of King Christian IV created by C.L. Jacobsen.

✳ **Cathedral** The cathedral (Domkirke), inaugurated in 1697, stands on the southeast side of the Stortorget. There are beautiful reliefs (1938) on the bronze doors at the main entrance. The pulpit, altar (both from around 1700) and organ (1725) have survived from the cathedral's early **interior furnishings**. The windows by Emanuel Vigeland (1910–16) date from more recent times, as does the ceiling fresco by Hugo Lous Mohr (1936–50). The octagonal Chapel of the Redeemer, added in 1950, contains a silver sculpture by Arrigo Minerbi entitled *The Last Supper*. The cathedral was also the venue for the marriage between Crown Prince Haakon and Crown Princess Mette-Marit in ⊙ August 2001 (opening times: daily 10am–4pm).

Bazaar Halls The Bazaar Halls, built in 1841–42, stand behind the cathedral now serve as a centre for arts and crafts shops, antique dealers, vegetable stalls, souvenir shops and cafés. The liveliest section of Karl Johansgate begins south of Stortorget. To the west lies **Egertorget**, a major junction for Oslo's rapid transit system, the T-bane.

Highlights *Oslo*

Karl Johansgate
Take a stroll and admire the magnificent buildings.
▶ page 310

Aker Brygge
Have fun shopping.
▶ page 314

Akershus Fortress
includes the Museum of Norwegian Resistance
▶ page 315

Oslo Opera House
A huge new project at the head of the fjord
▶ page 316

Munch Museum
Pure Edvard Munch
▶ page 317

Vigeland Park
Gustav Vigeland spent half a lifetime working on these sculptures.
▶ page 318

Bygdøy
Museum island: Vikings, polar explorers, seafarers
▶ page 319

Holmenkollen
Ski jump with view onto city and fjord
▶ page 326

It stays light till late during summer on Karl Johansgate.

The Storting, the **Norwegian parliament building**, stands to the left of the junction between Karl Johansgate and Akersgata. It was designed in a neo-Gothic style in 1861–66. In the conference hall hangs O. Wergeland's large painting portraying the assembly that established the constitution at Eidsvoll in 1814. Eidsvollplass Park stretches out in front of the building and contains a statue of the poet Henrik Wergeland designed by Bergslien. Beyond the Storting, the park goes by the name of Studenterlunden and its beer garden, shopping stalls, music pavilion and street musicians make it a popular meeting place during summer.

★ Storting

The Oslo Nye Theatre at Rosenkrantzgate 10, which crosses Karl Johansgate here, is a venue for new work and revues. It opened in 1929 with Knut Hamsun's *At the Gate of the Kingdom.* Numerous bars can be found in this neighbourhood.

Nye Teater

The classical building of the National Theatre, constructed in 1899, is situated to the northwest of Eidsvollplass. The main entrance is flanked by two bronze sculptures of Ibsen and Bjørnson. The partly art nouveau interior with a beautiful ceiling fresco in the large hall can be visited on request.

National Theatre

The buildings of the university, founded by Frederick VI of Denmark in 1811, were erected in 1854. They stand to the northeast of the theatre. Today the Faculty of Law is housed in this »old« university, while the new university is in the district of Blindern. In the lecture hall dating from 1911, the pictures by **Edvard Munch** (1926) are noteworthy.

Old university

Norske Teatret

Oslo's largest theatre, famous for its musicals and performances of Norwegian and foreign new drama, lies east of the university, on Kristian IV's gate.

✳
National Gallery

www.national
museum.no ►

Norway's largest collection of art is housed in the National Gallery at Universitetsgata 13. The fine museum building is from 1881 and presents an extensive cross-section of Norwegian painters from the 19th century to the present day. Works by the following artists can be viewed: J. C. Dahl (1788–1857), T. Fearnley (1802–42), H. F. Gude (1825–1903), H. O. Heyerdahl (1857–1913), C. Krohg (1852–1925), G. P. Munthe (1849–1929), E. Peterssen (1852–1928) and A. Tidemand (1814–76). Two exhibition rooms are dedicated to Edvard Munch. In addition, there are works by Danish and Swedish painters, as well as paintings by El Greco, Rubens and Rembrandt, and a collection of French art including Cézanne, Degas, Gauguin, Manet, Matisse and Renoir. There is also a room with casts of figures from antiquity (opening times: Tue, Wed, Fri 10am–6pm, Thu till 7pm, Sat–Sun 11am–5pm).

✳
Historical Museum

The Historical Museum (Historisk Museum; entrance at Frederiksgate 2) is behind the National Gallery and contains the Antiquities Collection of the University of History and Ethnology. Worth mentioning among the Nordic antiquities is the rich collection from the **Viking era** (around 800–1050), including a treasury, and an exhibition of **stave church** portals. Furthermore, there are exhibitions on the **Eskimos and Siberian peoples**, and the indigenous peoples of Africa, America and East Asia, as well as a coin collection (opening times: Tue–Sun 10am–4pm, from 11am in winter).

✳
Royal Palace

The long stretched out Empire style building of the Royal Palace (Det Kongelige Slott), built in 1825–48, is located on a hill in the middle of a large park at the northwest end of Karl Johansgate. The Swedish-Norwegian King Karl Johan, who commissioned this building but did not live to see it completed in 1848, dreamt of a palace where he could see the large parade ground and the entire city from the balcony. He therefore had the palace built outside the city gates at the time, a considerable distance away from the frequently poor housing of the local population (guided tours: mid-June–mid-Aug daily noon, 2pm, 4pm, Mon–Fri also at 10am).

A special attraction is the daily **changing of the guard** at 1.30pm.

Nobel Institute

Along the south side of the palace gardens runs Drammensveien and the Norwegian Nobel Institute stands at the junction with Parkveien. On 10 December every year, the festival hall within the city hall hosts the Nobel Peace Prize award ceremony, during which the individual or organization is named as the prizewinner. Candidates are suggested by parliamentarians from all over the world and chosen by the Norwegian Nobel Committee. Former prizewinners include Mar-

The royal palace at Oslo

tin Luther King Jr. (1964), **Mother Teresa** (1979), Mikhail Gorbatschev (1990), Nelson Mandela and Fredrik Willem de Klerk (1993), and **John Hume and David Trimble** (1998). In 2007, the prize was awarded to Al Gore for his work to promote awareness of climate change (all prizewinners can be found under www.nobel.no). A wealth of information regarding the Nobel Peace Prize can be found in the Nobel Peace Centre, opened in 2005 in the former Oslo West railway station (see below).

Henrik Ibsen's apartment, where he lived from 1895 until his death in 1906, can be found complete with its original interior south of the palace gardens at Arbins gate 1 (visits by guided tour only Tue–Sun noon, 1pm, 2pm).

Ibsen Museum

⊙

Heading south from the National Theatre, the monumental city hall comes into view, built in 1931–50 according to designs by Arnstein Arneberg and Magnus Poulson. This mighty concrete building with its two chunky towers clad in brick has become the city's emblem, despite always being controversial. There is a carillion in the east tower. The rich fresco ornamentation of the interior, the work of 28 artists including Henrik Sørensen, Per Krohg and Edvard Munch, is worth taking a look at (opening times: Mon–Sat 9am–5pm, Sun noon–5pm).

City hall

⊙

The Nobel Peace Centre was established in the old Oslo West railway station in July 2005. It contains information about Alfred Nobel and

Nobel Peace Centre

all the winners of the Nobel Peace Prize. Furthermore, there are lectures, seminars and exhibitions on peace campaigns around the world, as well as on current conflict zones. See www.nobelfredssenter.co for the events programme.

It is worth visiting **Aker Brygge** on the western shore of the Pipervika harbour, to the southwest of the city hall quay. The renovated halls of the former Aker shipyard have been transformed into a **modern shopping and cultural centre** with about 35 restaurants, as well as cafés, boutiques and galleries. It is the capital's liveliest and most popular shopping and leisure district, despite being **extremely expensive** by European standards.

Northern City Centre

Museum of Decorative Arts and Design

The Catholic St Olav's Church (1853) is located at the northern end of Akersgata opposite the Museum of Decorative Arts and Design (Kunstindustrimuseet), which offers insight into the development of Nordic arts and crafts. The most important exhibition centres on tapestries, including the Baldishol Tapestry (approx. 1180) taken from the Baldishol Church in the province of Hedmark. The exhibits also include metal and glass works, furniture and royal costumes (opening times: Tue–Fri 11am–3pm, Sat and Sun noon–4pm).

Damstredet

Behind St Olav's, Damstredet leads to the junction with Fredensborgveien. The small renovated wooden houses with their tiny gardens originating in the 18th and 19th centuries were once inhabited by poor craftsmen and workers. From 1839 to 1841, the poet Herik Wergeland (1808–45) lived at Damstredet 1.

The two-storeyed panelled wooden house dating from the early 19th-century at Damstredet 5 is also known as the »Rhubarb Palace« because large quantities of rhubarb were once cultivated in its garden. The sculpture of *Nils Holgerson's Goose* designed by Edvin Öhrström (1971) stands at the square a little further on.

Cemetery of Our Saviour

The Cemetery of Our Saviour (Vår Frelsers Gravlund) extends between Ullevålsveien and Akersveien to the north. The poets **Bjørnstjerne Bjørnson and Henrik Ibsen**, as well as the painter **H.F. Gude**, are buried in the »honorary glade« of Æreslunden in the middle of the cemetery.

Old Aker Church

Oslo's oldest building stands at the northern end of Akersveien. The Old Aker Church (Norwegian: Gamle Akerskirke) was probably built

by Olav Kyrre as a basilica in the Anglo-Norman style in 1150. The church gained its present, somewhat plain interior after the entire inventory was destroyed in a fire in 1703, though that was also when the present baptismal font and the beautiful **pulpit** were created. The building's acoustics are superb.

Southern City Centre

Oslo's old town extends to the south of the Storting and Karl Johansgate. The **stock exchange**, built in 1827 and extended in 1910, is located southwest of the central

Tempting delights in Oslo's shops

railway station. In response to a major fire in 1624, King Christian IV commissioned the construction of stone houses on a network of right-angled streets to the west of the stock exchange, known as Kvadraturen. Kongensgate was once the main entrance to the city. The oldest surviving building of the original Kvadraturen stands at Rådhusgaten 19 (1626), and today houses the **Oslo Art Association**. Kongensgate 1 now houses the **state theatre**. The building at Rådhusgate 7, whose oldest sections date from 1625–30, was used as the town hall from 1733 onwards, then as a prison, and also as a police station. Today it is the seat of the Norwegian Author's Association.

Further west, on Bankplassen, stands a large granite building (1902) in the Norwegian art nouveau style that was once the main seat of the Norwegian state bank. Since 1990, it has housed **Norway's largest museum for contemporary art** (Museet for Samtidskunst), with works by all of Norway's most important artists from 1945 onwards, as well as several by foreign artists such as Asger Jorn, Hanne Darboven, Sol LeWitt, Bill Viola and Günther Förg (opening times: Tue–Fri 10am–5pm, Thu till 8pm, Sat 11am–4pm, Sun 11am–5pm).

✳
National Museum of Contemporary Art

🕐

The Old Lodge dating from 1839 and containing a beautiful concert hall in Empire style is located at Grev Wedelsplaas 2. It is used for concerts and other events.

Old Lodge

Akershus Fortress stands on a spit of land (Akersnes) above the Oslofjord at the western edge of this quarter. Originally commissioned by Håkon V at the end of the 13th century, the medieval castle was turned into a Renaissance palace during the reign of Christian IV. The main area of the fortress is reached via the entrance at Festningsplassen. Christian IV's Hall and the palace church (which contains King Håkon VII's (1872–1957) tomb in the crypt) are open to the public. The other palace rooms are used a setting for various functions by the Norwegian government. There is a wonderful view

✳
Akershus Fortress

Akershus fortress *Plan*

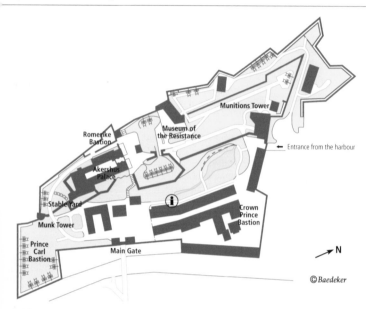

Munitions Tower

Romerike Bastion

Museum of the Resistance

← Entrance from the harbour

Akershus Palace

Stable Yard

Crown Prince Bastion

Munk Tower

Prince Carl Bastion

Main Gate

↗N

©Baedeker

across the Pipervika harbour, Aker Brygge and the entire city from the fortress.

A building in the upper part of the fortress contains the **Museum of the Norwegian Resistance** (Norges Hjemmefrontmuseum), documenting the resistance against the German occupation during the Second World War (opening times: daily 10am–4pm or 5pm).

The Armed Forces Museum (Forsvarsmuseet) is housed in the old arsenal. Its weapons and other exhibits illustrate Norwegian military history from Viking times to the present day (opening times: Mon–Fri 10am to 3pm, during summer till 6pm; Sat, Sun 11am–4pm).
Cruise ships dock below the Akershus and the Oslo Cruise Terminal has a large but expensive selection of typically Norwegian **souvenirs** of every kind.

★★
Oslo Opera House

www.operaen.no ►

Oslo's new opera house, whose artistic director is Bjørn Simensen, was opened in Bjørvika on 12 April 2008. The monumental building was the creation of the Snøhetta company of architects, who made generous use of marble, granite and glass. It bears a price tag of 500 million euros.Visitors are able to take a stroll along the impressive roof, which rises directly from the fjord and functions as a vantage point from which to enjoy the spectacular views. The main concert hall, with capacity for an audience of 1370, is decorated with a chandelier made of 17,000 pieces of glass that also function as acoustic reflectors. A smaller hall accommodates 400. The foyer is the work of Olafur Eliasson from Denmark, while the American Pae White created the large »MetaFoil« stage curtain.

What to See in the East and North

The Botanisk Have is located at the eastern edge of Oslo, with the entrance on Trondheimsveien. The alpine garden is especially pretty (opening times: Mon–Fri 7am–5pm or 8pm, Sat, Sun from 10am).

Botanical Garde

The rise above the Botanical Gardens contains a collection of three natural history museums: the Zoological Museum, the Mineral and Geology Museum, and the Palaeontology Museum (opening times: Tues–Sun 11am–4pm, Wed till 8pm).

Museums of natural history

The Munch Museum (Munchmuseet) can be found on the southern side of the Botanical Gardens at Tøyengata 53. Its exhibits are the legacy of Edvard Munch (1863–1944; ►Famous People) – Norway's most significant artist – and include paintings, prints, drawings and watercolours, as well as sculptures, from just about all of the artist's major artistic phases. Munch's work is characterized by love and death fantasies, Nordic melancholy and a mystical relationship with nature. The artist imbued his pictures with profound emotional content by using dark, depressing colours and simple shapes. Two of Munch's most famous pictures, *The Scream* (1893) and *Madonna* (approx. 1894), were stolen in the summer of 2004 and only recovered in 2006

✷ ✷ Munch Museum

> ## ! Baedeker TIP
>
> ### Still your »sult«
> The little restaurant of »Sult« (meaning hunger) offers good meals at sensible prices and is located in the cosmopolitan Grünerløkka quarter, »Oslo's Soho« in the eastern part of the city, where numerous foreign shops and bars can be found (Thorvald Meyers gate 26, tel. 22 87 04 67).

(►p.71). *The Scream* holds the distinction of being the best known picture in art history after the *Mona Lisa* by Leonardo da Vinci. Munch painted four versions of this picture, one of which can be seen in the National Gallery. The Munch Museum also owns other famous works by the artist, including *The Sick Child* (1886), *Girl on a Bridge* (1899), *The Dance of Life* (1900) and the *Frieze of Life* cycle of paintings (opening times: daily 10am–6pm, www.munch.museum.no). ⊙

The Norwegian Museum for Technology and Industry in Oslo's north, at Kjelsåsveien 143, is worth a visit and especially popular with children. The exhibits allow technology to be explored and understood in a playful way. In addition to the development of metal working (from smithies to modern factories) and gas and oil extrac-

Technology Museum

tion, the history of telecommunications is illustrated, from Viking fire signals to the internet (opening times: Tue–Sun 10am–4pm or 6pm, during summer incl. Mondays).

★ ★ Vigeland Park (Frogner Park)

650 sculptures

The beautiful Frogner Park, also known as Vigeland Park, is situated in the northwest of the city. It is reached via Drammensveien and Frognerveien; the main entrance is on Kirkeveien. The park has a restaurant as well as a very popular open-air swimming pool. Its main attraction, the Vigeland exhibition, was created by the sculptor **Gustav Vigeland** (►Famous People). The artist spent 40 years creating a total of 650 sculptures for the 600m/656yd-long exhibition (see image on p.59). The Vigeland Bridge alone is surrounded by 58 bronze sculptures; below the bridge are the child sculptures. One of the most famous figures at the installation is the *Little Angry Boy* (Sinnataggen) in the middle of the bridge. Adjacent is a bronze figure enclosed in a circle out of which it is desperately trying to escape which illustrates the recurring theme of the entire installation: namely that there is no escape from **the cycle of life**.

Bridge sculptures ►

Fountain group ►

The fountain is the oldest part of the installation and its figures also represent the cycle of life. Walking around the fountain, the first sculpture is of a small child sitting unselfconsciously in its tree of life; then comes the young pubescent person, followed by the meeting of the sexes. Marriage and birth follow and an exhausted mother can be seen in a tree of life. Finally comes old age. The grandfather bids farewell to his grandchild before death catches up with him. The transition from the world of the dead to the world of the as-yet unborn is seamless. The naked giants that stand in the middle of the fountain are condemned to carry the heavy water basin for eternity.

Cut from a single piece of stone, the 17m/56ft-high **monolith** is made up of 121 intertwined human bodies. Work on the giant block took from 1928 to 1942 and occupied several people at the same time. The sculpture installation is completed by the *Wheel of Life*, which contains seven intertwined bodies and was only completed after Vigeland's death in 1934. The park is open round the clock throughout the year.

The old Frogner Hovedgård manor house contains the **Oslo City Museum** (Oslo Bymuseum), which provides an overview of the capital's

Vigeland Exhibition Area Plan

Madserud Alle
»The Family«
Wheel of Life
Sundial
Monolith
Madserud Alle
Fountain (Circle of Life)
Frogner Pool
Frogner Lake
Bridge Sculptures
Frogner Stadium
Child Sculptures
Frogner Park
Tennis court
Triangle
Halvdan Svartes gate
City Museum
Main entrance
Kirkeveien
Essendrops gate
Middelthuns gate
Vigeland Museum
Nobels gate
Frogner plass
© Baedeker

history from the 13th century to the present; among other things, it documents the development of housing and transport (opening times: Tue–Fri 10am–4pm, Sat, Sun 11am–4pm).

Southwest of the Oslo City Museum, beyond Halvdan Svartesgate, is the former studio of the Norwegian sculptor Gustav Vigeland (1869–1943), now a museum. Vigeland's urn is in the tower (opening times: Tue–Sat 10am–6pm, Thu–Sun noon–6pm).

Vigeland Museum

The Emanuel Vigeland Museum (which also serves a as mausoleum) is dedicated to **Gustav Vigeland's brother Emanuel Vigeland** (1875–1948). It is located at Grimelundsveien 8 in the **Vinderen district** and can be reached via the Holmenkoll railway (alight at Vinderen station, and then walk around 700m/766yd along Holmenveien before turning right into Grimelundsveien). The museum is one of the city's curiosities. Vigeland's *Vita* fresco of naked bodies that are born, love, grow old and die is housed in a church-like, windowless stone building where every sound echoes endlessly (opening times: Sun noon–3pm).

★ Emanuel Vigeland Museum

Baedeker TIP

Children's art

At the International Museum of Children's Art, the world can be seen through the eyes of children. The museum at Lille Frøens vei 4 shows art by children from 180 countries, including drawings, paintings, sculptures and textiles. Lots of activities are on offer to ensure little ones don't get bored.

✳ Bygdøy Peninsula

During summer there are boats approximately every half an hour to the Bygdøy Peninsula in west Oslo from the city hall quay. Alternatively, it is a 6km/4mi bus ride. Several genuine highlights of any Oslo visit are gathered together here: namely the Norwegian Museum of Cultural History (Norsk Folkesmuseum), the Fram Museum (Frammuseet), the Kon-Tiki Museum and the Viking Ship Museum. Furthermore, there are several beaches (see p.307).

Getting there

The Fram Museum is located on the southeastern side of Bygdøy, where the motor boats moor. It contains the polar ship »Fram«, with which **Fridtjof Nansen** completed his drift through the Arctic Ocean in 1893–96 (►Famous People). Using a three-masted schooner fixed with an auxiliary 220 horsepower motor, Nansen wanted to prove that the polar ice drifts from Siberia through the Arctic Ocean past the North Pole and on to Greenland. Nansen and Hjalmar Johansen left the schooner at 84° northern latitude and 102° eastern longitude with 28 huskies, two kayaks, three sledges and equipment weighing 700kg/1543lbs in an attempt to reach the North Pole on skis, but they failed (opening times: May–Sept daily 10am–4.45pm, during high season 9am–5.45pm or 6.45pm).

★★ Fram Museum

Bygdøy Map

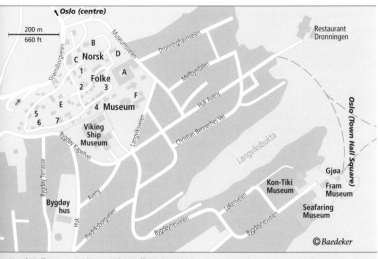

Norsk Folkemuseum (Norwegian Folk Museum)

		FARMS	
A Main Building (furniture, domestic items)	**D** Theatre	**1** Østerdalen	**4** Hallingdal
B Gol stave church	**E** Celebration area	**2** Numedal	**5** Vestlandet
C Restaurant	**F** Gamle byen (historic town houses)	**3** Telemark	**6** Jæren
			7 Østlandet

★
Norwegian Maritime Museum

The Norwegian Maritime Museum is adjacent to the Fram Museum and is a veritable goldmine for all those interested in shipping. There are models of all kinds of vessels, from small rowing boats to large oil tankers, as well as exhibitions on fishing, deep sea archaeology and meteorology, and multimedia shows. *Gjøa*, the polar ship used by the Norwegian polar explorer Roald Amundsen to travel the North West Passage between 1903 and 1906 stands on blocks in front of the museum (opening times: daily 10am–7pm, during winter 10.30am–4pm).

★
Kon-Tiki Museum

A building opposite the Fram Museum contains the balsa raft *Kon-Tiki*, with which the Norwegian anthropologist **Thor Heyerdahl** (► Famous People) travelled from Callao in Peru to the East Polynesian islands in 1947. In addition, there are prehistoric boats, an underwater exhibition and a reproduction of a family cave from Easter Island.

Visitors can also admire the 14m/46ft papyrus boat *Ra II*, with which Thor Heyerdahl and a group of men from eight nations crossed the Atlantic in 1970 (opening times: daily May–Sept 10.30am–5pm, June–Aug 9am–5.45pm).

The Norwegian Museum of Cultural History (Norsk Folkemuseum) is spread over several buildings and also encompasses a large open-air museum of around 150 houses from all corners of the country on an area of 14ha/35ac. It is thus **the largest such collection in Norway**. The main building exhibits folk costumes, domestic goods, carpets and old furniture with rose paintings; there is also a **Sami Exhibition** complete with traditional costumes, tents, equipment used in reindeer husbandry, and hunting and fishing tools. Directly behind the main building a street from the former Christiania has been re-created, in which small worker's apartments and little suburban houses, animal sheds, a sweet shop and fine 18th and 19th century houses can be viewed. The old pharmacy with its **Apothecary Museum** is especially appealing and includes mortar and herb vessels from 1867. A small herb garden lies a few steps away.

The main attraction of this museum is the open-air section that spreads out over a large park area. Here the visitor can experience fine bourgeois houses, country estates complete with barns (stabbur), stables, and servant housing from every district in the country. The Raulandstue (around 1300) from the Numedal valley is especially worth taking a look at. A further attraction is the Gol **stave church** from Hallingdal, which dates from around 1200, donated to the museum (founded in 1894) by King Oscar II. He bought the church when it was due for demolition. The interior is very well preserved, while the exterior was reconstructed using the stave church in Borgund as a model (opening times: mid-May–mid-Sept daily 10am–6pm, otherwise daily 11am–3pm, Sat/Sun till 4pm).

★ ★
Norwegian Museum of Cultural History

South of the Museum of Cultural History there is a large building (Vikingskiphuset) containing three 9th-century Viking ships that are named after the locations where they were discovered: Oseberg, Gokstad and Tune (►see p.322 for the Oseberg ship). The Vikings used all three ships for burials of chieftains, although the Oseberg ship and the Gokstad ship would still be seaworthy today.

★ ★
Viking Ship Museum

The Oseberg ship, found north of Tønsberg in 1903, was used for the burial of a Viking princess and is the most outstanding and complete pre-Christian find in northern Europe. Thanks to the damp, peaty soil, organic material such as wood and textiles were preserved (for more on the ship see the following pages).

◄ Oseberg ship

The ship unearthed near Gokstad in 1880 is 23m/75ft-long and 5m/16ft wide and, unlike the Oseberg ship, it was a lake vessel and therefore less richly decorated. It too was used for a burial. It was designed as a sailing and rowing vessel (the soldiers' shields were hung onto the highest plank). An exact replica of this ship sailed to America in six weeks in 1893, thereby proving that Vikings could have discovered America **before Columbus** did. The Tune ship, unearthed about 10km/6mi north of Fredrikstad in 1867, is the least well preserved; all that is left are the remains of the ship's floor (opening times: May–Sept daily 9am–6pm, otherwise daily 11am–4pm).

◄ Gokstad ship

OSEBERG SHIP

✳ ✳ A farmer at Oseberg came upon strange pieces of wood in the ground during agricultural work in the summer of 1903. These turned out to be a Viking ship that had been used for a burial in AD 834, and although the more valuable funerary goods had long since been stolen, the peat enveloping the ship had at least conserved the wood perfectly. Today the »Oseberg Ship« is the greatest treasure at the Viking Ship Museum in Oslo.

🕐 Opening times:
May–Sept daily 9am–6pm, otherwise daily 11am–4pm.

① Dragon head
The figurehead, a dragon or snake head with a spiralled throat had been hacked off the Oseberg Ship.

② Side rudder
Viking ships always have their side rudder at the steering end, to the right of the direction travelled. The hull is 21.4m/70.2ft long and 5.1m/16.7ft wide and the floor is flat. The ship can be rowed or sailed at up to 10 knots, although its delicate construction indicates that it was not used on the high seas, unlike the Viking warships. It was built between AD 815 and AD 820.

③ Oar
All 30 oars, each 3.18m/10.4ft long, survive. 30 men used them while seated on boxes.

④ Oxen as grave goods
The remains of an ox survive, whose last meal consisted of juniper, reeds, erica and rosehip.

⑤ The dead
The ship's bow pointed south and a chamber of 5.5m/18ft x 5.3m/17.3ft was constructed on deck: the tomb for two women. One, about 60–70 years old, suffered from pronounced arthritis; the other was 20–30 years old when she died. An oak trunk filled with ears of wheat, numerous wild apples and walnuts indicate that the funeral took place in autumn.

⑥ Runes
The front section of the ship contained a 2.42m/7.9ft -long spar that is embellished with Norway's oldest runic script: »litiluism«. Could it have been the name of the ship?

⑦ Planks
The decking planks were of pine and were fixed with nails made of ebony.

⑧ Mast
The mast was 20cm/7.9in thick and around 13m/43ft high. The roughly 90 sq m/969 sq ft sail was missing.

Final resting place in the Viking Ship Museum

Many Oslo residents are drawn out to the wonderful landscape on their days off: during winter on skis, and during summer on foot.

huts. During summer, these huts also make popular destinations for hikers and cyclists.

Heading south of Oslo, leave the E 18 that runs along the Bunnefjord and follow the RV 182 until the turning near Lake Gjersjøen to **Svartskog**. The former home of the polar explorer Roald Amundsen (1872–1928; ► Famous People) stands here, in an idyllic location right on the Bunnefjord, an arm of the Oslofjord. »Uranienborg« is a wooden villa in the Swiss style. Amundsen lived here from 1908 until his death, which occurred during an attempt to save the life of the Italian airship captain Nobile. In his bedroom, Amundsen had portholes instead of traditional windows installed. In addition to Amundsen's furniture, visitors can also see numerous souvenirs brought back from the South Pole (guided tours; opening times: mid-May–mid-Sept Tue–Sun 11am–4pm).

★
Amundsen's house

⏲

East Norway's most popular theme park lies directly at the junction of the E 18 and the E 6 and includes **northern Europe's largest wooden rollercoaster**. The »Land of the Vikings« is especially pretty and offers insight into Viking traditions. Children have their own park and also an aquapark (opening times: mid-June–mid-Aug daily 10.30am–7pm).

Tusenfryd

⏲

★ Oslofjord

Region: East Norway

The Oslofjord is the country's lifeline. About a third of all Norwegians live nearby and the capital city of Oslo lies at the fjord's far end. Nevertheless, there are still some quiet corners along its shores and many opportunities to have a swim.

Already popular in prehistoric times

Those arriving in Norway by boat should choose Oslo as their destination, which is where the Oslofjord (roughly 20km/12mi wide and 100km/62mi long) opens into the Skagerrak strait. The loveliest **summer destinations** are found along the western shore in particular. The 589km/368mi-long Glomma River empties into the fjord at ▶Fredrikstad on the eastern shore, to the north of the holiday islands of Hvaler with their strikingly smooth eroded rocks. The **oldest finds** proving human habitation in Norway have been found in this region and to the north as far as Svartskog: up to 9000 years old, they include **rock paintings** and burial sites. The earliest inhabitants followed the receding ice after the end of the last Ice Age. Norway's **most densely populated** area lies around the inner part of the Oslofjord. In addition to agriculture, there has been intense development of industry and important commercial centres and the coastal settlements are also home to a large merchant fleet.

What to See on the Western Shore of the Oslofjord

Horten

The first major settlement on the actual Oslofjord is the port of Horten (pop. 23,500, car ferry to Moss 30mins). The old marine buildings of Karljohansvern, north of the town centre, house the **Maritime Museum**. The world's oldest torpedo boat, the *Rapp*, dates from 1872 and can be seen in front of the museum. The internationally renowned **Preus National Museum of Photography** is in the same building complex and the only one of its kind in Norway. The exhibition halls were designed by the famous architect Sverre Fehn (opening times: June–Aug daily noon–6pm, otherwise Thu, Fri noon–4pm, Sat, Sun noon–6pm, www.preusmuseum.no). 4km/2.5mi south of town, near the medieval church of Borre, the new and artfully designed **Midgard Historical Centre** offers memorable documentation on the history of the Vikings. A visit is just as interesting for children as for adults (opening times: May–Sept daily 10am–5pm, otherwise Tue–Sun 10am–4pm). The small **Borre National Park** contains northern Europe's largest collection of royal burial mounds (six large ones up to 7m/23ft-high and 21 smaller mounds). A beautiful cycle track of about

● VISITING OSLOFJORD

INFORMATION

Horten og Borre Turistkontor
Tollbugt 1
3187 Horten
Tel. 33 03 17 08
Fax 33 03 17 09
www.vestfold.com
www.visithorten.com

Sandefjord Reiselivsforening
Thor Dahls gate 1
3210 Sandefjord
Tel. 33 46 05 90
Fax 33 46 06 20
www.visitsandefjord.com

Tønsberg Horisont
Tønsberg Brygge
3126 Tønsberg
Tel. 33 35 45 20
Fax 33 35 45 19
www.vestfold.com

WHERE TO EAT

► Moderate
Det gamle Bageri Ost &Vinhus
Drøbak
Tel. 64 93 21 05
This cosy, rustic tavern is a good place to have lunch after visiting the Drøbaker Christmas shop. The locals also like to meet here in the evenings for a glass wine.

► Inexpensive
Brygga Restaurant
Tønsberg
Nedre Langgate 35
(right on the quay)
Tel. 33 31 12 70
The large seafood plate in this harbour restaurant is not only of mighty proportions but also very reasonably priced. The large terrace right on the water is especially attractive.

WHERE TO STAY

► Luxury
Hotel Refsnes Gods
Moss, Godset 5
Tel. 69 27 83 00, fax 69 27 83 01
105 beds, www.refsnesgods.no
This luxury hotel on an island in the Oslofjord is set in a grand 18th-century country estate. Despite modern extensions, the hotel is still very quiet and has its own beach and boat jetty.

► Mid-range
Åsgårdstrand Hotel
Åsgårdstrand, Havnegata 6
Tel. 33 08 10 40, fax 33 08 10 77
70 rooms, www.asgardstrand-hotell.no
A comfortable hotel with a pleasant atmosphere right on the beach that pays homage to Edvard Munch, the most famous tourist to come to this small settlement.

Hotel Kong Carl
Sandefjord, Torvgt.9
Tel. 33 46 31 17
Fax 33 46 31 19
50 beds, www.kongcarl.no
This very centrally located historic house was built at the end of the 17th century. It has been an inn since 1721 and its cuisine is famous throughout the country.

Wassilioff Hotel
Stavern, Havnrgt. 1
Tel. 33 11 36 00
Fax 33 11 36 01
76 beds, www.wassilioff.no
This hotel in the old garrison town was founded by an immigrant from Riga in 1844. It is one of the most popular hotels on the Oslofjord.

In his studio in Åsgårdstrand on the Oslofjord, Edvard Munch concentrated not only on the dark side of human existence, but also painted happy scenes, such as »Three Girls on a Bridge«.

4km/2.5mi through forest leads from here along the waterside to Åsgårdstrand (coastal route 1).

Åsgårdstrand In the middle of the old village of this idyllic swimming resort and artists' centre there are several galleries, as well as the old Corsmeier Thuen clockmaker's workshop in which historic clocks and watches are restored. The white-painted wooden houses are very picturesque; in **»Munchs lille hus«** beyond the guest quay, Edvard Munch (►Famous People) painted *Girls on the Bridge*, one of the most famous images of Åsgårdstrand. The studio and old fishermen's cabin are from the 18th century(opening times: June–Aug, Tue to Sun 11am–7pm). The pretty beach can also be recognized on several more Munch pictures. The annual Åsgårdstrand Days in June celebrate this small resort's famous guest and include a revival of the scene portraying the three girls, when they can once again be seen posing just as in Munch's day. The **Oseberg ship** (► Oslo, Viking Ship Museum) was found in a 6m/20ft-high burial mound at Oseberg, 6km/4mi south of here, in 1904.

Tønsberg Tønsberg (pop. 34,500) is Norway's oldest town and was founded by Harald Hårfagre in 871. King Magnus Lagabøte resided in his brick fortress (1276) up on the rocky castle hill during the 13th century, when he wrote the country's first constitution. Today only ruins of the fortress remain in the castle grounds on the hill, but the **ruin-park** is one of northern Europe's largest. Håkon Håkonsson's 12th-century fortress of **Castrum Tunisbergis**, with its mighty buttress walls and bastions, was Norway's largest castle in the Middle Ages, but only a few partly reconstructed stone walls survive, as is the case with the St Michael's Church from 1150. A wonderful view onto Tønsberg and over the jagged skerry landscape can be enjoyed from the **lookout tower** (1888). This area is especially popular with Norway's high society during summer when hardly a seat can be found at the restaurant quay to the southeast of the historic Norbyen quarter. The **Vestfold Festival** at the end of June/early July is also popular and offers plays, concerts and exhibitions.

Odd Nerdrum (born 1944), one of Norway's best-known contemporary painters, has his own exhibition in the **Haugar Vestfold Art Museum**. The museum is located on Haugar Hill, which was the site of an important Viking »ting« (assembly). Until the mid-20th century, whaling in the southern ice floes was also a source of income for the town (► Baedeker Special p.400). More on whaling and Norway's great seafaring era can be found at the **Vestfold Fylkesmuseum**, at the foot of the castle hill (opening times: mid-May–mid-Sept Mon–Sat 10am–5pm, Sun from noon, otherwise Mon–Fri 10am–2pm). A tip for families with children: check out the wonderful long **sandy beaches** at Valløy (campsite) and Skallevoll to the west of Tønsberg.

The islands of Nøtterøy and Tjøme to the south of Tønsberg boast several sandy beaches and are popular holiday destinations (reached via the RV 308). A particularly pretty spot is Verdens End, »The End of the World«, in the south of Tjøme. Numerous coves, good for bathing, lie between the smoothly polished cliffs here. In fair weather, the 300-year-old Færder fyr lighthouse is visible in the middle of the mouth of the Oslofjord.

★
Islands of Nøtterøy and Tjøme

Those who fly to Oslo with Ryanair land southeast of Tønsberg, in the former whaling town of Sandefjord (pop. 39,000; for more on whaling see ►Baedeker Special p.400). The **Whaling Museum**, interesting not least because it is not one-sided, and the Seafaring Museum offer an insight into the old days; a whalers' memorial by Knut Steen stands at the harbour. Until the 19th century, the town was also a well-known spa. Opened in 1837, Sandefjord Spa played host to many a personality. The former wooden spa building was transformed into a **cultural centre** that

Sandefjord

> # Baedeker TIP
>
> ### Sail like the Vikings
> The *Gaia*, a replica of the approximately 1200-year-old Gokstad Ship, is anchored at the museum's quay at Sandefjord and makes occasional round trips out to sea.

has an exhibition on Sandefjord's past. In the south of the Østerøya Peninsula, beginning at the Tallakshamn beach, a narrow path leads to the **Tønsberg Tønne fire tower** (35mins), from where there is a good view towards the Skagerrak Sea. East of Sandefjord, it is possible to climb onto the Gokstad mound from which the Gokstad ship was dug out in 1880 (►Oslo, Viking Ship Museum).

✱
Viking town of Kaupang

One of the largest and oldest Viking trading posts can be found by following the road past the turning for **Ula pilots' harbour** and taking the road that branches off shortly before Larvik (in the direction of Bjønnes and Gloppe; in Kaupang in the direction of Lamøya). Along with Ribe and Hedeby in Denmark and Birka in Sweden, the Viking town of Kaupang, in an idyllic setting on the Viksfjord, was among the North's most important trading posts. Mentioned in the Yngling saga as **Sikringssal**, it was probably the **capital of the Norwegian Vikings**. Archaeological excavations have unearthed the remains of a royal hall, houses with fireplaces, workshops (smithies, weaving workshops and glass bead manufactories), streets and a port which all indicate a fixed settlement with a permanent market was located here between 770 and 920. Kaupang can therefore perhaps outdo Tønsberg, so far considered Norway's oldest town.

Larvik

The RV 303 ends at the former county capital of Larvik (pop. 40,000), where the ferry for Denmark departs once or twice a day. The sulphurous saltwater spring Kong Håkon's kilde, Norway's only natural **mineral spring** lies here. In the southeast of the town stands the stately Herregården estate that was constructed between 1670 and 1680 to serve as a residence for the Larvik counts and today houses the town museum. The interior of the 17th-century **Larvik Church**, to the south of the railway, is pretty. To the left of the altar there is a painting by Lucas Cranach the Elder portraying Martin Luther. **Bøkeskogen**, Norway's largest beech forest, stretches northwest of Larvik and contains around 90 burial mounds from the Iron Age.

✱
Stavern

200 days of sun per year – this bold claim is designed to tempt visitors to the seaside resort of Stavern to the south of Larvik. In the middle of the town stands the impressive maritime fortress of Fredriksvern, encircled by thick walls. It was built as a dockyard by King Frederik V in 1760. Artisans now work and exhibit in the former commandant's house.

What to See on the Eastern Shore of the Oslofjord

✱
Drøbak

Oslo's winter port was once located at the small seaside resort of Drøbak, at the narrowest point of the Oslofjord. When the fjord was frozen over, passengers and goods for Oslo had to be transported overland from here. Picturesque wooden houses and an aquarium stand by the small marina. Further north, by the bathing park, stands a pretty wooden church from 1736, while the attraction in the town centre is Norway's all-year-round **Christmas shop**, »Treegaardens julehus« (with its own special postmark).

Moss

One of eastern Norway's most famous galleries, the **F 15 Gallery** is housed in the Alby mansion on the island of Jeløy (bridge), which lies just offshore of Moss and is reached via the bathing resorts of Hvitsten and Son. There is a car ferry from Moss to Horten (duration 30mins, every 45mins). The personal union between Sweden and Norway was signed in the old estate located on the present site of the Moss paper factory on 14 August 1814.

✳ Romsdal

E 4/5

Region: West Norway

The mighty Romsdalshorn, the 1000m/3281ft-high vertical Troll Wall and, to top it all, the serpentine curves of the Trollstigen road. A visit to the Romsdal valley is a spectacular experience.

Cutting inland from Åndalsnes on the mighty Romsdalsfjord, the Romsdal valley is one of the most beautiful in western Norway. The Rauma river flows through the approximately 60km/37mi-long valley, which is embraced by magnificent mountains. Romsdal can either be reached from Åndalsnes or from the southeast through the ►Gudbrandsdal valley. The E 136 leads from the end of Gudbrandsdal across the watershed between the Atlantic and the Skagerrak Sea into the lower Romsdal valley.

Magnificent mountain valley

You just have to get through it: the Rondslottet in Romsdal.

► VISITING ROMSDAL

INFORMATION

Åndalsnes og Romsdal Reiselivslag
6300 Åndalsnes
Tel. 71 22 16 22
Fax 71 22 16 82
www.andalsnes.net

WHERE TO EAT

► Moderate
Trollstigen Fjellstue
Tel. 99 29 20 00
This modern mountain inn built in traditional blockhouse style on the Trollstigen pass offers seating for more than 300 people. Popular as a stop for tour buses, it is often full. Open from end of May to end of August.

Trollstigen Camping & Gjestegård
Åndalsnes
Tel. 71 22 11 12
Large inn and also a popular tour bus stop on the route from Åndalsnes to Trollstigen. Breakfast, lunch, coffee and cake, supper, and an extensive cold buffet are on the menu. The well-maintained campsite and comfortable cabins make this attractive to those wishing to stay longer.

Rød and Bare Blå
Molde, Storgt. 19
Tel. 71 21 58 88
The »Rød« is the town's most modern café and the »Bare Blå« the most popular coffee bar. With interiors are full of art works, they are found next door to each other inside the Hotel Molde. The Rød is a popular meeting place at lunchtime, while the Bare Blå is a good place to find a drink, even after midnight. A visit to the Hot Hat Jazz Club in the hotel basement is also recommended.

WHERE TO STAY

► Mid-range
Grand Hotel Bellevue
Åndalsnes, Åndalsgata 5
Tel. 71 22 75 00, fax 71 22 60 38
86 rooms, booking@grandhotel.no
This hotel, built in 1954, was recently refurbished to the latest standards so that all rooms give a modern impression. The excellent restaurant, pub, bar and nightclub are also popular.

Molde Fjordstuer
Molde, Julsundveien 6
Tel. 71 20 10 60, fax 71 20 10 61
18 rooms, www.havstuene.no
Newly-built hotel in the modern »Sjøbu style« located right by the water at the Hurtigruten quay. Bright and elegant rooms with lake views. The excellent restaurant is expensive, but the salt cod soup is authentic and affordable.

► Budget
Mjelva Camping Huts
Åndalsnes
Tel. 71 22 64 50, fax 71 22 68 77
www.mjelvacamping.no
This campsite was voted the region's best in 2004. Quiet location and beautiful views onto the spectacular Romsdal mountains. Space for mobile homes and tents; simple but comfortable cabins can be rented.

EXCURSIONS

Thanks to its beautiful beaches, the small island of Hjertøya in the Romsdalsfjord is ideal for day trips. A boat travels between Torget and Hjertøya between mid-June and mid-August, departing at 11am, noon, 2pm and 4pm (last return trip at 5.45pm)

What to See in and around the Romsdal Valley

The Romsdal valley, which can be followed on the E 136, gets narrower and narrower as it descends to the sea. The serpentine road regularly offers beautiful views down onto the churning Rauma river that has cut itself a dramatic chasm through the rock at the Slettafoss waterfall.

Down the Romsdal to the sea

The railway crosses the river on a 76m/249ft-long and 59m/194ft-high bridge, the Kylling bru at Verma (273m/896ft), from where the Vermafoss Power Station can be seen close to the road. A short drive further on, the road reaches the valley floor where it is flanked by rugged mountains on either side. To the left of the road at Flatmark, Døntind (1676m/5499ft) towers up into the sky. Where the valley widens at Malstein, the mighty 1799m/5902ft-high Kalskråtind catches the eye. Further north, Romsdalshorn towers 1550m/5085ft into the air, dominating the landscape. Pipes gather the water that flows inside the mountain to drive the turbines that produce electricity.

◄ Verma

✳ Romsdalshorn

Opposite Romsdalshorn stands the mighty Trollveggen (Troll Wall) crowned by the Trolltindene (Troll Peaks). It is **Europe's highest rock face** and measures 1800m/5906ft from its base to the summit, there being a 1000m/3281ft-high vertical part and an overhang of 50m/164ft. Several extremely difficult climbing routes lead up the Troll Wall, which was scaled for the first time in 1965. The first climbers needed two weeks to complete their mission. These mighty mountains are so high that the valley here sees no sun for almost five months of the year. The rock face used to present a challenge irresistible to sky divers, but jumping from the top of the wall with a parachute was prohibited after several fatalities.

✳ Trolltindene

At the Sogge bru bridge, the RV 63, the Trollstigen, branches off to the left and leads through the Isterdal valley to Valldal. In a series of eleven breathtaking bends and with a 12% slope, the Trollstigen winds 18km/11mi up the mountain, offering wonderful views of the wildly romantic mountain scenery. Earth slides have made it necessary to rebuild the road (visited by over half a million tourists each year) in several places. The road crosses the Stigfoss at the Stigfoss bru bridge before reaching Trollstigen Fjellstue at the top of the pass, from where there is a viewing point. Afterwards the road leads down into Valldal and the magnificent Tåfjord.

✳ ✳ Trollstigen

! **Baedeker TIP**

The sweetest fruit

Valldal, at the end of the Trollstigen, has been famous for its aromatic fruit since the importation of strawberries from Denmark about one hundred years ago. The »Syltetøybutikken« sell homemade juices and jams (tel. 70 25 75 11; opening times: Mon–Fri 10am–5pm, Sat till 2pm).

Åndalsnes The E 136 ends at Åndalsnes, a lively holiday resort with the picturesque Romsdalsfjord lying to its west. The town is connected to the railway network via the Rauma route and is suitable as a base for excursions into the fjords. A tourist train (departures daily 1pm) runs between Åndalsnes and Bjorli from the end of June to the end of August, and on several days a steam train is used.

Driving is sometimes a tight squeeze on the Trollstigen.

Molde (pop. 24,600) lies on the coast. It was given its nickname of »Rosetown« by Norway's well-known poet Bjørnstjerne Bjørnson (► Famous People), who went to school in Molde. Though located at 62° northern latitude, the effect of the Gulf Stream means the climate here is so mild that even chestnut trees, lime trees and, most of all, countless roses grow. Molde's panorama of 22 mountain peaks, sometimes covered in snow, on the other side of the fjord is truly beautiful. Jazz musicians from all over the world come to this lively resort every year at the beginning of August to take part in the international **Molde Jazz Festival**. Bjørnstjerne Bjørnson was a frequent visitor at the former magistrate's court of **Moldegården**, built in 1710, and the playwright Henrik Ibsen (► Famous People) wrote his play *Rosmersholm* there. The altar painting from the church destroyed in 1940, *The Resurrection* by Axel Ender (19th century), hangs in the aisle of the modern **cathedral** (1957), which has beautiful stained glass windows. In the west of town lies the Reknesparken forest park and the **Romsdal Museum**, a pretty open-air museum containing around 70 historic Romsdal buildings including the Synnøve Solbakken parlour that recalls Bjørnson's story about the farm girl Synnøve.

View of the sea Beautiful viewing points near Molde are Tusten (696m/2283ft; ascent 3hrs) and Varden (407m/1335ft), which can be climbed from the town centre in about one hour. There is also a road and panorama restaurant. On the RV 64 about 28km/17mi north of the town lies the Trollkirka grotto, which can be reached on foot via a steep path in one and a half hours (►Kristiansund, Atlantic Route).

Røros ✳

E 8

Region: Central Norway   **Population:** 5500

Røros, the only town in Norway located in the mountains, is often bitterly cold in winter, and yet it is one of the most beautiful places in the country. The historic town centre, whose wooden houses still date from the copper mining era, is on the UNESCO World Heritage List.

The last pit near the mining town of Røros was closed in 1977. An era that had lasted over 300 years and produced a total of 110,000 tons of copper was thereby ended. What remains are the large, dark brown **slag heaps** and the damage to the natural environment caused by centuries of **deforestation** around Røros. The town was founded in 1644 after large deposits of copper ore were found in the Arvedal pit, and in 1723 the Royal pit and the Christianus Sextus pit were also established (tours in summer). The »Rørosmartnan« folk festival, held in February every year, recalls the heyday of the mining town with concerts in the old smelting works and the miners' church, horse-drawn sled parades, ski races, dance and »miners' buffets«.

Fate of a mining town

What to See in Røros

The 75 listed buildings of the Bergstaden (old town) have been restored in a manner true to their original style and give an excellent insight into the local mining town architecture. The earliest examples of the characteristic dark brown workers' apartments were built at the end of the 17th century near the first smelting works at the Hitter River. A housing block often also included stables, bakeries and storage buildings. A good example is the 18th-century **Per Amundsa Court** at Bergmannsgata 37, where slag from the pits was used for the roofing. The wealthier citizens and pit directors settled in the lower part of the old town. The size and interiors of the houses are evidence of the class barriers that existed. The oldest testament to the town's history is the Aasengården. The estate stands on an area that was cleared in the 17th century by Hans Olsen Aasen, the first to discover that the region was ore-rich.

✳✳
Bergstaden

There is a fascinating **Mining Museum** on Malmplassen (Ore Square) with several models (1:10) showing old mining technologies. The museum's pit room installed in the reconstructed smelting block shows how the ore was extracted in the lower pits using explosives during the 18th century, and also how a pump was operated via a horse-drawn treadmill (opening times: mid-June–mid-Aug daily 10.30–6pm, Sat/Sun till 4pm, otherwise Mon–Fri 11am–3pm, Sat/Sun till 2pm).

✳✳
Røros Museum

🕓

✳
Røros Church

Built of stone in 1784, the octagonal Baroque church on Kjerkgata (also known as »Bergstadens Ziir«) is the town's emblem and remained the only stone building in Røros for a long time. The square tower is decorated with the hammer and mallet images of mining. The Baroque interior of this light and pleasant church contains a royal lodge decorated in real gold, the organ, and several portraits.

Falkeberg monument

The artist Sivert Donali created the Falkberget monument in honour of the writer Johann Falkberget (1879–1967), whose novels made a substantial contribution towards putting this, Norway's only high fjell town, on the map. The title of his Røros Trilogy is *Christianus Sextus*.

▶ VISITING RØROS

INFORMATION

Røros Turistkontor
Peder Hiortsgt. 2
7361 Røros
Tel. 72 41 11 65
Fax 72 41 02 08
www.rorosinfo.com

WHERE TO EAT

▶ **Moderate**

Vertshuset Røros
Kjerkgata 34
Tel. 72 41 24 11
A small restaurant in the centre with genuine Norwegian »rømmegrøt« sour cream porridge on the menu.

Kaffestuggu Røros
Bergmannsgata 18
Tel. 72 41 10 33
This café is housed in one of the town's oldest buildings. Its pastel coloured walls, old stove, portraits and rustic furniture make it a charming place for a snack.

Krambua Røros
Kjerkgt.
Tel. 72 41 05 67
Trendy restaurant in the town centre, good for steak and beer; occasional live music on the tiny stage.

Baedeker recommendation

Thomasgaarden
Kjerkegata 48
Tel. 72 42 24 70
The Thomasgaarden is a historic Røros building. Coffee and cake is served in the very cosy guest room.

WHERE TO STAY

▶ **Mid-range**

Vertshuset Røros
Kjerkgata 34
Tel. 72 41 93 50
Fax 72 41 93 51
Comfortable inn in the old town. The cellar bar hosts live music every week.

Erzscheidergården
16 rooms, Spell Olavn 6
Tel. 72 41 11 94
Fax 72 41 19 60
Small guesthouse with charming staff on a hill with views of Røros.

MARKET

The five-day »Rørosmartnan« is held in mid-February, with a winter market that attracts many traders, musicians and visitors.

Around Røros

The Olav Mine about 13km/8mi east of town is a copper mine that was discovered in 1936. There are daily guided tours of the mine during summer (mid-June–mid-Aug daily from 10.30am every hour till 6pm; May–Sept Mon–Sat 1pm and 3pm, Sun noon). The mine cavern, at a depth of 500m/547yd inside the mountain, also hosts concerts during summer. Inside, the temperature is a constant 5°C/ 41°F, so warm clothes are necessary. Norway's most southern Sami families still pursue a life of **reindeer husbandry** on the Rørosvidda mountain plateau.

Olav Mine

For those searching for even more obscure things, a detour into the **Hessdal** valley north of Røros is recommended. This is where **UFO hunters** study a phenomenon of mysterious appearances of lights and cigar-shaped objects in the sky. Their studies are frequently published and eye witnesses regularly report their sightings. A summary of mysterious happenings in Hessdal can be found at http://hessdalen.hiof.no/station/alarm.shtml.

? DID YOU KNOW ...?

■ ... that many street names in Røros are German in origin? Oskar Schwatz, the first director of the mines, was from Germany's Black Forest, and miners and engineers from both Norway and Germany flooded into Røros soon after cooper was discovered here.

★ Saltfjellet

Region: North Norway   **Height:** 0 - 1600m/5250ft

The sheer barrenness of the Saltfjellet plateau cannot fail to impress. Here, at the Arctic Circle, those who have not yet spotted a reindeer could be in luck: you may well encounter one while driving along the E 6. Of course the much larger attraction is the Svartisen glacier.

The 2250 sq km/869 sq mi of Saltfjellet (meaning »the salt mountain«) have consituted northern Norway's largest and most varied national park since 1989. Bordered by the North Sea and the Svartisen glacier to the west and the Swedish border to the east, it is also traversed by the **Arctic Circle**. The **only visible intervention** into the landscape is the E 6 running parallel to the railway line between Mo I Rana in the south and Bodø in the north; the most important road connection across the highland plateau, it becomes impassable during winter due to huge amounts of snow. Typical for Saltfjellet is the juxtaposition of a glacier landscape in the west with broad valleys and highlands to the east.

Primordial landscape

What to See on Saltfjellet

Saltfjellet is covered by a network of footpaths and self-catering huts that are each one day's walk away from the next. The best route into the area is via the E 6, travelling as far as Rognan and then taking the road that branches off to the west as far as Storjord. **Historic sacrificial sites**, hunting pits and stone walls prove that the indigenous Sami people were already using Saltfjellet as a **hunting and grazing ground** centuries ago.

Arctic Circle Centre The Arctic Circle (Polarsirkelen) in Norway is located around 80km/ 50mi north of Mo i Rana. At the spot where the E 6 cuts the Arctic Circle, the Arctic Circle Centre presents exhibitions on the culture and economy of northern Norway. The Arctic Circle Pillar stands in front of this architecturally interesting building and provides a popular photo opportunity (opening times: daily May–Sept 9am–6pm, July till 10pm).

Svartisen glacier An impressive draw for visitors to this region is the Svartisen glacier (»black ice glacier«), the largest of northern Scandinavia's ice massifs, which reaches all the way to the fjords in the west. Individual summits protrude from the 1200m/3937ft–1400m/4593ft-high plateau, including Snøtind (1599m/5246ft), Sniptind (1591m/5220ft) and Is-

Engabreen, a side arm of the Svartisen glacier, rolls majestically into the valley.

tind (1577m/5174ft). Coming from the south, it is advisable to head northwest via ► Mo i Rana in the direction of Svartisdalshytta or Melfjordbotn. Both roads end at the foot of a Svartisen outcrop. On no account should anyone venture onto the ice. During summer the ice moves several metres each day; fractures and splits can appear that are usually only noticed when it is too late. Coming from the north along the coastal route 17 (►Nordland) between ►Bodø and Glomfjord, it is possible to combine a glacier trip with a drive along what is probably **northern Norway's most beautiful coastal road**. Furthermore, the narrow Nordfjord, whose western shore falls steeply into the water and features countless waterfalls, numbers among Norway's most beautiful fjords.

Around 70% of Norway's natural caves are found here in the Saltfjellet region. The Grønli Cave north of ► Mo i Rana is a famous tourist attraction. The caves were created when the numerous water courses in the mountains dissolved the limestone and marble predominating in the region. In fact, at the edge of the national park the famous Saltfjellet marble is still mined today.

> ! *Baedeker* TIP
>
> ### Hiking made easy
>
> Bodø's hiking association (Bodø og Omegns Turistforening) runs 15 simple mountain huts that are ideally suited as accommodation during longer hikes: the Argaladshytta and Trygvebu are in the Junkerdal valley; the Bjellåvasstua, Lønsstua, Midtistua and Krukkistua are on Saltfjellet; the Tåkeheimen is at an elevation of 1100m/3609ft near the Svartisen glacier and the Lurefjellhytta is below Lurefjelltind near Bodø. Information at tel. 75 52 14 13; bot@online.no.

Beginning at Storjord on the E 6, the RV 77 leads through Junkerdal,   **Junkerdal**
a valley as dramatic as it is fertile, all the way to the Swedish border. Hiking in this densely forested landscape is a great way to spot local flora such as the **Arctic Orchid**, which belongs to a species that normally only grows in more southerly latitudes.

Near Fauske on the E 6 turn east onto route 830 and continue to Sulitjelma, where iron ore was mined until 1990. It was one of the Sami locals who discovered a seam here by chance in the 1880s. The **Mining Museum** in Sulitjelma bears witness to a unique epoch in the history of Norwegian iron ore mining. There are also guided walks onto the 1571m/5154ft-high **Blåmannsisen glacier** and ascents of Suliskongen at 1913m/6276ft on offer from Sulitjelma.

▶ SALTFJELLET

INFORMATION
Fauske Salten Reiseliv
Sjøgata 86
8201 Fauske
Tel. 75 64 33 03, fax 75 64 32 38
www.saltenreiseliv.no

✷ Senja (Island)

M 13-15

Region: North Norway

The coastal strips to the west and north of Senja Island are among the roughest mountain regions in the country. Sometimes the mountainsides rise vertically 1000m/3281ft out of the sea. A starker contrast to the flat, white, sandy beaches that can also be found on the island is hardly imaginable.

Treasure island for nature lovers Norway's third largest island after Spitsbergen and Hinnøya lies between Tromsø and the Vesterålen islands and is a veritable paradise for nature lovers. Steep mountainsides frame deeply cut fjords on the seaboard, while sheltered bays and forested hills characterize the landscape facing the mainland. All routes to Senja lead via Finnsness, where the region's only hotel can be found (airstrip at Bardufoss), and where the ▶ Hurtigruten ships also stop. Access to the island is made easy by the 1120m/3675ft-long Gisund Bridge.

The island has been inhabited since the end of the last Ice Age. The oldest surviving scripts tell of a nomadic tribe. Loot from one of their raiding trips to Friesland found under a stone by a farmer in 1905 is **Norway's greatest silver treasure** (including a ring with Runic inscriptions). King Ottar of Senja sailed to Nordkapp around 890, and then to England via Bergen and Stavanger. In the 16th and 17th centuries there were many Dutch settlements on the seaboard side of the island. The people lived from whaling and also fitted out ships for polar expeditions. Since 1993 the island's cultural emblem has been the 18m/59ft-high **Senja Troll**, the world's largest troll registered in the Guinness Book of Records. The troll is to be found in Berg in the island's northwest. Children especially enjoy visiting the inside of the troll, where exhibitions on Nordic mythology are on display (opening times: June–Aug daily 9am–9pm; www.senjatrollet.no).

▶ **SENJA**

INFORMATION

Destination Midt i Troms
Finnsnes
Tel. 77 85 07 30
Fax 77 85 07 31
mail@dmit.no

WHERE TO EAT/ WHERE TO STAY

Hamn i Senja tourist resort
Tel. 77 85 98 80
Fax 77 85 98 81
www.hamnisenja.no
Hamn is a fishing village that has been restored and turned into a comfortable holiday resort. Traditional Norwegian food is served at the Storbrygga Spiseri.

The pretty Torsken Church (1773), whose interior was donated by Hanseatic merchants from the northern German town of Lübeck, can be visited in the village of Torsken on the west coast near Gryllefjord.

The 68 sq km/26 sq mi **Ånderdalen National Park** is in the south of Senja Island. Its has a wealth of flora and bird species, including eagles. There are no footpaths or cabins, so visitors are dependent on their own tents, but mountain hikers really do get their money's worth here. Water sports enthusiasts can go canoeing, diving, and sailing, enjoy relaxing boat trips, and try both freshwater and sea fishing – Senja is a major fishing ground for halibut.

> **? DID YOU KNOW …?**
>
> ■ … that Cognac producer Jon Arne Berthelsen stores his French cognac in Senja with its coastal climate? The fine spirit is believed to develop a completely different – and hopefully even better – taste in the cool Norwegian conditions.

★ Setesdalen

A/B 4

Region: South Norway

For a long time, the Setesdal valley was remote and inaccessible. As a consequence many old farmsteads have survived here, and timeworn traditions preserved. The peace and quiet of the area has meanwhile been lost, however, because many have now discovered the valley's beauty.

In recent decades, the lovely and deeply forested Setesdal or Sæterdal valley has become the most important road connection between the south coast and ► Bergen and the ► Hardangerfjord. For centuries, though, the few inhabitants of Setesdalen lived in great isolation and developed their own customs and folk costumes: the women wore black, knee-length skirts with red borders. The railway and the road through the valley were built in the 19th century, but the latter has only been passable all year round since the 1960s.

Over the hills …

What to See in Setesdalen

The Setesdal valley lies north of ► Kristiansand on the RV 9. Many colourful minerals can be seen and a replica mine visited at the **Setesdal Mineral Park**, where there are also minerals for sale (opening times: mid-June–early Sept daily 10am–5pm). The **wooden Hornnes church**, 5km/3mi south of Evjes, is worth a visit. This octagonal building was erected between 1826 and 1829.

Evje

▶ VISITING SETESDALEN

INFORMATION

Evje / Setesdal Informasjonsenter
4735 Evje
Tel. 37 93 14 00, fax 37 93 14 55
www.setesdal.com

Hovden / Setesdal Ferie
4755 Hovden
Tel. 37 93 93 70, fax 37 93 93 77
www.hovden.com

WHERE TO EAT

▶ Moderate

Stigeren Restaurant
Evje, Tel. 37 93 08 28
A small and cosy restaurant in the middle of Evje, whose interior recalls the local mining history. An extensive menu offers fish and meat dishes, pizzas and snacks at affordable prices.

WHERE TO STAY

▶ Mid-range

Hovdestøylen Hotell & Hyttetun
Hovden
Tel. 37 93 95 52, fax 37 93 96 55
42 rooms, www.hovdestoylen.no
Modern comfortable huts and hotel rooms with wooden interiors close to the ski resort and the golf course; spectacular mountain location.

Rysstad Feriesenter
Rysstad
Tel. 37 93 61 30

www.rysstadferie.no
New and very comfortable cabins of varying sizes in a quiet location right by the water. There are also motel rooms and holiday apartments in the main building, and a cafeteria offering simple dishes. Good fishing, boat rental and a silver workshop.

▶ Budget

Neset Camping
Byglandsfjord
Tel. 37 93 40 50, fax 37 93 43 93
www.neset.no
This 4-star campsite is situated on a spit of land at the southern end of the Byglandfjord and offers sites for mobile homes and tents, many of which are right by the water. 20 cabins, a café and supermarket complete the pleasing picture.

LEISURE

Sport and excursions
During the summer season Troll Mountain offers daily three-hour tours on the Ortra at 11am and 3pm. Also on offer are a climbing wall, canoe and mountain bike hire, and elk and beaver tours (www.troll-mountain.no; tel. 37 93 11 77).
Mineral collecting
In Evje in the direction of Vikstøl, mineral collectors can find rare stones in six pegmatite pits.

Byglandsfjord Continuing, the Byglandsfjord (207m/679ft) is soon reached, marking the end of the Setesdal railway line, which was closed in 1962. Today the place is a winter sports resort with chairlifts and downhill pistes. Cruises on the Byglandsfjord on the historic »Bjoren« ship also set off from here. The steamship used to be a continuation of the Setesdal railway service and continued to ply a regular route across

the water until 1962 (tel. 37 93 42 52; July–early August daily 4pm). ⊙
The RV 9 – partly blasted out of the rock – now follows the eastern
shore of the Byglandsfjord with the 760m/2493ft-high Årdalsfjell
towering above. A **Runic stone** dating from 1100 in front of the
wooden church in **Årdal** (1827) is worth taking a look at. 300m/
330yd south of the church stands a mighty 900-year-old oak tree.

A nostalgic trip through the pleasant Otra valley in one of the lovingly restored carriages of the Setesdal Railway is sure to quicken the
pulse of every true railway fan. **Norway's oldest museum train** is
pulled by an engine dating from 1896. To reach the narrow-gauge
line's station in Grovane, turn off at Mosby and continue through
Vennesla. Trains travel to Beihøldalen and back (during summer
every Sun 10.30am, 2pm; in July
also Tue–Fri 6pm, Thu also at
noon).

★
A trip on the
Setesdalsbanen

The road crosses the lake at the
Storstraumen bru bridge and continues along the western shore. To
the left, the Reiårsfossen waterfall
descends. At the northern end of
the lake some historic storage
barns on stilts (»stabbur«) can be
seen. Following the course of the
Otra, the road leads around Rust-
fjell (1070m/3511ft) to the left and

> ! **Baedeker** TIP

Fine silver jewellery

Silver jewellery is made throughout Setesdalen.
In Nomeland the Bjørgum family runs the
Sylvartun silver workshop on a traditional
Setesdal farm and the business has long been
renowned for its high-quality, handmade silver
jewellery (opening times: during summer
Mon–Sat 10am–6pm, Sun 11am–6pm).

continues through a magnificent landscape to **Helle**, a traditional
centre for the art of silversmithing in the Setesdal valley.

South of Nomeland, the RV 45 – known as the Suleskardveg here –
winds its way up into the mountains, with its highest point at
1052m/3452ft (viewing point). It continues onwards into the **Sirdal**
valley and ►Stavanger.
During the drive, the 15m/50ft Hallandsfoss can be seen to the left,
with several deep potholes. **Valle** (307m/1007ft) is the main settlement in the valley, and has historic houses and a church from 1844.
It is situated where the valley widens. The **Setesdal Museum** with
old wooden houses can be reached on a side road (2km/1mi) that
turns off by the Flateland farm, 9km/6mi beyond Valle.

★
Hallandsfossen

The RV 9 route now travels high above the Otra, which cuts a ravine
into the rock here, and continues to the old farming settlement of
Bykle, not far east of Bossvatnet. The pretty interior of the 13th-cen-
tury church was painted with acanthus vines in the 19th century. To
the north of the church lies the Huldreheim Museum with wooden
houses dating from the 16th century. There are signposted footpaths
beginning in Bykle and leading into the mountainous surroundings,

Bykle

many of which are well worth the walk. To the north of Bykle, the valley becomes flatter, though the region takes on an increasingly mountainous character. The Otra is crossed once more at the Berdals bru bridge, where the road continues on the east side of the Harte-vatnet lake.

Hovden Located in an attractive position at the mouth of the Otra into the Hartevatnet, Hovden is Setesdalen's most important winter sports resort and mountaineering centre (lifts). At the Hovden **Jernvinne Museum**, visitors are transported back to the time of the Vikings with special effects produced with lighting, sound and smoke. The museum is small but memorable (opening times: mid-June–mid-Aug daily 11am–5pm). **Hovden Aqualand**, complete with water slide, sauna and solarium, is the right place to spend a rainy day (www.hovdenbadeland.no).

The lakes of Lislevatn, Breivatn and Sessvatn are situated along the road north of Hovden. The route reaches its highest point between Kristiansand and Haukeligrend here at 917m/3009ft. From Haukeligrend it is possible to drive to Haugesund on the ▶Haukeli Road.

✶✶ Sognefjord

C/D 1-3

Region: West Norway

None is mightier: with a length of 204km/127mi and a depth of 1308m/4291ft, the Sognefjord is rightly known as the »King of Fjords«. The mild climate allows walnut and apricot trees to flourish along its northern flank, and famous resorts and cultural monuments, such as the country's oldest stave church, line its shores.

Cruises Only the northern shore of the Sognefjord can be reached by car, but there are numerous ferries that penetrate back into even the tiniest nooks of the fjord. Cruise ships sail from Bergen all the way to Årdalstangen at the eastern end of the fjord. These ships stop off at all major settlements.

Furthermore, there are **several car ferries** in operation: Rysjedalsvika–Rutledal (on the outer Sognefjord, 30mins); Lavik–Oppedal (20mins); Nordeide–Måren–Ortnevik; Leikanger–Vangsnes–Balestrand–Hella–Fjærland (tourist ferry during summer); Hella–Dragsvik / Vangsnes; Kaupanger–Gudvangen (2hrs 20mins); and finally between Mannheller (south of Kaupanger) and Fodnes (north of Lærdalsøyri).

To the west, the Sognefjord splits into several narrower arms. →
This is the Naerøyfjord, surrounded by steep rock faces.

⏵ VISITING SOGNEFJORD

INFORMATION

Sognefjord Reiseliv BA,
Balestrand & Fjærland
6898 Balestrand
Tel. 57 69 12 55
Fax 57 69 16 93
www.sognefjord.no

WHERE TO EAT

▶ Moderate
Quality Hotel Sogndal
Tel. 57 62 77 00
The main Compagniet restaurant
serves mostly à la carte dishes; the Dr
Hagen offers light meals and refresh-
ments; and the Dolly Dimple has 20
pizzas on the menu.

▶ Inexpensive
Kringsjå Kjelleren
Balestrand
Tel. 57 69 13 03
Small restaurant with value for money
menu open daily June to August, from
6.30pm.

WHERE TO STAY

▶ Mid-range
Skjolden Hotel
Skjolden
Tel. 57 68 23 80, 55 rooms
www.skjolden.com/skjoldenhotel
Beautifully located hotel at the end of
the Lustrafjord, with a well maintained park and very comfortable day
rooms.

Balestrand Hotel
Balestrand
Tel. 57 69 11 38, fax 57 69 17 11
30 rooms, www.balestrand.net
Quiet hotel on the fjord in the centre
of Balestrand. Half the rooms face the
fjord and have balconies. There are
also panoramic views over the fjord
from the hotel terrace.

Munthehuset
Ytre Kroken, Skjolden
Tel./fax 57 68 37 25
10 rooms, kroken@muntehuset.no
The Munthehuset lies on the south
side of the Lustrafjord, on the way to
the Urnes stave church. Accommodation is neither cheap nor luxurious,
but the interior is worth seeing.

Baedeker recommendation

▶ Luxury
Kvikne's Hotel
Balholm
Tel. 57 69 42 00, fax 57 69 42 01
200 rooms, www.kviknes.no
Fantastic: a meal or a nostalgic night in th
magnificent building from 1894 standing
directly on the shore of the fjord, with its
own marina and bathing beach. The room
in the extensions built in the 1960s are
however rather disappointing. Wonderful
fishing and boat tours are on offer here, a
well as sightseeing flights by helicopter ov
Jostedalbreen.

▶ Budget
Marifjøra Sjøbuer
Marifjøra, at Gaupne
Tel. 57 68 74 05, fax 57 68 74 57
post@rorbu.net
Four new, comfortable huts accom-
modating four people each are lined
up directly on the shore of the fjord.
Boats and fishing equipment for hire.

What to See at the Sognefjord

The Sognefjord begins to the west of **Rysjedalsvika** in the midst of   Lavik
numerous skerries and islets that were rubbed smooth by glacial action in the Ice Age. The environment changes very rapidly, as the
rockfaces on either side of the fjord become ever higher and steeper.
Lavik is the main centre for the western Sognefjord region and has a
pretty magistrate's court dating from 1760 known as Alværen. Nearby is a mission centre with cheap accommodation. 15km/9mi further
on, at the Breivik farm, the deepest point of the Sognefjord is
reached (1308m/4291ft).

The romantic fjord resort of Balestrand is reached after driving   ✶
through the 8km/5mi long Høyanger tunnel. It was already a popu-   **Balestrand**
lar holiday destination with English and German tourists at the end
of the 19th century. Among its most famous guests were **Kaiser Wilhelm II**, who stayed several times at the magnificent **Kvikne's Hotel**,
built in Swiss style. The hotel festival hall still contains the chair in
which the emperor sat in 1914. The resort's famous guest donated
the statue of Bele, one time king of the Sogn fylke, that stands to the
west of the small St Olav church founded by the English in 1897.

In order to visit the Hopperstad stave church in **Vik**, it is necessary   ✶
to cross the fjord on the ferry from Vangsnes to Dragsvik. There is a   **Hopperstad
beautiful dragon portal on the west side of the church dating from   stave church**
1130. The pergola, roof structure and apse were reconstructed in the
style of the ►Borgund stave church. Nearby, there is also a Romanesque stone church. It is possible to continue driving to Bergen via
Voss from here.

A detour to the pretty Fjærlandsfjord – an approximately 26km/   ✶
16mi-long side arm of the Sognefjord – to the north of Balestrand, is   **Fjærlandsfjord**
highly recommended (cruise ship to Mundal). To the north of the
idyllic fjord settlement of Fjærland and its interesting glacier museum, it is worth visiting the Suphellebreen and Bøyabreen glaciers,
both arms of the large ►Jostedalsbreen. To the west of Suphellebreen, it is also possible to hike up to the Flatbrehytta, at a height
of 1000m/3281ft. Sogndal to the southeast can be reached via the
Fjærlandsvegen and the 7km/4mi-long Frudals tunnel, which passes
underneath a glacier.

The RV 55 leads along the serpentine north shore through one of   Leikanger,
Norway's largest fruit-growing regions before reaching Leikanger   Hermansverk
and Hermansverk. Even while snow still lies on the mountains in
May, **over 80,000 fruit trees** flower along the fjord shore. Due to the
influence of the Gulf Stream, even walnuts, apricots and peaches
ripen here during the short summer. No surprise then that Europe's
most northerly research institute for fruit and berries is stationed in

Hermansverk. Ten rare trees, including a 16m/52ft-high walnut tree and a 23m/75ft-high sequoia tree planted in 1980, stand near the parish house and the pretty stone church of Leikanger dating from 1250. According to an old Icelandic saga from the 13th century, the Viking Fridtjof once had a secret assignation with the married Ingebjørg in the beautiful orchard of Baldershage in Leikanger – a shrine to Balder, the god of light. There is a wonderful view into the Aurlandsfjord to the south from here.

Sogndal

Sogndal is the largest economic and educational centre of the region, as well as a major transport hub (air strip). Near the old people's home stands an almost 2m/7ft-high runic stone from around 1100 on which is inscribed: »King Olav shot between these stones«.

✳ Kaupanger

About 10km/6mi to the southeast, directly on the fjord, lies Kaupanger, an important trading centre in the Middle Ages. The stave church here, dating from around 1185, is worth taking a look at.

Wonderful carvings decorate the stave church at Urnes.

Even though it was later given windows and an extension, its interior is entirely authentic and includes high, mighty pillars connected by arches (restored in 1862). The remains of two even older churches were found underneath the present building, the oldest dating from 1000 (opening times: mid-June–mid-Aug 10am–5.30pm).

Also worth a visit is **»De Heiberske Samlinger«**, the local Kaupanger museum named after the teacher Heiberg whose collection formed its foundation. An **open-air museum**, it contains 30 buildings, including a medieval hut and a modern farmhouse from the 1980s. The museum also has displays of tools and machinery to do with ploughing, hunting, beer brewing and much more. The adjacent **Fjord Museum** near the ferry quay covers all questions on fjords, fishing and ferries (opening times: May and Sept daily 10am–3pm, June–Aug till 5pm).

12km/8mi north of Sogndal there is a turning to Svolvorn. Directly below the Walaker Hotel built in

1690 (with its own art gallery in an award-winning barn dating from 1863) a small ship sets off every hour (can also take a few cars) for the stave church of Urnes. **Norway's oldest surviving stave church**, it was built on a spit of land on the east shore of the 45km/28mi-long Lustrafjord (11th century, ►Baedeker Special p.175). A climb of around 20mins is necessary to reach the church, whose northern portal, from 1060, is especially worth seeing: it features lions, dragons and snakes locked in battle, as well as a gorgeous pattern in the so-called Urnes style. Inside the church, which is on the **UNESCO World Heritage List**, the high pillars with their ornate cubiform capitals are especially noteworthy (opening times: May–Sept 10.30am–5.30pm).

◄ Urnes stave church

The Urnes stave church can also be reached from **Skjolden**, located further in the interior of the picturesque Lustrafjord. Coming from that direction, the route follows the east shore and passes the 218m/715ft Feigunfoss waterfall.

? DID YOU KNOW ...?

■ .. that Austrian philosopher Ludwig Wittgenstein had a cabin near the Lustrafjord? A memorial to the Cambridge scholar stands at a rest stop on the Eidsvatn, shortly after Skjolden, on the way into the Jotunheimen mountains. What remains of his cabin on the other side of the lake can be reached via an incompletely signposted footpath leading from the campsite at the eastern end of the Eidsvatn.

Årdalstangen lies at the extreme eastern tip of the Sognefjord, where there is a loading station for the Hydro Aluminium smelter located in Øvre Årdal, 11km/7mi further north (visits are possible during summer). North of **Øvre Årdal** extends the Utladal valley, from where it is possible to hike from Hjelle through the Vettisgjel ravine up to the Vettishytta and the spectacular 275m/902ft-high Vettisfoss. The waterfall is in a protected area. It is another 6hrs to the Skogadalsbøen hut and then a further 5hrs to the Fannaråkihytta near Fannaråki (► Jotunheimen). The private road (toll payable) from Øvre Årdal to Turtagrø (► Jotunheimen, Sognefjell) – open during summer only – is worth the trip for its wonderful viewing points and the ice fields alongside the route. Warning: not suitable for mobile homes and caravans.

Arrival in the Aurlandsfjord – a southern branch of the Sognefjord – on board the ferry from Kaupanger or on a cruise ship is one of the most impressive experiences to be had in the west Norwegian fjord country. In some places the mighty rockface rises vertically out of the water and reaches heights of up to 1500m/4921ft (see photo p.405).

Aurlandsfjord

The ferry from Kaupanger to Gudvangen (2hrs 20mins) branches off into the imposing Nærøyfjord (►Voss, surroundings), which is one of the narrowest of the west Norwegian fjords. With a bit of luck, it is even possible to spot seals from the deck of the ferry.

Nærøyfjord

Spitsbergen · Svalbard

Population: 2700

Area of the archipelago:
62,700 sq km/24,200 sq mi

Spitsbergen is the only place in the world from which it is possible to penetrate so far and so easily into the Arctic. Yet the journey there is an adventure in itself: there are no roads and only a handful of places to stay, and anyone venturing into the surrounding country, the habitat of polar bears, must carry a gun.

Twice the size of Belgium

Svalbard, as the Norwegians call Spitsbergen, is just 1300km/8125mi from the North Pole, but the Gulf Stream ensures that the islands' waters are ice free from June to December. The arctic archipelago lies around 700km/440mi north of ► Nordkapp. With a total area of around 62,700 sq km/24,209 sq mi Svalbard is twice the size of Belgium, though only around 2500 people live here, spread over four settlements on the main island, Spitsbergen (39,000 sq km/15,058 sq mi), which is characterized by fjords that cut deeply into the land. To the northeast lies the glacier-covered Nordaustland (Nordaustland; 15,000 sq km/5791 sq mi), which is usually cut off by the frozen pack ice of the Hinlopen Strait. To the southeast lie Edgeøya (5000 sq km/1930 sq mi) and Barentsøya (1300 sq km/502 sq mi). To the far south lie the narrow long islands of Hopen and Bjørnøya (Bear Island), with weather stations.

What to See in Spitsbergen

Good planning required

In the meantime there are a handful of accommodations on the island, including the campsite by Longyearbyen airport, but there are still **no roads** between settlements. Visitors need to be sufficiently equipped to take care of themselves without outside help (including bringing items such as tents and sleeping bags). In particular **provisions for hiking tours** should be bought in advance, though it is a good idea to bring your own provisions in all cases. **Mobile phones** only work in Longyearbyen, Barentsburg and Svea. The importation of live **animals** is prohibited due to the risk posed by rabies. Every tour outside the settlements requires a **permit** and must be registered with the Governor of Spitsbergen. This includes tourists who wish to leave the Longyearbyen and Barentsburg area. In addition, every traveller is obliged to take out insurance against potential search and rescue costs. The governor has the right to issue restrictions or even ban tours, depending on individual circumstances, the travellers' level of experience, and the equipment taken. All those undertaking tours beyond the settlements are required to **carry guns**, because encounters with polar bears can happen any time. Weapons can be

Cruise ships bring visitors to the icy world of Svalbard in relative comfort.

hired locally. Environmental protection legislation from 2002 also allows **severe restrictions on shore leave** to be imposed on those on cruise ships.

The Vikings reached the archipelago as early as 1194, sending back the message: »Svalbardi fundinn« (»the cold coast has been found«). The Dutch seafarer **Willem Barents** did not discover the group of islands until 1596, another 400 years later, when he named it »Spitsbergen« (Dutch for »jagged mountains«). Instead of the hoped-for trading route to China, he found a wealth of seals and whales living on the edge of the pack ice; shortly afterwards, in the extreme northwest, the **whaling settlement of Smeerenburg** (Transtadt) was founded. The whaling era went into decline after just a few decades, however, as the whales and seals were quickly hunted to extinction. Peace returned to Spitsbergen, and it was only Fridtjof Nansen's polar expeditions at the end of the 19th century that revived interest in the islands. The Norwegian seafarer Søren Zachariassen discovered **rich coal deposits** in 1899 and the first coal mine was duly established in 1906, founded by the American millionaire John M. Longyear. The attached settlement was given the name Longyear City. The Norwegian coal mining company of SNSK then took over the pits and settlement in 1916, and Longyear City became Longyearbyen (byen = place). The rich coal deposits threw up the unresolved question of territorial rights. In the end, the archipelago came under Norwegian sovereignty in 1925, but most of the pits were already closed by the time of the Great Depression. Remaining today are

Longyearbyen (pop. 1800), the research station of Ny Ålesund (the world's most northern settlement), and the mining settlements of Svea Gruva (Norwegian) and Barentsburg (Russian).

Frosty climate Thanks to the Gulf Stream, Spitsbergen's average temperatures are substantially higher than those of comparable places, despite its arctic location. However, that does not mean the climate is comfortable! During winter temperatures sink to –8°C/18°F to –16°C/3°F. The record low lies at –49°C/–56°F, recorded in 1917. During July and August temperatures can rise to an average +5°C/41°F (the record high is +22°C/72°F). Frost and snow is possible throughout the year. Almost the entire east coast is covered by glaciers and there are only larger glacier-free zones in the central area. Thanks to the sea it is often foggy or cloudy, but **normally dry**.

 VISITING SVALBARD

INFORMATION
Svalbard (Spitsbergen) Reiseliv
Postboks 323, 9171 Longyearbyen
Tel. 79 02 55 50, fax 79 02 55 51
www.svalbard.net

WHERE TO STAY
▶ **Luxury**
Radisson SAS Polar Hotel
Longyearbyen, 99 rooms
Tel. 79 02 34 50, fax 79 02 34 51
The world's most northerly hotel was built in Lillehammer for the 1994 Olympic Winter Games; afterwards it was dismantled and rebuilt on the island of Spitsbergen.

▶ **Mid-range**
Gjestehuset 102
Longyearbyen
Tel. 79 02 57 16, fax 79 02 57 16
Simple guesthouse that used to house miners.

GETTING THERE
There are direct flights to Longyearbyen three to four times a week from Tromsø as well as from Oslo. Since 2008 the low cost airline »Norwegian« (www.norwegian.no) has been flying between Oslo and Longyearbyen on Thur and Sun. Arrival by sea is only possible on private vessels or cruise ships.

TOURS
Trekking, wilderness camps, husky or snowmobile tours, guided walks with snow shoes, and boat tours in the Isfjord are offered in Longyearbyen, for example by:

Nox Polaris
Tel. 79 02 18 69
www.nox.no

Spitsberg Tours
Tel. 79 02 10 68

Spitsbergen Travel
Tel. 79 02 61 00
www.spitsbergentravel.no

Svalbard Wildlife Service
Tel. 79 02 56 60
www.wildlife.no

MIDNIGHT SUN
Midnight sun: 19 April–24 Aug. Polar night: 27 Oct–15 Feb (Longyearbyen)

The arctic flora here encompasses 140 species: low growing flowering plants, ferns, mosses and lichen. The animal world is represented by more than 30 species of ocean birds, as well as seals, polar bears, reindeer and arctic fox. Polar bears have been protected since 1973 and their numbers have now reached several thousand, and they predominantly inhabit the frozen east coast of Spitsbergen. Nevertheless, it is possible to encounter polar bears on the west coast as well. Hungry bears are very aggressive and often attack without warning – the obligatory weapon rule therefore makes perfect sense.

Beware of the bear!

Almost half of Spitsbergen is environmentally protected. Every step taken by a tourist on the permafrost destroys the fragile vegetation for a long period. In these cold temperatures, rubbish takes many years to decompose. In order not to disturb the fragile ecological balance of the wilderness here, it is imperative to take all rubbish back home, including from multi-day boat tours.

Fragile nature

The tourist cruise ships usually only cover the west side of the Svalbard islands. They travel beyond Spitsbergen's Sørkapp (Southern Cape) and through the 15km/9mi Hornsund Fjord that is often thick with drift ice, even in summer. The coast is marked by the alpine summit of Hornsundtind (1431m4695ft) and the mighty peaks of Sofiekammen (925m/3034ft).

Hornsund

Around 50km/31mi north of the wide Bellsund lies the 100km/62mi-long Isfjord with its several fjord tongues. The northern shore is partly covered in glaciers, but the southern shore features steep mountainsides plunging down towards the fjord. This is where the two main settlements are located: **Longyearbyen** on Advent Bay, and Barentsburg on the Grønfjord. The museum on Spitsbergen, run by the author Bolette Petri-Sutermeister in Longyearbyen, is recommended and will tell you all you need to know about the islands.

✱
Isfjord

Those on a cruise along the west coast heading north will see the long, narrow island of Prins Karls Forland with its glacier-covered jagged mountain peaks (Monacofjell, 1084m/3557ft) as they sail up the Strait of Forlandsund. Heading around the northern tip the Kongsfjord becomes visible, beyond which the pyramids of Tre Kroner (Three Crowns, 1225m/4019ft) tower above a 14km/9mi-long ice front.

Kongsfjord

On the southern shore lies the former mining settlement of Ny Ålesund, where the Ny Ålesund railway can be visited – a monument to the history of mining here. The locomotive dates from 1909, built by Borsig in Berlin. The settlement has the **world's most northerly post office** (special postmark) and a **research station**. This is also where the landing mast from the 1920s for airships still stands today, from which the Norwegian polar explorer Roald Amundsen (► Famous

Ny Ålesund

People) set off with his airship *Norge* in 1926 (stone memorial). Two years later, the Italian Nobile's *Italia* crashed in the Spitsbergen pack ice and Amundsen disappeared during the rescue operation.

Krossfjord

To the north of the Kongsfjord lie the Krossfjord and the Bay of Møller, where the Møller port is located. About 30km/19mi further north, seven icy rivers empty over steep cliffs into the sea. Even further north lies the Magdalenefjord, whose eastern end is formed by the 2km/1.2mi-wide and up to 100m/330ft-high edge of the Waggonway glacier. At the northwestern corner of Spitsbergen nearby, the island of Danskøya (»Island of the Danes«) rises out of the sea. During the 17th and 18th centuries both Danskøya and Amsterdamøya opposite had whaling stations.

Spitzbergen Map

✦ Stavanger

Region: West Norway   **Population:** 111,000

Stavanger, Norway's oil boom town, is the most expensive city in the country. Nevertheless, it has many quiet and charming aspects, such as the historic town centre with its white-painted wooden houses. Visits to the Canning Museum and the Oil Museum are also very interesting. Stavanger was »European City of Culture« in 2008.

Stavanger is Norway's fourth-largest city and capital of the county of **Oil!** Rogaland. The pretty town on the Byfjord experienced a massive upturn at the beginning of the 1970s, when oil was discovered in the North Sea off Stavanger's shore. In Norway the inhabitants of Stavanger – along with those from Bergen – are considered especially cosmopolitan, not least because of the American, French and British working for the oil companies, as well as the students at the various higher education establishments. A bronze statue in honour of the poet Alexander Kielland (1849–1906), who was born in Stavanger, stands on the »Torget«, the fish and vegetable market. There are several dockyards in the harbour basin protected by outlying islands. The oil platforms built to service the oilfields of Tor, Ekofisk and Eldfisk, about 320km/200mi to the southwest of Stavanger, are located in the Gansfjord south of the city.

Stavanger played a vital role in the history of the Norwegian empire: **History** Harald Hårfagre (Harald Fairhair) vanquished the minor kings in a battle at the Hafrsfjord to the south of the city and thereby achieved the conditions that allowed Norway to be **united under one monarch**

Highlights Stavanger

Stavanger Domkirke
One of Norway's most important medieval churches. The magnificent Gothic choir was built in 1272.
▶ page 360

Gamle Stavanger
This idyll of white wooden houses, cobblestones and gas lanterns lies right on Vågen harbour, a lively district with historic buildings and many friendly bars.
▶ page 360

Oil Museum
Lots of technology and detail about »black gold« and the oil boom
▶ page 361

Canning Museum
Everything you always wanted to know about canning sardines
▶ page 359

Prekestolen
»Pulpit Rock« rising 600m/1969ft out of the Lysefjord
▶ page 363

● VISITING STAVANGER

INFORMATION

Destinasjon Stavanger
Rosenkildetorget 1, 4001 Stavanger
Tel. 51 85 92 00, fax 51 85 92 02
www.visitstavanger.com

WHERE TO EAT

► **Expensive**
④ **Jans Mat & Vinhus**
Breitorget
Tel. 51 85 45 85
Imaginative fish dishes can be enjoyed
by candlelight here. The most expensive but also the best gourmet restaurant in the city.

① **N.B. Sørensens
Dampskibsexpedition**
Skagen 26, Tel. 51 84 38 00
Gourmets dine in the »Directionen«
on the first floor. More affordable
meals are available in the Damp-
skibsekspeditionen restaurant on the
ground floor.

► **Moderate**
⑤ **Bølgen & Møi**
Kjerringholmen (in the Oil Museum)
Tel. 51 93 93 51
The snacks and delicious cheesecake
made by master chef Trond Moi can
be enjoyed with a fantastic view onto
the harbour at the museum café. In
the evening the prices are higher with
a menu for the gourmet.

② **Sjøhuset Skagen**
Skagenkaien 16
Tel. 51 89 51 80
The maritime interior is entirely
appropriate for this old house from
1770 where excellent meals are served.
Lunch dishes such as bacalao or
bouillabaisse are good value. On
Sundays between 2pm and 7pm there
is an affordable family menu.

► **Inexpensive**
③ **Newsman**
Skagen 14, Tel. 22 93 04 80
This is a good place for a relaxing read
of the Norwegian and foreign newspapers that are provided along with the
coffee or a glass of beer. Light snacks
from noon until the late evening.

WHERE TO STAY

► **Luxury**
③ **Comfort Hotel Grand**
Klubbgt. 3
Tel. 51 20 14 00, fax 51 20 14 01
90 rooms
www.comfort.choicehotels.no
Modern city hotel with a good
restaurant.

► **Mid-range**
② **Skagen Brygge Hotel**
Skagenkaien 30
Tel. 51 85 00 00, fax 51 85 00 01
www.skagenbryggehotell.no
110 rooms. A modern hotel with an
interesting façade right by the harbour. Attractive prices in July and
throughout the year at weekends.

① **Victoria Hotel**
Skansegt. 1
Tel. 51 86 70 00, fax 51 86 70 10
www.victoria-hotel.no
Venerable hotel in an ideal location,
completely modernized. Rooms are
elegant and welcoming and there are
value for money weekend prices. The
restaurant serves juicy steaks from the
grill.

ENTERTAINMENT

Those looking for nightlife stream
into the Vågen guest harbour and the
quarter that adjoins it to the east,
where there are any number of bars
and restaurants.

A picture-book façade hides Norway's most expensive city.

around 872. In memory of this event, **three oversized swords** were rammed into the rock at Harfrsfjord in 1983. The artist Fritz Røed created the handles of the mighty Viking swords from sword finds discovered in different parts of the country; the crowns represent the Norwegian districts that were involved in the battle.

The construction of the cathedral was begun in the year of the **city's foundation in 1125**. Stavanger quickly developed into an important religious centre. After major herring shoals appeared off the coast in the 16th century, the city also became an important **fishing centre**. However, after the herring stayed away for extended periods

 Baedeker TIP

All about sardines

Everything there is to know about sardine canning, which was Stavanger's most important industrial sector until the Second World War, can be discovered at the Canning Museum (Hermetikkmuseet) in the old town at Øvre Strandgaten 88a. On Tuesdays and Thursdays during summer, sprats are smoked here.

and the city suffered several fires, the bishopric was transferred to Kristiansand in 1672. The herring returned at the beginning of the 19th century, and **Norway's first canning factory** was opened in Stavanger in 1873. The last sardine was canned in the 1950s.

Stavanger Map

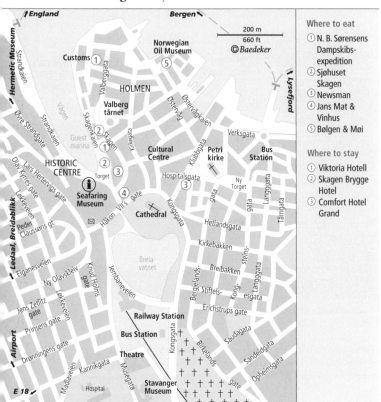

↑England

Bergen↘

200 m
660 ft
©Baedeker

Hermetic Museum
Strandkaien
Øvre Strandgate
Strandgate
Skagenkaien
Vågen
Guest marina
Lars Hertervigs gate
Olaf Kyrres gate
Løkkeveien
Peder Claussøns gt.
Ledaal, Breidablikk
Eiganesveien
Ny Olavskleiv
Knud Holms gate
Jernbaneveien
Jens Zetlitz gate
Prinsens gate
Dronningens gate
Airport
E 18↗
Maddlaveien
Kannikgata
Museigata
Hospital

Customs ①
HOLMEN
Valberg tårnet
Skagen
Skagenkaien
kirkegata
HISTORIC CENTRE ②
Torget ③
Seafaring Museum
✉
Håkon VII's gate
Cathedral
Kongsgata
Breiavatnet

Norwegian Oil Museum ⑤
Østervågkaien
Østervåg
Cultural Centre
Klubbgata
Petri kirke
Hospitalsgata ③
Ny Torget
Kirkebakken
Bergelands-gata
Stiftels-gata
Erichstrups gate
Railway Station
Bus Station
Theatre
Stavanger Museum
Birkelands gate
Kongsgata

Verksgata
Bus Station
Langggata
gata
steins-gata
Breibakken
Kongesgata
Langggata
Tårngata
Hetlandsgata
Saudagata
Sandeidgata
Opheimsgata

↑Lysefjord

Where to eat
① N. B. Sørensens Dampskibs-expedition
② Sjøhuset Skagen
③ Newsman
④ Jans Mat & Vinhus
⑤ Bølgen & Møi

Where to stay
① Viktoria Hotell
② Skagen Brygge Hotel
③ Comfort Hotel Grand

What to see in Stavanger

✱ Gamle Stavanger

The approximately 170 lovingly restored white painted wood houses complete with gas lanterns and attractively decorated windows and doors in the lanes of old Stavanger (on the west side of the Vågen harbour) recall the 18th and 19th century, when fishermen, craftsmen and seafarers lived here. Most of the houses on the Øvre Strandgaten are listed buildings.

✱ Stavanger Domkirke

Stavanger Cathedral stands above Vågen harbour, on the small urban lake of Breivatnet, and is considered Norway's most important medieval sacred building next to Nidaros Cathedral in Trondheim. The church was designed at the end of the 11th century as a triple-aisled basilica in the Anglo-Norman style and built under Bishop Reinald of Winchester with the help of English craftsmen. Its patron saint was St Swithin. After a fire in 1272, a **magnificent choir** was built in the Gothic style. The rich **interior** dates from the Baroque era and the entire building was renovated in the 19th and 20th centuries. The finely carved pulpit (1658) and the stone baptismal font from Gothic times are worth taking a look at inside. The east window with scenes from the New Testament was designed by Victor Sparre in 1957.

The architecturally striking **Oil Museum** (Norsk Oljemuseum), opened in 1999 on the Kjerringholmen quay north of the city centre, is the place to discover everything about the oil boom in Norway and the creation of natural gas and oil. Children can operate machinery on the replica oil drilling platform or be »saved« by the rescue net. There is a 3D cinema, too (opening times: May–August daily from 10am–7pm, otherwise 10am–4pm, Sun till 6pm).

Unusual: the Oil Museum in Stavanger

The Rogaland Art Museum near the Mosvannpark, to the southwest of the city centre, has an extensive collection of 2000 Norwegian paintings from 1900 to the present – though it exhibits only a certain number of them at any one time. The collection of frequently huge landscape paintings by the Stavanger artist Lars Hertervig (1830–1902) is unique (opening times: Tue–Sun 11am–4pm; www.rkm.no).

Rogaland Art Museum

A city stroll inevitably includes an encounter with the London artist **Antony Gormley's** *Broken Column* permanent installation. It consists of 23 iron statues placed throughout the city, all 1.95m/6ft 4in tall and all exact portraits of himself. The first stands by the Art Museum, 41m/134ft above sea level. Every additional sculpture is located precisely 1.95m/6ft 4 inches lower down, the last being on the Natvigs Minde skerry at the entrance to the harbour, which stands largely underwater. Some are found in rather strange places, such as the municipal swimming pool, a petrol station, a car park and a small shop.

Broken Column

The Stavanger Museum is on Muségata and contains collections on archaeology, natural history and ethnology, as well as a seafaring department. Exhibits from 15,000 years of natural and cultural history

Stavanger Museum

are shown in the **Archaeological Museum**, while the **Seafaring Museum** at Strandgata 17–19 illustrates 200 years of maritime and urban history.

Ledaal
The aristocratic Kielland family's Ledaal residence built in the Empire style in 1799 stands at Eiganesveien 45. Today it is the royal residence when the family is in Stavanger. The library on the first floor is in honour of the writer Alexander Kielland who featured Ledaal in his novels as »Sandsgård«.

Around Stavanger

✴ Beautiful views
The most beautiful view onto the city is offered by the 85m/279ft-high **Vålandshaug** at the southern edge of town, reached via Hornklovesgate. A wonderful view across Stavanger can also be enjoyed from the **Ullandshaug tower** located to the southwest in the municipal forest of Sørmarka; the view from the tower also takes in the flat Jæren landscape, the sea to the southwest, the mountainous Ryfylke region, the Boknafjord in the northeast and the Gansfjord in the east.

Not far to the west of the tower, the **Iron Age** (AD 350–550) **Jernaldergarden farm** has been reconstructed on its original site, the only such place in Norway. During summer the farm's rooms can be visited between 11am and 4pm, Sun from noon. Nextdoor are the remains of a Stone Age settlement, as well as Bronze Age and Viking graves (no. 78 bus).

> **! Baedeker TIP**
>
> **White sandy beaches...**
> ... just like those in southern Europe can be found in the region known as Jæren to the south of Stavanger. Solstranden by the airport, Hellestøstranden 30km/19mi southwest of Stavanger and Orresanden on the Jæren outcrop are among Norway's most beautiful beaches. The information centre by the car park at Orresanden provides information on the efforts to preserve the unique dune landscape from the wind and the weather.

Kongeparken leisure park
Kongeparken, »Norway's Disneyland«, lies on the E 39 by Ålgård, about 30km/19mi south of Stavanger (opening times: May–Sept daily 10am–6pm; www.kongeparken.no). The nearby **Havana Aqua Park** is one of the largest of its kind in Scandinavia (opening times: daily 10am–8pm).

✴ Utstein monastery
The island of Mosterøy can be reached from Stavanger via the almost 6km/4mi-long Byfjordtunnel which, at 223m/732ft below sea level, is the deepest underwater tunnel in the world, constructed 45m/148ft underneath the seabed. A ferry also makes the crossing between Stavanger and the Utstein monastery on the island. Since there are hardly any parking spaces in the near vicinity of the monastery, it is best to park the car 1km/0.6mi away and cover the final stretch –

through beautiful countryside – on foot. The Augustinian monastery of Utstein was first mentioned in the 13th century and is the best preserved of its kind in Norway. The setting is lovely: high trees and gentle hills with sheep grazing on meadows embraced by the blue sea. During summer, concerts are held behind the monastery's thick stone walls and it also functions as a hotel (reservations tel. 51 72 47 05; www.utsteinklosterhotell.no; monastery opening times: May–Sept Tue–Sat 10am–4pm, Sun noon–5pm, in July also Mon, Oct–April Sundays only).

Hå Gamle Prestegård (Hå old vicarage; 1637), one of the most popular excursion destinations around Stavanger, stands right by the open sea near a large Iron Age burial site. There is a small museum, a gallery and a friendly café. The Obrestad fyr lighthouse is a short walk further south (16km/10mi southwest of Bryne, turn off near Vigre; opening times: May––Sept Tue–Fri 11am–6pm, Sat/Sun from noon).

Prekestolen: a 600m/1969ft abyss

Beyond the Høgsfjord, the Lysefjord, located east of Stavanger (cruise ship from Stavanger), extends 37km/23mi inland as an up to 2km/1mi-wide and 457m/1499ft-deep gash penetrating the mountains. The fjord, light green of hue, is enclosed by steep, bare walls of rock on both sides that tower up more than 1000m/3281ft.

★
Lysefjord

Prekestolen (**Pulpit Rock**) is a cliff rising almost 600m/1969ft vertically out of the Lysefjord and is without doubt one of the most beautiful destinations in southwest Norway. Those who suffer from vertigo should on no account venture onto this platform above the abyss. Prekestolen can be reached from Stavanger via the RV 13 as far as Lauvvik on the Høgsfjord, from where the ferry departs for Jøssang. At Jøssang a road branches right for the Prekestolhytta, from which the cliff can be reached in about two hours on foot (good walking shoes required). There are several narrow stretches. The cliff can also be admired from the deck of a cruise ship (3hrs from Stavanger).

★ ★
Prekestolen

Lysebotn One of the most breathtaking experiences for drivers in Norway is the route near **Lysebotn** with 27 hairpin bends. Southwest of Lysebotn, the **Kjerag** cliff towers 1000m/3281ft into the sky, a popular destination for base jumpers (the riskier version of sky diving). The car park is near Øygardstøl (the challenging mountain tour takes approx. 5hrs there and back).

Sunndal

E 5/6

Region: Mid and West Norway

The romantic Sunndal valley with the river Driva flowing through it begins at the winter sports resort of Oppdal and extends west all the way to the industrial town of Sunndalsøra. The adjacent mountains are extremely beautiful areas for hiking, especially the Trollheimen mountains to the north.

The salmon's decline The Driva was once one of the best salmon rivers in Norway, but the legendary salmon stocks were destroyed by a parasite. Attempts are being made at present to reintroduce the fish with newly bred stock. Those who wish to benefit from the fruits of that labour need a fishing permit.

 SUNNDAL

INFORMATION

Sunndal Aktivum
Nordmørsvegen 2
6601 Sunndalsøra
Tel. 71 68 99 70
www.sunndal.com

WHERE TO STAY

► Mid-range
Sunndalsfjord Camping
On the RV 62 between Sunndalsøra and Eidsvåg
Tel. 71 23 31 12, fax 71 23 31 12
perlyhut@online.no
On offer are two large and comfortable cabins right on the fjord with pleasant interiors. Ideal for fishermen. There is also a small campsite on the property.

What to See in the Sunndal valley

The RV 70 leads from **Oppdal** down the valley of the Driva, past a burial site from Viking times, to Oppdal church (1651), whose pointed spire can be seen from quite a distance away. The interior of this pretty church with old paintings dates from the 17th–18th century.

A road branches off to the Gjevilvasshytta, a listed building, located 22km/14mi away near **Vognill**. It stands on the northern shore of the Gjevilvatnet at an elevation of 700m/2297ft. From here, it is possible to reach the Trollheimshytta to the northwest in 8–9hrs on foot. The mountains of Trollhetta

(1614m/5295ft; 7–8hrs there and back with a guide) and Snota (1668m/5473ft) can be climbed from there – these are the highest summits of the Trollheimen mountains (reached in 8–9hrs there and back with a guide).

The old **Gravaune** farm has an interesting collection of old tools and weapons. Near the Lønset Handel a footpath branches off for the Storfallet waterfall in Lønset. Those who fancy some Norwegian porridge can walk past the Dindalshytta to the Veggasetra (approx. 4hrs). The **Storlidal** valley is also beautiful. There are several places to stay the night along the route leading north from Lønset, including the Storli farm that makes a good starting point for hikes into the Trollheimen.

Casting out in the Sunndal valley

After crossing the county border the winding path continues downwards (viewing points) to Gjøra. To the left, a side road leads through the Jenstadjuvet ravine with the impressive 156m/512ft-high Svøufoss waterfall cascading into the Grøvudal valley, a beautiful hiking region with catered huts and interesting flora. The octagonal **Romfo church** (1820) has a beautiful carved altar panel and a medieval sculpture of St Olav, and to the west of it lies the Driva Power Station (140MW), inside the mountain. The villages of Fale and Grøa are popular bases with salmon fishermen.
An exhibition on the first English salmon fishermen who lived in the Elverøy House in the 19th century can be visited in the Sunndal Bygdemuseum, located 400m/438yd away from **Elvererhøy** bridge. Next to the school there is a large burial site dating from the Ice Age.

Gjøra

Sunndalsøra lies at the end of the Sunndalfjord, surrounded by snow-covered mountains. The large Aura Power Station (290MW) and an aluminium works – the largest industrial employment centre in the county of Møre og Romsdal – are of economic importance.

Sunndalsøra

Lake Aursjøen located approximately 39km/24mi south of Sunndalsøra (first 2km/1.2mi in the direction of Molde and then turning due south) is reached via the steep cliffs of the Litledal and then the Torbudal valley, whose highest point lies at 900m/2953ft. The Aursjøhytta is here, along with one of Norway's largest dams.

★
Aursjøen

Fun in the snow in Lofoten, on snowboards and skis: the very roots of snowsport lie in Norway.

THE SLALOM AND THE TELEMARK TURN

Telemark played an important role in the development of skiing. Sondre Norheim, the father of modern skiing, demonstrated for the first time how to turn elegantly downhill on skis with a cable binding around the heel in Christiania (Oslo), in 1868. The people of the Morgedal had already discovered at this point that it was also possible to jump small ramps with these skis.

The development of skiing began as far back as four thousand years ago. In Scandinavia, where there is often a great deal of snow for long periods, the inhabitants living predominantly from **hunting** were forced to construct aides for travelling in snow. Various finds from moorland excavations and rock art provide evidence that walking aides, oval and long in shape, were made of woven reeds, birch bark or pieces of wood. The old Norse expression of »skid« (piece of wood, plank) gradually established itself as the word to describe these winter walking aides. Linguistic studies have established that **snow shoes** were probably brought from their original Asiatic homeland by the **Finnish and Sami** peoples.

Kings of the piste

The earliest Norwegian historical documents also speak of skiing. **Kings Olav Trygvasson and Harald Hårdrade** (11th–12th century) are both lauded as good skiers. The **techniques of the Telemark** and elegant »Christiania« turn proved to be real strokes of genius: talented skiers could now

Norwegian invention: the »Telemark turn«

descend steep slopes at great speed and survive tight slalom turns. The breakthrough of skiing as a generally practiced sport was accelerated by the two polar explorers **Fridtjof Nansen** and **Roald Amundsen**, who described skiing as the ultimate sport and crossed the Greenland inland ice fields on skis in 1888. Amundsen reached the South Pole on skis in 1911.

Telemark starts a trend

Centres of Nordic skiing were soon established in Telemark, where an early skiing business established itself, as well as in the mountains around Oslo and Lillehammer, and in the Gudbrandsdal valley.

The ultimate Norwegian skiing mountain is the **Holmenkollen hill**, where the legendary ski jumping competition has been held since 1892. In 1952, Holmenkollen was one of the venues for the Winter Olympic Games. In 1994, world-class skiers attended the championships of the 17th Winter Olympics in Lillehammer to the north.

The new winter sport quickly spread from Norway, and the first skiers were already enjoying themselves in the southern Black Forest (Germany) and in the Alps (esp. around Arlberg) in the 1890s. Norwegian immigrants also brought skiing to **North America** and ensured the establishment of ski resorts such as those in Lake Placid, Aspen and Vail.

Typically Norwegian skiing disciplines are cross-country skiing, the slalom (»slalåm« = track on a slope) and jumping over a ramp, including ski jumping and ski flying. A combination of cross-country skiing and jumping is referred to as Nordic Skiing.

✴ Telemark

B 5/6

Region: South Norway

The birthplace of modern skiing is in the county of Telemark, where the »Telemark turn« was invented. Today, there are excellent ski resorts here. Those who visit during summer quickly discover that the forested central highlands have far more to offer than a trip on the Telemark canal.

Hustle and bustle or relaxation

Telemark covers a great area: the county stretches from the Skagerrak Sea to the south up to the south Norwegian highlands. There are numerous holiday cabins and pretty coastal towns with white-painted wooden houses along the jagged coast with idyllic **skerries**. During summer, Telemark's **marinas** are often overrun. Those looking for peace and relaxation find it in the mostly hilly forested landscape of the interior, as well as by hiking on the barren highland plateau of Hardangervidda to the north, with its crystal clear **mountain lakes** and streams.

What to See in Telemark

Skien

The capital of the county of Telemark and a lively industrial town, Skien (pop. 48,000) calls itself the »Ibsen town« because this is where Henrik Ibsen (► Famous People) was born, in 1828 at Stockmannsgården on the Torget. The building no longer exists, as it was destroyed in the town's large 1886 fire. Seven years later, the family moved to Venstøp farm (museum 5km/3mi north of Skien) with its famous loft that inspired the setting for the play *Wild Duck*. Finally, the Ibsen family moved to the Snipetorpgate (Ibsengården) quarter, with its pretty 18th-century wooden houses. There is also more to discover about the famous playwright in the **Telemark Fylkesmuseum**, which is the local museum set in the English garden style Brekkepark to the east of the town centre (restaurant and summer theatre). The open-air section of the museum contains several historic Telemark farms.

✴ Telemark Canal

Without doubt one of Telemark's finest attractions is a journey on the 110km/69mi-long Telemark Canal, also known as the Bandak Norsjø Canal. During summer, one of the historic motorboats, either the *Victoria* (built in 1882), the *Henrik Ibsen*, (1907) or the *Telemarken*, departs Skien each morning at 8.30am, arriving in the evening at the small settlement of **Dalen**, 110km/69mi away. Dalen is located on the west side of the Lake Bandak and surrounded by steep mountains up to 700m/2297ft high. The boat then quietly glides over Lake Norsjø to Ulefoss, where the striking blue dome of the small Empire castle of **Ulefoss Herregård** (1807), Norway's seminal example of Napoleonic architecture and open to the public, stands on the north side of the Eidselva. In the immediate vicinity lie the 11m/36ft-high **Ulefoss locks**. The most impressive lock, the Vrangfoss sluser, actually contains a total of six chambers. While the boat surmounts a

VISITING TELEMARK

INFORMATION
Skien Turistkontor
Nedre Hjellegate 18
3724 Skien
Tel. 35 90 55 20
Fax 35 90 55 30
www.grenland.no

WHERE TO STAY
► **Mid-range**
Gaustablikk Høyfjellshotel
Rjukan
Tel. 35 09 14 22
Fax 35 09 19 75
91 rooms, www.gaustablikk.no
The modern and spacious mountain hotel built in wood in the Norwegian style lies at the foot of Gaustastoppen and includes a swimming pool, saunas, tennis courts and a large sun terrace. Skiing region nearby.

Quality Lifjell Hotel
Bø i Telemark
Lifjellvegen 375
Tel. 35 95 33 00
Fax 35 95 33 00
150 beds, www.lifjellhotel.no
This very comfortable family hotel with indoor and outdoor swimming pool lies very centrally in the Telemark region. Nice tours to the Telemark canal and the Heddal stave church can be made from here.

Tuddal Høyfjellshotel
Tuddal
Tel. 35 02 88 88
Fax 35 02 88 89
23 rooms, www.tuddal.no

Hotel with a century of tradition. Elsa and Rune Gurholt ensure personal service and make good use of the historic furniture and antiques. Traditional Norwegian cuisine is served in the restaurant.

Baedeker recommendation

► **Mid-range**
Hotel Dalen
Dalen (near the Bø Sommarland leisure park)
Tel. 35 07 70 00
Fax 35 07 70 11
76 beds, www.dalenhotel.no
This hotel is an architectural jewel on the Telemark canal. The Swiss, Dragon and Romantic style combine in perfect symbiosis in this wooden palace – it is no surprise that several royals have stayed here. Even those who don't stay the night should at least indulge in tea and cake on the terrace, with its panoramic view of the extensive park.

► **Budget**
Sandviken Camping
Tinn Austbygd
Tel. 35 09 81 73
Fax 35 09 41 05
www.sandviken-camping.no
Small campsite with a familial atmosphere on the northern shore of the Tinnsjø, containing 12 simple huts, some of which are right on the sandy beach with views onto the lake.

height difference of 23m/75ft, passengers can disembark and take photographs from the steps or the bridge over the canal. From **Lunde**, passengers can either return to Skien by bus or on another boat. Alternatively they can slowly chug across the lakes of Flåvatn, Kviteseidvatn and Bandak. At the northern shore, near Dalen, a road winds up to the 13th-century **Eidsborg stave church** (small open-air museum nearby). The west portal displays glorious vine ornamentation and capitals with standing lions (information on local tours and cruises from Telemarkreiser, Skien, tel. 35 90 00 20; www.telemarkreiser.no).

! **Baedeker TIP**

Thrills at the gorge
The quickest road between Dalen and Åmot is route 38, but a small detour on a partly unmade parallel road leads to the Ravnejuvet gorge, which is well worth seeing. A short footpath leads to a viewing point offering broad vistas down into the valley and from which you can carefully look into the void below an overhanging rockface.

There's fun in the water for children and adults alike at the **Bø Sommarland** aqua park near Bø. The park has developed into one of Telemark's major attractions and offers more than 20 different water activities – including a giant waterslide, of course (opening times: daily from mid-May–mid-Aug; www.sommarland.no).

Heddal stave church

The stave church at Heddal (Hitterdal) to the west of the small industrial town of Notodden, 50km/31mi north of Skien on the E 134, dates from the mid-13th century. It was reconstructed in 1849–51, and has been restored several times, but it is the largest surviving stave church in Norway (detailed information on p.372).

Gaustatoppen

About 16km/10mi west of Heddal stave church, a road turns off to the north into the romantic Tuddalsdal valley and on to Rjukan. Beyond **Tuddal** with its pretty wooden church (1796), the occasionally steep road winds its way up to the 1275m/4183ft pass, with wonderful views along the way, and onwards to the foot of the mighty Gaustatoppen (hiking and skiing region) that, at 1883m/6178ft, is the highest summit south of the Bergen railway. From the car park right next to the road a marked footpath leads almost as far as the summit, from which there is an awe-inspiring **view over Hardangervidda**. Good hiking boots are recommended (no trainers!) as extensive expanses of scree have to be crossed. The round trip takes around 3hrs (delicious waffles are served at the summit hut). East of Gaustatoppen lies the **Gaustablikk** ski resort with lifts, numerous ski runs, a hotel and comfortable cabins.

Rjukan

Directly below Gaustatoppen, the industrial town of Rjukan (pop. 7500) lies in a deep and long valley whose inhabitants have to make do without sun for several months a year. Rjukan was designed and built at the beginning of the 20th century when the large Vemork hydroelectric power station and the sodium nitrate factory were built in 1911. The »Krossobanen« cable car leads up into the mountains from the town centre. Norway's first cable car was built in 1928 by Norsk Hydro so that workers could enjoy sun and fresh air at the weekends.

The Mår power station 5km/3mi east of town (Dale junction), whose construction was begun by the Germans during the Second World War, produces 1 billion kWh annually and has three dams. There are beautiful hiking and skiing regions around Lake Møsvatn above Rjukan and in the area around Rauland (RV 37).

Rjukan became notorious during the **Second World War** when the Germans showed a special interest in the deuterium oxide (heavy water) that was being produced there. Several sabotage efforts were carried out by the Allies – among others, the sinking of the *Hydro* ferry on Lake Tinnsjøen that was loaded with heavy water, so as to prevent the valuable water reaching Germany for the **production of atomic bombs**. More about the battle for the heavy water can be found on the Sabotage Trail and in the nearby Norwegian Industrial Workers' Museum (incl. old BBC films) housed in the Vemorker hydroelectric power station, which was the world's largest of its kind at the beginning of the 20th century. The mighty interior with its giant turbines is impressive (opening times: June–mid-Aug daily 10am–6pm, mid-Aug–Sept till 4pm, otherwise Sat/Sun 11am–4pm).

✱
◄ Norsk
Industriearbeider-
museum
🕐

Seljord, which is idyllically located on the Seljordvatn, can be reached via the E 134. It is a major centre for agricultural products. In **Seljord church**, dating from 1180, take a look at the 17th-century chalk paintings and Norway's oldest altar panel from the time after the Reformation. To the east of the idyllically situated Lake Seljordsvatnet embedded among steep forested hills rises Lifjell, from whose summits one can see as far as the Skagerrak Sea in clear weather. Seljordsvatnet has a famous »lake monster«, and several eye-witness accounts have even drawn interest from foreign researchers.

Seljord, Lifjell

The Norwegian Skiing Museum (Norsk skieventyr) in the small resort of **Morgedal** (22km/14mi west of Seljord) takes the visitor on a journey through 4000 years of Norway's skiing history with the help of light and sound effects. There is also an exhibition of equipment used by Olav Bjaaland's South Pole Expedition that he undertook together with Roald Amundsen. A bauta stone in honour of Sondre Norheim, the father of modern skiing, stands in front of the museum.

✱
**Norwegian
Skiing Museum**

HEDDAL STAVE CHURCH

✴ ✴ Heddal church – the »cathedral« of Norwegian stave churches – stands right next to the E 134, to the west of Kongsberg and Notodden. Building began in 1147, and the church was dedicated to the Blessed Virgin Mary in 1241. The pillar stave church with its striking three-tier roof is a masterpiece of wood architecture.

Opening times:
20 May–19 June 10am–5pm
20 June–20 Aug 9am–7pm
21 August–10 Sept 10am–5pm
Sun after services from 1pm

① Nave

Stave churches are not stone churches in wood, but an original form with a mighty central area which is presumed to recall Nordic royal halls. The interior of Heddal contains, among other things, a carved 12th-century bishop's throne with scenes from the Sigurd Saga. Sigurd and King Gunnar set off to bring the Nibelungen Ring to Brunhild. Heddal is Norway's largest stave church: built of pine, it is 24m/79ft long, 14m/46ft wide, and 26m/85ft high.

② The »staves«

A frame of square planks lies on a square stone foundation, on which staves (»stav« in Norwegian), vertical masts or posts, were erected. At the base they are set in the wooden frame and at the top they are held in place by an additional square frame that also carries the gable. This perfect wooden construction has survived 850 years.

③ St Andrew's Cross

The diagonal St Andrew's Crosses are typical of stave churches. Fixed at the height of the first roof section, they ensure additional stability.

④ Sval gallery

A roofed gallery runs around the church (»sval-gang«), where men once had to leave their weapons before attending religious services.

⑤ Roof shingles

Scale-like overlapping shingles cover the five roof tiers. Half of the shingles at Heddal were replaced between 1998 and 2004. Handmade shingles based on the medieval model were used. In addition, the church needs tarring at regular intervals to preserve its ability to withstand the weather. As scaffolding is not allowed to be fixed to the church, mountaineers do that job.

⑥ Church spires

Like the roof, Heddal's spires are also on several levels. The towers are empty, as the bell tower stands apart from the church.

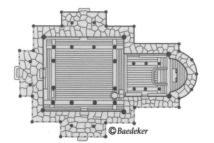

© Baedeker

Heddal ground plan. Like all Christian churches, it is orientated east to west. The choir in the east (right) is the oldest part of the church, and has a semicircular apse.

▶ VISITING TROMS

INFORMATION

See Tromsø and Harstad

GETTING THERE

Troms is not connected to the railway network. The nearest stations are Narvik and Fauske. Airports are at Tromsø, Bardufoss, Sørkjosen and Harstad (in Evenes).

WHERE TO EAT

▶ Moderate

Vollan Gjestestue

Nordkjosbotn

At the junction of the E 6 and E 8

Tel. 77 72 23 00

The meat balls here are especially popular: 15,000 portions are sold annually. The menu also features nettle soup, herring soup, fish balls, cod tongues and a whale meat terrine.

WHERE TO STAY

▶ Mid-range

Euro Hotel Maritim

Skjervøy , Strandveien 35

Tel. 77 76 03 77

Fax 77 76 07 16

31 rooms, www.hotell-maritim.no

This hotel is located in the centre of Skjervøy, by the harbour. The menu changes daily – the selection of dishes is always a pleasant surprise. There is a good view onto the harbour and the passing Hurtigruten ships from the restaurant.

RAFTING, FISHING

Permits for salmon fishing in the Målselv river can be purchased in Andselv. The river is also ideal for rafting and kayaking (Målselv Turist-kontor, tel. 77 18 10 97).

Following the Målselv upriver as far as Øverbygd, a side trip into the densely forested Dividal is an option. One of Europe's last wilder-nesses, and a wealth of plants and animals, can be found here. The Øvre Dividal National Park covers an area of 750 sq km/299 sq mi and is easily accessible to all who wish to stay in the cabins provided by the Troms Turlad hiking association. Guides are available to lead expeditions into rough terrain and territories inhabited by beasts of prey such as **wolves and bears**. The guides can also provide horses or dog sleds, as well as Sami tents. Adventurous visitors can also ar-range guided canoe and rafting tours (May–June) in Rundhaug and Øverbygd along the RV 87.

✱ **Øvre Dividal National Park**

En route from Tromsø to Alta, the E 6 follows the shoreline of the broad ▶ Lyngenfjord. At Storslett, the RV 865 leads into the pretty Reisadal. It is possible to travel upriver on the Reisa, for example, as far as the Mollisfoss in the Reisa National Park. This waterfall has not been regulated by human intervention of any kind and its 269m/883ft free falling flow makes it **Norway's second highest waterfall**.

Mollisfoss

The E 6 continues along the coast and reaches a height of 402m/1319ft on the Kvænangsfjell mountain plateau. During summer there

Kvænangsfjell Sørstraumen

are numerous Sami tents to be seen here and the view onto the Kvænangenfjord is impressive. A short while later the road descends steeply down to the fjord. The Sørstraumen bridge crosses the tidal strait of Sørstraumen, which is rich in fish. At Burfjord, the Kvænangstindan (up to 1175m/3855ft) mountain range can be seen to the west; its north face has still to be scaled.

✴ Tromsø

M 15

Region: North Norway   **Population:** 62,000

Tromsø likes to refer to itself as the »Paris of the North«, and rightly so, because the pretty port city surprises visitors with a very lively cultural and restaurant scene, vibrant nightlife included. It also has something that Paris cannot offer: the midnight sun during summer and a magical arctic light during winter.

Gateway to the Arctic   Tromsø is located between Narvik and Hammerfest on a small island connected with the mainland by the striking 43m/141ft-high Tromsø

Tromsø is known as the »Paris of the North«.

Bridge, at one end of which the white Arctic Cathedral impressively stands. The city that emerged around the site of a 13th-century church and received its municipal charter in 1794 is known as the »Gateway to the Arctic«. Once the first fishing boat had successfully been sent into the Arctic Sea in 1820, **seal hunting** quickly established itself as the most important economic sector for the city. Furthermore, it was from Tromsø that Fridtjof Nansen, Roald Amundsen (► Famous People) and other **polar explorers** set off on their great expeditions. A memorial on the harbour breakwater recalls Amundsen's flight with the water plane *Latham*, on which he set off in search of Umberto Nobile in 1928. During the 19th century, numerous rich businessmen lived in Tromsø, whose continental lifestyle and tastes acquired during their journeys abroad brought the city the fashionable moniker the **»Paris of the North«**. Today it is the roughly 4000 students that enrich the lively restaurant and nightlife scene. Tromsø is northern Norway's largest city, capital of the county of Troms and a significant fishing centre.

Tromsø palms

During summer, the temperatures can reach 25°C/77°F, so that the vegetation is positively exuberant. The front gardens of houses are notable for their displays of flowering plants, and 2m/6ft–3m/10ft-high »Tromsø palms« are common in the city. This sub-species of Heracleum sibiricum (eltrot) has stands with broad pinnate leaves (hence »palm«) and white blossoms, and can grow up to 10cm/4in per day; this flowering plant of the Umbelliferae, or carrot family, can occasionally snap under its own weight after two months of growth.

What to See in Tromsø

★ Arctic Cathedral

Still on the mainland, right next to the Tromsø Bridge, stands Tromsdalen church, otherwise known as the Arctic Cathedral. This architecturally interesting building was designed by Jan Inge Hovig in 1965 to symbolize the dark time of year and the Northern Lights. The Return of Christ is symbolized by Norwegian Victor Sparre's wonderfully colourful 23m/75ft-high stained glass window with a total of 86 panes (opening times: June–Aug Mon–Sat 10am–5pm, Sun from 1pm).

Perspektivet

The municipal museum has exhibits at three locations. In the city centre, there is an exhibition on the city's history and youth culture (Storegata 95; opening times: Sept–mid-June Tue–Fri 11am–3pm, Sat/Sun noon–4pm, mid-June–Aug daily 11am–5pm). At the **Folke-parken** open-air museum in the south of the city, 13 different farms and mansions are exhibited, and there is a fascinating display on the Lofoten fishing industry. The **Straumen gård** on the island of Kvaløya (see below) houses 19th-century farms (opening times: June–Sept daily, depending on the weather, www.perspektivet.no).

▶ VISITING TROMSØ

INFORMATION

Destinasjon Tromsø AS
Storgt. 61-63
9253 Tromsø
Tel. 77 61 00 00
Fax 77 61 00 10
www.destinasjontromso.no

WHERE TO EAT

▶ Expensive

② *Peppermøllen*
Mat & Vinhus
Storgate 42, tel. 77 68 62 60
While enjoying the fine fish or
vegetarian dishes here, patrons in the
Amundsen Room, where Roald
Amundsen and his friend Zapffe once
dined, can study pictures of his
adventures.

▶ Inexpensive

③ *Blå Rock Café*
Strandgata 14/16
Tel. 77 61 00 20
An institution in Tromsø and probably the world's most northerly
rock'n'roll café. Lots of little cosy
rooms on several floors with authentic interiors from around the world.
DJs ensure a great atmosphere at the
weekends. Occasionally there is also
live music.

① *Kaffe å Lars*
Kirkegata 8
Tel. 77 63 77 30
This miniscule café on the second
floor of Emm's Drømmekjøkken opposite the cathedral serves breakfast as
early as 7am. In the evening there is
often live music, especially jazz. Light
meals at affordable prices make this a
popular meeting place, including at
lunchtime.

Baedeker recommendation

▶ Moderate

④ *Arctandria Sjømat Restaurant*
Strandtorget 1
Tel. 77 60 07 20
There are no less than three restaurants
here: the Vertshuset Skarven awaits guests
with simple but exotic small dishes; the
Arctandria is a highly praised fish and
shellfish restaurant with regional and Sami
specialities; and the Skarvens Biffhus serve
up juicy steaks in varying sizes.

WHERE TO STAY

▶ Luxury

① *Scandic Hotel*
Heiloveien 23
Tel. 77 75 50 00
Fax 77 75 50 11
315 beds, www.scandic-hotels.com
This hotel, opened in 1986, offers a
high level of comfort and houses three
renowned attractions with its Måken
restaurant, Pelikanen bar and Pingvi-
nen nightclub.

▶ Budget

② *Hotel Nord*
Parkgata 4
Tel. 77 66 83 00, fax 77 66 83 20
22 rooms, nord@tromso.biz
This small hotel near the centre has
been offering clean and affordable
rooms for years. Simple breakfast.
Advance booking essential!

GETTING THERE

The Hurtigruten ships arrive in the
port daily. During summer Tromsø is
also the final destination for Spitsbergen cruises. There are flights to
Longyearbyen/Spitsbergen, Oslo and
other larger cities.

FESTIVALS

International Film Festival
Every year during the third week in January, Norway's largest film festival takes place here (www.tiff.no).

Northern Lights Festival
The Northern Lights Festival at the end of January concentrates on innovative music, in particular, especially cross-over music with traditional music styles (www.nordlysfestivalen.no).

SPORT

Polar Night Half Marathon (Mørketidsløp)
This unique winter race is held in Tromsø during the first weekend in January. Start and finish lines are in the city centre. The distance to be covered is either 10km/6mi or a half marathon.

Tromsø Ski Marathon
Tromsø invites participants to the Ski Marathon at the beginning of April. The cross-country route lies in truly beautiful landscape outside the city and is 40km/25mi long.

Midnight Sun Marathon
This, the world's most northerly marathon, is held in mid-June; information at www.msm.no.

MIDNIGHT SUN
from 21 May to 23 July

EXCURSIONS
Take the Fjellheisen cable car to the 420m/1378ft-high viewing point at Storsteinen. Timetable: May–Sept 10am–5pm; in fine weather also from 9pm–12.30am.

Polar Museum ⊙
Located on the fjord, the Polar Museum is well worth seeing and includes items from Amundsen's South Pole Expedition (opening times: mid-May–mid-Sept daily 11am–3pm, otherwise only Mon–Fri).

Cathedral
To the southwest of the ships' landing area in the city centre of Tromsø stands the 1861 cathedral with attractive stained glass windows. King Håkon Håkonsson had the first church built here in 1250, around which a settlement gradually developed. Today the Lutheran cathedral is Norway's largest neo-Gothic wooden church.

★ Tromsø Museum ⊙
The Tromsø Museum is 2km/1.2mi further to the southwest, past the university. Located in a park, its natural and cultural history collections with a special focus on Sami culture and arctic nature are also interesting for children. Archaeological finds testify to the fact that people were already living by hunting and fishing in the Troms region as much as 10,000 years ago (opening times: June–Aug daily 9am–8pm, otherwise Mon–Fri 8.30am–3.30pm, Sat/Sun from noon/11am respectively).

Elverhøy church
Elverhøy church (1802) to the west of the city centre served as Tromsø's Lutheran cathedral from 1803 to 1861 and was moved here in 1975. The interior of this wooden church contains a noteworthy altar and a medieval Madonna, also made of wood.

Tromsø Map

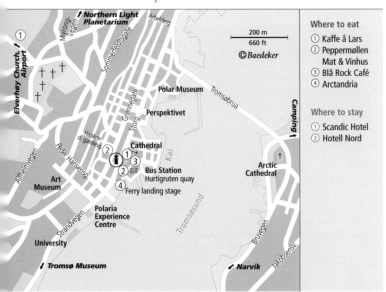

Where to eat
① Kaffe å Lars
② Peppermøllen Mat & Vinhus
③ Blå Rock Café
④ Arctandria

Where to stay
① Scandic Hotel
② Hotell Nord

200 m
660 ft
©Baedeker

Nordnorsk Art Museum

Very close to the world's most northern brewery with its own beer cellar (»Mack« on Storgata), lies the modern north Norwegian museum of art (Muségata), with works by north Norwegian artists from the early 18th century to the present day (opening times: mid-June–mid-Aug Mon–Fri noon–6pm, Sat/Sun till 5pm, winter season Tue–Fri 10am–5pm, Sat/Sun from noon).

Polaria Adventure Centre

Southeast of the Nordnorsk Art Museum, at Hjalmar Johansgata 12, visitors to the Polaria Adventure Centre, opened in 1998, can discover everything about life in the arctic. A panoramic film carries spectators off to the islands of Svalbard, while arctic fish and other sea animals can be seen in the large aquariums. It is fascinating for old and young alike (opening times: May–Aug daily 10am–7pm, Sept–April noon–5pm).

Nordlys Planetarium

At the world's northernmost planetarium (Northern Lights Planetarium) on the university campus in Breivika, visitors can experience a variety of meteorological phenomena, including the Northern Lights, on the big screen.

Catholic church

At the Stortorget, the »Large Market«, reached via Skippergata and Havnegata, stands the 19th-century Catholic church. The Norwegian Catholic diocese was established in 1843 after catholicism was banned during the Reformation.

Around Tromsø

The base station of the Fjellheisen cable car route up the 420m/   ✴
1378ft Storsteinen is located in a side street behind the striking Arc-   **Storsteinen**
tic Cathedral. In fine weather, there is a fantastic view from up here,   **viewing point**
and it is also a good place to experience the midnight sun. The
»Fjellstua« mountain restaurant is there for hungry souls (timetable: ⏲
May–Sept 10am–5pm, in good weather also 9pm–12.30am).

Mountain hikers can ascend the 1238m/4062ft-high Tromsdalstind   **Hikes**
east of Tromsdal, as well as explore the Tønsvikdal valley. There are
three cabins offering accommodation: Skarvassbu, Nonsbu and
Blåkollkoia. During winter, there are several cross-country skiing
routes. More information is available from the Tromsø tourist office.

The island of Kvaløya (»Whale Island«) lies to the west of Tromsø   **Kvaløya Island**
and its moist meadows facing the Sandnessund Strait can be reached
via the Sandnessund Bridge that leads across it. The German
battleship *Tirpitz* was sunk by the British to the south of Kvaløya in
1944. A memorial for the 2000 victims was set up on Hakøy in the
year 2000 (turning about 7km/4mi south of the bridge). Near the RV
862 at the southern end of the is-
land, the 2500–4000-year-old
Skavberg **rock paintings** are worth
seeing; as is the pretty village of Hella, located right by the tidal waters
of the Rystraumen, where there is a
small open-air museum with several
beautiful historic houses from
Tromsø. Hillesøy church (1880) at
the far western side of the island has
two German altar panels dating from
around 1500. In the fishing village of
Hillesøy, further north, there is also
a wonderful view of the sea. Kvaløya
Island is connected to its northern
neighbour of **Ringsvassøy** by the
Kvalsund Tunnel (1630m/1783yd).
Deep-sea fishing tours set off from
Hansnes on Ringsvassøya, which is
about an hour's drive from Tromsø.

About 70km/44mi southeast of
Tromsø, the peninsula of Lyngen is
an natural arctic paradise complete
with the almost 2000m/6562ft-high
snow-covered summits of the »Lyngen Alps« (►Lyngenfjord).

Bears still live in the wild and lonely region around Tromsø.

✦ ✦ Trondheim

Region: Central Norway   **Population:** 161,700

Norway's third largest city boasts a picturesque location on a southern bay of the Trondheimfjord. Trondheim was the country's first capital. St Olav died here, and the Nidaros Cathedral, Scandinavia's most magnificent church in which Norway's monarchs are crowned, was built over his grave.

City on a peninsula

Trondheim's old town is bounded by the Nidelv river and is therefore a peninsula that is only connected to the mainland in the west. All the sights are easily reached on foot. The capital of the county of Sør-Trøndelag is also the seat of both the Protestant and Catholic bishops. The favourable temperatures (average January temperatures rarely fall below −3°C/27°F) always leave the fjord **free of ice** and allow a wealth of flora to grow. Trondheim is not only an important industrial city (engineering, food industry and fish processing), but has also made a name for itself as a centre of university research and learning. Norway's largest technical college is here, as well as a university and **Scandinavia's largest technological research centre** SINTEF.

History of a royal town

Originally Trondhjem, Trondheim was once the name for the entire region around the Trondheimfjord, which is considered the cradle of the Norwegian empire. This is where Norwegian monarchs were chosen by the Øreting. Olav Tryggvason (or Tryggvessøn) had the **royal residence of »Nidarnes«** built as early as 997, but the real founder of the city, in 1016, is considered to be **St Olav**. From then until the 16th century, the city was known as **»Nidaros«** (mouth of the Nid). After St Olav's death in 1030, hordes of pilgrims came to see the shrine of the canonized king and it was through this cult that Trondheim became the largest and **richest city in the land**. Apart from the cathedral, another nine churches and five monasteries were built. The Reformation put an end to the pilgrimages; the saint's shrine was carried off to Denmark and destroyed there, and the body was buried at an unrecorded spot inside the cathedral. The number of churches and monasteries declined, and Trondheim's heyday came to an end.

> **! Baedeker TIP**
>
> **The Middle Ages brought to life**
> The best time to visit Trondheim is during the St Olav Days at the end of July/beginning of August, when a variety of churches and public buildings host numerous concerts, exhibitions, and music and theatre performances. A medieval market held in the courtyard of the Archbishop's Palace (Erkebispegård) includes demonstrations of traditional trades and Norwegian crafts, such as ceramics, candles and carvings are sold.

VISITING TRONDHEIM

INFORMATION
Trondheim Aktivum
Munkegt. 19, Torget
7411 Trondheim
Tel. 73 80 76 60
Fax 73 80 76 70
www.trondheim.com

WHERE TO EAT
► Expensive
① **Palmehaven**
Dronningensgate 5
Tel. 73 80 08 00
Very fancy restaurant in the Britannia Hotel. Stylish atmosphere among the palms and fountains.

► Moderate
② **Abelone Mat & Vinkjeller**
Dronningens gate 15,
Tel. 73 53 24 70
Stylish 150-year-old cellar restaurant with good cuisine and fine wines on the menu.

③ **Erichsen Konditori & Restaurant**
Nordre gate 8, tel. 73 87 45 50
Genteel ladies from the Singsaker neighbourhood meet for coffee and cake in this traditional café dating from 1856.

► Inexpensive
④ **Daily Bakklandet**
Øvre Bakklandet 66
Tel. 73 87 42 42
Pizza, pasta, wok dishes, salads and soups are served in this friendly restaurant.

WHERE TO STAY
► Luxury
② **Britannia Hotel**
Dronningensgate 5
Tel. 73 80 08 00, fax 73 80 08 01
247 rooms, www.britannia.no

First class comfort is offered here, as well as the Palmehaven restaurant, a piano bar, a cellar restaurant and an English pub.

③ **Clarion Hotel Grand Olav**
Kjøpmannsgt. 48,
Tel. 73 80 80 80
Fax 73 80 80 81
106 rooms, www.choicehotels.no
First-class hotel in the busy city centre with popular and outstanding gastronomic services (restaurant, café, bar, night club).

④ **Radisson SAS Royal Garden Hotel**
Kjøpmannsgt. 73
Tel. 73 80 30 00, fax 73 80 30 50
297 rooms, www.radissonsas.com
This modern hotel with giant lobby has architectural appeal as well as a beautiful location on the river, not far from the harbour.

► Mid-range
① **Munken Hotel**
Kongensgt. 44
Tel. 73 53 45 40
Fax 73 53 42 60
19 rooms, www.munken.no
Small, central hotel in a newly renovated wooden house.

► Budget
⑤ **Singsaker Sommerhotel**
Rogerts gate 1
Tel. 73 89 31 00, fax 73 89 32 00
105 rooms
www.sommerhotell.singsaker.no
The value for money alternative is a simple hotel in a very quiet location on a hill near the Kristiansten fortress.

MARKET
There is a daily vegetable, fruit and flower market on the Torget.

After repeated fires – the last in **1651, when the entire old city was destroyed** – the Luxembourg general Caspar de Cicignon was given a contract by Christian V to design a new city. Inspired by **Versailles**, he built broad boulevards that led off in all directions from the market square. He also built the **Kristiansten fortress**, which was to withstand several Swedish attacks. The increase in wood trading at the beginning of the 17th century resulted in an upswing for the city and numerous rich Swedish families settled here. The population increased fourfold within 100 years and, by the beginning of the 19th century, Trondheim's 9500 inhabitants made it just as large as Kristiania, today's Oslo. The city received a further boost in growth when it was connected to the rest of the Norwegian and then the Swedish **railway network**, in 1877 and 1881 respectively.

Inspired by Versailles

What to See in Trondheim

The heart of Trondheim is the Torget market square where the two main roads of Kongensgata and Munkegata converge. A tall octagonal pillar with a statue of Olav Tryggvason (1923) stands on the square. In the paving stones below the memorial, it is possible to see the four points of the compass (N–V–S–Ø).

Torget

The Arts and Crafts Museum (Nordenfjeldske Kunstindustrimuseum), founded in 1893, exhibits historic furniture and domestic items dating from the 16th century to 1930 (including, among other things, 17th–18th-century Trondheim silver), objects from the Arts and Crafts Movement of the turn of the 19th century, an art nouveau collection, Scandinavian design (1950–65), tapestries by Hanny Ryggen, folk costume and a Japanese collection (opening times: June–Aug Fri 10am–5pm, otherwise till 3pm, Sun from noon).

Arts and Crafts Museum

Nidaros Cathedral (Nidarosdomen) was founded **on the site of St Olav's grave** by King Olav Kyrre (1066–93), and substantially extended in 1151 after the establishment of the archbishopric of Nidaros that encompassed all of Norway. The building complex and its artistic execution make it the most magnificent church in all of Scandinavia and Trondheim's most important sight (see also photo p.54). The transept, chapter house and the splendid early Gothic octagonal dome are characterized by a **late Romanesque transitional style** influenced by Anglo-Norman thought at the time. The cathedral's building material was the blue-grey soapstone from the area around Trondheim. The **long choir** with its beautiful south portal was built in the early 13th century, the mighty **nave** and spire in the Gothic style in 1280. After several fires, the western section, starting with the transept, was left in ruins. But the nascent national consciousness of the 19th century saved the cathedral from oblivion: **reconstruc-**

★ ★
Nidaros Cathedral

← *Norway's kings are crowned in the Nidaros Cathedral.*

Nidaros Cathedral Trondheim Plan

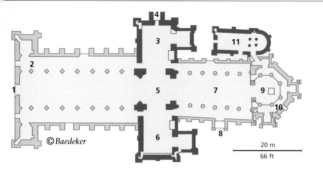

■ Romanesque
□ Gothic

1 West portal
2 Coronation ins
3 Northern transe
4 North portal
5 Crossing
6 Southern transe
7 Long choir
8 Southern choir
9 High choir
  (octagonal don
10 St Olav's well
11 Sacristy
  (chapter house

© Baedeker

20 m
66 ft

tion began in 1869 and on 28 July 1930, in time for the 900th centenary of St Olav's death, the church was reconsecrated. The **organ**, with its Baroque styling built by Steinmeyer from Oettingen in Swabia in 1930, was moved to stand below the window rosette in 1963. The west wall was restored in the period 1914–68; the cathedral's **west façade** is very beautiful with its statues of Norwegian kings and bishops, along with biblical figures.

Coronation insignia ▶ The cathedral served as the final royal resting place in the 11th and 12th centuries. Several kings were crowned here in the 15th century and, since 1814, it has been constitutionally set that Norwegian kings must be crowned in Trondheim's cathedral. The coronation insignia are also kept here and are on display to the public (opening times: June–Aug Mon–Thu, Sat 9am–12.30pm, Sun 1pm–4pm, otherwise only Fri noon–2pm).

Stained glass windows ▶ On entering the cathedral, the ceremonial atmosphere immediately impresses the visitor. The only sources of light are the colourful stained glass windows (1913–34) by Gabriel Kielland and the luminous blue and red tones of the glass rosette above the organ.

14 pillars separate the 43m/47yd-long and 20m/22yd-wide nave from the aisles. The octagonal dome in high Gothic style rises above the high choir, where the 26m/28yd long choir with its beautiful baptismal font adjoins. The southern side chapel in the Romanesque transept was consecrated as early as 1161 (cathedral opening times: June–Aug Mon–Fri 9am–6pm, Sat till 2pm, Sun 1pm–4pm).

Archbishop's Palace ▶ Nextdoor stands the Archbishop's Palace (Erkebispegård), a medieval stone building that once served as home for the bishops. It is northern Europe's oldest secular building. Originally it was encircled by thick walls; after the Reformation it served as an aristocratic seat for the Danish overlords and, from 1660, it housed military munitions. The magnificent **Knights' Hall** (1180), used for official occasions and celebrations by the city of Trondheim, is open to the public. The storage buildings of the bishops' seat burnt down to their foundations in 1983 and valuable collections were destroyed. Today a large **museum centre** is housed here with interesting exhibitions on the history of Norway and Trondheim, a weapons collection, and the Museum of the Resistance (1940–45).

On Bispegate, northwest of the cathedral, stands the building of the **Art Association** (Kunstforening) which has a picture gallery and changing exhibitions (opening times: June–Aug daily 10am–5pm, otherwise Tue–Sun 11am–4pm).

There is an attractive view towards several 18th–19th century **old warehouses** (largely restored) set **on posts** from the **Bybrua**, a red wooden bridge (1861) that crosses the Nidelv to the northeast of the cathedral. Today there are several **good fish restaurants** here. Olav Tryggvason had the first warehouses built by the Nidelv on Øvre Elvehavn about one thousand years ago, but they quickly burnt down again. On the east side stand historic, mostly restored, wooden houses that were once workers' apartments.

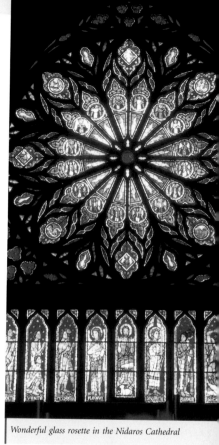

Wonderful glass rosette in the Nidaros Cathedral

The **Kristiansten fortress**, built in the European Baroque style by General Caspar de Cicignon in the 17th century, can be reached by walking across the Bybrua and up through the suburb of Bakklandet onto the hill, from where there is also a panoramic view of the city. The view is most beautiful during the early morning or at sunset (opening times for the rooms: June–Aug Mon–Fri 10am–3pm, Sat, Sun 11am–4pm).

Kristiansten fortress

Ⓟ

A wonderful view of Trondheim and the fjord landscape can also be enjoyed from the 80m/262ft-high rotating restaurant inside the Television Tower (Tyholttarnet; 120m/394ft), to the east of the city centre.

Television Tower

North of the market square, on Munkegata, stands the mighty yellow wooden house of the Stiftsgården, built in 1770, whose approxi-

★

Stiftsgården

Trondheim Map

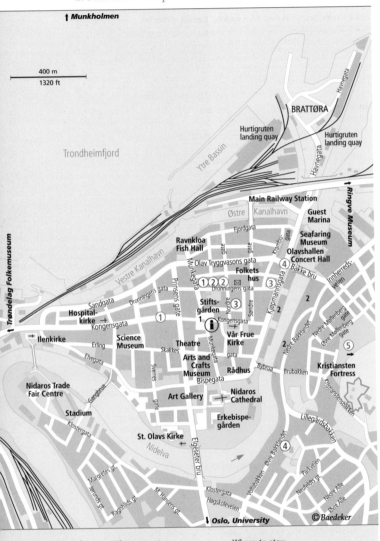

400 m
1320 ft

↑ *Munkholmen*

BRATTØRA

Hurtigruten
landing quay

Hurtigruten
landing quay

Trondheimfjord

Havnegata

Main Railway Station

Østre Kanalhavn

Guest
Marina

Ringve Museum

Fjordgata

Seafaring
Museum

Ravnkloa
Fish Hall

Olavshallen
Concert Hall

Olav Tryggvasons gata

Folkets
hus

Bakke bru

Innherredsveien

Vestre Kanalhavn

Trøndelag Folkemuseum

Munkegata

Prinsens gate

Dronningens gata

① ② ②

Dronningens gata

③

Kjøpmannsgata

Stifts-
gården

Nordre gate

Søndre gate

1

ⓘ

2

Sandgata

Hospital-
kirke

Kongensgata

Dronningens gata

①

Kongensgata

Vår Frue
Kirke

2

Nedre Møllenberg gate

Øvre Møllenberg gate

Ilenkirke

Erling

Science
Museum

Theatre

Skakkes

gata

⑤

Elvegata

Sverres

Arts and
Crafts
Museum

Rådhus

Bybrua

Brubakken

Kristiansten
Fortress

Nidaros Trade
Fair Centre

Bispegata

Art Gallery

Nidaros
Cathedral

Kongens gata

gate

Gangbrua

Erkebispe-
gården

Lillegårdsbakken

Kristianstenbakken

Stadium

Klostergata

Margretes gt.

St. Olavs Kirke

Nidelva

Elgeseter bru

④

Jonrnuds gt.

Ragnhilds gt.

Mt. Hansens gt.

Klostergata

Høgskoleveien

Voldsbakken Øvre Bakklandet

Parkveien

Nedre Alle

Neufelds gt.

Øvre Alle

↓ *Oslo, University*

© *Baedeker*

1 Olav Tryyvason Column

2 Historic warehouses

Where to eat
① Palmehaven
② Abelone Mat &
Vinkjeller
③ Erichsen Konditori &
Restaurant
④ Daily Bakklandet

Where to stay
① Munken Hotel
② Britannia Hotel
③ Clarion Hotel Grand Olav
④ Radisson SAS
Royal Garden Hotel
⑤ Singsaker Sommerhotell

mately 140 rooms serve as the royal seat when the Norwegian king visits Trondheim. When the widow **Cecilie Schøller** commissioned this building – one of the largest wooden buildings in northern Europe – she intended to outshine her rivals who lived in the urban mansions of Hornemannsgården and Harmonien. Sure enough, this small palace became Trondheim's finest building.

The coronation celebrations for kings Karl XIV Johan (1818), Karl XV (1860), Oscar II (1873), Håkon VII (1906), Olav V (1958) and latterly Harald V (1991) took place here. The building can only be visited during the one-hour guided tours (opening times: June–Aug Mon–Sat 10am–5pm, Sun not before noon).

A little way outside the centre, several buildings belonging to the University of Trondheim on Erling Skakkes gata house divers collections, including an important library with ancient manuscripts and an exhibition of sacred art. There is a mineral, botanic, zoological (incl. bird diorama) and archaeological collection.

Science museums

A particularly well executed exhibition is »Medieval Trondheim«, opened in 1997, in a former warehouse from 1843. The visitor is taken through the city's history during a tour complete with audio effects, beginning with the Vikings, continuing with the foundation of the city in the 10th century by Olav Tryggvason, and through to the 17th century. Everyday life from that era is made real with the help of archaeological finds as well as reconstructed workshops and domestic interiors (opening times: May–mid-Sept Mon–Fri 9am–4pm, Sat, Sun 11am–4pm, mid-Sept–Dec Tue–Fri 9am–2pm, Sat, Sun noon to 4pm).

★
◄ **Medieval Trondheim**

On a hill in the southwest of the city, where King Sverre's (1177–1202) Sverresborg once stood, there is a huge area with a fine view that is now the Folklore Museum (Folkemuseet). There are farms from the 18th to the 20th century from the district of Trøndelag, as well as the 12th century Haltdalen stave church and buildings from Trondheim's old town (opening times: June–Aug daily 11am–6pm, otherwise 11am–3pm).

Folklore Museum

Around Trondheim

The fortified island of Munkholmen lies in the Trondheimfjord and can be reached by boat from the Ravnkloa fish market at the northern end of Munkegata (hourly, 10mins). There was a place of execution here during the reign of Olav Tryggvason; the king had the heads of the executed mounted on poles right by the water so that enemies penetrating the Trondheimfjord would be frightened off. The round tower of the Benedictine Nidarosholm monastery built at the beginning of the 11th century can still be seen on the island. From 1658 onwards, a fortress and prison stood here, but times change: today there is an open-air swimming pool and a restaurant.

Munkholmen

★ ★
**Ringve
Museum**

Following the E 6 out of the city centre in the direction of Narvik and then taking a left turn after about 2km/1mi (signposted), drivers reach the Ringve Gård farm where the bold sea hero and adventurer Tordenskjold grew up in the 17th century. The Ringve farm is idyllically located in an artistic botanical garden and has served as a museum for a noteworthy collection of musical instruments since 1952. Furnished true to their time, the interiors of the rooms of the composers F. Chopin (including the composer's death mask), Edvard Grieg (original photos), Beethoven and Mozart are worth taking a look at. The presentations on the historic instruments by the museum guides enhance the exhibition's impact.

A particular attraction for music fans is the music history museum opened in the hay loft in 1999, which has a wonderful collection of keyboard, wind and string instruments from all around the world, as well as a representative collection of Norwegian folk music instruments. Examples of diverse music styles ranging from classical to jazz and contemporary pop underline the museum's educational appeal (opening times: mid-April–mid-Sept daily 11am–3pm, July, Aug till 5pm, during winter till 3pm; the main building can only be visited as part of a guided tour).

**Excursion to
Gråkallen**

A pleasant excursion runs from Trondheim to Fjellseter (skiing region, ski jump) on the Fjellsetervei and then to Fjellseter chapel 8km/5mi west of the city. From there, a footpath (15mins) can be taken to the summit of Gråkallen (556m/1824ft) and the incredible views over the Trondheimfjord and onto the Trollheimen mountains. It is also possible to take the **Gråkall railway** from Trondheim (departures from St. Olavsgate) or a bus from the city's Dronningensgate to Lian (30mins) and walk via Fjellseter and Skistua to ascend Gråkallen – a beautiful walk that takes 2.5hrs there and back.

**Rock art by
Hegra**

Hegra is reached on the E 14. About 2km/1mi beyond Hegra a country path turns off to the left, signposted »Bergmuseet«, to Leirfall, one of northern Europe's largest sites containing Bronze Age (1500–500 BC) rock art. At the site, for example, is a group of 13 people that walk behind each other, as in a **procession**.

The figure at the forefront and the three smallest ones represent »masked men« who were probably responsible for encouraging plants to grow. Furthermore, ships, sun symbols and a group of horse riders (approx. 600 BC) can be seen at Leirfall. Aslo near Hegra are the remains of the 1911 Hegra fortress, where 200 Norwegians held out for 27 days during the Second World War before capitulating to the Germans.

Steinkjer

Steinkjer lies 125km/78mi northeast of Trondheim on the E 6. The town on the Breistadfjord was already an important trading centre in ancient times, but lost its historic buildings in two devastating fires. Today it is the relatively unspectacular administrative centre for the region of Nord-Trøndelag. The **Steinkjer church**, consecrated in 1965, is located on the former farm of Steinkjer. Its unusual stained glass windows and frescoes are by the locally born artist Jakob Weidemann. The modern **»Dampsaga« cultural centre**, created from three old sawmill buildings and a modern annex, is located on the Sagmester-vegen, to the north of the Steinkjerelva river. Further north lies the appealing **Egge open-air museum** which has 11 historic farms and also the Eggevammen burial mounds on both sides of the E 6, where finds from AD 200 up to the Viking era testify to the fact that there was a lively trade with England and other countries here.

Around 400 rock paintings at Bardal, about 11km/7mi northwest of Steinkjer, show images of hunting scenes (human figures, elk and reindeer) from the Stone Age, and also sun symbols from the Bronze Age.

Norway's most beautiful rock paintings

The site of perhaps the most famous rock painting of hunting scenes (*c*3000 BC) in Scandinavia is located about 30km/19mi north of Steinkjer (RV 763), near the southeastern shore of the idyllic Snåsa-vatn: the life-sized **»Bøla Reindeer«**.

33km/21mi south of Steinkjer lies the Stiklestad national cultural centre, with an open-air museum and the Stiklestad hotel in the middle of the historic site. The annual St Olav's festival takes place here in the middle of summer. At the spot where the altar of the Sti-klestad church (1128, with inter-esting chalk paintings) now stands, the national patron saint King Olav, alias **Olav Haraldsson** (995–1030), received a fatal shot from his arch enemy Tore Hund on 29 July 1030. Olav's body was later taken to Trondheim.

★ Stiklestad

> **! Baedeker TIP**
>
> ### Spectacular theatrical thunder
> Norway's largest open-air stage is in Stiklestad. Each year on 29 July – the anniversary of Olav Haraldson's death – 5000 spectators relive the Battle of Stiklestad at close quarters, with 300 actors taking part. Visitors to the Stiklestad Nasjonale Kulturhus can also follow the course of the battle along a walkway where they are inundated with violent light and sound effects.

About 10km/6mi south of Stikle-stad lies the little town of **Le-vanger**, where people have been meeting at the popular **»Levanger-martan«** market every August since the early 15th century. During the »Marsimartnan« market in late February there is a torchlight procession with music and festivities.
The stone church of Alstadhang (*c*1150) about 5km/3mi further south is particularly worth seeing and contains interesting 13th cen-tury chalk paintings, though it is open only when services are taking place. It was built close to a large burial mound on the site of a hea-then temple. 8km/5mi to the east of town stand the ruins of the Cis-tercian Munkeby monastery (1155–1200), one of eight monasteries located on the Trondheimfjord.

✳ Valdres

C/D 5-7

Region: East Norway

Farms and green meadows characterize the scenery of the Valdres valley, in the vicinity of which are several stave churches. The open-air museum, with its many historic houses from the region, in the main settlement of Fagernes is among the most notable sights here.

The fertile Valdres landscape of southern Norway extends on both sides of the Begna river that comes from the southern Jotunheimen mountains and empties into Lake Tyrifjord near the Hønefoss waterfall.

What to See in the Valdres Valley

✳
Hadeland glass works
Norway's most famous glass works is located at the southern end of the Randsfjord, at Jevnaker about 23km/14mi northeast of Hønefoss. Hadeland Glassverk was founded as early as 1762 and is Norway's oldest industrial firm. Visitors can watch glass-blowers at work, purchase glass products, take a journey through history and design in the exhibition sites, and admire the artfully designed glass
⏲ products (opening times: Mon–Fri 10am–5pm, Sat to 4pm, Sun 11am–5pm, www.hadeland-glassverk.no).

▶ VISITING VALDRES

INFORMATION
Fagernes Turistkontor
2900 Fagernes
Tel. 61 35 94 10
Fax 61 35 94 15
www.visitvaldres.com

WHERE TO STAY

▶ **Mid-range**
Valdres Hytteutleie
Fagernes Skysstation
Tel. 61 35 94 40
Fax 61 35 94 15
www.valdres-hytteutleie.com
There is a large selection of holiday cabins available in all the Valdres valley communities. Most are well provisioned, though guests must bring their own bedding. The extensive website has detailed descriptions of all cabins which can be booked online.

▶ **Budget**
Fagernes Camping
In the centre
Tel. 61 36 05 10
Fax 61 36 07 51
www.fagernes-camping.no
Not just for those under canvas: at this campsite with a pretty and central lakeside location, simple and value-for-money cabins can also be rented.

North of Hønefoss travelling up the valley, the E 16 runs along the eastern shore of the 23km/14mi-long Lake Sperillen. The RV 243 turns off to Hedalen (25km/16mi) after the church and village of **Nes** at the northern end of the lake, not far from the mouth of the Begna. The oldest stave church in the Valdres valley stands here (not to be confused with the similarly-named Heddal stave church; see p. 372). Originally built in the 12th century, it was remodelled in 1738 and restored in 1901. A **bear skin** in the church recalls the rediscovery of the church in around 1500, when it is said that two hunters pursued a bear into the church and killed it there. Before that the church had stood empty ever since an outbreak of plague 150 years earlier. The **valuable interior** includes a Madonna statue and a medieval reliquary shrine.

✷
Hedalen stave
church

The E 16 follows the Begna through forested landscape via Begndal to Bagn, a pretty, drawn out settlement (radio transmitter). Take a look at the 18th-century wooden church here. Near Bagn a secondary road turns off to the small 12th-century stave church of Reinli, from which there is a marvellous view.

Bagn

The much-visited settlement of Fagernes, also popular with fishermen, lies picturesquely between forested hills at the mouth of the Neselv river that forms beautiful waterfalls here as it empties into the Strandefjord. In Fragernes it is worth visiting the **open-air folk museum** with its numerous historic farm buildings from the Valdres region complete with historic domestic items, textiles, musical instruments and hunting weapons. From Fragernes, the RV 51 leads north to the famous ► Jotunheimen mountain massif.

✷
Fagernes

> **!** *Baedeker* **TIP**
>
> **Delicious rømmegrøt**
> The Nystøga café in the Valdres Folkemuseum is housed in a 250-year-old building that once served as an inn for travellers to the Filefjell. Traditional Norwegian fare is served here, such as alpine pancakes and sour cream waffles. »Rømmegrøt«, Norway's calorie-heavy sour cream porridge is definitely worth tasting here. The farmer's plate of ham, dried leg of lamb and dried sausage is also a regional delicacy (opening times: mid-June–mid-Aug; tel. 61 35 99 00).

It is worth paying a visit to the 13th-century stave church at **Lomen**, which lies on the E 16 en route to **Lake Vangsmjøsa**.
Vang, where the local church is also worth a visit, lies along the southern shore of the 19km/12mi-long lake. Once upon a time there was a stave church here, but it was carried off to Silesia in 1841 and replaced by the white wooden church seen today. The runic stone in front of it carries the inscription: »Gose's sons erected this stone for Gunnar, their brother's son«.
In **Øye** – at the west end of the Vangsmjøsa – stands a stave church that was rebuilt from the remains of a 12th-century church.

Varanger Peninsula

N 26

Region: North Norway

The peninsula of Varanger is a treeless expanse of scree, blasted by arctic storms. Travellers break their journey here at Vadsø, the administrative centre for Finnmark, or in Vardø, where the world's most northerly fortress stands.

Finnish enclave
The Varanger peninsula is separated from the mainland by the Tanafjord and the Varangerfjord, the latter of which has tidal waters that have a differential of up to 4m/13ft during full moon and a new

 VISITING VARANGER

INFORMATION

▶ **Vadsø**
Kirkegata 15
Tel. 78 94 04 44, fax 78 94 04 45
www.vadso-tourism.no

▶ **Vardø**
c/o Vardø i Vekst
Skolegt.
Tel. 78 98 69 07, fax 78 98 69 08
kontakt@vardovekst.no

GETTING THERE

Hurtigruten ships arrive daily in
Vadsø and Vardø. There are flights to
Kirdenes and Båtsfjord from Svartnes
Airport 4km/3mi outside Vardø.
There are also daily bus connections
to the rest of Finnmark.

WHERE TO EAT
▶ **Inexpensive**
Nordpol Kro
Vardø, Kaigt. 21
Tel. 78 98 75 01
Northern Norway's oldest guesthouse
is near the quay. It does not look like
much from the outside, but it is an
atmospheric English pub with lots of
local colour. The live concerts in the
Nordpol are renowned.

WHERE TO STAY
▶ **Luxury to mid-range**
Nobile Hotell
Vadsø, Brugata 2
Tel. 78 95 33 35
Fax 78 95 34 35
29 rooms, www.noblilehotell.no
Whether in the restaurant or the
hotel, everything is themed on the
airship pioneer Nobile. There are
historic photos of him and his
exploits everywhere. The restaurant is
also popular with locals for its
excellent fish dishes. The menu also
always offers a traditional regional
dish on Sundays.

FESTIVALS

The Varanger Jazz Festival, the largest
of its kind in the high north, is held at
Vadsø in mid-August. It is followed by
the King Crab Festival in October,
during which all the events revolve
around the king crab (www.polar-
spectacle.no).

MIDNIGHT SUN

The midnight sun shines from 16 May
to 29 July. From 23 November to 21
January, on the other hand, there is
no sun at all.

moon. Norway's most easterly point lies on the island of Hornøya near the town of Vardø. At 31° 10' eastern latitude, its location is further east than St Petersburg or Istanbul.

During the 19th century, so many Finns moved to Vadsø, on the northern coast of the Varangerfjord, that the fishing settlement was also known as the »Finnish capital« in Norway. In 1875, over 60% of the population in the administrative centre for the county of Finnmark spoke Finnish.

For centuries there was a lively trade along the coast of the Barents Sea between Russians, Norwegians and Sami, which only came to an end with the onset of the Russian revolution. This so-called »**Pomor trade**« – the word comes from the Russian phrase for the coastal inhabitants – involved the bartering of fish, grain and wood between northern Norwegians and Russians from the White Sea region. Since the dismantling of the Soviet Union these old trading relationships of the high north have been revived – and are duly celebrated in July on the Varanger peninsula during the **Pomor Festival**, with numerous cultural events and attractions.

What to See on the Varanger peninsula

Vadsø (pop. 6000) is the administrative centre of the county of Finnmark. This is where the expeditions by Umberto Nobile and Roald Amundsen, the first man to reach the South Pole (►Famous People), set off in 1926 with the intention of reaching the North Pole with their airship, the *Norge*. Two years later, Nobile set off on a North Pole journey once again. When he did not return, Amundsen went in search of him, also never to return. The anchor mast for the two airships remains on the island of Vadsøya, a memorial to the tragedy. | **Vadsø**

Varanger's most interesting attraction is the **Vadsø Museum** with the Tuomainen building, which predominantly covers the history of Finnish immigration; the Danish Norwegian aristocratic mansion of Esbensengården, a merchant house dating from 1850 and the only building of its kind in the county of Finnmark, is also worth a visit (opening times: mid-June–mid-Aug Mon–Fri 11am–6pm, Sat/Sun till 4pm). The architect Magnus Poulsson called the Vadsø church of 1958 the »**Arctic Ocean Church**«. Its two spires are meant to represent icebergs. | **Vadsø Museum** ⏱

The idyllic fishing settlement of Ekkerøy lies on a peninsula around 14km/9mi east of Vadsø (turn-off from the E 75). There is the grave of a woman here that dates from Viking times. The »bird mountain« of Flåget offers the chance to see arctic bird species, such as auks, puffins and kittiwakes. | **Ekkerøy**

Vardø – one of Norway's easternmost settlements – lies just off the coast on an island in the Arctic Ocean that is connected with the | **Vardø** mainland via a 3km/2mi-long underwater tunnel. Until the October Revolution of 1917, there was a lively trade with the Pomors of the Kola Peninsula (►Finnmark). During the Cold War, Vardø played an important role in NATO's early warning system. Today, though, the domes that dominate the town's picture also serve civilian interests. Two thirds of the town was destroyed during the war years between 1942 and 1944, but it has now been rebuilt.

✳
Vardøhus fortress ► Vardøhus fortress, the world's northernmost fortress, was originally built in the 14th century and redesigned in 1734–38 in the form of an eight-pointed star by Denmark's King Christian. When the long, dark, polar night of winter is over and the sun rises over the horizon again around the 22 January, the fortress cannons are fired and children get a day off school. The **Vardøhus Museum** dates from the time before the Second World War and contains the only surviving port in Finnmark. Norway's most carefully cared for tree must surely be the mountain ash at the fortress that soldiers wrap up in protective layers in October and unpack in April.

Domen The Domen mound rises 127m/417ft above Vardø. It is associated with many **tales of witches**. 80 »witches« were burnt here in the 17th century, the last in around 1700. It is said that these »witches« met to party with the devil here the night before the midsummer solstice and during Christmas.

✳ Vesterålen

L 11-13

Region: North Norway

The Vesterålen islands to the north of Lofoten are rather unfairly overshadowed by their famous neighbours. Of particular interest is an excursion to Andenes, the islands' northernmost settlement: on the famous whaling tours that set out from here there is a near guarantee of sperm whale sightings.

Picturesque landscape The Vesterålen mountains are not as rugged and mighty as those of Lofoten, but rather covered in green meadows up to quite high elevations. However the landscape of the islands is very appealing and definitely worth a visit. The island group consists of Andøya, Langøya and Hadseløya, as well as parts of the islands of Hinnøya und Austvågøya.

What to See on the Islands of Vesterålen

Hinnøya The many sections of Hinnøya combine to make it Norway's second largest island after Spitsbergen. The main settlement on the island is ►Harstad. The route that runs right along the water to the west of

On the island of Andøya you could almost imagine you were in the Caribbean – if it weren't so chilly.

Harstad is also known as the »Midnight Sun Route«. The 1266m/4154ft-high Møysalen in the south of the island is **Vesterålen's highest summit**. It offers an appealing panorama over Vesterålen and Lofoten, the view extending all the way to the mountains in the direction of Sweden. The ascent can be made from Kaldjord, at the end of the RV 822; there and back 9hrs). From Lødingen in the south of the island (RV 85), it is possible to catch a ferry to Bognes and the E 6.

The old trading settlement of **Risøyhamn** perches on the middle of a bare cliff right next to the sound. The Andøy Museum, with numerous cultural and historical objects, is located here. Up to 600m/1969ft-high mountains rise out of Andøya's extensive moorland and, in the east, an unexploited bed of coal stretches into the sea. The fishing village of **Andenes** (pop. 4200) lies at the northern tip of the island and has a 2.5km/1.5mi-long jetty. A polar and fishing museum is located in one of the historic homes.You can find out everything you need to know about whales at the Whale Centre in Andenes or, alternatively, live during a whale safari (see below), where you come face to face with 20m/66ft-long sperm whales – as well as smaller species.

Andøya

★
◄ Whale safaris

The fishing village of Bleik and the sugarloaf bird island of Bleikøya a short distance from the coast (boat tours) are also worth a visit. Puffins, guillemots, shags and kittiwakes live on the island.

Bleikøya

Langøya and its many peninsulas and fjords forms the largest section of west Vesterålen. **Sortland** (pop. 3000) is an old trading settlement and harbour for the Hurtigruten ships. Around 20km/13mi west of Sortland, the breathtaking needle-like peak of Reka reaches to the sky. Its steep 607m/1992ft-high southwest face has never been climbed. Around a century ago, **Nyksund**, in the north of Langøya, was one of Vesterålen's largest settlements, a canning factory provid-

Langøya

▶ **VISITING VESTERÅLEN**

INFORMATION

Sortland / Vesterålen Reiselivslag
Kjøpmannsgt. 2
8401 Sortland
Tel. 76 11 14 80
Fax 76 11 14 81
www.visitvesteralen.com

WHERE TO STAY AND EAT

▶ **Mid-range**
Strand Hotell Sortland
Strandgata 34
Tel. 76 11 00 80
Ffax 76 11 00 88
37 rooms
www.strandhotell.no
This hotel in the centre cannot be missed due to its striking blue colour. Several of its rooms were designed by the Norwegian Academy for Interior Decoration, so the hotel has an original character. The Spisestua restaurant serves arctic fish and meat dishes and has made a name for itself with north Norwegian cuisine.

Sjøhus Senteret
Ånstadsjøen, Sortland
Tel. 76 12 37 40
Fax 76 12 00 40
sjoehus@online.no
Seven comfortable wood cabins right by the water, with two bedrooms each. The large wooden hot tub can be fired up on request. The main building has the Sjøstua restaurant, which offers a beautiful view of the midnight sun as well as freshly prepared fish dishes.

▶ **Budget**
Holmvik Brygge
Nyksund
Tel. 76 13 47 96
Fax 76 13 17 09
post@nyksund.com
Simple, value for money accommodation in an old fisherman's house in Nyksund.

Nyksund Ekspedisjonen
Tel. 76 13 27 00
www.nyksund.biz
Clean and value-for-money single or family rooms. The restaurant, with a view of the harbour, serves up regional dishes.

GETTING THERE

Thanks to bridges and tunnels from the mainland, all the Vesterålen islands can be reached by car. The Hurtigruten ships dock at Stokmarknes, Sortland, Risøyhamn and Harstad.

EVENTS

An international cultural festival with concerts and theatre performances is held at Melbu on Hadseløya in July each year.

MIDNIGHT SUN

The midnight sun shines from 16 May to 29 July; from 23 November to 21 January there is no sun at all.

WHALE SAFARIS

A special attraction: whale safaris out of the former whaling station of Andenes from June to mid-September (reservations at least two days in advance; Andøy Reiseliv, tel. 76 11 56 00, tour 5hrs). Tours are accompanied by employees of the whale research institute and the World Wildlife Fund (WWF). They can also be booked in Stø on the island of Langøya.

Pretty fishing boats at the harbour at Nykvåg.

ing employment. However the place then fell into steady decline and became a ghost town. In the meantime, a little life has returned to Nyksund; accommodation is available, a café has opened and in summer a few tourists are attracted to the place.

One of northern Europe's largest bird colonies can be found near Nykvåg on the Fuglenyken and Måsnykas cliffs facing the open sea to the west. Vesterålen also boasts northern Europe's largest numbers of sea eagles who still find plenty of food here, though they suffer greatly from nest robbers.

★ Nykvåg

Swimmers will enjoy the 800m/875yd-long sandy beach at Fjærvoll, south of Føre. The writer Knut Hamsun (►Famous People) was a police assistant in this area for two years, until he tried his luck as a teacher and storyteller.

Stokmarknes on the island of Hadseløya is an economic centre with an important merchant fleet and also serves as departure point for cruises into the Trollfjord (► Lofoten), one of the most beautiful fjord cruises Norway has to offer. The Hurtigruten Museum was founded in honour of the shipping line's founder Captain Richard With (►Baedeker Special p.237). Hadsel church (1824), south of the town centre, is also worth seeing: it contains an altar panel from around 1500.

Hadseløya

The port of **Melbu**, where an important fishing fleet is based, lies in the south of the island. The historic Melbu Hovedgård (1830) with its beautiful warehouse (»stabbur«) is notable, as is the 200-year-old Rødgården, where changing exhibitions are held during summer. There is a wonderful view of the islands from **Husbykollen** (513m/1683ft), and there are also beautiful views of the sea and islands from the road that runs along the west coast from Melbu back to Stokmarknes. There is a lovely **sandy beach** near Taen, where swimmers can enjoy the midnight sun.

Whalers used to pursue their prey for many months.

WHALE HUNTING

Whaling has played a role in the economic foundation of Norway since time immemorial. This is particularly true for the settlements of the north Norwegian coast. After stocks of all large whale species were substantially decimated throughout the world due to overfishing, the International Whaling Commission (IWC) banned whale hunting and the export of whale meat in 1986. Norway does not recognize this ban and continues whaling.

A telltale blast of condensed water vapour shoots out of the sea. The ship will now pursue the whale for as long as it takes to have it in front of its bow, so that it can be killed by the **harpoon** cannon. Once the harpoon has embedded itself in the body of the ocean-going mammal, a small grenade explodes inside the animal at a depth of around 60cm/24 inches. On average, the animals are dead within three minutes, but sometimes the battle with death can also take up to an hour. The cadaver is then brought alongside the ship with the harpoon rope before being heaved on board where it is immediately quartered. The whale, a resource for humans for generations, supplies not only oil and blubber but also the raw materials for industrial products such as perfume, cosmetics, shoe polish, cod liver oil, glue, gelatine, fertilizer, animal feed and hormone pills. **Norway and Japan** are among the few nations that still hunt whales.

Norway swims against the tide

When, in 1993, the Norwegian government decided to permit once more the hunting of up to 800 minke whales annually, and despite the fact that the real quota lay well below that figure, a cry of outrage rang out among the international animal protection community. Foreign firms answered with a **boycott** of Norwegian products. European politicians saw the country's membership application for the EU endangered. The Norwegian government insisted, however, that whaling was not only a matter of economic interests, but also a matter of principle: Norway must be allowed to administer its ocean resources independently and responsibly. Meanwhile, the **International Whaling Commission (IWC)** added further restrictions to the 1986 **prohibition of commercial whaling** in 1993. A limited number of whales may be hunted for research purposes. This **loophole**

allows the Japanese to kill 440 minke whales annually, supposedly for research purposes.

What is the purpose of whaling?

Norway returned to whaling with the justification that minke whale stocks are not endangered, since there are around 750,000 animals of this species found throughout the world. The country is the only one that is not tied to the decisions of the IWC, because it exercised a veto against the whaling ban. Furthermore, the kill quota clearly lies below the rate of reproduction. The hunting of the larger and rarer species of whale, such as sperm whale, blue whale, fin whale and humpback whale continues to be strictly forbidden in Norway, just as in the rest of the world. Despite these figures, which are basically accepted by Greenpeace, it was of all countries Norway – normally considered advanced in ecological matters – that

suffered a severe blow to its image due to its decision to **recommence whaling**. From a strictly economic point of view, whaling makes no sense in a country that has become rich from North Sea oil. The profits from whaling are estimated to be over 4 million pounds annually and no more than 100 people still work in the business, many of them second-jobbers. In spite of decreasing demand for whale meat the Norwegian government allows up to 1052 minke whales to be killed annually – although the actual figure for each of the hunting seasons of 2006 and 2007 was less than 600 animals.

Whale hunts once took months

The era of widespread whale massacres had already come to an end in the 1960s, simply because it was **no longer economically viable**: only a few hundred individual animals of the large whale species remained in Ant-

Bloodless exploitation: whale-watching.

arctic waters. Even today, there are still only a few thousand of the up to 40m/131ft-long blue whales, when once there were 250,000. Parts of the whaling fleets from all the industrial nations, with Norway leading the way, had moved out of their coastal waters to the Arctic and Antarctic oceans by the turn of the 19th century, in order to hunt down the animals that supplied so many raw materials during expeditions that took many months. But the range of products produced by the synthetic industries eventually made these gruelling whaling journeys pointless. What is hunted today is the relatively small minke whale (10m/33ft). However, due to the **violent protests** and occasionally militant obstruction efforts mounted by foreign »whale kissers« – as fishermen disparagingly call them – the relations between whalers and animal rights activists have become strained. This is the reason there is probably no chance that any tourist would succeed in coming along on a whaling ship.

Whale safari

In order to enjoy the majestic ocean animals first hand, a bloodless »whale safari« is recommended, such as those offered from the small port of **Andenes** on the Vesterålen island of Andøya. As with the inhabitants of California, the locals have discovered the financial benefits of whale tourism as an alternative to hunting. Not far north of Andøya the flat continental shelf meets the deeper waters of the Atlantic. Warm and cold ocean currents meet here, which draws ocean life of many different species, among them the 20m/66ft sperm whales that can be observed rising from the deep to breathe. During summer, these large whales leave their territories near the equator and migrate to Norway's coast to eat their fill there. Sperm whales have teeth, so their diet includes fish, as well as plankton. A whale safari costs around £70 and lasts several hours, requiring appropriate clothing for the weather and good sea legs. Some people may suffer many hours of sea sickness on the small former whaling craft before a whale is seen. The sight of such a giant is compensation enough, though, for any hardships suffered; which explains the growing number of whale watching fans.

★ Voss

C 3

Region: West Norway   **Population:** 14,000

Architecturally, Voss has little to offer due to its many plain post-war buildings, but its location is unique. Located on the shores of Lake Vangsvatn and surrounded by high mountains, the town is an ideal base for active holidays.

Voss is not only a significant industrial town and transport hub on the Bergen railway line, but also a busy tourist and winter sports resort with a large selection of hotels and guesthouses. Above the railway station, a cable car leads up the approximately 700m/2297ft-high Hangursnolten mountain. The town is an excellent base for excursions to the ►Sognefjord and the ►Hardangerfjord.

What to See in and around Voss

One of the few buildings to survive the German aerial bomb raids of 1940 unscathed is the early Gothic **Vangs church** dating from 1277, situated in the centre of Voss. The formerly late Gothic altar cupboard received a Baroque restyling in the 17th century to create an altar panel that was painted by Bergen-born Elias Figenschoug, a pupil of Rubens. The chandelier in the choir comes from Holland and dates from 1614. The stone Olav Cross was erected to the southeast of the church to recall the region's Christianization during the 11th century. Norway's oldest secular wooden building, the **Finnesloftet** guild hall built in 1250, is located 15mins walk from the centre, to the west of the railway station, at Finnesveien.

Voss

> ### ! Baedeker TIP
>
> **Breathtaking views**
>
> At Vinje it is worth making a side trip to Stahlheim and one of Norway's most famous viewing points. There is a breathtaking view of the Nærøy valley, 550m/1804ft down below, from the terrace of the Stahlheim Hotel (open access), which once inspired J.C. Dahl to paint his famous picture *Stahlheim* (1842) that hangs in the National Gallery in Oslo.

The open-air museum is set in a wonderfully panoramic location to the north of the railway station. The 16 wooden buildings of the Mølsterhof reflect the traditional building arts of the 17th to the 19th century, as well as the people's way of life in the fjord regions (opening times: during summer daily 10am–7pm).

The internationally renowned wood carver **Magnus Dagestad** (1865–1957) established a museum that exhibits much of his work (opening times: during summer Tue–Sun 11am–3pm/5pm; Gjernes, Helgavangen).

⏵ VISITING VOSS

INFORMATION

Voss Turistinformasjon
Uttrågata 9
5701 Voss
Tel. 56 52 08 00, fax 56 52 08 01
www.visitvoss.no

WHERE TO EAT

▶ **Inexpensive**
Ringheim Café
Vangsgata 32
Tel. 56 51 13 65
Baguettes, pizza, pasta, a typical
Norwegian Smørebrød and home-
made cake are served here.

WHERE TO STAY

▶ **Luxury**
Fleischers Hotel
Evangervn. 13
Tel. 56 52 05 00, fax 56 52 05 01
172 beds, www.fleischers.no
The Belle Epoque façade dating from
1889 has lost something of its beauty
because of the modern annex.

Nevertheless, this hotel built in the
Swiss style is still one of the town's
architectural jewels.

▶ **Budget**
Tvinde Camping
12km/8mi north of Voss
Tel. 56 51 69 19
Fax 56 51 30 15
www.tvinde.no
This campsite by the 150m/492ft-high
Tvindefoss also rents out cabins and
holiday apartments of varying levels
of comfort.

LEISURE AND SPORT

The tourist office in Voss can provide
info on white-water rafting, sea
kayaking, rafting, riding on fjord
horses, fishing and skiing. One of
Norway's top alpine ski centres is at
Bavallen (cable car) to the northwest
of Voss, where there are opportunities
for cross-country skiing, alpine skiing,
biathlons and trick skiing.

** ✱ ✱ **
Nærøyfjord

The Nærøyfjord, a southern arm of the ▶Sognefjord, can be reached
via the E 16 from Vinje. A cruise on this, Norway's narrowest fjord,
is breathtaking. In some places it is only 250m/820ft wide and embraced by almost vertical walls of rock. During winter, the sun remains invisible for months at a time. At its end lies the settlement of
Gudvangen. Buses travel between Voss and Gudvangen.

** ✱ ✱ **
Aurlandsfjord

The Aurlandsfjord, another branch of the Sognefjord, lies east of the
Nærøyfjord. This gash in the mountains, less than 2km/1mi wide, is
flanked by rockfaces 900m/2953ft–1200m/3937ft high. **The region's
oldest stone church** (around 1200) is in **Aurlandsvangen**, the administrative centre for the district of Aurland. The little stave church
at Undredal, rebuilt in around 1700, is less than 4m/13ft wide and
has 40 seats.

The journey through the Aurlandsfjord is one →
of the most beautiful fjord journeys in all Norway.

The fjord horse is no longer a workhorse. Today it is predominantly used for riding.

★ ★
Flåm railway

At the southern end of the Aurlandsfjord lies the tourist resort of Flåm, at the exit of the Flåmdal valley, south of Aurlandsvangen. This is the end of the Flåm railway line, a branch line of the Bergen railway that leads to Mydal station, to the east of Voss. This is probably Norway's most spectacular railway line. Built between 1920 and 1940, the route has the distinction of being the world's steepest railway line to run without the help of rack-wheels. There are 22 tunnels on the route and an elevation differential of 864m/2835ft over a distance of just 20km/13mi is covered during the 50-minute journey from Flåm to Mydal (connections to the Bergen line). The views change constantly, from snow-covered mountains to wild waterfalls and green meadows. An intermediate stop is made very close to the mighty Kjosfossen waterfall. The Flåm train runs hourly between mid-June to mid-September, and otherwise about four times a day. It is often very crowded.

> **! Baedeker TIP**
>
> **The Rallarvegen**
>
> A beautiful hike can be made from Mydal down into the Flåmdal valley along the Rallar footpath. The first section is especially spectacular, with 21 hairpin bends and a slope of 15%. The mountains rise up almost vertically. After about 2.5hrs of walking, Berekvam station is reached, where the next Flåm train can be caught.

★
Skjervet

About 11km/7mi southeast of Voss, the RV 13 leads in the direction of the Hardangerfjord at the southern end of the Opelandsvatnet. It passes through the Skjervedal valley enclosed by mighty rock faces. This section of road, about 3km/2mi long, was built as early as 1863–70; this is where the Skjervefoss waterfall, formed by the Granvinelva, cascades down into the valley.

*Cyclists are welcome on
the Bergen Railway.*

A TRAIN THROUGH THE
HIGH MOUNTAINS

It is only 470km/294mi long and its highest point lies at just 1301m/4269ft, yet the Bergen railway route that connects Bergen with the capital city of Oslo is considered one of the most fascinating rail journeys in Europe.

The Bergen railway, which also stops in **Voss**, is largely famous thanks to the fantastic route it follows, which passes through almost all the types of landscape that Norway has to offer: forests and lakes in the east, the cultivated land of the Hallingdal valley, the high mountains and plateaus of Hardangervidda, and the fjords to the west.

Leisurely tempo

The entire journey takes nearly seven hours – hardly a record-breaking time in this era of high-speed trains. The most beautiful section runs through the high mountains. The train travels above the tree line, which in southern Norway lies at around 900m/2953ft, and is exposed to the whims of nature while crossing a barren highland plateau on a 100km/63mi stretch between Ustaoset and Myrdal. In the area around the small village of **Finse** (only accessible by train) in particular, storms and snow with up to 15m/49ft drifts make life difficult for the railway staff during the dark season of the year. Here, at the watershed of the damp western Norwegian climate and the drier one of the east, it can snow hard, even during the summer months. The creation of the Bergen railway line is thanks in great part to interested parties in western Norway at the end of the 19th century, who sought a definite cross-country connection to the capital of Kristiania. Enthralled by the technological innovations of the time, they were convinced the train was the answer. Fifteen years was spent building the route, during which engineers created a logistical masterpiece: the route was designed in such a way that neither superfluous stone materials were left over nor additional material brought in. All the required shoring up was achieved using rock from tunnel excavations. The **inaugural journey** in January 1908 was the first to fall victim to the vagaries of nature: the train got stuck in snow on the fjell and it took tremendous effort to rescue the passengers. Half a year later they tried again – and this time passengers were safely conveyed from the Oslofjord to Bergen in 21 hours.

INDEX

PHOTO CREDITS

LIST OF MAPS AND ILLUSTRATIONS

PUBLISHER'S INFORMATION

Illustrations etc: 189 illustrations, 32 maps and diagrams, one large map
Text: Astrid Feltes-Peter and Anja Carstanjen Schroth, with contributions by Achim Bourmer, Dr. Helmut Eck, Dr. Cornelia Hermanns, Johannes Holzleiter, Helmut Linde, Hilke Maunder, Hans Molter, Dr. Christian Nowak, Nordis Redaktion, Guido Pinkau, Dr. Madeleine Reincke, Dina Stahn, Werner Strasdat, Christine Wessely und Reinhard Zakrzewski
Editing: Baedeker editorial team (Robert Taylor)
Translation: Natascha Scott-Stokes
Cartography: Franz Huber, Munich; MAIRDUMONT/Falk Verlag, Ostfildern (map)
3D illustrations: jangled nerves, Stuttgart
Design: independent Medien-Design, Munich; Kathrin Schemel

Editor-in-chief: Rainer Eisenschmid, Baedeker Ostfildern

1st edition 2009
Based on Baedeker Allianz Reiseführer »Norwegen«, 8. Auflage 2009

Copyright: Karl Baedeker Verlag, Ostfildern
Publication rights: MAIRDUMONT GmbH & Co; Ostfildern

Printed in China

BAEDEKER GUIDE BOOKS AT A GLANCE

Guiding the World since 1827

- Andalusia
- Austria
- Bali
- Barcelona
- Berlin
- Brazil
- Budapest
- Cologne
- Dresden
- Dubai
- Egypt

- Florence
- Florida
- France
- Greece
- Iceland
- Ireland
- Italy
- Japan
- London
- Mexico
- New York

- Norway
- Paris
- Portugal
- Prague
- Rome
- South Africa
- Spain
- Thailand
- Tuscany
- Venice
- Vienna

DEAR READER,

We would like to thank you for choosing this Baedeker travel guide. It will be a reliable companion on your travels and will not disappoint you.
This book describes the major sights, of course, but it also recommends the most beautiful excursions and tours, as well as hotels in the luxury and budget categories, and includes tips about where to eat or go shopping and much more, helping to make your trip an enjoyable experience. Our authors ensure the quality of this information by making regular journeys to Norway and putting all their know-how into this book.

Nevertheless, experience shows us that it is impossible to rule out errors and changes made after the book goes to press, for which Baedeker accepts no liability. Please send us your criticisms, corrections and suggestions for improvement: we appreciate your contribution. Contact us by post or e-mail, or phone us:

▶ **Verlag Karl Baedeker GmbH**
  Editorial department
  Postfach 3162
  73751 Ostfildern
  Germany
  Tel. 49-711-4502-262, fax -343
  www.baedeker.com
  www.baedeker.co.uk
  E-Mail: baedeker@mairdumont.com